# RESTAURANT MANAGEMENT
## Customers, Operations, and Employees

*Third Edition*

# Robert Christie Mill

School of Hotel, Restaurant, and Tourism Management
Daniels College of Business
University of Denver

PEARSON

Prentice
Hall

Upper Saddle River, New Jersey 07458

**Library of Congress Cataloging-in-Publication Data**
Mill, Robert Christie.
  Restaurant management : customers, operations, and employees / Robert
Christie Mill.—3rd ed.
    p. cm.
Includes bibliographical references and index.
ISBN 0-13-113690-9
1.  Restaurant management.  I. Title.
TX911.3.M24M55 2007
647.95068—dc22

                                            2006017886

*Dedication*
*For Christian, Jordan,*
*Mikayla, Andrew,*
*and Gabriel*

**Editor-in-Chief:** Vernon R. Anthony
**Senior Editor:** William Lawrensen
**Managing Editor-Editorial:** Judith Casillo
**Editorial Assistant:** Marion Gottlieb
**Executive Marketing Manager:** Ryan DeGrote
**Senior Marketing Coordinator:** Elizabeth Farrell
**Marketing Assistant:** Les Roberts
**Director of Manufacturing and Production:** Bruce Johnson
**Managing Editor-Production:** Mary Carnis
**Production Liaison:** Jane Bonnell
**Production Editor:** Jessica Balch, Pine Tree Composition
**Manufacturing Manager:** Ilene Sanford
**Manufacturing Buyer:** Cathleen Petersen
**Senior Design Coordinator:** Miguel Ortiz
**Cover Designer:** Anthony Gemmellaro/Solid State Graphics
**Cover Image:** SIME s.a.s/eStock Photo
**Composition:** Pine Tree Composition
**Printer/Binder:** R. R. Donnelley & Sons Company

Text photo credits appear on p. 438, which constitutes a continuation of this copyright page.

Pearson Education, LTD.                 Pearson Education Australia PTY. Limited
Pearson Education Singapore, Pte. Ltd.   Pearson Education North Asia Ltd.
Pearson Education Canada, Ltd.           Pearson Educación de Mexico, S.A. de C.V.
Pearson Education—Japan                  Pearson Education Malaysia, Pte. Ltd.

10  9  8  7  6  5  4
ISBN 0-13-113690-9

# CONTENTS

Preface      xi

From Concept to Completion: The Shaping of a Restaurant      xiv

**Chapter 1**
**Introduction**      1

Learning Objectives   1

The Foodservice Industry   2

Industry Trends   4
     *Sources of Information, 5*

Common Denominators   7
     *Utility versus Pleasure, 7 • Service and Menu Price, 8 • Food Preparation*
     *Method, 9 • Menu Development, 10*

Overview of Restaurant Chains   12
     *Sandwich Chains, 13 • Dinnerhouses, 13 • Major Contractors, 15 •*
     *Pizza Chains, 16 • Family Chains, 16 • Chicken Chains, 17 • Hotels, 17 •*
     *Grill-Buffet Chains, 17*

Why Restaurants Fail   19
     *The Restaurant Industry Dollar, 20 • Failure to Increase Sales, 21 •*
     *Failure to Control Costs, 22*

Success Factors   24
     *Right Concept, 24 • Careful Expansion, 24 • Skillful Execution, 24 •*
     *Service, 24*

Endnotes   27

Internet Resources   28

Quick Quiz Answer Key   28

 **C h a p t e r   2**
**Understanding the Customer**                                                            **29**

Learning Objectives   29

Introduction   31

Market Categories   31
*Captive Market, 31 • Mass Market, 32 • Status Market, 32*

Trend Analysis   33
*Trend Spotters, 33 • Trends: Early Adopters, 35 • Trends: Traditional
Research, 35*

Meal Occasion   42
*Breakfast, 42 • Lunch, 43 • Dinner, 45*

Endnotes   50

Internet Resources   51

Quick Quiz Answer Key   51

**C h a p t e r   3**
**Developing a Marketing Plan**                                                          **52**

Learning Objectives   52

Marketing Defined   53

Developing a Marketing Plan   55
*Conduct a Marketing Audit, 55 • Select Target Markets, 60 • Position
the Property, 64 • Determine Marketing Objectives, 69 • Develop and
Implement Action Plans, 70 • Monitor and Evaluate the Marketing Plan, 75*

Endnotes   77

Internet Resources   78

Quick Quiz Answer Key   78

**C h a p t e r   4**
**Promoting the Operation**                                                              **79**

Learning Objectives   79

The Promotional Process   80
*Objectives of Promotion, 80 • Steps in the Process, 81 • Customer Use
of Information, 86*

Advertising Agencies   86
*When to Use an Agency, 86 • How to Select an Agency, 87*

Advertising   88

*Functions of Advertising, 88 • Types of Campaigns, 88 • Media Selection Criteria, 89 • Newspapers, 90 • Radio, 91 • Television, 92 • Magazines, 92 • Yellow Pages, 93 • Signs and Billboards, 94 • Direct Mail, 94*

Internet   96

Personal Selling   97

Sales Promotion   97

*Incentives, 97 • Key Steps, 100*

Merchandising   103

*Purpose, 103 • Effectiveness, 103 • Merchandising of Beverages, 104*

Public Relations and Publicity   104

*Word of Mouth, 105 • Implementation, 106*

Endnotes   108

Internet Resources   109

Quick Quiz Answer Key   109

## Chapter 5
## Pricing and Designing the Menu

**110**

Learning Objectives   110

Importance of the Menu   112

Menu Content   112

Menu Pricing   114

*Pricing Philosophies, 114*

Pricing Methods   117

*Factor, Cost-Multiplier, or Mark-Up System, 117 • Prime Cost, 118 • Actual Pricing or All Costs Plus Profit, 120 • Gross Mark-up or Gross Profit, 120 • Base Price, 121 • Texas Restaurant Association, 121 • Marginal Pricing, 122 • Daily Pricing, 122 • Handling Price Increases, 122 • Listing Prices, 123*

Measuring Menu Strength   126

*Average Check, 126 • Range, 126 • Menu Scoring, 127 • Menu Engineering, 128*

Menu Design   130

*Cover, 131 • Size, 132 • Materials, 132 • Placement, 132 • Specials, 135 • Menu Descriptions, 135 • Typeface, 137 • Verbal Pictures, 137 • Menu Pricing, 138 • Packaging, 140 • Wine Menus, 140 • Menu Alternatives, 141*

Endnotes   143

Internet Resources   144

Quick Quiz Answer Key   144

### Chapter 6
## Delivering High-Quality Service
**145**

Learning Objectives   145

The Service Encounter   146

*Enduring Insights, 147 • Service Problems, 148 • Assessing Customer Satisfaction, 149*

Service Gaps   150

*Lack of knowledge, 152 • Lack of Standards, 153 • Setting Service Standards, 155 • Lack of Performance, 165 • Promising Too Much, 172 • Planned Attack, 173*

Endnotes   174

Internet Resources   174

### Chapter 7
## The Physical Facility
**175**

Learning Objectives   175

Front of the House: Layout   176

Front of the House: Atmosphere   178

*Table Arrangements, 178 • Furniture, 182 • Surface Materials, 183 • Entertainment, 184 • Space, 186 • Lighting, 187 • Color, 189 • Accessibility, 192*

Back of the House: Space Requirements   192

Back of the House: Workplace Design   193

*Systematic Approach, 194 • Layout of Functional Areas, 197 • Arranging Functional Areas, 201 • Comparing Systems, 201 • Ergonomics, 202*

Improving Existing Layouts   203

*Individual Movements, 204 • Product Flow, 206*

Task Planning   206

Endnotes   211

Internet Resources   211

### Chapter 8
## Food and Beverage: From Supplier to Customer
**212**

Learning Objectives   212

Steps in the Process   213

Purchasing   213

*Importance, 213 • Process, 213 • Buying Methods, 214 • Standards, 216 • Control, 218*

Receiving   219
  *Methods, 219 • Space Requirements, 221 • Practices, 220*

Storage   221
  *Space Requirements, 221*

Issuing   223
  *Control, 224*

Preparation   224
  *Function, 224 • Space Requirements, 224*

Cooking   226
  *Service Systems, 226 • Space Requirements, 227 • Principles of Cooking, 228 • Control, 231*

Service   231
  *Service Styles, 231 • Space Requirements, 232 • Portion Control, 234*

Dishwashing   234
  *Pot and Pan Washing, 236*

Waste Disposal   236

Endnotes   236

Internet Resources   237

## Chapter 9
## Kitchen Equipment and Interiors: Selection, Maintenance, and Energy Management    **238**

Learning Objectives   238

Equipment Selection   239
  *Basic Considerations, 239 • Materials Used, 242 • Energy Sources, 243 • Specifications, 244*

Equipment Types   244
  *Dry-Heat Cooking Equipment, 244 • Steam Equipment, 247 • Fryers, 248 • Small Equipment, 248 • Dishwashers, 249 • Refrigeration Equipment, 249*

Interior Surfaces   250
  *Materials, 250*

Equipment Maintenance   253
  *Stainless Steel Surfaces, 253 • Equipment, 253*

Energy Management   259
  *Comprehensive Program, 259 • Lighting, 262 • Water, 263 • Heating, Ventilation, and Air Conditioning (HVAC) System, 264*

Endnotes   265

Internet Resources   266

## Chapter 10
## Sanitation and Food Safety

Learning Objectives   267

Role of the Manager   268
 *Allergies, 269*

Major Sanitation Problems   271
 *Foodborne Illnesses, 271 • Biological Sources, 274 • Chemical Contamination, 275 • Physical Contamination, 275*

Taking a Proactive Stance: HACCP   275

Preventive Procedures   277
 *Purchasing, 277 • Receiving, 277 • Storage, 279 • Preparation and Serving, 280 • Reheating, 281 • Bars, 283 • Equipment, 283 • Rodent and Insect Control, 284 • Crisis Management, 285*

Employee Habits   286
 *Employee Health, 286 • Safety and Accident Prevention, 288*

Endnotes   291

Internet Resources   291

Quick Quiz Answer Key   291

## Chapter 11
## Controlling Costs

Learning Objectives   292

Financial Statements   293
 *Statement of Income, 294 • Balance Sheet, 297*

Analyzing Financial Statements: Statement of Income   298
 *Systematic Approach, 298 • The Three-Part Method, 300*

Analyzing Financial Statements: Balance Sheet   306
 *Current Assets, 306 • Fixed Assets, 309 • Liabilities, 309 • Solvency Ratios, 310*

Cost–Volume–Profit Analysis   310
 *Break-Even Chart, 310*

Capital Budgeting   316
 *Determining Priorities, 316*

Endnotes   320

Internet Resources   320

# Chapter 12
## Employee Selection

**321**

Learning Objectives    321

Supply of Labor: The Changing Picture    322
*Women, 324 • Minorities, 325 • Immigrants, 326 • Older Employees, 326 • Part-Time Employees, 327 • Employees with Disabilities, 328*

The Regulatory Environment: Equal Employment Opportunity    330
*Federal Laws, 330 • Bona Fide Occupational Qualification (BFOQ), 333 • Sexual Harassment, 333 • Affirmative Action, 334*

Recruiting Employees    336
*Job Analysis, 336 • Analysis Process, 336*

The Hiring Process    339
*Preliminary Interview, 340 • Completing the Application Form, 341 • Employment Tests, 341 • Interview in the Human Resources Department, 346 • Background Investigation, 350 • Medical Examination, 353 • Preliminary Selection in the Human Resources Department, 353 • Supervisory Interview, 353 • Realistic Job Preview, 353 • Hiring Decision, 355*

Endnotes    355

Internet Resources    357

# Chapter 13
## Training and Development

**358**

Learning Objectives    358

Employee Orientation    360

Employee Training and Development    363
*Importance of Training, 363 • Responsibility for Training, 364*

Training Process    366
*Needs Assessment, 366 • Learning Objectives, 368 • Training Program, 368 • Training Lessons, 370 • Conducting the Training, 370 • Evaluation, 370 • Follow-Up, 371*

Principles of Learning    371
*Intention to Learn, 371 • Whole Learning, 372 • Reinforcement, 372 • Practice, 372 • Spaced versus Massed Practice, 372 • Learning Curve, 372 • Behavior Modeling, 374*

Training Methods    374
*Learner-Controlled Instruction, 374 • Individual Training, 377 • Group Training, 378*

Career Development   379
    *Employee Development, 379 • Management Development, 380*
Endnotes   383
Internet Resources   384

## Chapter 14
## Motivating the Employee                                           **385**

Learning Objectives   385
Employee Motivation   386
    *The Role of Managers, 386 • Theories of Motivation, 388*
Organizational Climate   394
    *Dimensions of Climate, 395*
Developing a Productive Organizational Climate   397
    *Management by Objectives, 400 • Implementing the Concept, 401 • Job Redesign, 405 • Punishment, 410 • Positive Reinforcement, 410 • Development of Trust, 413*
Leaders and Managers   415
    *Leadership Theories, 415*
Endnotes   420
Internet Resources   421

## Chapter 15
## Restaurant Manager 2010                                           **422**

Learning Objectives   422
Industry Challenges   423
    *Nutrition/Obesity, 423 • Smoking Prohibition, 424 • Animal Rights, 426 • Human Resources, 426 • Food Safety, 426 • Food Technology, 428 • Serving Alcohol, 428 • Food Sustainability, 428*
Industry Solutions   428
    *The Manager's Job, 428 • The Bottom Line, 435*
Endnotes   436
Internet Resources   437

## Photo Credits                                                     **438**

## Index                                                            **439**

# PREFACE

In writing this book I wanted to identify the crucial elements involved in the successful operation of a restaurant and show their inter-relationships. In providing what John Fuller, the former head of the Scottish Hotel School, called "The Meal Experience," the restaurant manager brings together three elements—customers, the operation (consisting of food and beverage items as well as the physical facility), and employees. The operator's task is to manage these elements to produce satisfied customers. How to do this is the thrust of this book.

Chapter 1 provides a financial overview of the restaurant industry while looking at the major factors affecting the growth of the business and considering the factors that make the difference between success and failure in running a restaurant.

Chapters 2 through 6 consider the first of the three elements of The Meal Experience—the customer. The eating habits of the various segments of the market are described in Chapter 2 and the major trends in customer behavior that will impact the business are identified. Chapter 3 shows how to develop a marketing plan to attract one or more of the segments identified in the previous chapter. The importance of promotion as a marketing tool is recognized in Chapter 4 as we consider how and when to use various types of advertising to bring people in the front door. The role of the menu as a crucial part of the marketing effort is covered in Chapter 5, with important sections on pricing and design to develop the strongest possible promotional vehicle. The culmination of the marketing effort to the customer is the provision of quality service—the topic of Chapter 6. The features that make the service encounter unique are identified and strategies developed to provide service to the customer that will result in satisfied patrons who want to return—and who will tell their friends to visit.

Chapters 7 through 11 deal with the physical facilities. Chapter 7 shows how the front of the house can be designed to positively impact the psychological needs and behavior of the customer. The impact of design of the back of the house on employee productivity is also covered. Chapter 8 follows the flow of food and beverage items from supplier to customer through the various departments within the operation in developing procedures for the effective purchasing, receiving, storing, and issuing of items used in the operation. The various production and service systems are compared within the context of developing effective cost control. Chapter 9 focuses on kitchen equipment and interiors. Guidelines are given on the proper procedures to follow in selecting, cleaning and repairing kitchen equipment. Readers are shown how to develop a comprehensive energy management program. The importance of sanitation and food safety is stressed in Chapter 10. The major sanitation problems faced by restaurant managers are identified and procedures developed for preventing foodborne diseases. A program to build effective employee habits is presented. The final chapter in this section shows how to systematically analyze financial statements in order to determine the profitability of the operation.

The final chapters of the book examine the role of employees. Chapter 12 deals with employee selection, identifying the work groups that managers will increasingly turn to in the next decade. The legal environment within which managers must operate is described and the steps involved in staffing the operation are noted and guidelines given for each step on how to improve the quality of employees selected. The design of effective orientation, training, and development programs is covered in Chapter 13 together with tips on how to develop the skills necessary to be an effective trainer. The topic of employee motivation is dealt with in Chapter 14. Suggestions are given as to why employees behave the way they do and techniques are developed that will allow managers to channel and maintain employee behavior through the implementation of various process theories of motivation. Chapter 15 examines the challenges facing the restaurant industry and identifies the skills and knowledge required of restaurant managers to respond to these challenges.

A number of video cases are available as a supplement to the third edition of this text. These cases have been produced for the Cornell Entrepreneurship and Personal Enterprise Program (EPE) by Peter Rainsford, Director of the School of Hotel, Restaurant and Tourism Management at the University of Denver. The cases serve as real-life examples of many of the principles outlined in the text. A teaching note for each is included as part of this book's instructor's manual. The cases can be ordered individually for $19.95 each from John Jaquette, Director, Cornell Entrepreneurship and Personal Enterprise Program, Cornell EPE, 51 Warren Hall, Cornell University, Ithaca, NY 14853.

One distinctive feature of this book is the use of sidebars throughout. Most are tied to a specific learning objective of the chapter and serve to illustrate, either from research journals or the trade press, how theory is applied in practice. It is hoped that, through the principles and procedures identified in the text and the practices covered in the sidebars, readers will leave this book knowing what is needed to run a profitable restaurant. While this book can provide a blueprint on how to be successful, that success will come only when readers put these ideas into practice.

## SUPPLEMENTS

The comprehensive supplements package includes the following:

**Instructor's Manual with Test Item File**—available both online and as a print version

**TestGen**—a computerized test generation program featuring test questions for each chapter, enabling instructors to select questions and create their own tests

**PowerPoint Presentation**—available to instructors both online and on the Instructor's Resource CD-ROM

**Instructor's Resource CD**—includes all of the aforementioned materials on one CD-ROM

## ACKNOWLEDGMENTS

I am grateful to Professor John Fuller, who, as head of the Scottish Hotel School, first brought the phrase "the meal experience" to my attention.

The people at Prentice Hall have been a delight to work with. In particular, I owe a debt of gratitude to Eileen McClay, Marion Gottlieb, Judy Casillo, and Jane Bonnell, as well as Jessica Balch and the team at Pine Tree Composition.

The reviewers gave feedback that was detailed, insightful, and added greatly to this new edition: Margaret Condrasky, Clemson University; T. F. Gaddis, Pellissippi State Technical College; Lisa R. Kennon, University of North Texas; and Gary Ward, Scottsdale Community College.

Last, but by no means least, I have had the good fortune to have two superb research assistants—Laura Johnson and Kirstin Stengel—who updated quick bites, quotations, and the instructor's manual. Many of my students at the University of Denver assisted in updating the manuscript. Special mention goes to Venice Adams, Cassie Dando, Lisa Zinna, and Miguel Vega. I, of course, take full responsibility for any and all errors.

*Robert Christie Mill*

# FROM CONCEPT TO COMPLETION: THE SHAPING OF A RESTAURANT

Allison Connolly

FIRST MEAL: Serving a private party of 100 guests, Thomason, a graduate of the prestigious Parisian culinary school Le Cordon Bleu, prepares roast beef tenderloin Wednesday night at his restaurant, Vintage Kitchen, in Norfolk. After almost two years of preparation, he will officially open the restaurant Sept. 6.
(Hyunsoo Leo Kim photos/the virginian-pilot)

Phillip Craig Thomason made his first buck as a restaurateur four days ago. With the guests gone and his restaurant, Vintage Kitchen, closed for the night, he savored his achievement at the copper bar with a mint julep, made with Virginia Gentleman.

He was tired, but it felt good.

It has been a whirlwind five months since he signed the lease for space on the first floor of Dominion Tower on Waterside Drive in Norfolk. Most nights he slept a scant few hours on the leather banquettes. But he made his deadline, opening Wednesday night with a party for 100 from the accounting firm KPMG LLP, which has offices upstairs.

Thomason, 35, spent most of the night in the kitchen with his staff, doing what he does best: roast beef tenderloin with tomato preserves and horseradish sour cream; homemade pimento cheese with Marshall Farms cheddar and smoked chilies; wild mushroom strudel with blue cheese, caramelized onion and applewood-smoked bacon; and for dessert, lavender butter cookies with raspberry, bittersweet chocolate brownies and lemon squares.

He stocked the bar with Virginia wines and beers, in keeping with the restaurant's regional theme.

A graduate of the prestigious Parisian culinary school Le Cordon Bleu, Thomason can cook. But he knows it takes a lot more to run a restaurant, especially in the most competitive area of Hampton Roads.

"The reason I came back here is I saw a need in this market," he said.

A year and a half ago, Thomason was one of a dozen aspiring entrepreneurs in a class offered in Chesepeake by the Small Business Development Center of Hampton Roads. Over the course of 11 weeks, he would learn the difference between a debt-to-asset ratio and a cash-flow projection.

As a consultant, Thomason had helped other chefs open restaurants around the world: Portugal, Cyprus, Russia, Venezuela. He felt it was time to open his own. But he knew the odds were against him—four out of five new restaurants fail in the first three years.

Thomason was out to prove the statistics wrong.

He brought his 130-page business plan to the first three-hour session.

Tall and thin, with dark hair and a boyish face, Thomason long knew what he wanted to do. The Portsmouth native earned his bachelor's degree in French literature from the University of Virginia and spent his junior year at the Sorbonne. There, he developed a passion for French cuisine.

He wanted a place where people could eat several times a week. A place that gave back to the community. A place that served homegrown products.

In Paris, he once saw two women so wanting to eat at a certain restaurant that they took seats on the floor when no tables were available.

"You open a restaurant in the States, and everyone is looking for the big bang," he said. "We've moved away from having that neighborhood restaurant."

Others in the class—a stained-glass artist, an accountant, an executive coach—had their own dreams.

Their teacher, Sheila Guillette-Moore, shared her war stories and gave advice:

"Hire an attorney. The sooner the better, to prevent you from going into the ditch."

"You can be making money and still go out of business."

And, "Fear of failure is great motivation."

Guillette-Moore was part mother, part drill instructor. Her motto: "Don't ask me if you don't want to know." She learned about running a small business the hard way.

Several years ago, her then-husband asked her to do the books for the family business, a lawn and garden company. She quickly realized it was in debt and revenue had been on the decline. The bank gave them six months to show a profit or it would begin foreclosure. Guillette-Moore decided to buy it outright and turn it around.

She not only made it profitable, she doubled the business in 18 months hawking her wares the old-fashioned way.

"If I saw a guy in a tree, I would stand at the bottom of the tree and yell. 'Hey! Get down here!'"

The property was later taken by eminent domain, and she had to close the company. But in that time she learned a lot.

"When I had the lawn and garden business without a business plan, the business ran me," she told her students.

Businesses can fail for a number of reasons, Guillette-Moore said. Entrepreneurs don't make a profit the first week. Sometimes it can take months to break even, and many aren't prepared for that.

Guillette-Moore dedicates a full three-hour class to cash-flow projections. Students must detail what costs they will incur in opening their business, from stocking shelves to keeping lights on to cleaning bathrooms.

They add it up and determine how much capital will be needed to open and to keep the business going until it breaks even. It can be a real eye-opener for students, Guillette-Moore said. Some don't take it as seriously as they should.

"They say, 'I'm different. I'm going to show you,'" she said. "When people have a dream, they are so sure."

More than 150 businesses have come through her classes, but only 20 percent have succeeded, she said. She's had to tell students she doesn't think their ideas will work. Some take her advice, others don't.

One, a chiropractor, had to liquidate a year after opening her business because she didn't factor in having a baby, something Guillette-Moore had asked her to consider early on.

"Entrepreneurs, we're an independent sort. We don't want to hear anything negative," she said.

From the start, Guillette-Moore was impressed with Thomason because he had done his homework, she said. And he brought experience to the table. But she said a restaurant is one of the most difficult small businesses to start.

"Rapid growth can kill you just as quickly as no business," she said.

When choosing space, Thomason knew what he wanted the restaurant to look like, but he would have to create it from what was available.

In February 2004, he was shown 3,200 square feet in Town Center, then a promising new development in Virginia Beach with high-rise office, retail and restaurant space. But unlike other places Thomason had seen, this one was just white walls and concrete floors. Without a space that had previously held a busi-

FALSE START: Phillip Craig Thomason discusses the floor plan for a 3,200-square-foot space in Town Center in Virginia Beach with an architect in early 2004. Later he changed direction and secured a different space at Dominion Tower in Norfolk.

ness, he would have to install his own pipes, vents and fixtures. It would take three months to build out, pushing his opening until Thanksgiving or so.

Thomason hired an architect to design a floor plan so he could talk costs with the developer. To get financing from a bank, he needed a lease.

On a gray May morning, he and architect Randy Hicks pored over sketches of the restaurant. The plans showed seating for about 50 in the main room, with a table in the window looking out at the street. There was a small bar at the front. The kitchen took up a third of the space, and it was open so diners could see in.

By July, Thomason was starting to think a new space might not be the best option. It was going to cost him half a million dollars—three times what he had estimated—to build out, before ordering furniture or fixtures.

Cost wasn't a problem for large chain restaurants such as The Cheesecake Factory and California Pizza Kitchen, which were moving to the Town Center block.

"You don't want to be working for a bank for 10 years," Thomason said.

In December, a friend told him about space in Dominion Tower in Norfolk.

The competition would be greater, and the venue did not benefit from walking traffic like businesses on nearby Granby Street. But it was formerly a restaurant, so Thomason wouldn't have to spend as much on construction.

It had been vacated by Metro Cafe, which largely catered to the business crowd in the building. The owners apparently left in a hurry: There were commercial-size boxes of sugar, grits and muffin mix on the shelf, brownie batter in the walk-in refrigerator and french fries in the deep-fryer.

The space itself needed work. The walls were light purple with dark purple trim. The carpet was green and threadbare in places.

It was almost 900 square feet bigger than the space at Town Center and seated 80 instead of 55. The bar was in front, the kitchen was in the middle and seating was on the side and back. There was enough room for a private dining room off the kitchen, as he wanted, with a library of collectible cooking books.

It was only January, but Thomason could see people sitting out on the terrace on a sunny Sunday afternoon, with Bellinis and eggs Benedict, listening to music and looking out at the water.

"That's a perfect day for me."

Thomason found that a lease is more than just signing on the dotted line. It is weeks of negotiations over dates, rates, hours of operation, escalation of rent and various security deposits.

"It's important to find what your limitations are, where you can bend, where you can't bend," he said. "And then you meet in the middle."

On March 1, Thomason had a final 30-page lease from Harbor Group International, owner of the building.

"It took four weeks to put together, and they wanted it back in two days," he said.

Because the former tenant left, Thomason was able to negotiate a 3 percent annual rent increase on the multiyear lease, down from 4.5 percent. He also got a 90-day window to open the restaurant instead of the typical 60-day default period.

He went with his hometown bank, Towne Bank, which guaranteed him a credit line—tough for a lot of first-time restaurateurs to get, he said.

Overall, he said, the space was 10 times less expensive than developing a restaurant from scratch.

OPEN SPACES: Long before Vintage Kitchen became reality, Thomason stands at the center of an empty room and explains his vision for the restaurant.

As soon as he signed the lease, the clock began ticking. It was time to find a contractor.

"Everyone said, 'Expect a price and tack on 40 percent,'" he said. "But it went far beyond my expectations."

The quotes he received to repaint and re-floor the space averaged between $150,000 and $160,000—much more than his max of $60,000. There were a lot of extras he hadn't bargained for: One contractor required about $450 a month for cell phones for the crew. Another wanted him to cover workers' transportation, at $150 a week. One wanted $3,500 a week for a part-time supervisor to check on the project from time to time to make sure work was being done.

To save money, Thomason did a lot of rehabbing himself. He relied on friends and friends of friends for help.

"I don't want to do any more finish work unless it's on a plate," said one of those friends, Christian Davis, who will be working in the restaurant's kitchen.

In late April, dressed in a charcoal gray jumpsuit, the kind worn by a mechanic, Thomason was sanding down the bar.

"To see it come together under your own hand, there's nothing like it," he said at the time.

He also learned it pays to shop around. For the same set of blinds, for example, he received bids of $2,500 to $8,000 from distributors. A lot of entrepreneurs don't have time to make comparison calls, but Thomason said it was worth it.

Then he had to make sure the suppliers delivered what they said they would.

People say, "You're opening a restaurant? How glamorous,'" he said. 'Well, there's a toilet seat in the back of my car."

And he was continually reminded of his instructor's message: Expect the unexpected.

Thomason heard through the grapevine that a couple of his friends were opening a restaurant in Suffolk with an all-too familiar name: "Vintage Tavern." He said he had long ago told them he would open a restaurant called Vintage Kitchen, and he couldn't believe it was a coincidence that the name sounded so similar.

He tried to reason with them—even offering a list of 125 other names. But he said they refused to change the name. He is considering taking legal action.

Then, during a rainstorm, the glass wall facing the terrace leaked. Fortunately, Thomason hadn't yet tiled the floor. He also had negotiated in the lease that the management company would be responsible for structural problems. But the situation forced him to push back his opening date by a couple of weeks.

The floor tiles proved to be a challenge. During his inspection, he found about 400 of the white, square-inch tiles had chips in the corners. Most people might not have noticed, he said. But he did. He made the workers replace the chipped ones.

"No one is going to be as passionate about your business as you are," he said.

Thomason had hoped to open by the end of June to take advantage of Harborfest at Town Point Park just a few doors away. But as he has learned, everything takes time.

When he wasn't in the space, he visited prospective suppliers at vineyards and farms. He cooked for private parties, testing recipes. He traveled to other cities with regional flair for inspiration, including Mexico City and Dublin, Ireland.

The week leading up to the party Wednesday night was dizzying. If he didn't pass inspections by the health board and fire department, he couldn't get a business license and open. And he had to have all the equipment and fixtures in place for inspections.

The health board flagged him on 50 minor things, such as not having drain screens, which he said he was able to fix in a day. But the fire inspector was going to fail him because one of his workers hadn't taped over the sprinklers properly when painting the ceiling, leaving paint on them. She did inspections only on Fridays, which meant he would not be able to get reinspected in time for Wednesday's party.

Thomason was able to persuade her to come back later that Friday, after his workers had cleaned the sprinkler heads. He got his business license Tuesday and his permit to serve alcohol just three hours before his first customers arrived.

On his opening night, he ran out of chardonnay. He bought three cases of white and three cases of red, but bartender Jamal Giles didn't empty a single bottle of red.

"How do you predict something like that?" Thomason said.

So with just two bottles of white remaining, he slipped out to Total Wine and picked up six more.

Several guests said they liked the dark wood, the chocolate brown walls and the retro decor and said they would return. But they've seen three restaurants open and close in the Dominion Tower space in five years.

Thomason is confident he's there to stay and is looking forward to his official opening Sept. 6, when he'll start serving breakfast and lunch. He plans to open for dinner later that month.

He's managed to stay within his budget of $250,000 from start to finish. Riding high from Wednesday's debut, he's eager to get started.

"You're only as good as your last meal," he said.

AFTER PARTY: Standing next to the copper bar with a mint julep after closing for the night, Thomason, second from left, discusses the first night with his crew, from left, Nate Stauty, Christina Cole, Rachel Sears and Jamal Giles.

# INTRODUCTION

"A successful restaurant makes everything in it, including the
patrons, seem a little better than they are."
Mason Cooley, U.S. aphorist

## learning objectives

*By the end of this chapter you should be able to*

1. Identify the major factors affecting the growth of the restaurant industry.

2. Identify the common denominators of restaurants.

3. Provide a financial overview of the restaurant industry in the United States.

4. Identify the reasons that restaurants fail.

5. Identify the major reasons contributing to the financial success of a
   restaurant.

## THE FOODSERVICE INDUSTRY

The importance of the foodservice industry can be seen from the following figures:[1]

- There are about 900,000 foodservice outlets in the United States, a number expected to reach 1 million by 2010.
- 12.2 million people, about 10 percent of the workforce, are employed in restaurants, making the industry the nation's second largest employer after the military. By 2010 the number is expected to reach 13 million.
- Approximately one-third of all U.S. adults have, at one time or another, been employed in the restaurant industry.
- On any given day in the United States, about half the population will be customers of the foodservice industry and will spend over $1 billion.
- Customers buy an average of 4.2 commercially prepared meals each week (218 a year).
- The percentage of revenues from food away from home compared to food at home has increased from 25 percent in 1955 to 47 percent in 2005 and is expected to reach 53 percent by 2010.

The foodservice industry as a whole had 2005 food and drink sales of almost $477 billion. Full-service restaurants account for almost 36 percent of the total, while limited-service restaurants make up an additional 28 percent of overall sales.

The vastness of, and job opportunities in, the various segments for 2005 can be seen from the following figures:[2]

**Restaurant Industry Food and Drink Sales—2005**

| Segment | 2005 (projected dollars in billions) |
|---|---|
| **Group I—Commercial Restaurant Services** | |
| **Eating Places** | |
| Full-service restaurants | $164.8 |
| Limited-service (quick-service) restaurants | $134.2 |
| Commercial cafeterias | $ 2.5 |
| Social caterers | $ 5.3 |
| Snack and nonalcoholic bars | $ 16.9 |
| TOTAL EATING PLACES | $326.4 |
| Bars and taverns | $ 15.2 |
| TOTAL EATING AND DRINKING PLACES | $341.8 |
| **Managed Services** | |
| Manufacturing and industrial plants | $ 6.6 |
| Commercial and office buildings | $ 2.2 |
| Hospitals and nursing homes | $ 3.8 |
| Colleges and universities | $ 9.0 |
| Primary and secondary schools | $ 4.1 |
| In-transit restaurant services (airlines) | $ 1.8 |
| Recreation and sports centers | $ 4.2 |
| TOTAL MANAGED SERVICES | $31.6 |
| **Lodging Places** | |
| Hotel restaurants | $24.8 |
| Other accommodation restaurants | $ 0.39 |
| TOTAL LODGING PLACES | $25.2 |
| Retail-host restaurants | $22 |
| Recreation and sports | $ 5.6 |
| Mobile caterers | $ 0.87 |
| Vending and nonstore retailers | $ 9.8 |
| TOTAL GROUP I | $436.9 |
| **Group II—Noncommercial Restaurant Services** | |
| Employee restaurant services | $ 0.62 |
| Public and parochial elementary, secondary schools | $ 5.1 |
| Colleges and universities | $ 5.3 |
| Transportation | $ 1.5 |
| Hospitals | $ 12.5 |
| Nursing homes | $ 6.2 |
| Clubs, sporting, and recreational camps | $ 4.3 |
| Community centers | $ 1.6 |
| TOTAL GROUP II | $ 37.1 |
| TOTAL GROUPS I AND II | $474 |

*(continued)*

**Group III—Military Restaurant Services**

| | |
|---|---|
| Officers' and NCO clubs (open mess) | $ 1.2 |
| Military exchanges | $ 0.56 |
| TOTAL GROUP III | $ 1.8 |
| GRAND TOTAL | $475.8 |

## INDUSTRY TRENDS

The restaurant industry does not operate in a vacuum. Industry trends directly reflect changes in the society within which the business operates. The manager who is aware of (and, better still, able to anticipate) these trends is in a position to take advantage of opportunities in the marketplace. This involves conducting a scan of the environment. The National Restaurant Association (NRA) offers periodic analyses of trends as they affect the restaurant industry.[3]

A recent survey of tableservice operators and their patrons is instructive.[4]

- Growth in sales and the number of customers is driven by the increased number of higher income households and consumer need for convenience and value.

- Most customers are satisfied with how often they eat out. However, 25 percent are not eating out as often as they would like while 20 percent would like to buy takeout or delivery food items more often.

- Almost half of the customers surveyed feel that restaurants are an essential part of their lifestyle while 40 percent agree that eating out is as cost effective as cooking at home and cleaning up. Two-thirds say that restaurants provide flavor and tastes not easily duplicated at home.

- Twenty percent of restaurateurs offer a frequent diner program in an attempt to maintain customer loyalty. Over half of those who offer such a program report an increase in the number of customers who participate in the program. Approximately 12 percent of restaurant customers participate in such a program. There appears to be unmet demand for customer loyalty programs.

- Parties with children are an increasingly important segment of the restaurant business. Forty percent of respondents say they are offering a larger variety of healthy menu items for children.

- Takeout is another segment that is growing in importance. Eighty percent of respondents, largely family and casual dining, offer takeout. About 60 percent of consumers say they would use curbside takeout if it were available.

- Valet parking is offered by 40 percent of the fine dining respondents. Twenty-five percent of consumers say they are more likely to eat at a restaurant if free valet parking is offered.
- Most restaurants use the Internet for marketing, and two-thirds have their own Web site.
- The major challenges faced by operators are competition, operations costs, and the economy.
- Although the labor shortage is less of a problem than in it was the 1990s, it remains an important issue for operators. Other operational problems are food safety and remodeling.
- Menu items gaining in popularity include entrée salads, vegetarian entrées, side salads, and side vegetables.

## Sources of Information

How can an operator be proactive by identifying changes before they occur rather than reactive and attempting to respond to changes after they happen? The key is to become a trend watcher. In its formal setting, trend watching involves reading or watching news media, keeping track of issues and events, noting the data, and using them to predict what might happen in the future.

In one study,[5] restaurateurs were given a choice of the following sources of information:

- Family members and personal friends
- Other restaurant owners
- Trade associations
- Printed sources
- Customers
- Food and equipment vendors
- Bankers, lawyers, or accountants

The most frequently used sources were family and friends, food and equipment vendors, and printed materials. A complete watch of printed and other media would involve keeping track of events as reported by the four major television networks: ABC, CBS, NBC, and Fox; the three national news magazines: *Newsweek, Time,* and *U.S. News & World Report;* and several influential newspapers, including the *Chicago Tribune, Los Angeles Times, New York Times, Wall Street Journal,* and *Washington Post.* For busy restaurateurs such a watch could become a full-time job. For the specialist, trends can be evaluated by reading trade magazines, the front page of the *Wall Street Journal* and *USA Today,* and a technical precursor publication. Precursor publications are those that influence mainstream journalists by uncovering trends before they occur. The *Wall Street Journal* is not particularly good at forecasting what might happen in the future because by the time an item appears in the *Journal,* it is already fact. For general issues, magazines such as *Demography, Science News,* and *Utne Reader* have been found to be useful precursor publications.

**Restaurant Industry Growth**

**Learning Objective:** Identify the major factors affecting the growth of the restaurant industry.

Over the past two decades, the U.S. restaurant industry has undergone continual growth. In fact, the National Restaurant Association's 2005 Industry Forecast expects that the nation's restaurants (approximately 900,000 venues) will finish the year with $475.8 billion in total sales. This represents an increase of almost 5 percent from last year.

What is driving this incredible growth? Why is the restaurant industry doing so well when compared to other industries? The answer is clear: consumer demand has never been greater. U.S. consumers are not cooking at home as often, as busy schedules have them out of the house for large periods of the day, and they're eating out more than ever.

This growth is a definite plus for the industry, but it does pose some problems that must be addressed. To increase the profit that can be derived from the industry's growth, restaurants should look into investing in newer, better technologies that can cut labor costs and improve efficiency. And restaurants must keep on top of current food trends to ensure that they draw those demanding consumers.

Gerald White, associate publisher of sales development of *Nation's Restaurant News,* says "just take a look at the breadth and depth of ethnic cuisines that have exploded onto the marketplace. It's no longer just Italian, but Tuscan. It's no longer Mediterranean, but Moroccan." This new interest in specialized exotic cuisines coincides with a rise in consumer demand for healthier options, forcing many restaurants to significantly change their menus.

With such a huge consumer base, how can new players in the game tap ensure that they get a cut of the profits? The answer is to take advantage of industry trade shows and conventions, which provide an excellent face-to-face selling opportunity not available on the streets.

*Source:* Slavens, Roger, "How to Reach Restaurants," *BtoB,* January 17, 2005, vol. 90, no. 1, p. 18.

**Discussion Question:** What steps might a new operation take if it wanted to take advantage of the restaurant industry's large customer base?

Bruegger's Bagel Bakery

## COMMON DENOMINATORS

A useful way to explore the industry is to consider the factors that are common to all restaurants.[6]

### Utility versus Pleasure

Restaurants are built for utility or pleasure. Utility restaurants are filling stations, seeing to the need we all have for periodic refueling during the day. Restaurants that are built for pleasure appeal to more than the need to refuel. The importance of good food and wine is shared with the desire to dine in comfortable surroundings. Up to 75 percent of meals eaten away from home in the United States are for utilitarian purposes, and the other 25 percent are for pleasure.

Imagine the following progression of foodservice operations:

- Vending machines
- Fast-food operations
- Cafeterias
- Coffee shops

- Family restaurants
- Dinner houses
- Luxury restaurants

As the utility of a concept decreases, the pleasure component increases. Going from high utility to high pleasure, we move from vending machines through luxury restaurants.

> High utility/low pleasure
>> Vending machines
>> Fast-food operations
>> Cafeterias
>> Coffee shops
>> Family restaurants
>> Dinner houses
>> Luxury restaurants
> High pleasure/low utility

## Service and Menu Price

Restaurants can also be classified on the basis of the degree of service offered. The level of service offered can range from full service to self-service. In full- or table-service operation, servers take menu orders from customers and deliver those items to the table. This level of service requires more square feet of space per seat than that required by any other type of operation.

Counter service allows customers to sit at a counter facing the production area. A minimum of space is needed because the production area where the food is prepared and the service area where the food is served are one and the same. Tray service is used in such operations as airlines and hospitals. Food is delivered to the passenger or patient already plated on a tray. Room service is common in hotels. Orders are placed from the room by the guest, and the meal is arranged on a tray or table and delivered to the room by service personnel.

In self-service operations customers serve themselves. This type of service is appropriate for serving large numbers of people in a relatively short period of time. Self-service operations may be found in cafeterias, where customers pick up a tray and serve themselves from items displayed in a cafeteria line or in several areas in freestanding style. Buffet service is increasingly popular for breakfast at hotels, as it allows customers to get what they want for one price and to serve themselves as quickly as they wish. Some restaurants use buffet service for a particular meal, typically lunch or Sunday brunch.

Takeout service allows customers, for example, to pick up something on the way home from work and to enjoy it wherever they wish, whether in the privacy of their own homes or in their cars. Vending machines serve in-between meal snacks or simple meals that can be served cold or cooked by the customer in a microwave oven provided at the scene.

An increase in service typically comes with an increase in menu prices. The vending machine, relatively inexpensive, is totally self-service; a luxury restaurant may offer table-side carving. The progression from low prices and low levels of service to high prices and maximum service is the same as before.

Low service/low prices
    Vending machines
    Fast-food operations
    Cafeterias
    Coffee shops
    Family restaurants
    Dinner houses
    Luxury restaurants
High service/high prices

Menu prices are also a function of when a meal is eaten, the cost of labor, the space per customer, and the cost of that space. Meals taken in the evening, when customers are more likely to stay longer, cost more than lunch meals, when customers stay for less time and the restaurateur can increase customer and seat turnover by selling the table again.

Since the restaurant business tends to be highly labor intensive, the cost of labor is a major determinant in the price of a meal—the more service, the greater the labor cost and the higher the price. There is also a relationship between the cost of space and menu prices. The cost of a facility is, in great part, determined by the size of the facility—the larger the operation, the more it costs to build. Part of the decision that must be made is how much of the facility should be revenue producing (where customers are served) compared to non–revenue producing (for example, kitchen, storage, and service areas). Less space given over to producing revenue means that more revenue per square foot must be generated from that space. In addition, the more square footage per customer (for example, greater space between the tables), the more it will cost the customer in menu prices.

## Food Preparation Method

Restaurants have the option of preparing food from scratch or buying convenience items and finishing them in the operation. The decision as to which mix to operate under has many ramifications. Using convenience items will result in greater food cost but lower labor cost. The level of expertise needed by employees will be less if convenience items are used. The experience of the prevailing labor force may thus be a factor in the decision whether to make or buy. Different types of equipment may also be needed, depending on whether items are prepared from scratch or purchased as convenience items. Finally, the image of the

## The Common Denominator of Successful Restaurants

**Learning Objective:** Identify the common denominators of restaurants.

One word: food. Well, two actually: good food. From the earliest European taverns to the posh high-dining establishments of metropolitan centers, one thing has been the largest part in determining whether a restaurant succeeds or fails. The most successful restaurants serve the food that consumers want; it's as simple as that. Keeping up with what consumers want is a bit more difficult.

During the first 70 years of the 20th century, grocery stores were not a source of culinary excitement for most. The glitz and dazzle of fine eating belonged to the restaurant world, and it was there that the idea of food as fashion first took hold. Nowadays restaurateurs do their best to keep on top of eating trends.

For a long time French food was in high demand, and then Americans discovered the joys of pasta, olive oil and garlic. In the early 90's, the Olympics took place in Spain, making way for a fascination with Iberian cuisine. Low-fat, heart-healthy options could be seen on every menu as Americans became more health-conscious. Now the demand is for low-carb entrées and sophisticated ethnic cuisines.

Trends come and go quickly. The best plan is to keep a thumb on the pulse of the industry, and cater to the desires of the consumers.

*Source:* Mellgren, James, "Restaurant Trends a Menu for Success," *Gourmet Retailer*, January 2005, vol. 26, no. 1, pp. 82–88.

**Discussion Question:** What are some food trends that have become popular today? What are some food trends that have died out in the last 10 years?

operation may be a factor in this decision. A luxury restaurant, seeking an upscale image, may advertise preparation from scratch as part of its message. Most operations make some items while purchasing others in a convenience form.

## Menu Development

All restaurants have menus. However, the format of the menu will vary greatly depending on a variety of factors.

**Frequency of Change.** Menus can range from those that are completely fixed to those that change completely daily. The former is simpler to plan for than the latter. Menus that are completely fixed are used in fast-food and specialty operations. Changes are made only when individual menu items are dropped or added for reasons of popularity or profitability.

In some operations the menu is essentially fixed but changes are made depending on the season of the year or when daily specials are added. In the former case menus may change two or four times a year to accommodate seasonally popular items. Salads and lighter items may predominate in the summer, while stews and other hearty items provide the mainstay in the winter. Certain popular items may be kept year-round.

Daily specials help where there is repeat business. Customers who tire of the regular menu may find the specials appealing. The appeal to the customer also comes from the perception that if a dish is prepared that day, it is fresher or specially prepared. For the operator, daily specials can be a way of recycling leftovers. The baked chicken from one day becomes chicken à la king the next.

Daily changes can be cyclical or complete. Cyclical changes are used when the customer base is captive: that is, when they are tied to a particular operation such as in institutional feeding such as college dorms or prisons. In such an operation a menu is repeated on a cycle that can range from two to six weeks in length. A complete change would be appropriate for a captive audience in a resort setting where people stay for two weeks at a time. In this situation the entire menu is often changed daily.

**Types of Offerings.**   Menus tend to be à la carte, table d'hôte, or some combination of the two. On à la carte menus, items are priced individually. The appetizers, entrées or main course, potatoes, vegetables, and desserts are priced separately. A table d'hôte menu features a complete meal at a set price, with, for example, a choice of appetizer, main course, and dessert from several options. A combination menu might price appetizers and desserts separately while including salad, bread, potato, and vegetable in the price of the entrée. An advantage of à la carte menus is their perception of being classier. They certainly tend to be more expensive. By packaging a dessert in with the main course, the average check—total revenue divided by the number of customers—can be increased. People are "forced" to buy an item—the dessert—they might not purchase otherwise. If they feel the value is there, they will be satisfied and the restaurateur will have sold an item that would not have been purchased had it been priced separately.

**Size of Menu.**   Restaurants range from those that have a limited menu to those that offer an extensive menu. A limited menu offers fewer choices to the customers and relies on creating a large number of customers willing to purchase a small number of menu items. Care must be taken that the items offered are desired by a relatively large percentage of people.

A limited menu restricts the number of customers. If all the restaurant offers is salads and a party of four is eating out together, one person in the party who does not like salads can lose the restaurant four customers. For this reason fast-food operations tend to start out with a basic product and as the concept moves through the life cycle, add items to the menu to attract a larger base of people.

A limited menu allows people to make a very quick decision as to what to eat. This may appeal to customers who do not want to make extensive decisions at mealtimes. It also speeds customer turnover.

A limited menu also means less waste. For every item on the menu, there is a waste factor. It may occur as spoilage in storing; it may be that too much is made of a particular item and the remainder must be thrown out. Thus the more items on the menu, the more items will have to be ordered, stored, issued, prepared, and served. Inventory costs will be higher, as will waste costs.

The major advantage of an extensive menu is that there is a greater chance that one or more items on the menu will appeal to more people, thus increasing the menu range.

---

quick quiz

In what country and in what year was the first restaurant opened?

a. Italy, 1802
b. France, 1765
c. England, 1621

*Source:* Hickok, Allan F. and Lana E. Lazarus, *Restaurant Industry Review,* U.S. Bancorp Piper Jaffray Equity Research, March 2003, pp. 54–55.

---

## OVERVIEW OF RESTAURANT CHAINS

America's 100 leading foodservice chains produce U.S. systemwide sales of $171.26 billion.[7] Revenues from the top 100 represent 36 percent of the estimated $475 billion U.S. consumer foodservice market.

The Top 100 chains break down by market share in the following way:[8]

| Chain | Market Share |
| --- | --- |
| Sandwich chains | 41% |
| Dinnerhouses | 15 |
| Major contractors | 11 |
| Pizza chains | 7 |
| Family chains | 6 |
| Chicken chains | 6 |
| Hotels | 3 |
| Snack | 3 |
| Coffee | 2 |
| Grill-buffet chains | 2 |
| Convenience store | 1 |
| Fish quick-service restaurant | 1 |

*Note:* Does not total 100 percent because of rounding.

## Sandwich Chains

Sandwich chains account for 40 percent of Top 100 chains U.S. systemwide sales. The first edition noted that customers have difficulty differentiating among the various sandwich chains and that, to do well, they must return to identifying what differentiates them from the competition. The answer, according to industry practice as outlined in the second edition, seems to be promotional tie-ins. Noting the move by sandwich chains to highlight promotional tie-ins, many industry observers joke that some restaurants are toy stores that sell food on the side. The lack of differentiation in the sandwich market may mean that the toy becomes the deciding factor, particularly when children exert a major factor in the choice of restaurant.

McDonald's pioneered the movement in 1997 with its Teeny Beanie Babies promotion. By making the premium appealing to collectors, return sales were all but assured. The challenge for management became how to turn the customer, initially attracted by the promotion, into a long-term returning customer after the toys are gone. The competition to design toy tie-ins leaves the smaller chains at a distinct disadvantage. Reaching a deal with Hollywood or a TV network is something that only the larger chains can pull off.

In recent years sandwich chains have responded to customer demand for healthier items by downplaying fried items and focusing on more nutritious and "gourmet" items such as salads and frilled chicken. Burger King, for example, replaced its "flame broiled" slogan with the healthier-sounding "fire grilled" while, in addition to adding healthy items, McDonald's is encouraging its customers to exercise. Attempts have also been made at attracting traffic through eye-catching design. McDonald's is experimenting with updated designs featuring shingle roofs, brick and wood exteriors, and more natural colors to replace the standard red and white pattern.

The 18 sandwich chains in the Top 100 account for 72,862 units and produce an average $1,064,800 in sales.

The top five sandwich chains ranked by Top 100 market share are as follows:[9]

| Rank | Chain | Annual Market Share |
|------|-------|:-------------------:|
| 1 | McDonald's | 35% |
| 2 | Burger King | 11 |
| 3 | Wendy's | 11 |
| 4 | Subway | 9 |
| 5 | Taco Bell | 8 |

## Dinnerhouses

The 22 dinnerhouses in the Top 100 consist of just under 9000 units and produce average annual revenue of slightly less than $3.4 million. Successful operations are expanding revenues through menu development and product diversity. New products are seen as a high-volume, low-investment way to make income.

**A Day in the Life: How to Turn a Restaurant Around**

When a restaurant is in trouble, employees can see the signs, and are often reluctant to share information for fear that they will make things worse. To turn around a struggling business, you must be able to communicate with your employees and have their full support. Here are ten steps to turning a restaurant around in a short amount of time:

1. Investigate. Review old reports and plans to see if you can catch what went wrong, and perhaps find a previously disregarded suggestion that could prove a lifesaver.

2. Analyze. You cannot develop a clear summary of a business's vital signs without the help of employees, so you must share what you know with your employees.

3. Communicate. As early as possible, hold company-wide meetings that summarize data developed to date. Employees are often ignorant of the severity of the situation, although they recognize that something is amiss.

4. Share. Sharing the information may be painful, but it's necessary. The more a leader shares, the more help he or she gets in return.

5. Gather. Now that everyone is on board, you must gather information. Anonymous surveys are best for gathering the most candid, helpful information from your employees. One-on-one interviews should not be used, as employees may be reluctant to volunteer information that they think might cost them their job.

6. Match. Now address your employees and ask them to identify their skills, knowledge, and abilities. Try to identify which skills are underused, so that you can match the right people to the right positions.

7. Compile. Create a chart detailing employees, their strengths and their pay. Keep this confidential. This will be an essential tool in meeting with people and rethinking organizational structure.

8. Interview. Armed with your information, you can ask your employees revealing questions with the target of closing gaps in the organization.

9. Implementation. This is where most plans fall short. Employees are unwilling to help implement changes if they have not been consulted all along. Change is always easier when it is imposed from the top, because you can create an environment of employee-driven change.

10. Update. If everyone is kept abreast of developments in the company, they will keep coming back with good ideas to help the business through the turnaround.

*Source:* Murak, Gerry, "Turnaround with Help from Your Staff," *Restaurant Hospitality,* July 2004, vol. 88, no. 7, pp. 68–71.

**Discussion Question:** Why is it so essential to include employees when trying to turn an operation around?

Bennigan's, for example, recently added the Irish haystack to its menu—well-seasoned, deep fried, thinly sliced red onions served in a basket with stout ketchup—while California Kitchen increased sales through the addition of a jerk chicken pizza. Chains have also been adding a takeout option designed to attract sales from customers who would not have come into the restaurant. There are two schools of thought in the segment in regard to the breadth of the menu. Some, like segment leader Applebee's, attempt to be all things to all people, while others, like Chevy's, concentrate on adding new and unique flavors to take their menu to the next level (e.g., Chevy's Fresh Tex menu items).

The top five casual dinnerhouse chains in terms of annual market share are as follows:[10]

| Rank | Chain | Annual Market Share |
| --- | --- | --- |
| 1 | Applebee's Neighborhood Bar & Grill | 15% |
| 2 | Chili's Grill & Bar | 11 |
| 3 | Outback Steakhouse | 10 |
| 4 | Red Lobster | 9 |
| 5 | Olive Garden | 9 |

## Major Contractors

The 14 contract caterers in the Top 100 represent over 45,000 contract venues. Recent gains in education and health care contracting have offset difficulties in the business-and-industry and airline sectors. The greatest recent growth has been in primary- and secondary-school markets, which long resisted outsourcing their meal services. On the other hand, the airline sector has suffered as airlines have cut meal service in an attempt to reduce costs. Some airlines are experimenting with partnerships with chains like T.G.I. Friday's and Wolfgang Puck to sell meals on board flights.

A growing trend is to award multisite contracts—where a corporation bids all its foodservice at the same time. This tends to favor the largest national contractor over the smaller regional operator.

The top five contractors in terms of annual market share are as follows:[11]

| Rank | Chain | Annual Market Share |
| --- | --- | --- |
| 1 | Aramark Global Food/Leisure Services | 29% |
| 2 | Canteen Services | 10 |
| 3 | Sodexho Healthcare Services | 9 |
| 4 | Sodexho Campus Services | 8 |
| 5 | Sodexho Corporate Services | 8 |

## Pizza Chains

The six pizza chains in the Top 100 consist of just over 19,000 units producing an average of $733,000 per unit. In recent years pizza chains have pursed a strategy of competing on price by targeting college students and young families. While some marketing consultants disagree with such a strategy, the chains have responded by attempting to get out of competing on the basis of price by competing on the basis of new products. Many see that as a reactionary tactic rather than a well-thought-out long-term strategy. As a result of engaging in price wars, chains have been unable to build their brand. As a result, pizza is seen as a commodity product rather than a branded product. One effect is that pizza chains are facing competition from supermarkets that are selling branded, frozen pizzas.

The chains seem to be going for a "national taste" rather than taking regional preferences into account. As a result, the mom-and-pop units that add more oregano in the Northeast or spice things up in the southwest tend to produce better-tasting pizza.

The top five chains by annual market share are as follows:[12]

| Rank | Chain | Annual Market Share |
|------|-------|--------------------|
| 1 | Pizza Hut | 42% |
| 2 | Domino's Pizza | 26 |
| 3 | Papa John's Pizza | 14 |
| 4 | Little Caesar's Pizza | 10 |
| 5 | Chuck E. Cheese's | 4 |

## Family Chains

The nine family market chains in the Top 100 consist of just over 7000 units producing average revenue of over $1.6 million per store. The family market is not easily swayed by new trends. As such, the chains tend toward subtle changes in menu, design, and advertising. A number of chains have been working to update their nighttime images as a way of increasing sales.

The top five family chains in the Top 100 are as follows:[13]

| Rank | Chain | Annual Market Share |
|------|-------|--------------------|
| 1 | Denny's | 22% |
| 2 | IHOP/International House of Pancakes | 19 |
| 3 | Cracker Barrel Old Country Store | 16 |
| 4 | Bob Evans Restaurants | 10 |
| 5 | Waffle House | 8 |

## Chicken Chains

The seven chicken chains in the Top 100 consist of 10,697 units producing an average of just over $1 million per unit.

The top five chicken chains by annual market share are as follows:[14]

| Rank | Chain | Annual Market Share |
|---|---|---|
| 1 | KFC | 49% |
| 2 | Chick-fil-A | 17 |
| 3 | Popeye's Chicken & Biscuits | 13 |
| 4 | Church's Chicken | 7 |
| 5 | Boston Market | 7 |

## Hotels

There are seven hotel chains in the Top 100 with over 4000 units that average over $2.9 million. Hotel occupancy has suffered through a poor economy, cutbacks in corporate travel, various levels of terrorist alert, and problems in the airline industry. To counter these events some hotels are outsourcing their restaurant operations while others seek to appeal to the leisure market. Some are taking the opportunity to upgrade facilities in anticipation of better times while others are developing concepts to appeal to local residents as well as in-house guests. An increasing number of hotels are opening with no foodservice as part of a "suite" or "express" brand.

The top five hotel chains in terms of annual market share are as follows:[15]

| Rank | Chain | Annual Market Share |
|---|---|---|
| 1 | Marriot Hotels, Resorts, and Suites | 22% |
| 2 | Hilton Hotels | 19 |
| 3 | Sheraton Hotels | 17 |
| 4 | Holiday Inns | 12 |
| 5 | Radisson | 11 |

## Grill-Buffet Chains

There are three grill-buffet chains in the Top 100 consisting of over 1000 units with average revenue of just over $2.2 million. The chains market a combination of self-service, broad menus, and budget price points. The chains have been getting a smaller share of Top 100 revenue in recent years as they compete with fast-casual restaurants for the same customers.

The three grill-buffet chains in the Top 100 have market share as follows:[16]

| Rank | Chain | Annual Market Share |
|------|-------|---------------------|
| 1 | Golden Corral | 51% |
| 2 | Ryan's Family Steak House | 29 |
| 3 | Ponderosa Steakhouse | 20 |

*Note:* Does not equal 100% because of rounding.

---

### quick bite 1.5
### American Restaurants in the Global Restaurant Industry

**Learning Objective:** Provide a financial overview of the restaurant industry in the United States.

Across the world, the restaurant industry has slowed in recent years due to a poor economy. In Western markets, fast food has fallen in popularity due to a new interest in healthier eating. Despite this downward turn in fast food popularity, American and European consumers still enjoy eating out, and their Asian-Pacific and South American counterparts are increasingly spending their time and money in bars and restaurants.

The global restaurant sector was worth an estimated $1.4 trillion in 2003. The compound annual growth rate of 3.8 percent has gone down from 4.9 percent in 2000, but has begun to increase once more. Looking ahead, the fast food segment is expected to drive the growth of the industry, despite its slowing in the Western world. The growth in fast food is primarily the result of its popularity in developing markets.

The United States' McDonald's Corporation is the world's biggest fast food chain and seems likely to keep that spot for some time. However, recent U.S. consumer demand for healthier options has created a structural problem for the company, leading many to speculate that McDonald's biggest market in the future will be overseas.

The largest market for the restaurant sector is, unsurprisingly, the United States, with about 32 percent of the sector value share. The U.S. is closely followed by Europe with 30.3 percent and Asia-Pacific with 27.3 percent.

*Source: DataMonitor,* "Restaurant Industry Profile: Global," May 2004, pp. 1–18.

**Discussion Question:** What do you think accounts for the decrease in popularity of fast food in the Western world and the increase in its popularity in developing countries? What should fast-food venues do in response to these trends?

## WHY RESTAURANTS FAIL

By some estimates, one out of every three restaurants fails in the first year of operation. One study of publicly held companies identified the following events described as unique in the bankruptcy process of restaurant firms:[17]

- Net losses
- Management turnover
- Loan default
- Royalty default
- Credit accommodation
- Decline in unit sales
- Renegotiation of franchise contract

There are a variety of reasons for the high failure rate in this business.[18] Simply put,

Profit = sales – costs

Thus, to achieve profitability it is necessary to increase sales while reducing costs. By increasing costs through such things as bigger portion sizes or more service, a restaurant becomes more attractive to customers, thereby increasing sales. The reverse is also true. Costs can be trimmed by having fewer employees or cheaper cuts of meat, which might lead to the loss of customers, thereby reducing sales. We focus our discussion of the reasons that restaurants fail on the two sides of the profit equation: sales and costs.

## The Restaurant Industry Dollar

The following statements of income and expenses give a statistical overview of the restaurant industry dollar. All figures are medians based on 2004 data. All ratios are based on a percentage of total sales except food and beverage costs, which are based on their respective sales. A represents full-service restaurants, average check per person under $15.00; B represents full-service restaurants, average check per person $15.00 to $24.99; C represents full-service restaurants with an average check over $25.00; D represents limited-service restaurants that serve both food and beverage.

|  | A | B | C | D |
|---|---|---|---|---|
| **Sales** | | | | |
| Food sales | 82% | 78% | 71% | 85% |
| Beverage sales (alcoholic) | 18 | 22 | 29 | 15 |
| Total sales | 100 | 100 | 100 | 100 |
| **Cost of sales** | | | | |
| Food cost | 34 | 37 | 34 | 30 |
| Beverage cost | 30 | 28 | 30 | 29 |
| Total cost of sales | 33 | 34 | 33 | 30 |
| Gross profit | 67 | 65 | 67 | 69 |
| **Operating expenses** | | | | |
| Salaries and wages (including employee benefits) | 34 | 34 | 32 | 33 |
| Direct operating expenses | 7 | 7 | 6 | 6 |
| Music and entertainment | 0.3 | 0.4 | 1 | 0 |
| Marketing | 2 | 2 | 2 | 2 |
| Utility services | 3 | 3 | 3 | 3 |
| Restaurant occupancy costs | 5 | 5 | 7 | 8 |
| Repairs and maintenance | 1 | 2 | 1 | 1 |
| Depreciation | 2 | 2 | 1 | 2 |
| Other expense/(income) | 0.2 | 0.2 | 0.4 | 2 |
| Administrative and general | 3 | 3 | 3 | 3 |
| Corporate overhead | 4 | 2 | 2 | 3 |
| Total operating expenses* | 60 | 60 | 62 | 60 |
| Interest expense | 1 | 1 | 0.3 | 1 |
| Other expenses | 0.3 | 0.3 | 0.6 | — |
| Income before income taxes | 5.5 | 4 | 3 | 6 |

*Many do not total correctly because of rounding.

Source: *Restaurant Industry Operations Report, 2005* (Washington, DC: Deloitte & Touche and the National Restaurant Association, 2005), pp. 29, 57, 85, 113.

It is perhaps surprising that food costs are relatively similar across all four categories. We might expect that food costs in limited-service restaurants would be much less than in full-service operations. It may be that convenience food—which costs more than items prepared from scratch—is used more in limited-service restaurants. This is offset by having lower labor costs in limited-service restaurants.

Many students like the prestige of working in restaurants that have a higher average check. Notice, however, the difference in income before income taxes across all four categories. Higher check does not necessarily translate into higher income.

---

### quick fact

One of the latest concepts seeking to capture the breakfast niche is taking traditional breakfast and the idea of fast food a step further. Cereality is a cereal bar and café founded in 2005. At Cereality, customers choose from their favorite brands and toppings. Pajama-clad Cereologists™ fill the orders and customers choose and add their own milk, just the way they like it. To see how this concept is creating a new spin on one of America's life-long breakfast staples, visit *http://www.cereality.com/*.

*Source: http://www.cereality.com/comp.php.* Accessed October 30, 2005.

---

## Failure to Increase Sales

**Same Concept.** Many failures occur because management stays with the same concept for too long. Like other products and services, restaurants have a life cycle. In the early stages of a new operation, the restaurant goes through an introductory stage in which the concept is introduced into the marketplace. If all goes well, the operation experiences a period of growth, in which sales are increasing at an increasing rate. As the concept matures, sales continue to increase but at a decreasing rate. If no action is taken, a period of decline sets in, during which sales fall. Throughout the life-cycle curve, profits lead sales. That is, a downturn in profits precedes a downturn in sales. In this way it is possible to get advance warning about where the restaurant is in the cycle.

If advance notice is given and the operation changes, it is possible to go through a period of rejuvenation rather than decline. Fast-food restaurants attempted this a few years ago when they added breakfast items to their menus as a response to a slowdown in sales. One way to rejuvenate an operation is to sell a product or service at additional times: hence the breakfast menu. Fast-food restaurants made a similar decision when they expanded internationally. The domestic market was becoming saturated, and future growth necessitated overseas expansion. This is another way to rejuvenate—sell to another market.

**Lack of Creativity.** Lack of sales often comes from a lack of imagination and creativity in developing new ideas. We are conditioned to believe that "new is good." Increasingly, the public is looking for new ways to do things, new items on the menu, new experiences in general. Managers cannot afford to rely on the status quo. Flexibility is the key—operators need to adopt an attitude that encourages them and their employees to seek constant improvement in their restaurants.

Falling sales may be due partially to the human tendency to react to new situations rather than to anticipate them. There are constant changes in the marketplace. Changing economic conditions may include a demand for less expensive menu items; increased concern over alcohol abuse leads to less consumption of alcohol. The reactive manager waits until trends work their way through society and manifest themselves in a different, reduced, or nonexistent customer base. The proactive manager reads newspapers and magazines, attends industry forums where trends are discussed, anticipates the likelihood of events happening, identifies their potential effects on the business, and changes the operation accordingly before the effects of the changes are felt. In other words, the proactive manager plans rather than simply operates the business.

## Failure to Control Costs

Most restaurants operate on relatively small profit margins. Cost control is very important in ensuring a profitable margin. In foodservice operations, the principal areas of cost are labor, food, and beverages. Keeping a close watch on these three areas helps ensure profitability.

**Productivity.** To a large extent, high employee costs are a result of poor productivity. Productivity is the ratio of outputs (sales, profits, etc.) to inputs (time, costs, etc.). Typically, this ratio is less for service industries than for manufacturing concerns. In fact, the National Restaurant Association has estimated that the restaurant industry is only half as productive as the manufacturing industries. To

> "It's a sad commentary on the state of franchise relations...that in many cases the franchisor is the franchisee's biggest competitor."
> —GARY AUSTERMAN,
> FRANCHISEES' ATTORNEY

Problems between franchisor and franchisee is one of the causes of restaurant failure. *Source: Nation's Restaurant News,* October 9, 1995, p. 118.

the extent that service is important to customers, it is difficult to achieve a sales increase by reducing staff. However, labor cost savings of 10 to 20 percent can be expected through improved employee scheduling alone, resulting in a savings of 3 to 6 percent of sales.[19]

**Cost Cutting.**   Many operators fall into a cost-cutting mode that is counterproductive. When sales drop, managers are often tempted to cut costs to compensate for reduced sales. Advertising may be reduced; employee uniforms are not laundered as frequently; less expensive cuts of meat replace menu staples. As a result, the customers who remain become disenchanted with the operation and leave. The focus often is on cutting costs when it should be on increasing sales.

This comes about because of the cost structure of restaurants. So many of a restaurant's costs are fixed; they do not vary as sales volume varies. The mortgage or lease payment must still be made whether there is one customer or a thousand; the restaurant must be lit regardless of the number of patrons. As a consequence, only a limited amount of cost cutting can take place. In operations where a high proportion of costs are fixed, the break-even point—the point at which sales generated exactly equals costs incurred—is higher than for businesses in which a large proportion of the costs are variable. A variable cost is one that varies proportionately with sales volume (Figure 1.1).

However, once the break-even point has been passed, the only costs incurred are variable costs. In restaurants, the variable costs are relatively small compared to the fixed costs. As a result, once an operation has reached a sales volume above the break-even point, the profit potential from a relatively small increase in sales volume becomes great. Managers might therefore better focus their attention on increasing sales rather than on spending time seeking to minimize

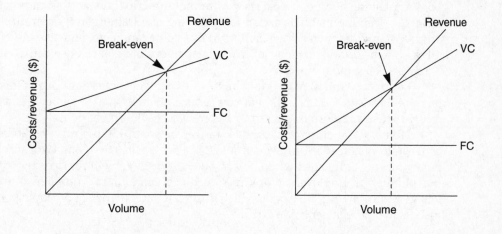

(a) High proportion of fixed costs relative to variable costs

(b) High proportion of variable costs relative to fixed costs

**Figure 1.1**   Break-even chart.

costs. This is not to negate the importance of cost control; it is, rather, to suggest that with a finite amount of management time available, profits might be increased more by focusing on the sales side of the profit equation than on the cost side.

## SUCCESS FACTORS

The key to a successful operation is to develop the right concept, expand carefully, execute the concept skillfully, and deliver quality service.

### Right Concept

Almost 30 percent of new, independent restaurants fail in the first year while as many as 60 percent go out of business in the first five years. The restaurants that do succeed begin with a great concept and brand. The former require tightly run operations and a motivated team from top to bottom that delivers consistent quality.

### Careful Expansion

Another success variable is careful expansion. This begins with site feasibility and the "economies of gain" that come from operating and marketing efficiency. Above all, however, the success or failure of an operation depends on hiring, training, and motivating a team of employees.

### Skillful Execution

To ensure that employees have the skills to perform to standard, employers should provide a full range of activities for employees. This begins with a handbook explaining company policies, written job descriptions, and an orientation program. Training manuals are an integral part of a training program, but films or videos are used increasingly in part to overcome language difficulties. A complete system includes regular job performance evaluations to ensure that standards are being maintained.

From the standpoint of profitability, one of the best measures of an effective team is turnover. Restaurants that can reduce turnover have a better chance to return a positive return on investment compared to those that do not.[20]

Hourly wage employee turnover ranges between 150 percent and 200 percent while managerial turnover of about 50 percent is common. Two hundred percent turnover means that, in any given year, management replaces two times the number of employees employed by the operation. The problem is made worse by a shrinking labor pool, which is expected to go from 11.3 people per job in 1990 to 6 people per job in 2010.[21]

### Service

Service is a major concern for both customers and operators. Indeed, service complaints dominate, far exceeding customer complaints about food or atmosphere. Five elements have been identified as important: providing timely service,

## quick bite 1.6
### Why Restaurants Fail—and Succeed

**Learning Objectives:** Identify the reasons that restaurants fail. Identify the major reasons contributing to the financial success of a restaurant.

In the restaurant industry, there's a long-standing myth that 90 percent of restaurants fail within the first year. This myth has been picked up by the public and by bankers, who are understandably reluctant to give loans to budding restaurants. However, this figure has been proved wrong in many studies. It's not 90 percent; it's more like 57–61 percent.

That's still a high rate of failure. What causes restaurants to fail anyway? There are many factors that can lead to the demise of a restaurant. Howard Gordon, the senior vice president of business development for The Cheesecake Factory, believes that restaurants fail because they've lost focus: "The only restaurants [who fail] are the ones who no longer deliver on what they originally promised."

New restaurateurs with no idea of how to market a concept or handle front-of-house communications are ill-equipped to deal with the instabilities of the restaurant industry. They are also generally unprepared for the difficulties of working in the business, like working 65-hour weeks, working holidays, and committing to philoxenia—the love of strangers.

According to Ken Fredrickson, a partner and master sommelier at Adega Restaurant & Wine Bar in Denver, new restaurants fail because the owners are undercapitalized and inexperienced. Fredrickson is confident that Adega will succeed, although it occupies a space where several restaurants have failed before. "We have incredible experience and are very well-capitalized," he said.

Obstacles can be overcome, and the best teacher in the restaurant industry is experience. It's most often the ones who do not give up who succeed in the end.

*Sources:* Sanson, Michael, "The 90% Restaurant First-Year Failure Rate Is a Myth," *Restaurant Hospitality,* November 2003, vol. 87, no. 11, p. 8. Walkup, Carolyn, "Newcomers Have No Reservations About Plans of Success," *Nation's Restaurant News,* August 12, 2002, vol. 36, no. 32, pp. 20, 103. Watson, Dave and Karousos, George, "The Failure Rate Is Bogus," *Restaurant Hospitality,* January 2004, vol. 88, no. 1, p. 10.

**Discussion Questions**: Are the difficulties of running a restaurant mostly internal (inability to communicate, difficulty working long hours) or mostly external (difficulty in getting loans, difficulty in attracting customers)? Which are easier to solve?

answering customer questions, handling complaints, delivering accurately to-taled guest checks, and recommending appropriate menu items. Customers seem most satisfied with the accuracy of the check and the server's ability to answer questions, although only 75 percent rated staff as "good" or "excellent" on these items. Almost two-thirds of respondents rated servers "good" or "excellent" in recommending appropriate menu items.

The two most common complaints in the aforementioned categories concern speed of service and inattentive staff. The former can involve service that is too slow or the feeling of being rushed. It is important to tailor the speed of service to the individual and the occasion. In the latter case, customers are upset by having to summon employees to give an order or by waiting for a check. For cus-

Boston Market

tomers, the wait seems longest after the meal is over. Delays during a meal seem shorter than waits either before or after the meal. Customers are most dissatisfied with the way that complaints are handled. The subject of service is dealt with in more detail in Chapter 6.

## ENDNOTES

1. Allan F. Hickok and Lana E. Lazarus, *Restaurant Industry Review*, U.S. Bancorp Piper Jaffray Equity Research, March 2003, p. 9.
2. National Restaurant Association, *2005 Restaurant Industry Forecast* (Washington, DC: National Restaurant Association, 2005), p. 2.
3. See *www.restaurant.org*, the official site of the National Restaurant Association, for detailed reports.
4. National Restaurant Association, *Tableservice Restaurant Trends, 2005* (Washington, DC: National Restaurant Association, 2005), pp. 3–4.
5. Claire D. Schmelzer and James R. Lang, "Networking and Information Sources of Independent Restaurateurs," *Hospitality Research Journal*, vol. 14, no. 2, 1990, pp. 327–338.
6. Donald E. Lundberg, *The Restaurant: From Concept to Operation* (New York: John Wiley & Sons, 1985), pp. 18–22.
7. "NRN Top 100," *Nation's Restaurant News*, vol. 39, no. 26, June 27, 2005.
8. Ibid., p. 152.
9. Ibid., p. 98.
10. Ibid., p. 106.
11. Ibid., p. 114.
12. Ibid., p. 118.
13. Ibid., p. 126.
14. Ibid., p. 132.
15. Ibid., p. 140.
16. Ibid., p. 150.
17. Francis A. Kwansa and H. G. Parsa, "Business Failure Analysis," *Hospitality Research Journal*, vol. 14, no. 2, 1990, pp. 23–34.
18. Lewis J. Minor and Ronald F. Cichy, *Foodservice Systems Management* (Westport, CT: AVI Publishing Company, 1984), pp. 18–23.
19. Robert Christie Mill, *Managing for Productivity in the Hospitality Industry* (New York: Van Nostrand Reinhold, 1989), p. 53.

20. Allan F. Hickok and Lana E. Lazarus, *Restaurant Industry Review,* U.S. Bancorp Piper Jaffray Equity Research, March 2003, pp. 6–7.
21. Ibid., p. 22.

## INTERNET RESOURCES

| | |
|---|---|
| National Restaurant Association | *http://www.restaurant.org/* |
| U.S. Chamber of Commerce | *http://www.uschamber.com/* |
| *Nation's Restaurant News* | *http://www.nrn.com/* |
| Food Franchise | *http://www.foodfranchise.com/* |
| Pizza Hut | *http://www.pizzahut.com/* |
| Applebee's Neighborhood Grill & Bar | *http://www.applebees.com/* |
| McDonald's | *http://www.mcdonalds.com/* |
| Marriott Hotels | *http://www.marriott.com/* |

## QUICK QUIZ ANSWER KEY

p. 4—Ordinaires.
p. 12—b. France, 1765.

# CHAPTER TWO

# UNDERSTANDING THE CUSTOMER

"A restaurant is a fantasy—a kind of living fantasy in which diners are the most important members of the cast."
Warner LeRoy, founder,
Maxwell's Plum restaurant, New York City

## learning objectives

*By the end of this chapter you should be able to*

1. Identify the three market categories of the foodservice industry in terms of the physical and psychological needs customers seek to satisfy.

2. Compare and contrast recent trends in the industry identified through trend spotters and traditional research.

3. Suggest how restaurants can respond effectively to recent trends in the marketplace.

4. Compare and contrast the 1996, 2002, and 2005 consumer behavior studies conducted by the National Restaurant Association, and suggest implications for restaurants.

### Hot Concept: Hospitals in Search of Culinary Success

Hospital cafeteria food has been traditionally known as bland and unappealing. For most patients receiving meals from the hospital, the food is neither tasteful nor fulfilling. At most hospitals, food is served buffet-style. Customers see what food has been prepared and then select the food of their choice.

Hospitals often fall short in the task of understanding the foodservice preferences of patients and other customers. Since most hospitals do not address their clients' culinary desires, it's not surprising that patients often resort to other means of satisfying their hunger.

Customer expectations have changed; today, instead of canned foods or prepared frozen foods, customers are insisting upon fresher food and ingredients and a variety of menu choices served in a comfortable atmosphere. Sarosh Mistry of Healthcare Support Services stated that "today's patients are picking the place they want to go to get a procedure done, especially if it's an elective procedure. A hospital has to be good all the way around. It truly is survival of the fittest."

Hospitals are limited in what they are able to serve; therefore, some hospitals are getting help from Aramark, a Healthcare Support Services' World Class Patient Service program which focuses on improving the foodservice at hospitals. Aramark utilizes a variety of elements to improve service, from color-coordinated tray mats and menu materials to room service.

With the help of Aramark's Design Solutions and Culinary Solutions divisions, Healthcare Support Services are trying to create modern, more updated facilities in hospitals and other long-term care centers. Aramark is trying to meet expectations by providing surveys to visitors, patients and employees to measure their levels of satisfaction in the hope of improving service.

Health care providers are looking for foodservice companies that can facilitate improvement in the quality of their services, not just to attract patients but also to attract and retain nurses, doctors, and other employees. Some hospital cafeterias are now receiving better ratings and have shown improvement in food sales since they have changed their focus and are now meeting their market/customer base needs.

*Source:* Berta, Dina, "Hospital Corner: Flavorful Food the Rx for Success in Health Care Dining." *Nation's Restaurants News*, vol. 37, no. 33, August 18, 2003, pp. 66, 68.

**Discussion Question:** How might hospitals meet their market/customer base needs?

## INTRODUCTION

An understanding of the restaurant customer is useful as long as the limitations of such a study are appreciated. It is useful as a way of seeing the big picture: Why do people eat out, and what are the characteristics of this activity? However, any attempt to characterize the restaurant customer will result in a picture that, although valid in the aggregate, will probably not be accurate for any particular operation. Thus, although this chapter will be useful to managers overall, it will be necessary to develop a marketing plan (Chapter 3) to make the picture relevant to the individual operation.

## MARKET CATEGORIES

One way to make market categories relevant is to think of the foodservice industry as being arranged in three general categories: the captive market, the mass market, and the status market (Figure 2.1).

### Captive Market

The captive market—in institutions, industrial or school settings, and airplanes—is limited in the choice of what is available. These customers have little choice in what to eat, when and where to eat, and the price if a charge is made. The primary concern here is "how we eat."

When people are given little or no choice in the mechanics of the eating experience, there is a tendency to rebel. Having little or no choice in these matters is like being treated as a child. As a child, adults told us when to eat, what to eat, how to eat, and how much to eat. When people grow up, they want to make these decisions for themselves and resent being put back in the role of a child. Take, for example, eating on a plane. Passengers are served when it is convenient for the cabin staff to do so, and remain trapped in place until the staff decides to collect the platters.

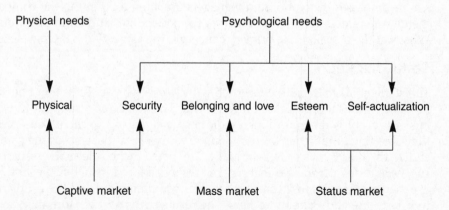

**Figure 2.1** Needs and the foodservice industry.

Research in British mental institutions has shown some rather sophisticated behavior on the part of patients regarding food. Hoarding of food, midnight snacks, and secret parties allowed the patients to exhibit some degree of control over their food intake—control that was not allowed in the way they were served their meals.

There is some indication that traditional complaints about institutional food have less to do with the food and more to do with the way the food is served and the lack of control the customers have in that process. Allowing some degree of choice in how, when, and where food is served may result in fewer complaints and more satisfied customers.

McDonald's is one company that combined cost and availability in its initial marketing thrust. The first national advertising campaign for McDonald's did not mention food or beverage. It said, "You deserve a break today; so get out and get away—to McDonald's." The ads were talking to the busy mother, trying to balance the needs of home, children, and, often, a job outside the home. This person was hungry, the children were hungry, and the conflicting demands of the mother's life left her exhausted. The "solution" was a trip to McDonald's. Catering to physical needs, McDonald's offered a break from the work of preparing food by serving food at low cost to the customer.

---

### quick quiz

What was the original meaning of the word *restaurant?*

a. Meeting house
b. Place of rest
c. Restorative broth

---

## Mass Market

The mass market looks for food in a social setting. This large segment of the market encompasses everyone from teenagers grabbing a burger in the company of friends and families eating out together to special dates and anniversary dinners. Whatever the occasion, the primary concern is the same: with whom we eat.

## Status Market

The status market is more concerned with where we eat. To see and be seen is more important than what is on the menu. The choice of restaurant to which a business client is taken for lunch indicates what status the client "deserves." At the same time, the prices on the menu are, in part, a measure of the status accorded the host by his or her company. The person who selects the restaurant or suggests an item from the menu takes responsibility for that suggestion. If the experience is good, the recommendation is complimented and the recipient gets to bask in the admiration of others. The reverse is also true: More than an overcooked steak is on the line.

Men prefer red meat!

It should be emphasized that at different times of the week, the same person can be concerned with the satisfaction of different needs. An executive may grab a salad at Wendy's for lunch on Monday, dine with her husband at a romantic getaway on Tuesday, and treat a business client to lunch in an upscale club on Wednesday. In the first instance the concern is physical—to refuel; in the second it is belonging and love—to create the mood for romance; and in the third it is esteem—to impress the client. The key for the operator is to understand the underlying motivation for the dining experience and to organize all elements of the marketing mix to meet those needs and wants.

## TREND ANALYSIS[1]

The relatively new concept of trend analysis involves identifying the behaviors of trendsetters or early adopters (consumers who are among the first to try/buy new products). Such people tend to be under age 30. Trend analysis can be effective method of successfully launching a new menu item, restaurant concept, or advertising campaign.

### Trend Spotters

In the 1960s, market-research firms began taking a scientific approach to opinion polls, surveys, and focus groups in an attempt to help businesses anticipate trends. These methods are a reliable way to research behaviors of specific demographic groups.

Although traditional research remains the most reliable method of obtaining market data, a number of researchers—termed "cool hunters" or "trend

**Customer Satisfaction**

**Learning Objective:** Identify the three market categories of the foodservice industry in terms of the physical and psychological needs customers seek to satisfy.

Customers come to restaurants looking for psychological as well as physical satisfaction. To fulfill the psychological needs of a customer, extraordinary service is in order. The following explains the dimensions of psychological needs of the customer how these needs should be met:

| Dimensions | The Extraordinary Meal Experience |
|---|---|
| Motivation | De-routinization of consumption/escape |
| Expectation | No script |
| | Curiosity |
| | Capacity to act |
| Interaction | Being part of the production |
| | Opportunities for action |
| | Recognition |
| Involvement | Absorption |
| | Familiarity |
| | Emotion |
| Satisfaction | Surprise |
| | Pleasure |
| | Enjoyment |
| | Memorable |

*Source: Journal of Business & Management,* Summer 2003, vol. 9, issue 3, pp. 249, 22p.

**Discussion Question:** Looking at the dimension table, how might a server anticipate and meet the needs of the customer?

spotters"—attempt to divine the trends that will develop to fruition in the next 5 to 10 years by observing the behaviors of early adopters.

Work tends to focus in the key markets of New York City, Miami, Chicago, Seattle, San Francisco, and Los Angeles. Instead of using focus groups of 10 or so target customers in a discussion group or surveying many people to get quantitative scores, these researchers hire "urban pioneers" who conduct one-on-one, on-the-street interviews with 18- to 30-year-olds. The technique looks at behavior rather than opinions. It is common for people to say one thing yet do something else.

## Trends: Early Adopters

Early adopters being tracked in New York City are expressing particular interest in childhood foods and Indian and East Asian influences. Some believe that many of today's high-profile restaurants are successful in part because they tap into current cultural values. Asia de Cuba in New York City, for example, uses its Latin/Asian fusion cuisine and its popular communal table to express recent popular trends. The first of these is called "cultural infidelity"—an interest in mixing and blending different cultural influences. The second trend, "merit badges," is the desire for unique experiences that cannot be duplicated. This might involve eating with an interesting group of total strangers from various countries.

"Customization" has recently been identified as a current cultural value that has contributed to the popularity of such things as tasting menus in restaurants. Tasting menus offer patrons the opportunity to try smaller portions of a variety of dishes. Customers enjoy having more choices and a greater chance to experiment. There is also less risk involved in ordering a smaller portion compared to eating a regular-size entrée. If the customers orders three items, they might not like one of them but are rewarded with two good experiences. At the same time, customers do not want to customize if the task appears too challenging. A tasting menu is an easy way to offer the customer the opportunity to customize.

## Trends: Traditional Research

Results from more traditional market research indicate four customer trends will be key in shaping the restaurant industry over the next 10 years:[2]

1. Aging of baby boomers
2. Increase in the ethnic population
3. Increase in women in the workforce
4. Decrease in both customers and employees under 25 years of age

**Aging Baby Boomers.** America is getting older and richer. While the fast-casual sector is enjoying great growth, some analysts view the "modern family" as the key to the future. The *modern family* refers to baby boomers, their parents, and their children. This segment is growing older and has the financial resources to demand more from the meal occasion. They want fuller flavors as they seek value for money. Boomers will use quick service less and replace it with full-service alternatives that offer a wider menu variety and higher quality. Consider the following:[3]

- Ten thousand Americans turn 50 every day.
- Six thousand Americans turn 65 every day; by 2010 that number will be 9000.
- Americans over the age of 50 control more than three-quarters of the country's financial assets.
- The over-50 population will increase from 26 percent of the U.S. population in 1997 to over one-third in 2012.

According to the U.S. Census Bureau, there will be 96.3 million Americans in the 50-plus age group by 2010. This number will increase to 115.4 million by 2020.[4] Today's seniors are more active, knowledgeable, and financially secure than in the past. Willing to spend money, they are interested in the price–value relationship being offered. They also tend to be very loyal once they find a restaurant they like.

It is wrong to assume that seniors represent a homogeneous segment of the market. A segmentation approach known as "gerontographics" believes that needs and life circumstances make those 55 and over more or less receptive to marketing offerings. There are, in fact, four distinct segments of the over-55 market. The segments are as follows:[5]

- Healthy hermits are in good health but are socially withdrawn. Their time is taken up with day-to-day tasks. They deny that they are old and resent the fact that others expect them to behave like old people. Healthy hermits are well educated and have the highest income of any of the four groups. There are an estimated 20 million people in this segment.
- Ailing outgoers are health conscious and seek to remain socially active. They tend to be retired yet still interested in learning new things. They are approximately 18 million people in this segment.
- Frail reclusives are inactive and have one or more chronic ailments. Spending most of their time at home, the 18 million reclusives are concerned with personal an physical security.
- Healthy indulgers have a lot in common with baby boomers. The 7 million adults in this segment are relatively wealthy and want to make the most of life.

The most important reasons the over-55 groups give for visiting one restaurant over another are the availability of senior-citizen discounts, finding a comfortable place in which to socialize, and the proximity to the residents' home or workplace.

Operators need to be aware of the concerns of these segments and make the necessary adjustments. As seniors get older they appreciate the things that add to their comfort. Restaurants need to go beyond complying with the minimum legal requirements of the Americans with Disabilities Act to make the restaurant attractive and comfortable for seniors.

Seniors appreciate subtlety. They do not want to be reminded continually that they are getting older and need assistance with such things as reading the menu. Make sure that customers can safely and comfortably navigate the restaurant. Changes in elevation need to be marked with lighting. Alternatively, there can be a change in texture such as moving from a wood floor to a carpet. As obvious as it may seem, all stairs should include a handrail. Cluttered, busy patterns are especially distracting to older people. Simple designs make getting around easier for seniors.

According to research conducted for the National Restaurant Association (NRA),[6] full-service restaurants with an atmosphere that allows for quiet conversation are appealing to 81 percent of adults age 55 to 64 and 72 percent of those age 65 and older. Sound barriers and sound-absorbing materials throughout the restaurant are particularly helpful.

Seniors are more concerned with food quality than price, service, or location. Only 20 percent have a special diet. A menu can be made more senior friendly by:[7]

- Offering choices. Some seniors prefer simpler, low-fat foods while others will want to try new dishes and flavor combinations.
- Serving smaller portions at lower prices. Some restaurants create a special senior menu while others offer half-portions of standard dishes. Many seniors may resent being singled out by means of a special seniors menu.
- Targeting promotions. Operators may advertise in senior-related magazines and in senior-living facility newsletters. NRA research indicates, however, that when choosing a new restaurant, seniors are most likely to use recommendations from family and friends and least likely to use the Internet as the basis for their dining decisions. They also are influenced more by restaurant reviews and guides than print and broadcast advertisements.
- Implementing early-bird specials. Seniors (and families with young children) often prefer to dine early. Special promotions during the pre-prime-time hour appeal to this group and provide additional sales during slow time slots.
- Providing a senior discount at times that are particularly slow.
- Creating an easy-to-read menu. Use simple fonts and a type size that can be read easily by people who have vision difficulties. Bold type and graphics are also helpful.
- Installing legible signage around the facility.
- Targeting the level of service. Seniors expect a certain level of respect from (younger) servers, who may be used to giving more casual service to younger customers.
- Adding community tables to appeal to seniors and singles of all ages that prefer not to eat alone.
- Offering transportation for those who no longer drive or who prefer not to.
- Adding easy to-go options. Seniors are not the strongest segment of the takeout market. However, according to National Restaurant Association research,[8] 15 percent of the 50 and older age group are daily takeout users, 18 percent are frequent users, 28 percent are moderate users, and 35 percent are light users.

**Growing Ethnic Population.** By 2010 Caucasians will represent 72 percent of the U.S. population compared to 77 percent in 1990. By 2020 the three largest minority groups in the United States—African Americans, Hispanics, and Asian Americans—will make up 35 percent of the population.[9] In the next few years the largest increase in the minority population will come from the Latino population, who will make up 12 percent of the population by 2010. These second- and third-generation Latinos will be more likely to eat out than their first-generation parents. Restaurant operators will need to consider language and marketing that is culture specific; menus will have to incorporate ethnic flavorings; staffing and training will have to accommodate different languages.[10]

Table 2.1 indicates food categories that particularly appeal to the three largest minority groups in the United States.

In the 1990s restaurants began to respond to the preferences of the ethnic population. In fact, the market for ethnic food has grown to such an extent that Italian, Mexican, and Chinese (Cantonese) cuisines have joined the mainstream

**Table 2.1 Critical Ethnic Brand Categories**

| Categories | Hispanics | Asian Americans | African Americans |
|---|---|---|---|
| Rice | X | X | |
| Noodles | | X | |
| Sauces | X | X | X |
| Canned juices | X | X | |
| Canned fruit | X | X | |
| Corn products | X | | X |
| Spices | X | X | X |
| Flours | X | | X |
| Canned vegetables | X | X | X |
| Sodas | X | X | |
| Legumes | X | | X |
| Juices | X | | X |

*Source:* "Grow with America: Best Practices in Ethnic Marketing and Merchandising," from The Coca-Cola Retailing Council, undated, reprinted in a Hobart advertising supplement to *Nation's Restaurant News,* 2003.

American culture and are no longer considered ethnic. Compared with data from 1994, six cuisines have grown significantly in popularity—Italian, Mexican, Japanese (sushi), Thai, Caribbean, and Middle Eastern—while four—French, German, Scandinavian, and Soul Food—have undergone a decline in popularity.

As a result of the assimilation of ethnic cuisines into American culture, customers now judge ethnic restaurants in the same ways that they evaluate other establishments. Gone are the days when customers would accept poor service for the chance to try something new and exotic.

In addition to the ethnic population itself, there are two additional segments that are very involved with ethnic cuisine: "internationalists" and "urban professionals."[11] Internationalists are younger individuals who live in major metropolitan areas. They are people who search for a foreign experience. They appreciate authenticity and have a taste for hot, spicy foods. Urban professionals are older than internationalists. They enjoy experimenting with new restaurants and cuisines but they are careful about what they are eating and want to know unmistakably what it is that they are eating.

Internationalists look for the following:[12]

- A menu of unique tastes related to regions of the country producing the ethnic cuisine
- Sophisticated cultural cues in the decor and atmosphere
- Servers able to speak the language of the country producing the ethnic cuisine
- Special cues that make natives of the country producing the cuisine feel welcome
- Cues of authentic cooking

Urban professionals are interested in the following:[13]

- A menu that explains the dishes' ingredients in understandable English
- Changing menus and extensive specials
- Dramatic, unusual food presentations
- Involvement with environmental and health issues
- Affiliation with the local fitness/jogging community

**Women in the Workplace.** Almost two-thirds of all married-couple households have two or three paycheck earners.[14] This increases the amount of money available for spending on restaurant-prepared meals.

Additionally, the income gap between men and women has narrowed in recent years. The median income of females continues to rise. An increasing number of working women in two-earner households bring home bigger paychecks than their husbands. Higher incomes and busier lifestyles of families bringing in more than one paycheck mean more money spent in restaurants.

Households with two or more persons and two paycheck earners spend more than 40 percent above the spending by households with one earner.

Households with three or more earners spend more than 30 percent more than two-earner households.

**Fewer Under-25s.**   The number of people in the under-25 group, the highest users of fast-food meals, will be reduced. It was noted in the previous chapter that casual restaurants are offering takeout options in direct competition to the convenience offered by quick-service restaurants. Both trends will put increased pressure on the quick-service segment of the industry. One long-term approach to the problem is to grow the market from childhood—appeal to the children's segment.[15] As a group, children represent three different markets. They spend $8 billion of their own money on food and beverages and are a strong influence on the food and beverage expenditures of their parents. Research by the NRA indicates that families with children account for 40 percent of spending on food away from home. Children make the choice at least half the time.

Independent operators cannot afford many of the kid-friendly items—play-grounds, colorfully packaged meals, and special giveaway promotions—that the quick-service chains provide. A minimum is to provide a children's menu—even if the child cannot read. The children's menu shows that the restaurant is interested in children. The most common promotion restaurants offer to attract families with kids is child-size portions at lower prices. Ninety percent of restaurants with an average check size of less than $15 and nearly 70 percent of operations with average checks of $25 or more do so.

Menus need to be designed with children in mind. The children's menu at Bob Evans Farms utilized input from both children and their parents to develop tater tots shaped like the letters of the alphabet (so kids can spell out their names on the plate), chicken nibbles, grilled cheese sandwiches, and macaroni and cheese. Employees of the Hyatt Regency Scottsdale in Arizona went to a third-grade classroom to get some ideas. After the chef developed the recipes, the kids came in for a taste test. Food items are given names that tie them to the region of the country. For example, the most popular item on the menu—chicken fingers with fries—is called the "Coyote Special."

While children tend to order foods they are familiar with, they sometimes eat what their parents order in restaurants. By adjusting ethnic recipes to meet children's tastes, operators can help educate a future generation of diners. For example, El Torito Express, a division of Irvine, California–based El Torito Restaurants, has a special menu for children that includes kid-size quesadillas, tacos, and burritos. At the other end of the price range, the $30-per-person check average restaurant Mia Cucina in Palatine, Illinois, has a children's menu of simple Italian dishes like cheese pizza, linguine Alfredo, penne marinara, and rigatoni Bolognese.

Dealing with children can be a challenge because of their short attention spans. Giving the child something to do while the table is waiting for food helps keep children occupied and happy. According to the NRA, almost three-quarters of restaurants with average checks in the $8.00 to $14.99 range offer entertainment, such as coloring books, to children.[16]

## quick bite 2.3
### Baby Boomers Taking Control

**Learning Objectives:** Compare and contrast recent trends in the industry identified through trend spotters and traditional research. Suggest how restaurants can effectively respond to recent trends in the marketplace.

Adults who were born in the United States between 1946 and 1964 are known as the baby boomers. Due to the massive size of the boomer market, it is hard to ignore the demands of a demographic that has such power in the restaurant industry. According to Allan Hickock, restaurant analysts for U.S. Bancorp Piper Jaffray, the future of dining out will rely on the baby boomers. Operators will need to pay attention to the boomers' wants and needs as never before.

The Happy Meal was once a favorite of the baby boomers, but as they age, baby boomers are becoming more aware of what they are putting in their bodies. While boomers may have some dietary restrictions, they still desire sophisticated flavors. Baby boomers enjoy traveling, which would explain why they are more adventurous when it comes to trying new tastes and ingredients. In response to this behavior, development departments are creating menus that appeal to the boomers' sense of adventure.

Baby boomers control more than 77 percent of the nation's financial assets. When they demand their food on their own terms, restaurants have no choice but to respond to their demands. To do otherwise would be bad business.

Boomers do not possess the time to sit down in a casual-dining restaurant, especially when the restaurant is crowded and service is slow. This has led to the growing proliferation of fast-casual or quick-casual restaurants that provide casual-dining-quality food in a modified counter-service format.

Casual-dining operators like Chili's Grill and Bar and Outback Steakhouse have developed sophisticated to-go programs in order to meet the baby boomers' service demands. As with all businesses operating in the hospitality industry, it is especially important that restaurants listen to their customers, determine what customers want, and assist with those wants. In order to be successful, restaurant operators must determine how to stay ahead of the demographic curve and be prepared to provide the boomers what they want.

*Source:* Allen, Robin Lee, "Sonic Boomers: Those Babies Have a Loud Cry That Restaurant Operators Must Heed," *Nation's Restaurant News,* vol. 37, no. 17, p. 43.

**Discussion Question:** Why do casual-dining establishments appeal to baby boomers?

## MEAL OCCASION

Another way to examine the various market segments for meals is to break down customers by meal occasion. Adults average 5.3 restaurant occasions per week.[17] More than 1 billion commercially prepared meals are eaten each week. This number has increased steadily over the past 20 years. It is estimated that, in 2005, over 51 percent of all meals prepared outside the home were for dinner, 38 percent were for lunch, and 12 percent were for breakfast.[18]

Men are more likely than women to eat commercially prepared meals—an average of 4.6 meals a week compared to 3.8 for women. Additionally, a higher proportion of men compared to women eat out frequently: 12.8 percent of men compared with 8.5 percent of women.

Age and income are also factors that influence eating behavior. Males between the ages of 25 and 34 eat out most frequently, while the highest average among females is in the under 18 segment. Finally, as might be expected, people with higher household incomes are more likely than those with lower incomes to eat out.[19]

### Breakfast[20]

In four of the past six years, morning-meal traffic has outpaced total traffic growth. It should be noted, however, that morning-meal business accounts for less than 10 percent of restaurant industry sales. Sales from 11:00 A.M. to 5:00 P.M. make up just under 40 percent of total sales. As might be expected, sales from 5:00 P.M. to 11:00 P.M., with larger average dinner checks, account for just under half of all restaurant industry sales.

Several points can be made about the morning meal:[21]

- Per-person check size is relatively small.
- Quick-service restaurants get 75 percent of morning-meal traffic.
- Customers order more individual menu items when they purchase their morning meal at a full-service restaurant than they do at a quick-service establishment.
- Twenty-five percent of breakfast-oriented servings are purchased using a deal or promotion.
- The largest proportion of breakfast-oriented items are ordered on Sunday, followed by Saturday, Friday, and Thursday.
- Seventy-five percent of breakfast-oriented foods are ordered by parties that do not include any children.

- Purchasing the morning meal at a restaurant is more popular with men than women and with customers older than 35. The morning meal is most popular with customers in the South.
- The most popular breakfast food is the breakfast sandwich, followed by eggs.
- Bacon ranks first in the breakfast-meat category, followed by sausage.
- Doughnuts lead the bread/sweet-roll category, followed closely by bagels and sliced bread/toast.
- There are distinct regional favorites among breakfast-oriented items. The bagel breakfast sandwich is most popular in the East, while in the West it is the breakfast wrap/burrito.

An NRA analysis of research data identifies the following breakdown of who orders what for breakfast:[22]

| Breakfast Item | Appeals Disproportionately to . . . |
| --- | --- |
| English muffin | Males; age 35 and older; upper income; Eastern and Western states |
| English muffin breakfast sandwich | Males; age 35 to 49; central states |
| French toast | Age 50 and older; upper income; Eastern and Western states |
| Grits | Males; age 50 and older; middle income; Southern states |
| Hash browns/ house fries | Males; age 35 and older; middle income; central states |
| Hot cereal | Males; age 50 and older; Western states |
| Muffin | Upper income; Eastern states |
| Pancakes/waffles | Males; age 50 and older |
| Sausage | Males; age 35 and older |
| Toasted/sliced bread | Age 50 and older; Eastern and Western states |

## Lunch

According to the NRA, an increasing number of full-time employees are doing things other than eating during their lunch breaks.[23] Over one-quarter of full-time employees report that they frequently spend their lunch break doing things other than eating, while 4 out of 10 say they do not take a "real" lunch break.

Lunch is increasingly seen as something that is done while doing something else. Twenty years ago it was common for people to take a full hour for lunch, often having a cocktail and a meal. Now the average worker spends 42 minutes on a lunch break. Two-thirds eat lunch at their desks while over 60 percent say they stay at their workstation to snack.[24]

Some restaurants have responded by improving speed of service. Bennigan's, for example, introduced its Time Crunch Lunch a number of years ago. If the time from ordering the food to its arrival on the table is more than 15 minutes, the meal is free. Bennigan's claims a 99 percent efficiency rate. Le Bernardin

### Differences in Consumer Behavior between 1996, 2002, and 2005

**Learning Objective:** Compare and contrast the 1996, 2002, and 2005 consumer behavior studies conducted by the National Restaurant Association, and suggest implications for restaurants.

According to the National Restaurant Association, consumer behavior in 1996 showed the following:

- Twenty-four hour operations recorded a 31 percent food cost, which is substantially below the 35 percent averaged by restaurants serving two or three meals a day.
- Smaller average check size of $5.34.
- Consumers eat an average of 4.1 meals per week away from home.
- Breakfast as the meal most likely to be skipped and least likely to be prepared commercially.
- Lunch was most likely to be commercially prepared and least likely to be privately prepared.
- Dinner was most likely to be privately prepared and least likely to be skipped.
- Males aged 18 to 24 average nearly six commercially prepared meals a week—the highest among all groups.
- Males and females aged 65 and older reported eating the lowest number of commercially prepared meals per—2.5 and 2.3, respectively.
- Residents of households earning more than $75,000 annually consume an average of 5.0 commercially prepared meals per week.
- Members of households earning less than $25,000 annually consume 4.1 commercially prepared meals per week.
- Other groups less likely to consumer commercially prepared meals include unemployed females and households without children.

The National Restaurant Association showed that consumer behavior in 2002 demonstrated the following:

- The average per-person check increased 2 percent to $5.85 during the spring quarter of 2002.
- Traffic growth was the strongest in the higher-check upscale segment estimating 6 percent, followed by the casual segment estimating 4 percent.
- Lunch and evenings meals each posted a 2 percent increase.
- Breakfast traffic increased a relatively weak 1 percent, while P.M. snack traffic declined 4 percent.

- On-premises traffic rose 2 percent during the spring quarter of 2002 after posting a strong 6 percent gain during the winter quarter while off-premises traffic remained virtually unchanged in the spring quarter of 2002.
- Drive-thru was the only off-premises segment to post an increase in traffic during the spring quarter of 2002.
- Carryout traffic growth remained flat and delivery fell 6 percent.
- The number of consumer-reported deals rose to 25 percent of all occasions during the spring quarter of 2002.
- Higher-check-upscale establishments posted a 5 percent increase in average check size, reaching $29.18.
- Average check increased 3 percent to $7.44 at mid-scale restaurants.
- Quickservice and casual-dining restaurants each posted increases of 2 percent to $4.42 and $11.16, respectively.

*Sources:* Ebbin, Robert, "CREST 2002—Spring-Quarter Report," *Restaurants USA,* August 2002. Mills, Susan, "The Daypart Difference," *Restaurants USA,* May 1997. "¡NEWS!" National Restaurant Association Releases New Consumer Study. *http://www.foodnet.com/epr/sections/new/study.html* (May 15, 2004).

**Discussion Question:** How is this information helpful to foodservice operations?

in New York City aims to serve its $32.00 Timely Lunch—appetizer, entrée, and coffee—in 30 minutes.

At the same time customers are looking for value. The "1999 Lunch Study" indicates that employees who buy lunch away from home spend $4.00 to $5.00 a day. An increasing number of employees use carryout for lunch. Convenience stores offering made-to-order sandwiches and salads are competing with restaurants for this business. The Internet may be an increasingly important competitive tool for restaurants. With online ordering it is possible to allow customers to save their last several orders and favorite meals for easy ordering. About 20 percent of employees would like to order online but lack the access to do so. About 14 percent of full-time employees frequently use the phone to call in their orders.[25] Fax is another option that is used.

## Dinner

The vehicle used to explore the characteristics of the dinner market will be a series of national studies prepared by the National Restaurant Association.[26]

**Decision Scenarios.** A 1996 report divides all dinner decisions into six basic decision scenarios that seek to satisfy three goals:[27]

The goal of social pleasure or togetherness is met through

*Celebration/special occasion,* where the accent is on enjoying each other's company. These meals tend to be on Saturdays, the decision is made well in advance, the meals last one and a half hours, the party is large, and coupons are not used.

*Kids,* where the (adult) decision maker is primarily concerned with pleasing one or more children. The size of the group is large, the decision is made that day (50 percent of the time an hour or less in advance), hamburger and pizza are the favorite choices, and coupons are used. Customers tend to be younger parents of children and females.

The goal of eating pleasure is met through

*A craving,* where the focus is on satisfying the desire for a particular type of food, irrespective of how healthy it might be. Cravings occur every day of the week, early in the evening. Asian, pizza, and general menu are the typical choices, the average time spent at the restaurant is one hour, and children are typically not present.

*Home cooking,* where the desire is for healthy, wholesome food. Meals are taken before 6:00 P.M., and the decision is made not very far in advance.

The goal of lifestyle support or convenience is satisfied through

*Pressed for time,* when the customer is in a hurry and has little time available. These visits tend to be on weekdays, early in the evening. Children are part of the group one-third of the time, hamburgers are the most common menu choice, and the average time spent is less than half an hour.

*No energy/fatigue,* when the diner is tired and wants to take it easy. Weekdays, relatively early in the evening, is the common pattern where the decision on where to go is made at the last minute. Hamburger and pizza are, again, the most common choices. Meals last about half an hour and coupons are used relatively often. Most customers are young couples without children.

## quick bite 2.5
### A Day in the Life: How to Be a Restaurant Designer

All right, so your restaurant is making and selling great food. You've got a lot of customers, but one thing's missing: atmosphere. That's right, your restaurant is an everyday, ordinary-looking space. It needs some spice, some sophistication, to cater to the aesthetic needs of your customers. What do you do? Call in a restaurant designer.

Good lighting is one of the best ways to create an agreeable atmosphere in a restaurant. Keith Youngquist of Aumiller Youngquist PC in Chicago recommends using attractive lighting and ornamental fixtures to help create a relaxed experience for customers.

To create a more upscale and inviting atmosphere, restaurateurs should tone down flamboyant colors. California Pizza Kitchen toned down its signature yellow at its new prototype store in Irvine, Calif., as part of an effort to increase dinner business and position itself in the upscale casual dining segment.

To help highlight the cuisine of a restaurant, one should use a mixture of textural elements. Bold, geometric architecture combined with ancient legendary art helped Parisi Design of Del Mar, Calif., accent the contemporary Pacific Rim cuisine of Roppongi Restaurant & Bar.

Giving guests control over the space they occupy at a restaurant may prolong their visit. Many fast-food restaurants bolt tables and chairs to the floor to encourage rapid table turns.

*Source:* Lohmeyer, Lori, "Ambience, design Key to Attracting Consumers' Palates," *Nation's Restaurant News,* October 4, 2004, vol. 38, issue 40, p. 68.

**Discussion Question:** How can poor restaurant design create a bad dining experience?

The breakdown of dinner need by type of restaurant is shown in Table 2.2. The indications are as follows:[28]

| When customers eat dinner at . . . | The needs they seek to satisfy are . . . |
| --- | --- |
| fast-food restaurant | pressed for time/kids/no energy/fatigue |
| self-service cafeteria/buffet | home cooking/craving |
| sit-down restaurant (under $10) | home cooking/craving/celebration |
| sit-down restaurant ($10–$20) | craving/celebration |
| sit-down restaurant ($20+) | celebration/craving |

The *2005 Restaurant Industry Forecast* identifies two major factors that influence food choices: how adventurous customers are about foods and how much

Table 2.2    Dinner Need States by Type of Restaurant

| | Fast-Food Restaurants | Self-Service Cafeterias | Sit-Down Restaurants | | |
| --- | --- | --- | --- | --- | --- |
| | | | Under $10 | $10–$20 | Over $20 |
| **Social pleasure** | | | | | |
| Celebration | 3% | 14% | 17% | 38% | 55% |
| Kids | 19% | 12% | 7% | 3% | 1% |
| **Eating pleasure** | | | | | |
| Craving | 10% | 18% | 28% | 43% | 38% |
| Home cooking | 13% | 39% | 29% | 11% | 3% |
| **Lifestyle support** | | | | | |
| Pressed for time | 37% | 10% | 9% | 2% | 2% |
| No energy/fatigue | 18% | 8% | 10% | 3% | 2% |

*Source:* National Restaurant Association, *Dinner Decision Making* (Washington, DC: National Restaurant Association, 1996), pp. 49–50.

they care about health, nutrition, or diet. Four broad "food attitude segments" of approximately the same size are identified:[29]

- Adventurous diners are most enthused about trying new types of foods and ingredients. They have the highest exposure to different foods and are the most active restaurant diners. They are upscale, educated and tend to live in urban areas.
- Traditional diners, by contrast, are the least experimental. They tend to be found in smaller cities, are older, are less likely to visit restaurants and prefer comfort food.
- Health-conscious diners are more concerned about what they eat. They may have health problems or concerns or are following special diets. They want a variety of foods but are more selective than adventurous diners.
- Carefree diners want to forget about eating healthy when dining out. Nutrition is not important to them. They are more likely to be males under 50 years of age.

**Celebrations/Special Occasions.**    Americans also dine out when celebrating holidays and special occasions. The National Restaurant Association's Holiday Dining—2000 report finds birthdays top the list for restaurant dining, followed by Mother's Day and Valentine's Day.[30] This order has remained the same in recent years.

Over half of all survey respondents report that they had eaten at a restaurant on their birthday. Those with income over $35,000, those living in two-member and dual-income households, and college graduates are more likely than average to eat out on their birthdays. Three out of ten married respondents report dining out on their spouse's birthday. Males are more likely to eat out on

## quick bite 2.6
### Road to the Top: Julia and Tony Amato

Julia and Tony Amato are the parents of three grown children. When the children were young the couple would have a hard time escaping to evening dinners. Finding a babysitter was a continuous struggle, but when the couple did manage to locate a babysitter and retreat to an intimate dinner, they would feel guilty for leaving the kids at home. As a result of this ongoing problem the Amatos opened Villa Bella, a casual Italian restaurant. What makes Villa Bella a unique restaurant is its ability to serve all its customers. The restaurant features a supervised room where kids can eat dinner and watch cartoons, while their parents enjoy a meal alone close by.

Some of the deterrents for foodservice operations considering whether to offer such services may include: liability, labor and loss of valuable restaurant space. Most casual restaurants that accommodate kids are places like McDonald's and Burger King. Finding a restaurant where both the adult and the child are able to sit down and be taken care of is a rare occasion, which is why Villa Bella is receiving so much success. "It's not a play room, but a miniature replica of our main dining room," says Amato.

There is also a children's menu, which includes pizza, spaghetti, and chicken strips along with other child favorites. As entertainment the restaurant provides coloring books and crayons along with a big screen television that broadcasts cartoons.

Villa Bella's children's dining room serves an estimated 300 children aged 3 to 10 years old per week. A plaque next to the door displays a list of the room's rules, stating that children may come and go from the room only if accompanied by a parent and that parents must escort their children to the rest room.

The supervisors who monitor the children in the dinning area are CPR-certified and trained in basic security and safety procedures. There is a one way mirror inside the children's dinning room so that parents are able to monitor the activity of their children if they choose.

*Source:* Duecy, Erica, "Baby's Day Out: Restaurateurs Feed Child Care Needs of Parents, Kids," *Nation's Restaurant News,* vol. 37, no. 46, November 17, 2003, pp. 4, 59.

**Discussion Question:** How does Villa Bella include children throughout its operation?

their wife's birthday than females on their husband's birthday. Three out of ten report eating out to celebrate a child's birthday in the past 12 months.

After birthdays, Mother's Day is the next-most-popular dining-out occasion. Almost 40 percent eat at a restaurant on Mother's Day, while about 25 percent eat out on Father's Day. In both cases the percentage increases with household size.

Valentine's Day ranks third among the holidays. Almost one-third eat at a restaurant on Valentine's Day. Eating out on Valentine's Day is especially popular with those under age 35. About 20 percent of Americans dine out on New Year's Eve, and about one in ten do so on New Year's Day. Those between the ages of 18 and 24 are more likely to do so, while those with children are less likely to do so.

The Super Bowl is a time when family and friends get together. More than one-quarter of those who watch the televised event order takeout or delivery food from a restaurant for a gathering at their home or someone else's home.

## ENDNOTES

1. Donna Oetzel, "The New Breed of Market Researchers: Forecasting the Future of 'Cool,'" *Restaurants USA*, June/July 2001, www.restaurant.org/rusa.
2. Allan F. Hickok and Lana E. Lazarus, *Restaurant Industry Review*, U.S. Bancorp Piper Jaffray Equity Research, March 2003, p. 19; National Restaurant Association, *2005 Restaurant Industry Forecast* (Washington, DC: National Restaurant Association, 2005); National Restaurant Association, *Tableservice Restaurant Trends, 2005* (Washington, DC: National Restaurant Association, 2005).
3. Hickok and Lazarus, *Restaurant Industry Review*, p. 47.
4. Jacquelyn Lynn, "Silver Dollars: Operators Find That Serving Seniors Just Makes Good Cents," *Restaurants USA*, November 2000, www.restaurant.org/rusa.
5. George Mochis, Carolyn Folkman Curasi, and Denny Bellenger, "Restaurants-Selection of Mature Consumers, *Cornell Hotel and Restaurant Quarterly*, vol. 44, issue 4, August 2003, pp. 51+.
6. Lynn, "Silver Dollars: Operators Find That Serving Seniors Just Makes Good Cents."
7. Ibid.
8. Ibid.
9. M. Pina, "Profiling Ethnic Travelers," *Travel Weekly*, August 22, 1996, p. 3.
10. Hickok and Lazarus, *Restaurant Industry Review*, p. 9.
11. Susan Mills, "A Cultural Melting Pot," *Restaurants USA*, May 2000, www.restaurant.org/rusa.
12. Ibid.
13. Ibid.
14. Robert Ebbin, "Multipaycheck Households Spark Sales," *Restaurants USA*, April 1998, www.restaurant.org/rusa.
15. Suzanne Hall, "Marketing to Children: Growing the Customers of Tomorrow," *Restaurants USA*, November 1999, www.restaurant.org/rusa.
16. Ibid.
17. National Restaurant Association, *2005 Restaurant Industry Forecast* (Washington, DC: National Restaurant Association, 2005), p. 23.
18. John McPherson, Adrian Mitchell, and Mark Mitten, "Speed It Up, Buddy: Overcoming Hurdles to Fast Casual a Quicker Way to Maximize Profits," *Nation's Restaurant News*, vol. 37, no. 32, pp. 27–28.
19. Robert Ebbin, "American's Dining-Out Habits," *Restaurants USA*, November 2000, www.restaurant.org/rusa.
20. Susan Mills, "What's for Breakfast?" *Restaurants USA*, May 2002, www.restaurant.org/rusa.
21. Ibid.
22. Ibid.
23. Sarah E. Smith, "1999 Lunch Study: Restaurateurs Put Food Back Into Lunch Hour," *Restaurants USA*, October 1999, www.restaurant.org/rusa.

24. Karen Dybis, "Restaurants Dangle Cheap Eats for the Lunch Crowd," *The Detroit News,* November 6, 1999.
25. Smith, "1999 Lunch Study: Restaurateurs Put Food Back into Lunch Hour."
26. National Restaurant Association, *Dinner Decision Making* (Washington, DC: National Restaurant Association, 1996); National Restaurant Association, *2005 Restaurant Industry Forecast* (Washington, DC: National Restaurant Association, 2005); National Restaurant Association, *Tableservice Restaurant Trends, 2005* (Washington, DC: National Restaurant Association, 2005).
27. National Restaurant Association, *2005 Restaurant Industry Forecast* (Washington, DC: National Restaurant Association, 2005), p. 11.
28. National Restaurant Association, *Dinner Decision Making* (Washington, DC: National Restaurant Association, 1996), pp. 6–7.
29. National Restaurant Association, *2005 Restaurant Industry Forecast* (Washington, DC: National Restaurant Association, 2005), p. 25.
30. Robert Ebbin, "Eating Out for the Holidays," *Restaurants USA,* October 2000, www.restaurant.org/rusa.

## INTERNET RESOURCES

| | |
|---|---|
| Restaurant News Resource | *http://restaurantnewsresource.com/* |
| Iconoculture, Inc. | *http://www.iconoculture.com/* |
| Style Report (Lambesis Research Group) | *http://www.lstylereport.com/* |

## QUICK QUIZ ANSWER KEY

p. 32—c. Restorative broth.
p. 38—c. 66%.

# CHAPTER THREE

# DEVELOPING A MARKETING PLAN

"Nobody goes there anymore because it's always so crowded."
Yogi Berra, American baseball player, manager,
and coach of the New York Yankees

## learning objectives

*By the end of this chapter you should be able to*

1. List the steps involved in producing a marketing plan.

2. Describe how to conduct a customer, property, and competitor analysis.

3. Compare and contrast the various ways by which a market can be segmented.

4. Identify the elements of the marketing mix for restaurant operations.

5. Describe how to monitor each step of a marketing plan to ensure its effectiveness.

### quick bite 3.1
### Hot Concepts: Restaurants Required to Serve More Than Food

In the past foodservice operators were evaluated by the quality of the food they served in their restaurant, but today restaurant owners are finding that it takes more than serving good food to keep up the value of their company. Advertising their businesses on billboards is no longer as effective. Today, in order for restaurants to be somewhat successful they must viewed by others as being good Samaritans both nationally and internationally. Now, some foodservice operators are promoting children's welfare to help combat obesity and present their operations as caring, concerned and connected—to the entire world.

For example, McDonald's Corp., which is the world's burger giant with more than 30,000 restaurants in 100 countries, was selected to sponsor their second annual World Children's Day in November. Within 24 hours McDonald's helped to raise $12 million during the event. Funds that were collected from this event were distributed to more than 20 orphanages throughout Eastern Europe for the provision of aid, 1,300 hearing aids where given to children in Mexico, and assistance was given to some 70 children's hospitals worldwide.

Despite the fact that some restaurants do receive impressive bottom line numbers from their outstanding cuisine, smart companies know this is not enough for sustaining long-term momentum. While restaurants are not applauded for these fundraisers, they are expected, and successful operators know that being a good corporate citizen is one business plan component whose results can be pocketed worldwide.

*Source:* Allen, Robin Lee, "Serving Meals Just Isn't Enough Anymore as Industry Must Sandwich in Good Works Globally," *Nation's Restaurant News,* vol. 37, no. 47, November 24, 2003, p. 31.

**Discussion Question:** How might such efforts as those displayed by McDonald's Corporation help with the positioning of a property?

## MARKETING DEFINED

The American Marketing Association defines marketing as the "process of planning and executing the conception, pricing, promotion, and distribution of ideas, goods, and services to create exchanges that satisfy individual and organizational objectives."[1] This definition indicates that marketing is much more than advertising, much more than sales promotion. Marketing encompasses everything from developing the concept, product, and/or service to how it should be priced, promoted, and made available to people. Marketing works only if an exchange is made between buyer (the individual) and seller (the organization) that benefits both. The buyer receives something of value and the organization receives revenue.

Robert Reid developed a definition that brings together the financial concerns of management and the need to satisfy consumer needs. His definition encompasses three items:[2]

1. Determining the needs and wants of consumers
2. Creating the mix of products and services that will satisfy these needs and wants
3. Promoting and selling the product–service mix to generate a level of income satisfactory to the management and stockholders of the organization

J. C. Penney put it this way: "If you satisfy the customers but fail to get the profit, you'll soon be out of business; if you get the profit but fail to satisfy the customers, you'll soon be out of customers." The idea is to generate profits by producing satisfied customers.

Inherent in these definitions are several ideas. First, there is the focus on the customer. Marketing is a way of thinking about the business that makes satisfying customer needs paramount. Second, there is the practical implication that businesses cannot be all things to all people—they cannot satisfy all the needs and wants of all the people. Some choice must be made as to which segments of the market are to be targeted. Third, there is an appreciation of research to determine customer needs and wants. The idea of sequential steps—that products and services are developed only after customer needs and wants have been identified—is a fourth idea. Customer satisfaction is the fifth idea. It is not enough to promote and sell the service. Customer satisfaction implies that the operation must not only bring customers in, it must bring them back. Finally, the idea of exchange means that the satisfaction of customers' needs must bring economic benefit to the organization.

---

quick quiz

What percentage of beef consumption away from home is composed of hamburgers and cheeseburgers?

  a. 55%
  b. 62%
  c. 76%

*Source:* Hickok, Allan F. and Lana E. Lazarus, *Restaurant Industry Review,* U.S. Bancorp Piper Jaffray Equity Research, March 2003, pp. 54–55.

---

# DEVELOPING A MARKETING PLAN

Six steps are involved in developing a marketing plan:[3]

1. Conduct a marketing audit.
2. Select target markets.
3. Position the property.
4. Determine marketing objectives.
5. Develop and implement action plans.
6. Monitor and evaluate the marketing plan.

## Conduct a Marketing Audit

There are three parts to the marketing audit; it is an analysis of the customers, the property or operation, and the competition. Given the foregoing definitions of marketing, it is appropriate to look first at customers.

**Customers.**    The purpose of the customer, property, and competitive analysis is to develop a profile of the customers and to evaluate, in an unbiased way, how the operation stacks up relative to the competition in providing what customers want.

Information about the customers breaks down as follows:

- Who are they?
- Where do they come from?
- When do they visit, and when is the decision made?
- How do they reach us?
- Why do they come and how satisfied are they?

This information can come from sales histories, employees and management staff, the customers themselves, and outside research sources. Sales histories should be kept for six distinct dining segments:[4]

1. Weekday breakfast: Monday–Friday
2. Weekday lunch: Monday–Friday
3. Weekday dinner: Monday–Thursday
4. Weekend breakfast: Saturday and Sunday
5. Weekend lunch: Saturday and Sunday
6. Weekend dinner: Friday–Sunday

Note that while weekday breakfast and lunch run from Monday through Friday, weekday dinner runs from Monday through Thursday. The breakdown is in terms of the characteristics of the meal. Friday dinner is regarded by customers as part of the weekend.

For each day it would be appropriate to collect data on the following:

- Number of customers
- Total sales in dollars
- Number of meals sold
- Number of beverages sold
- Number of appetizers sold
- Number of side items sold
- Number of desserts sold
- Number of breakfast customers
- Breakfast sales in dollars
- Number of lunch customers
- Lunch sales in dollars
- Number of dinner customers

---

**quick bite 3.2**
**Making a Marketing Plan**

**Learning Objectives:** List the steps involved in producing a marketing plan. Describe how to monitor each step of a marketing plan to ensure its effectiveness.

Every marketing plan has to fit the needs and conditions of an operation. Even so, there are standard components a company cannot do without. A marketing plan should always include a situation analysis, marketing strategy, sales forecast, and expense budget.

- Situation Analysis: Normally this will include a market analysis, a SWOT analysis (strengths, weaknesses, opportunities, and threats), and a competitive analysis. The market analysis will include market forecast, segmentation, customer information, and market needs analysis.
- Marketing Strategy: This should include at least a mission statement, objectives, and focused strategy including market segment focus and product positioning.
- Sales Forecast: This would include enough detail to track sales month by month and follow up on plan-vs.-actual analysis. Normally a plan will also include specific sales by product, by region or market segment, by channels, by manager responsibilities, and other elements. The forecast alone is a bare minimum.
- Expense Budget: This ought to include enough detail to track expenses month by month and follow up on plan-vs.-actual analysis. Normally

- Dinner sales in dollars
- Average entrée in dollars
- Average check in dollars
- Number of beverages, appetizers, side items, and desserts per customer
- Average breakfast, lunch, and dinner check
- Daily sales as a percentage of the week
- Breakfast, lunch, and dinner sales as a percentage of day's sales
- Weekend and weekday sales as a percentage of week's sales

The information collected basically breaks down into how many people the restaurant serves, how much customers spend, what they order, and how the restaurant's business is spread throughout the week. From this analysis we can see when business is strong and, more important, when it is weak. In addition, specific objectives can be set to improve sales of specific items or numbers of customers.

a plan will also include specific sales tactics, programs, management responsibilities, promotion, and other elements. The expense budget is a bare minimum.

### Are They Enough?

These minimum requirements listed above are not ideal, they are just the minimum. In most cases a marketing plan will being with an Executive Summary, using the same essentials as described above to review organizational impact, risks and contingencies, and pending issues.

### Include a Specific Action Plan

You should also bear in mind that planning is about the results, not the plan itself. A marketing plan should be measured by the results it produces. The implementation of your plan is much more important than any creative ideas or massive market research. You can influence implementation by designing a plan full of specific, measurable and concrete proposals that can be tracked and followed up. Plan-vs.-actual analysis is critical to the final results, and you should try and build it into your plan.

*Sources:* Berry, Tim, and Wilson, Doug, "The Essential Ingredients of an Effective Marketing Plan," *http://www.marketingsurvivalkit.com/marketing-plan-tips.htm* (May 26, 2004). Manktelow, James, "Understanding Strengths, Weaknesses, Opportunities, and Threats. SWOT Analysis," *www.mindtools.com/pages/article/newTMC_05.htm* (May 26, 2004).

**Discussion Question:** Why are these components of the marketing plan so important to operations?

A core store panel provides the head office with information from the field through the collection of data from a representative sample of stores. The sample chosen should be representative of the company's geographic distribution and sales volume. Data should be collected on the following:[5]

- Sales by day and week
- Transaction count
- Product sales mix
- Advertising activities
- Promotional activities
- Competing activities
- Weather

On an informal basis, management and staff can provide information about the customers because they are constantly in contact with them. While such data are not scientific, they can give a picture of the items that are selling and why, what customers like and do not like, and what types of people visit at different times during the week. In addition to providing useful information, asking the opinion of employees makes them feel important and can serve as a motivational tool.

More formal questionnaires can be used to collect information on the customer base. The key in developing a questionnaire is to develop the research objectives first, decide on the questions that will provide answers to the information being sought, select an appropriate research methodology, and conduct the research.

A simple category of data that can easily be collected and is very useful is customer zip codes. Most restaurants attract customers from a relatively small area. Some consultants estimate that 80 percent of a restaurant's business comes from within a 3-mile radius. By instructing servers and/or cashiers to ask for customers' home and work zip codes, management can readily identify where customers come from.

The best way to find out what a restaurant is doing well and poorly is to ask customers. The key to increasing sales and customer count is to identify the characteristics of existing customers and to use that profile as a basis for attracting more customers who fit that profile.

One way to get this information is from a focus group. A focus group consists of six to ten former or existing customers, led by a discussion leader, who express their feelings about various aspects of the operation. Questions go from the general to the specific and concentrate on motivations, feelings, and gut-level issues. Although not statistically reliable, such sessions can indicate a great deal about what motivates customers.

Customer comment cards are a favorite way of collecting information. There is probably a positive bias built into any research conducted in the restaurant. Most customers will not complain in the restaurant unless there is something really wrong. An average or mildly unpleasant experience may not result in negative comments from the customers until they leave the operation.

**Property.**   The property analysis is an unbiased evaluation of the strengths and weaknesses of the operation. A "typical" checklist would evaluate the property and the competition as to the following factors:[6]

- Menu variety
- Menu appeal
- Food/beverage quality
- Food/beverage taste
- Food/beverage consistency
- Portion size
- Pricing
- Service speed
- Service quality
- Service friendliness
- Cleanliness
- Promotional activity
- Visibility
- Image
- Atmosphere
- Facility
- Sales level
- Point of sale
- Happy-hour offerings

The problem is that such a list does not indicate how important these things are to the customer. A better starting point is to look at the operation from the viewpoint of the customer. By identifying the factors important to customers and using these items as a checklist to evaluate both the operation and the competition, a focus on the customer is assured. For example, if a restaurant features an excellent salad bar but that factor is unimportant to the customers, is the salad bar a strength, a weakness, or a neutral factor?

Suppose that one segment of the dinner market seeks out places that excel in five things:

1. Food quality
2. Nice place
3. Cleanliness
4. Friendly people
5. Fresh food and ingredients

If the operation appeals to this segment of the market, it could identify from its customers just what is meant by each of these five factors and use the resulting list as the basis for evaluating the property and the competition.

Some restaurants use mystery shoppers to evaluate the operation. These people should always remain anonymous and conduct random evaluations. There are typically three or four visits the first month, followed by monthly visits thereafter. Management receives a report on the exterior, interior, and signage of the facility in addition to comments on the appearance, performance, and service provided by the employees.

**Competition.**   A competing facility is any operation that seeks to attract the business being sought by the restaurant under consideration.

A competitive analysis compares competing facilities with the operation under study. The purpose of such an analysis is to discover the following:[7]

1. Profitable market segments being served by competitors that are not being served at the operation under study
2. Some competitive benefit or advantage the property has that cannot be matched by the competition
3. Weaknesses in the marketing strategy of the competition that can be capitalized on

A competitive analysis involves getting as much relevant information as possible and includes eating at the facility and evaluating the advertising.

## Select Target Markets

The idea behind selecting market segments is that people are different in what they want from a dining experience and that it is not possible to be all things to all people. Market segmentation involves dividing a heterogeneous market into smaller homogeneous segments. While the members of a segment have characteristics similar to each other, they differ from people in another market segment. In this way operators can more effectively target marketing efforts to those people who are most likely to patronize the restaurant.

**Segmentation Variables.**   Marketers segment the market on the basis of one or more variables. The major variables used are geographic, demographic, psychographic, usage or behavioral, and benefits sought. Geographic segmentation involves identifying the geographic limits of the trading area and appealing to people within the boundaries of that area. The National Restaurant Association estimates that people will travel an average of 15 to 18 minutes for special-occasion meals. A radius of 18 minutes' driving time from the operation would be a geographic segmentation of the market.

Demographic segmentation involves dividing the market on the basis of such things as age, income, gender, family size, stage in the family life cycle, educational level, occupation, ethnicity, religion, nationality, and social class. The most important demographic today and for the immediate future is the baby boomer segment—defined as those born between 1946 and 1964. The strength of this segment can be seen from the following:[8]

- There are more than 76 million boomers in the United States.
- Boomers are currently in their peak earning years—ages 37 to 55—and have a great deal of disposable income.
- Most baby-boomer families have dual incomes.
- Boomers expect to continue working during their retirement years, to receive inheritances that will have a positive impact on their retirement planning, and to live longer and more self-indulgently than did their parents.

Psychographic segmentation divides people based on their attitudes, interests, and opinions. Many marketers are using psychographic research on the aforementioned baby boomers to enhance the marketing effort. Research indicates that boomers overwhelmingly feel "young at heart." This attachment to the youth culture means that they are, among other things, traveling and eating with their kids in record numbers. This segment, seen as individualistic and self-indulgent, is also family focused—part of their desire to "have it all."[9]

Restaurants seeking this segment of the market must offer variety: more choices, more menu items, more seating arrangements, and more types of entertainment. This duality of interest may explain the increased popularity of quick-casual or fast-casual restaurants, which attempt to bridge the gap between quick-service and full-service restaurants.

Another major difference between the boomers and their parents is the extent to which they utilize restaurants as a source of daily meals. This comes about largely because of the pressure of time—they do not have the time or energy to cook. Those who do cook see it as a hobby rather than a daily chore. However, boomers in general are more knowledgeable and interested in food compared to their parents.

As boomers age, their concerns will shift to health and retirement issues. However, their basic attitudes that drive purchase decisions will likely remain the same.

Segmenting on the basis of use or behavior is based on the oft-quoted 80–20 rule. This rule states that 80 percent of the business comes from 20 percent of the customers. If the operator can identify the frequent customers who make up a substantial part of the business, he or she can do a more effective job of marketing.

The Simmons Market Research Bureau, Inc. breaks restaurant use into five segments: nonprospects (those who are never likely to become users), prospects (those who might become users), light users (1 to 5 times per month), medium users (6 to 13 times per month), and heavy users (over 14 times per month). Heavy users account for 44.8 percent of total restaurant revenue in a typical month, medium users account for 40.8 percent, and light users bring in the remaining 14.8 percent of revenue. Giving the light user an index of 100, the heavy user has an index of 522. For every $1 spent by a light user, a heavy user spends $5.22.[10]

## quick bite 3.3
### Analysis Checklist

**Learning Objectives:** Describe how to conduct a customer, property, and competitor analysis. Compare and contrast the various ways by which a market can be segmented.

The following is a checklist to help businesses collect and analyze information as part of a restaurant market analysis—since market conditions have a significant impact on the profitability of any foodservice operation, this checklist serves a guide to help operations analyze the market so that they can make more informed operating and investment decisions.

## Competition Checklist

*Location*

✓ Community traffic patterns
✓ Proximity to sources of demand
✓ Sign visibility
✓ Accessibility
✓ Parking availability

*Appearance/Comfort*

✓ Exterior appearance and theme
✓ Interior appearance and theme
✓ Ambiance
✓ Cleanliness

*Menu*

✓ Theme
✓ Variety and selection
✓ Signature items
✓ Beverage service
✓ Price range and value

*Food Quality*

✓ Taste
✓ Portion size
✓ Presentation
✓ Consistency

*Service*

✓ Days open
✓ Hours of operation
✓ Speed of service
✓ Extra services offered
✓ Service style
✓ Quality of service

*General Information*

✓ Seating capacity
✓ Banquet facilities
✓ Entertainment
✓ Reviews by food critics/ratings
✓ Local reputation
✓ Advertising and promotion methods used
✓ Is business increasing or decreasing?
✓ Types of guest served (age, income, origin, etc.)
✓ Number of customer served each meal period

## Location Checklist

*Description of Immediate Area*

✓ Residential and commercial profile

✓ Special appeal
✓ Surrounding business

*Proximity to Customers
and Competition*

✓ Major demand generators (retail, offices, lodging, hospitals, etc.)
✓ Number of potential customers by segment within one-, two-, three- mile radius, etc.
✓ List of direct competitors

*Traffic Volume*

✓ Street and road patterns
✓ Highway/street traffic counts
✓ Pedestrian traffic counts
✓ Peak and off-peak traffic periods

*Accessibility*

✓ Proximity to major streets and highways
✓ Ease of entrance and exit
✓ Pedestrian accessibility
✓ Americans with Disabilities Act (ADA) compliance

*Visibility*

✓ Visibility from highways
✓ Effectiveness of sign
✓ Landscaping

*Other Issues*

✓ Environmental issues
✓ Growth patterns of surrounding areas

## Market Area Checklist

*Geographic Market Area*

✓ Market area radius (one, two, three miles, etc.)
✓ Plot market area boundaries on a map

*Demographic Characteristics*

✓ Population
✓ Gender
✓ Ethnic groups
✓ Household income distribution
✓ Martial status
✓ Education

*Economic Characteristics*

✓ Eating and drinking place sales
✓ Restaurant Activity Index (RAI)
✓ Restaurant Growth Index (RGI)
✓ Employment levels
✓ Seasonality and tourism visitation

*Labor Market Characteristics*

✓ Local wage rates
✓ Availability of labor
✓ Types of labor available

*Dining Out Preferences and Lifestyles
of Local Residents*

✓ Interview with local residents
✓ Observe eating habits in other restaurants

*Source:* Michigan State University Extension. "Restaurant Market Analysis." *http://www.msue.msu.edu/msue/imp/modtd/33702004.html* (May 12, 2004).

**Discussion Question:** How is this market analysis checklist helpful to businesses?

Benefit segmentation separates people out on the basis of the benefits sought from the meal experience. As identified in Chapter 2, there are five different decision scenarios for people dining out:

1. Fun time
2. Nice meal out
3. Craving
4. Making sure that everyone is getting something to eat
5. Easiest thing available

Those eating out for a "fun time" believe that they deserve a treat or reward and feel like having fun. They have the time to plan the event, and price is not very important to them. On the other hand, the "easiest thing available" group eat out when they are tired and pressed for time. They choose options with the least number of hassles. For them, speed of service and a convenient location are important benefits.

Market segments should be selected on the basis of size, likelihood of growth, competitive position, the cost of reaching the segment, and how compatible the segment is with the company's objectives and resources.

**Revenue Grid.**   For an existing business a revenue grid and an analysis of activity can be helpful in selecting workable market segments. A revenue grid identifies how much revenue is brought in from the various segments of the market presently being served. A useful rule of thumb in marketing is, "Attract customers similar to those already being attracted." For some reason the restaurant attracts a certain kind of clientele. An examination of the existing customer base broken down by how much sales each segment brings in is an excellent start to identifying future potential. In other words, find out who the customers are and seek to find more people with similar characteristics.

An analysis of business activity will tell when business is good and, more important, when it is bad. This can suggest areas of importance for increasing sales. The marketplace can then be searched for prospective market segments consisting of people who eat out when the operation needs the business. The segments are then evaluated relative to the criteria noted previously to determine their suitability.

## Position the Property

**Positioning Statement.**   The image that customers have of an operation is its position in the marketplace. A good positioning statement accomplishes several things. First, it creates an image in the minds of the customers as to what it stands for. In the foodservice business, as in any other, image is reality. People make decisions based on their perceptions rather than on the reality of the situation. If the image is positive—that the restaurant offers good value—the decision may be made to eat out there. Image alone will not induce the customer to buy. That willingness comes from a variety of promotional means, described later.

The actual meal experience offers a reality check to the guest. The actual experience may be less than expected. The result is a disappointed customer. The image portrayed by the operation must be positive enough to encourage people to visit the operation. To satisfy the customer, the actual meal experience must be equal to or greater than the image.

Second, the positioning statement will describe the benefits the restaurant offers to the guests. Restaurants offer features but people buy benefits. Customers, in fact, "buy" a bundle of benefits. When going out for a meal, different people look for different things. For some, a large variety of menu choices is important. For others, price is a major concern. Still others emphasize privacy. Since people buy benefits, the operation must communicate what benefits it offers to its potential customers.

Third, the positioning statement differentiates the property from the competition. Everyone offers "good food," "atmosphere," and "value." But just what is it that makes one restaurant different from the other? Why should I come to your place rather than the restaurant across the street?

The key is to find a difference, an advantage, that is difficult for the competition to replicate. Every business seeks a unique selling point or a competitive differential advantage, something that makes it different from the competition that can be used to advantage. The nature of business means that unique selling points are subject to the principle of perishable distinctiveness. If one restaurant develops an advantage that makes it more attractive to customers, the competition becomes aware of that advantage and seeks to copy it, thus neutralizing the previously unique selling point. That which made the restaurant distinctive is gone; it is perishable. "What can separate me from my competition that is difficult, if not impossible, for competitors to copy?" This is the third element that must be answered from a positioning statement.

A positioning statement can come only after an analysis has been made of the market, the property, and the competition. The key is to identify what the target market wants (the benefits) from a dining-out experience and how one operation is perceived (in the minds of the customers) as providing these benefits compared to the competition.

**Perceptual Maps.** Perceptual maps can be useful tools in developing a positioning statement. A perceptual map is a visual representation of two elements: the relative importance of various benefits to guests and guests' perception of how well a facility does in providing these benefits. In essence, customers from the market segment being sought are asked two questions: "What things are important to you when dining out?" and "How well do you think restaurant X does in providing these things?" The benefits considered important to customers can be identified from informal discussions with guests or from a focus group session. The focus group can identify what the members like and dislike about the company and the competition. The results are qualitative rather than quantitative. Focus group results will not disclose percentages, but they will indicate "gut issues." From such a group a list of benefits sought when dining out can be obtained. For example, it may be that customers decide that the benefits they are looking for when dining out are

| | |
|---|---|
| A  Prices in their range | K  Consistency |
| B  Nice place | L  Special deals and coupons |
| C  Cleanliness | M  Variety |
| D  Friendly people and service | N  No lines and no waiting |
| E  Extensive choice | O  Size of the portions |
| F  Speed of service | P  Food presentation |
| G  Food quality | Q  Convenience of location |
| H  Value for money | R  Comfortable seating |
| I  Kids like it | S  Fresh food and ingredients |
| J  Hours open | T  Unique or original food |

This list can then be used to construct a questionnaire to be presented to a sample of present and prospective customers who are asked to rate the importance of these items to them on a scale of 1 (very important) to 5 (not important). Those customers are then asked how well the restaurant under study does in providing these things, again on a scale of 1 (totally) to 5 (not at all). The resulting scores can be placed on a matrix as in Figure 3.1.

Crosshairs are drawn on the graph such that half of the 20 items are above the horizontal line and half below, and half of the 20 items are to the left of the vertical line and half to the right. The result is four quadrants. In the upper right section, quadrant 1, are items that are not important to the customers and that they think the restaurant does not satisfy. In this example guests say that the following factors are not important to them and, furthermore, the restaurant does not, in their mind, provide these things:

- Prices in their range
- Extensive choice
- Kids like it
- Hours open
- Variety

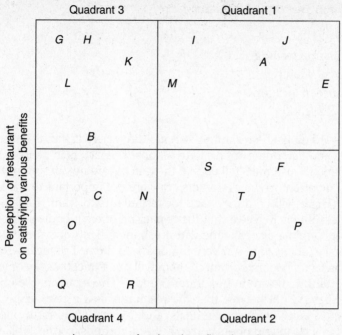

Quadrant 3                    Quadrant 1

Perception of restaurant on satisfying various benefits

Quadrant 4                    Quadrant 2

Importance of various benefits when dining out

**Figure 3.1**   Perceptual map.

Quadrant 2 contains factors that, again, are not important to the guests. However, in this case they do think that the restaurant provides these:

- Friendly people and service
- Speed of service
- Food presentation
- Fresh food and ingredients
- Unique or original food

Quadrants 3 and 4 are made up of factors that customers consider important. In quadrant 3 are factors that guests perceive the restaurant does not do a good job of providing. In quadrant 4 are factors the customers think the operation does do well on.

The factors in quadrant 3 are:

- Nice place
- Food quality
- Value for money
- Consistency
- Special deals and coupons

The remaining factors, in quadrant 4, are

- Cleanliness
- No lines and no waiting
- Size of the portions
- Convenience of location
- Comfortable seating

From these findings the restaurant can identify where it stands in the minds of its customers and determine appropriate actions. The factors in quadrants 1 and 2 should be ignored. Customers tell us that these items are not important to them. If they are not important to the customers, they are not important to the foodservice operation. There will be a tendency for restaurants to want to play to their strengths. The customers perceive that the restaurant offers friendly service that is fast and includes original dishes made with fresh ingredients and presented well. However, these factors just are not very important to them. The facility that markets to guests on factors not important to them will not attract those people.

The important items are in quadrants 3 and 4. These factors are important to guests. But they do not believe that the restaurant is a nice place that offers consistent, good-quality food, special deals, and delivers value for money. They do believe that it is clean and offers correctly sized portions, comfortable seating, and a convenient location with no lines.

At this point it is necessary to do a reality check. How accurate are the customers' perceptions? The answer will determine the appropriate action. Where the image is negative but the actual situation is positive, we need to improve the image. For example, it may be that special deals are offered but customers are unaware of them. Where the image is negative and the actual situation is negative, or when the image is positive but the actual situation is negative, the product or service must be changed. For example, if people believe that consistency is a problem and it really is a problem, the food served must be improved so that it is consistent. Similarly, if the perception is that the seats are comfortable, but in reality they are not, that also must be changed. If customers are drawn to a restaurant expecting comfortable seats, the visit will show that the seats are not comfortable and the customer will be dissatisfied. Finally, where the image is positive and the actual situation is positive, we have the basis for a positioning statement.

Similar perceptual maps can be drawn for the competition to determine where, in the minds of the customers, we are perceived as doing a better job of providing benefits important to them. The resulting positioning statement will be based on research that has identified the benefits the customer is looking for, what is provided to satisfy these desired benefits, and how the restaurant differs from the competition in providing these desired benefits. In essence, the positioning statement says, "For _____ seeking _____, we provide _____."

The first blank should be filled with the segment of the market being considered, the second blank identifies the benefits being sought, and the third space says what will be provided to satisfy customers.

## Determine Marketing Objectives

**Criteria.**   The very act of setting objectives increases the likelihood that the objectives will be achieved. The reason is that management now has something to work toward. Developing objectives gives managers a way to determine the extent to which they are moving forward and to allow them to change strategies if positive movement is not being made. It allows for a way of keeping score. This in itself is a motivational tool as well as a method of assigning responsibility and rewarding the achievement of results.

To be useful, objectives should be set for each segment of the market to which the restaurant is appealing. Each market segment is different in terms of dining and spending patterns and the extent to which the operation is presently successful in its marketing effort. For seniors it may be appropriate to increase the number of such customers, whereas for businesspeople it may be more appropriate to have existing customers patronize the operation more frequently.

Second, objectives should be results oriented. This usually means specifying an improvement in volume, revenues, or market share. It is only by identifying the desired results that management can set targets and, later, measure to see whether the effort has been successful.

Objectives should also be set in quantitative rather than qualitative terms. The problem with qualitative objectives (for example, "to improve service") is that the measurement of such objectives is open to subjective judgment.

There should be a time element to each objective. It is not enough to say that the foodservice operation wants to increase its customer count by 100 customers a week. A time limit must be set as to when this objective should be achieved.

**Life-Cycle Curve.**   Objectives must be set consistent with where the operation is in the product life-cycle curve. The concept of a product life cycle is that a business goes through various stages during its lifetime. A business is introduced into the marketplace and will grow, mature, and decline. Different marketing objectives are appropriate at the various stages of the life cycle. In the introductory stage, the key is to create awareness and trial on the part of customers; in the growth stage, sales are increasing at an increasing rate and market share should be maximized; in the maturity stage, sales are increasing but at a decreasing rate and profits should be maximized while market share is defended; and finally, in the decline stage of the life cycle, sales are decreasing and expenditures are reduced and as much is extracted from the business as possible.

**Buying Process.**   It is also important to set objectives that are consistent with where customers are in their buying process. The concept of a buying process is that potential customers go through a series of stages in their minds before making a purchase. They must first be made aware of the existence of the operation. Then they need to have information outlining the operation's benefits to them. At this point, if the campaign is successful, customers form a positive attitude about the restaurant, develop a preference for it, are convinced they should go there, actually visit the restaurant, and, if satisfied, return. The objectives set will vary depending on where the market is in this process.

At the awareness stage, the objective is to expose people to the operation. How successful we are can be measured by identifying the number of people exposed to the message: number of readers, viewers, and so on.

At the knowledge or comprehension stage, when customers are trying to identify what the restaurant can offer them, the objective is to transmit information. How well this has been accomplished can be determined by measuring the percentage of readers or viewers who remember essential parts of the message.

The objective in the attitude stage is to changes people's attitudes about the operation. The success of a program can be determined by measuring consumer attitudes before and after the campaign to determine whether or not a change has occurred. Similarly, during the preference stage—where the objective is to create a preference in the mind of the customer—preference surveys before and after the campaign can be done. It may be, for example, that prior to the campaign one restaurant places sixth out of ten on a list of preferred operations. If the restaurant places third, after the program, the campaign can be called a success.

The conviction stage seeks to have customers do something. The number of actions taken—phone reservations made, for example—can be measured. Purchase is measured by the number of people who come in the door or who order the item being promoted. Finally, adoption—where the objective is repeat purchase—can be measured by the percentage of customers who are repeats.

## Develop and Implement Action Plans

Implementing an action plan actually involves developing and executing a specific marketing mix for each segment of the market being sought. It involves developing the means to carry out the job, developing a budget to accomplish the plan, and assigning responsibility for the plan.

The marketing mix has been variously defined by different authors. Originally comprised of product planning, pricing, distribution, promotion, servicing, and market research, it has been standardized into the "four Ps" of product, price, promotion, and place. Other elements have been suggested to make the four Ps suitable for the hospitality industry. It is suggested that the marketing mix for foodservice operations consists of four elements: product–service mix, price, promotion–communication, and place–distribution mix.[11] The mix chosen will vary depending on the industry, the position of the operation in the marketplace, and how it fares presently relative to the competition.

**Product–Service Mix.** The product–service mix consists of the various products and services offered by the operation in an attempt to satisfy customer needs. It covers such things as the options on the menu, quality, reputation, image, the furnishings and decor, the exterior structure and interior layout, and the various service features of the operation. It includes elements that the customer pays for either directly or indirectly. The price charged for the steak on the plate covers not only the meat itself but also the plate it is served on, the napkins used, the background entertainment, and even the view from the table, the "price" of which is reflected in the cost of buying the facility and is passed on to the customer in the prices charged. Even the status of visiting a particular restaurant is something that is paid for in increased prices.

According to Lewis and Chambers,[12] the following factors are associated with successful new products and services:

- The ability to identify customer needs
- Using existing company know-how and resources
- Developing new products in the company's core markets
- Measuring performance during the development stage: screening and testing ideas before spending money on development
- Coordinating between research and development and marketing
- An organizational environment that encourages entrepreneurship and risk taking
- Linking new product development to corporate goals

**Price.**  Several points regarding price bear mentioning. First, the importance of price comes from the fact that it is one-half of the price–value relationship that customers seek. If, in the minds of the guest, the value received is less than the price paid, the experience will be viewed negatively. Second, in the foodservice business much of the pricing that goes on is product-driven pricing. That is, restaurants often have a particular facility that has various fixed costs and items on the menu that can increase in their cost to the restaurateur. The operator must meet these costs by finding a segment of the market willing to pay the price for the product. However, it should always be remembered that the customer is the final arbiter of whether the price charged is acceptable. The latter concept, consumer-driven pricing, has often been ignored in the restaurant industry.[13] In the 1970s, restaurants responded to price increases of various food items by raising prices—in effect, passing their price increases on to the customer. After a while, customers decided that the prices charged were more than the value received. As a result, many customers traded down. Fast-food restaurants gained business from table-service restaurants, and convenience stores benefited from customers who saw fast-food prices increase. Many customers decided to stay home and eat, satisfying their desire for quality by eating better at home. The smarter operators recognized this customer resistance and adjusted concepts and prices accordingly. The point is that the customer, not the product cost, will determine whether an item will sell.

**Promotion–Communication Mix.**  The promotion–communication mix consists of all of the communications between the company and the customer and consists of media advertising, word of mouth, merchandising, promotion, public relations, publicity, and personal selling. These items are covered in greater detail in Chapter 4.

**Place–Distribution Mix.**   The channels that connect the company and its various customers are referred to as the distribution mix. Channels can either be direct or indirect. A direct channel of distribution means that the restaurant communicates directly with its customers. In indirect distribution there are one or more intermediaries between the restaurant and its customers. For example, a restaurant may decide to be listed in a discount book sold by high school students as a fundraising device. A restaurant may decide to become part of a package tour being promoted by a tour operator. The decision to accept credit cards also brings an intermediary—the credit card company—between the restaurant and the customer.

There are several factors to consider before deciding on the form of distribution. If there is an existing or a proposed distribution network, it may be in the interests of the operator to use it. If the seniors in the local high school propose to sell discount books as a fundraiser, it is probably easier to tap into that effort than to duplicate it by distributing fliers about the restaurant directly to the parents and friends of the students.

Several years ago the Scottish Tourist Board began a program called A Taste of Scotland. Restaurants were asked to provide a special menu using locally produced items and to price the menu items within a certain range. In return, the Scottish Tourist Board listed the restaurants in a booklet distributed to tourists that informed them of the operations participating in the scheme. Again, the network provided by the board was not available to the individual operation.

People in the indirect channel of distribution between the restaurant and the customer make their money by helping generate sales. They do not get paid unless a sale is made. Thus the selling cost for the restaurant is a variable one. This compares to the selling cost for direct distribution, which is a fixed cost. The promotion is directed by the operator directly to the customer and must be paid for in full whether it attracts one customer or a thousand. On the other hand, it must be remembered that everyone between the restaurant and the customer must get a cut of the selling price charged by the operation. If a menu item regularly sells for $18 and the restaurant sells that item directly to the customer, it receives $18. However, if a credit card is used, a percentage of the sale is paid to the credit card company and the bank handling the collection. The bus operator willing to bring in two busloads of tourists three times a week during the season will pay less than the $18 because he or she is buying in bulk and expects to pay less by buying wholesale. Every restaurant manager would prefer to sell every meal for the retail price. At times during the day, or the week, or the year, however, the business is not there to pay the full asking price. This is when, and only when, discounts paid to intermediaries can be justified.

The key for the operation is to know when it wants the business and to know the cost structure sufficiently well to realize how low it can price the product and still make money. As a minimum, it is important to know what the break-even point is. As discussed in Chapter 1, the break-even point for a food-service facility is that point at which the operation exactly breaks even. No profits are made; no costs are incurred. At the break-even point, total revenues taken in exactly equal total costs incurred. The important distinction here is that after the break-even point, the only costs incurred by the operation are variable costs. If break-even can thus be assured, the product can be priced to cover variable costs. Anything over the variable cost is profit.

A third factor to consider is the image of the intermediary. The image of the people or organizations distributing the product represent, for the customer, the image of the restaurant being sold. Operators want to ensure that this image is consistent with the one they want to portray.

When sales are made directly, they are made through the employees of the restaurant. Those employees are employed by the operation and should therefore be more motivated to ensure the success of the restaurant than others in the channel who are not employees. The operator needs to determine the needs and wants of those in the channel to ensure a match with her or his own needs.

A final factor to consider is who has the power in the channel. To the extent that a restaurant relies on a tour operator to bring in a significant amount of business, that operator has increased power to demand better prices and services at the risk of taking the business to another restaurant. Recently, a number of restaurants in the Northeast were successful in their attempts to reduce the percentages paid to American Express. The individual operation must balance the various forms of direct and indirect distribution in such a way that it feels in charge of its own destiny rather than being at the mercy of others in the channel.

**Budget.** A crucial part of the action plan is the budget that is developed to carry it out. Various means have been used to develop a budget. A common way of developing a budget is to base it on a percentage of sales. Restaurants typically spend from 0.4 to 6.8 percent of sales on marketing depending on whether it is a full- or limited-service, limited-menu with no table-service facility, or a cafeteria. This option can work with businesses with a high percentage of repeat business. However, if sales go down in a particular year, the following year's marketing budget will be cut when it should probably be increased.

Another option is to spend in line with what the competition is spending. This effectively puts one's fate in the hands of the competition, who may not know what they are doing.

**College Cuisine 2010**

**Learning Objective:** Identify the elements of the marketing mix for restaurant operations.

The college student of 2010 will likely be a highly cosmopolitan person, with knowledge of the world and with an incredible level of technological literacy who would rather eat spontaneously than in a planned manner.

These things are good to know, especially since the industry relies heavily on the 16–24 age bracket for employees. Restaurateurs should look to this age bracket for customers, too. Many college students eat out on a regular basis, especially when they feel that on-campus dining does not provide them with adequate service. Restaurant owners would do well to cater to this age group. How can a restaurant create the proper marketing mix to attract college age students?

The college student of 2010 will have been raised in single or double-parent homes and eaten out more than the previous generation, creating a more sophisticated palate. The college student of 2010 will prefer an unstructured schedule in place of the traditional breakfast, lunch, dinner routine. Rather, due to exposure to the world at large, college students will eat on a more European schedule, with more fruits and breads at breakfast, a large lunch, a quick bite in the early evening, and a late dinner. College student employees may have troubles adjusting to a fixed work schedule due to these lifestyle preferences.

A restaurateur seeking out college-aged customers must start with product, price, promotion, and place. To cater to this age group, restaurants should look into 24-hour service, more food delivery options, and intelligent meal choices. College-aged employees would be helpful in implementing these strategies and coming up with new ideas to make the company appeal to their peers. Foods that are nutrient-enriched, genetically engineered and flavorful will entice the palate of the college student of 2010. Vegetarian options will also draw customers from this age bracket.

*Source:* King, Paul, "NACUFS Presentation Looks at the College Student of 2010," *Nation's Restaurant News,* July 19, 1999, vol. 33, no. 29, p. 16.

**Discussion Question:** Should managers make concessions to create less structured schedules for college-aged employees?

---

A third option is to spend what the business can afford. This approach is a reactive way of deciding action plans.

The fourth approach is the best but also the most difficult. Action plans are developed that will be successful and an amount budgeted to ensure their completion. At this point the desired budget may have to be modified in light of the amount of money available. However, the point is first to determine how

much is needed to do the job, then determine if the business can afford it, rather
than vice versa.

## Monitor and Evaluate the Marketing Plan

It is easy to see when a marketing plan is successful—there are more customers
coming in more often and paying a higher average check. Equally, it is easy to
determine when a plan has not worked—there are fewer customers coming in
as often and they are spending less. What is difficult, however, is to determine
why the plan failed. The exciting part of putting a marketing plan in place is the
operation of the plan. But the most important and most overlooked part is

determining whether or not it was successful and how and where it succeeded or went wrong. Even when the plan is evaluated, it is often done after the event as a kind of postmortem. This may help ensure the success of the next marketing effort. However, it does nothing for the existing campaign.

The marketing plan must be monitored at each step of the way to ensure that it is on track, and corrective action must be taken at each step of the way if it is off track. The first point at which a plan can falter is in the selection of the correct market segment. No matter how good an advertising campaign, if it is directed at the wrong people, it will not work. For control purposes, the restaurateur needs to ask,

- Do I know what my customers want?
- Do I know what people in the marketplace, who are not yet my customers, want?
- Do I know the characteristics of the target market I want to attract?

Assuming that the answer to all the questions above is "yes," the next step is to evaluate the objectives that have been set. The objectives should be

- Specific
- Measurable
- Achievable
- Realistic
- Time based
- Consistent with the operation's place in the product life-cycle curve
- Consistent with the customer's place in the buying process

In monitoring the theme of the program, research is essential to determine the extent to which it is desirable and believable in the eyes of the target market. Additionally, it must be action oriented. In other words, will it produce action on the part of potential customers?

In selecting the appropriate promotional mix, the key concern is whether or not the message is being placed where it will be seen, heard, and/or read by the target market. Media planning involves making decisions on the timing, frequency, size, and position of promotional messages. At this stage messages should be tracked to see whether they meet the objectives set earlier. Were customers exposed to the message? Did the message convey to them the necessary information about the operation? Were customers' attitudes about the facility changed as a result of the message? Did they develop a preference for the operation because of the message? Were they driven to action by the message? Will they come back again? Finally, the budget must be examined along two lines: (1) Is it sufficient to meet the objectives set, and (2) is it an amount that the business can afford?

## quick bite 3.6
### Road to the Top: Mike Scruggs

What do you do when your operation has suffered a setback? Get back to your roots, according to Mike Scruggs, senior vice president for global operations for Little Caesars Enterprises.

"We put together a plan several years ago when we were down in the dumps," he said. "We felt that we needed to take a good hard look at what we were selling, and we found that we were not proud of the product that we were putting out." To fix the problem, the pizza chain made several menu changes, focusing especially on cheeses, pizza sauce, and dough. For example, frozen cheese was phased out in favor of fresh cheese.

"We went back to the roots of what Little Caesars was years ago," Scruggs said. "That has probably been one of the most important aspects of our sales growth."

Often it can be difficult to remember one's roots once one has reached the top, but in order to bring back the freshness of earlier days, it's a necessary step. Besides going back to a higher-quality product, Little Caesars instigated better manager training and a campaign to enhance the restaurant's image.

It paid off; the chain's sales jumped 15.5 percent in the first half of 2003. Sometimes you just have to get back to your roots.

*Source:* Garber, Amy, "Pizza Players Eye New Products, Demographics to Increase Sales," *Nation's Restaurant News,* September 8, 2003, vol. 37, issue 36, p. 4.

**Discussion Question:** When can "getting back to your roots" prove to be a bad strategy?

## ENDNOTES

1. "AMA Board Approves New Marketing Definition," *Marketing News,* March 1, 1985, p. 1.
2. Robert D. Reid, *Hospitality Marketing Management,* 2nd ed. (New York: Van Nostrand Reinhold, 1989), p. 8.
3. James R. Abbey, *Hospitality Sales and Advertising* (East Lansing, MI: Educational Institute of the American Hotel and Motel Association, 1989), p. 34.
4. Tom Feltenstein, *Foodservice Marketing for the '90s* (New York: John Wiley & Sons, 1992), pp. 51–54.
5. Ibid., p. 29.
6. Ibid., p. 23.
7. Abbey, *Hospitality Sales and Advertising,* p. 37.
8. National Restaurant Association, "The Business of Keeping Baby Boomers Happy," *Restaurants USA,* December 2001, www.restaurant.org/rusa.
9. Ibid.
10. Eric N. Berkowitz, Roger A. Kerin, Steven W. Hartley, and William Rudelius, *Marketing,* 3rd ed. (Homewood, IL: Richard D. Irwin, 1992), p. 204.
11. Abbey, *Hospitality Sales and Advertising,* p. 20.

12. Robert C. Lewis and Richard E. Chambers, *Marketing Leadership in Hospitality: Foundations and Practices* (New York: Van Nostrand Reinhold, 1989), p. 327.

13. Ibid., p. 354.

## INTERNET RESOURCES

| | |
|---|---|
| American Marketing Association | *http://www.marketingpower.com/* |
| Simmons Market Research Bureau | *http://www.smrb.com/* |
| Nation's Restaurant News | *http://www.nrn.com/* |
| U.S. Census Bureau | *http://www.census.gov/* |

## QUICK QUIZ ANSWER KEY

p. 54—c. 76%.

p. 65—d. $2211.

# CHAPTER FOUR

# PROMOTING THE OPERATION

"I went to a fancy French restaurant called 'Deja Vu.' The
headwaiter said, 'Don't I know you?'"
Steven Wright, Canadian comedian

## learning objectives

*By the end of this chapter you should be able to*

1. Describe the various stages in the promotional process.

2. Compare and contrast the various methods of establishing a promotional budget.

3. Describe the functions of advertising.

4. Identify the criteria used in selecting which media should be used.

5. Compare and contrast the effectiveness of various media.

6. Identify the key parts of a successful sales promotion: merchandising effort and public relations campaign.

**Learning Objective:** Compare and contrast the various methods of establishing a promotional budget.

When you have dozens of units in your restaurant chain, it can be difficult to synchronize marketing efforts. However, a new Internet technology is changing that by allowing businesses to introduce new advertising campaigns and promotions from an internal website.

These sites operate as order centers for marketing-related supplies, like promotion materials, business cards, and signage. "It is one-stop shopping," said Jim Fox of Denver-based Aerios Direct. Aerios Direct is a private marketing-services firm whose speciality is creating customized Web-based order centers for multiunit chains. The order centers help large chains like Noodles & Company streamline marketing efforts and reduce costs.

Susan Touchette Aust, director of creative services for Noodles & Company, is more than pleased with the site that Aerios Direct created. "We want to make sure we can service the field as we grow," she said, "but our corporate staff may not be expanding as fast as the number of stores." While the Web site was originally a large investment—these systems can run from $10,000 to $45,000—in time and effort, it's paying off. Noodles expects to reduce the number of wasted promotional materials by 20 percent. "By measuring better, you manage better, and by managing better, you can serve the field better," Fox said.

*Source:* Garber, Amy, "Online Order Centers Save Advertising, Promotion Time," *Nation's Restaurant News,* June 14, 2004, vol. 38, issue 24, p. 90.

**Discussion Question:** Why is Noodles & Company's setup—very little corporate staff relative to the 90-unit chain—ideal for using online ordering?

## THE PROMOTIONAL PROCESS

### Objectives of Promotion

Modern marketing calls for more than developing a good product, pricing it attractively, and making it available to target customers. Restaurants must also communicate with their customers.

Management communicates with customers—both existing and potential—through what is known as the promotional mix. The end goal of promotion is behavior modification: We want to initiate or change the behavior of customers such that they will dine with us.

Specifically, promotion seeks to inform, persuade, and remind. For new or remodeled restaurants the task is to inform the public about the operation; for existing operations the job is to persuade customers to visit; for existing customers the goal is to keep them aware of the operation so that when they think about eating out, one restaurant immediately springs to mind.

## Steps in the Process

The promotional process is illustrated in Figure 4.1. A target market is identified, objectives set, the content and form of the message established, the promotional mix determined, appropriate media selected, and a budget established. It is important to set up controls at each step of the way to determine whether the campaign is on track.

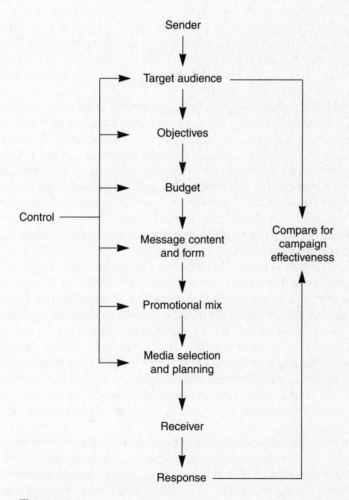

**Figure 4.1** The promotional process. *Source:* Adapted from Robert Christie Mill and Alastair M. Morrison, *The Tourism System: An Introductory Text,* 2nd ed. (Upper Saddle River, NJ: Prentice Hall, 1992), p. 448.

**Target Market.**   The various segments of the market have been covered in earlier chapters. To determine whether the correct market has been chosen, the operator must answer the following questions:

- Do I know what my customers want?
- Do I know what the marketplace wants?
- Do I know the characteristics of the target market I want to attract?

**Objectives.**   To determine the objectives of the campaign, it is important to determine where the operation is in the life-cycle curve and where the customers are in the buying process. The concept of a life-cycle curve involves the notion that a business goes through various stages. The length of time in each stage will vary from business to business. At each stage, different operational strategies are important. Typically, a business will be introduced into the marketplace, then go through stages of growth, maturity, and decline or rejuvenation. In the first stage, the new or remodeled concept is introduced into the marketplace. At this point, potential customers are unaware of the operation. The objective is to inform customers of the restaurant's existence.

If all goes well the restaurant goes through a period of growth. One characteristic of the operation is that sales or customers are increasing at an increasing rate. Perhaps there was a 5 percent increase in sales last year, a 7 percent increase this year, and a projected 8 percent increase next year. At this point, customers are obviously aware of the operation and the objective is to persuade.

In the mature stage of the life cycle, sales and/or customers are increasing but at a decreasing rate—last year's growth of 6 percent is replaced this year by a growth of 5 percent and a projected growth next year of 3 percent. Profits begin to peak before sales decline. The promotional objective is to differentiate the operation from the competition.

If no remedial action is taken, the business will go into the decline stage of the cycle. Sales and/or customers are going down. At this point it is important to take the appropriate steps to get out of that particular business segment.

Remedial action can be taken to rejuvenate the business to produce another spurt of growth. This might involve getting existing customers to come in more often and/or at different times of the day, going after another segment of the market, or introducing new items on the menu (or a change of theme). A number of the fast-food chains noticed a slowdown in sales as the industry entered the mature stage of the life cycle and introduced breakfast menus as a way of rejuvenating sales. In addition, many expanded overseas to reach an entirely new market.

For control purposes objectives should be SMART—that is, they should be *s*pecific, *m*easurable, *a*chievable, *r*ealistic, and *t*ime-bound. To make the objective specific, it is necessary to quantify it. It is not enough to "increase awareness"; it is necessary to "reach 1000 prospects." The sheer fact that a specific target has been set increases the chances of reaching it.

Similarly, objectives must be measurable. There is no way that an objective of "increasing awareness" can be measured; it is just too vague. It is possible, however, to determine whether or not 1000 people have been exposed to a promotional message. Newspapers count circulation, radio stations count listeners, and direct mailings can be tabulated.

If objectives are not achievable, setting them becomes a meaningless exercise. Objectives must also be realistic in the eyes of the people whose job it is to meet the objectives. If objectives are set at an unrealistically high level—"we want to sell an additional 200 bottles of wine next week"—the servers who are charged with the task of selling the wine will not even try, realizing that it is impossible.

Finally, objectives must be time-bound. There must be a time frame within which the objective is to be achieved. If there is no time frame, it becomes impossible to determine whether the objective has been reached.

**Message Content and Form.** A variety of themes can be developed as part of a promotional campaign. A restaurant may stress reputation, food taste or type, quality, or service. The "proper" message is one that is desirable, believable, exclusive, and action oriented. It must make the customer want what is being offered; it has to be believed; it should "belong" to one operation and no one else; and it should induce action on the part of the customer.

**Promotional Mix.** The major elements of the promotional mix are as follows:[1]

- *Advertising:* Any paid form of nonpersonal presentation and promotion of ideas, goods, or services by an identified sponsor
- *Personal selling:* Oral conversations, either by telephone or face to face, between salespersons and prospective customers
- *Sales promotion:* Short-term incentives to encourage purchase or sales of a product or service
- *Merchandising:* Materials used in-house to stimulate sales, including brochures on display, signs, posters, tent cards, and other point-of-purchase promotional items
- *Public relations and publicity:* The nonpaid communication activities involved in maintaining or improving relationships with other organizations and individuals

The principles and practices involved in the proper selection of the various parts of the promotional mix will make up much of the remainder of this chapter.

**Media Selection and Planning.** Various elements of the promotional mix involve using paid or unpaid media. While selecting appropriate media will be covered in more detail later, the key control question is this: "Is my message in a place where it will be seen, read, and/or heard by my customers?"

**Budget.** The place of budgeting in the promotional process will depend on the approach to promotion taken by the operation. In a bottom-up approach, objectives will be set, the methods of reaching the objectives determined, and a

**Learning Objective:** Describe the various stages in the promotional process.

How can an old restaurant invite in new customers? By changing its look. With the constant influx of new competition into the foodservice industry, restaurants must update themselves to keep ahead.

Ryan's Family Steakhouse Inc. is seeking to gain new customers by making some new changes, both on the inside and the outside of the restaurant.

The first step was redesigning the space to make the restaurant feel more like a lodge. Natural effects and a lot of woodwork add a woodsy flavor to the atmosphere of the steakhouse. Although such remodeling is costly, the new design has generated a 10-percent increase in sales over typical volumes at standard branches, according to management. "Our remodeled exterior lets the customer know that there is something new inside the store," said Fred Grant, Ryan's chief financial officer. "We think we're getting a little bit more upscale customer."

*Source:* Spielberg, Susan, "Ryan's Get More Upscale with New Look, Name," *Nation's Restaurant News*, vol. 38, no. 7, February 16, 2004, p. 4.

**Discussion Question:** Why is this more complicated than it sounds? What does a remodeled exterior do?

budget agreed upon that will do the job. All too often, however, a top-down approach is used whereby the budget is determined first and objectives set relative to the amount of money available. Budgets can be set according to industry standards, to what the competition is spending, to what amount of money is available, or to meet the agreed-upon objectives.

Restaurants across the board spend an average of 2 percent of sales on marketing expenses.[2] The problem with an average is just that—it is an average. This figure represents a number for newly opened operations (which probably need to promote more) and established facilities, which may not need to promote as much. This figure should only be used as a very rough starting point.

Often a manager, noticing that the competition has taken out an advertisement in the local paper, responds with an ad of his or her own. Although it can be important to match the competition, this policy has two major drawbacks: It means that the manager's actions are being "controlled" by the competition, and it assumes that the competition knows what the manager's establishment is doing!

For many managers promotion is seen as a cost of doing business rather than as an investment. Too often the refrain is, "I can't afford to advertise," to which the answer is, "You can't afford not to." Promotional expenses must be planned for in advance as a part of doing business rather than being relegated to

Mathew Tivvy usually specializes in French cuisine. However, Metro Diet, his latest venture, focuses on health rather than on the rich butter and cream sauces common in French food. Metro Diet caters specifically to the needs of customers who find it difficult to eat out or to stick to a restricted diet; the chef-driven operation offers gourmet personalized meals for those on low-carb diets or other specialized diets. These meals are delivered to the customer at work or at home.

Over the course of his 20-year career in the foodservice industry Tivvy says he has learned the importance of catering to the consumer's desire for lean offerings. Although he loves making and eating French food, he says that he has learned as he has grown older that although the meal is important, how you feel after eating the meal is more important. Feeling satisfied and healthy after eating a light meal is more pleasant than the gorged, unpleasant feeling following a very heavy meal.

*Source:* Lohmeyer, Lori, "Mathew Tivvy: Tipping the Scales in Favor of Good Health," *Nation's Restaurant News,* vol. 38, no. 1, January 5, 2004, p. 24.

**Discussion Question:** Why did Tivvy lean away from French cuisine toward leaner cuisines? Do you agree that the feeling after eating a meal is more important than the meal?

the category of an "extra" for which money may or may not be available after all other bills have been paid.

The best and most difficult method of establishing a budget is to identify the objectives and set a budget sufficient to meet the objectives. At the same time, it must be an amount that the business can afford. Promotion is more art than science. There is no scientific way to determine how many advertisements it will take to produce $x$ number of customers. For this reason alone, there is a common tendency to view budgeting as a top-down effort.

**Response.**   If promotion is communication, it does not work unless communication occurs, unless the object of the communication receives it and responds. If each step of the process has been controlled, there is a greater chance that the campaign will be a success and that customers will respond to an advertisement, buy the bottle of wine from the server, or order the appetizer noted on the tent card.

This final part of the control process is vital. Did the promotion do what it was intended to do? Can we trace the impact on sales to a particular effort? Only through such tracking can a cost–benefit analysis be done in an effort to measure the effectiveness of the various parts of the promotional effort.

## Customer Use of Information

According to the National Restaurant Association,[3] while restaurateurs typically use advertisements in magazines and newspapers or direct mail to tempt customers into their restaurants for the first time, these types of information sources are used by fewer than one out of five adults who are looking for a new restaurant. Twenty-eight percent of adults report that they are likely to select a new table-service restaurant on the basis of a television advertisement while one-third are likely to use a restaurant guide. Eight percent are likely to use the Internet, a figure expected to increase dramatically in the future. Word of mouth remains the most popular source of information used by prospective customers in selecting a new restaurant. Younger people and those with lower incomes are less likely to use the recommendations of friends than are older people and those in higher income brackets. However, across all age and income groups, personal recommendations are overwhelmingly the most used information source. This emphasizes the importance of providing excellent value and service, the subject of Chapter 6.

# ADVERTISING AGENCIES

## When to Use an Agency

A foodservice company can handle its own promotional campaign or it can hire an advertising agency. Some owners, managers, and key personnel are clever with words and ideas. They may actually be better than some professionals at creating ads and promos. They may need only occasional outside services and suppliers to help them promote their businesses. Other operators may not be so fortunate or creative; they may wish to contract with outside companies for publicity services and suppliers to help them promote their businesses. Another option could be to create an in-house advertising agency—that is, an agency within the firm.

Operators of many small or beginning businesses have little choice. Their advertising budget is not big enough to justify hiring an independent agency, much less setting up a house agency. These operators must look after their own promotion, calling on representatives of local media for expertise. Fortunately, many local broadcast or print media prepare advertising competently. The restaurateur has only to coordinate the themes and timing of the various efforts—and be sure that he or she is buying what is needed. It is always worth remembering that advertising salespeople are paid for selling advertising, and, believing in their service, they will sell as much as they can.

Agencies are paid in a variety of ways.[4] Often, they receive commissions from the media in which the message is placed. The usual commission is 15 percent of the cost of the advertisement. If an advertisement cost $400, for example, the client would pay the agency the $400. The agency would subtract 15 percent ($60) and pay the media $340.

Agencies also charge the client for production and creative services involved in creating the advertisement. Typically, these fees consist of monthly retainers in addition to hourly charges for creative work, photography, and type-setting. Finally, agencies charge for advertisements on which commissions are not paid, such as direct mail and local newspaper advertising.

## How to Select an Agency

When an agency wants a restaurant's business, or a restaurateur wants to hire an agency, it is customary to arrange an agency presentation. The larger the account and billing, the more attractive the company will be to agencies.

An agency presentation can be accomplished over a simple lunch or may take the form of a full-blown display of what the agency can do. A presentation will include a description of the personnel of the agency and some representative work they have performed successfully for others. A list of past and present clients will usually be offered for reference checks. The pitch can be conducted in the client's offices or at the agency. Most agencies prefer to use their facilities to avoid interruptions and to put on a proper show.

Presenting agencies will try to sell an entire marketing plan rather than just a media plan. Even if they do not know the idiosyncrasies of the business, they may be able to lay out a plan of attack to help a restaurateur get more mileage out of an ad budget.

If the restaurateur's budget is large enough to interest agencies, it is wise to listen to more than one agency's presentation. It is not wise to make a hasty decision. References of past and present clients of the agencies that are being considered should be checked before committing to an outside agency.

Most agencies will not represent more than one client in a given business or industry. If an agency already has a restaurant or hospitality account, it will probably be prepared to quit or lose it before taking another.

Before making a decision, the agency offices should be toured and meetings held with the personnel. The person who will be working with the account representing the client should be identified. Agency personnel who do not own a piece of the action in their agencies tend to move about in their industry just as restaurant people change jobs in theirs. It may become an important issue if an account executive leaves the agency. An account may be bound by an employment agreement that forbids agency personnel from taking clients along to a new agency.

Studying how an advertising agency works will help improve cooperation with the agency's efforts. An outside agency representative can instruct a client in how the agency operates, purchases media, performs research, orders graphic artwork and photography, handles copyrighting, and conducts publicity. In the process a restaurateur will sign all insertion orders and okay all copy. It is important for clients to receive copies of all work done on their behalf.

The agency relationship should begin with a complete understanding of how all items, services, and media are to be purchased. Both parties must exert every possible effort to be open to what the other is doing for their mutual good. Both client and agency must anticipate problems and discuss them beforehand to establish the best possible relations and to achieve the best results.

Most client–agency relationship and agreements, either oral or written, can terminate almost immediately. Agencies know that they cannot work where they are not wanted. There should be one item that should be understood when a split occurs—all bills and invoices should be paid by the client to the agency or be guaranteed to all other suppliers and media. When this is fully done, the agency should relinquish all the materials and support information that belong to the client.

---

quick quiz

In the 1920s, hamburgers had another nickname, which came from an insatiable hamburger addict in the Popeye comic strip. What were they called?

*Source:* Hickok, Allan F. and Lana E. Lazarus, *Restaurant Industry Review,* U.S. Bancorp Piper Jaffray Equity Research, March 2003, pp. 54–55.

---

## ADVERTISING

As noted previously, advertising can be defined as any paid form of nonpersonal presentation and promotion of ideas, goods, or services by an identified sponsor.

### Functions of Advertising

Advertising seeks to inform, persuade, and remind. It can accomplish a number of things:[5] It presents information to the customer about the operation, it encourages first-time visits, it enhances the image of a particular company or operation, and it reinforces the behavior of customers who have eaten at the restaurant in the past.

### Types of Campaigns

**National/Local.**  Advertising campaigns can be either national or local. National advertising uses network media—television, radio, and magazines—to reach a national audience. The effort is essentially directed toward promoting the general name or image of the company rather than toward any one establishment. At the local level promotions are tailored to the local market in an attempt to promote specific restaurants. The only way that local operators can compete against major chains is to target their marketing efforts to those people within a three- to five-mile radius of the restaurant.[6]

**Cooperative Agreements.**  To maximize use of the promotional dollar, individual restaurants can enter into cooperative agreements whereby a number of individual operations pool their resources to produce an advertisement promoting eating out in general or restaurants in a geographic area. This allows an individual facility to advertise in media that it could not afford on its own. Individual managers must determine whether or not the benefits of inclusion outweigh the costs.

Another example of cooperative advertising is when restaurants who are members of chains cooperate with the corporate office in producing a promotion. A national chain would pay the "national rate" for a series of advertisements in print, television, or radio. This rate is higher than the "local rate," that paid by a local business. By splitting the cost of the campaign 50–50 and having the local business book the advertisement, the company gets a lower rate while the individual business effectively doubles its advertising budget.

## Media Selection Criteria

A variety of criteria are used to determine which media should be used. The most important criteria are the cost per contact, total cost, market selectivity, geographic selectivity, source credibility, visual quality, noise level, life span, pass-along rate, and timing flexibility.

---

### quick bite 4.4
**Skills: Health Concept**

**Learning Objectives:** Describe the functions of advertising.

It seems that Red Lobster, one of the most popular seafood chains in America, does not have the most popular brand. "The brand is not getting tired, but the brand is in need of a little polishing. We need to be known more as a place that offers a great experience where you can reconnect with family and friends," said a Red Lobster marketing executive.

While that could be said with most brands, it rings especially true with Red Lobster. Different promotions are planned but they will most likely still have their annual lobster-fest. What might help more, according to Gregg Cebrzynski, is to stop focusing on the lobsters and crab legs, and start focusing on the other seafood that they sell.

With a name like Red Lobster, it's understandable that one would think that it is a high scale lobster restaurant. But that's not the case. "It's not a lobster restaurant," said marketing strategist Al Ries. "They can't sell lobsters at lobster prices. They're selling lobster at shrimp prices, which is not the way to make money."

Because their seafood is healthy (and health sells in the current market) then they might have better luck promoting that idea. "Compared to every other restaurant out there, Red Lobster is the healthiest," said Ries. "Why not sell that?"

*Source:* Cebrzynski, Gregg, "Red Lobster May Not Be a Tired Brand, but It Looks Sleepy," *Nation's Restaurant News*, vol. 38, no. 1, January 5, 2004, p. 14.

**Discussion Question:** Do you agree that Red Lobster should shift its advertising focus to health instead of lobster? Why or why not?

---

The cost per contact, usually expressed as cost per thousand (CPM), refers to the cost of reaching 1000 people. The total cost is the actual cost of the message. *Market selectivity* refers to the extent to which an advertiser can reach a specific market segment. In recent years magazines aimed at a general readership have given way to a variety of magazines targeted toward specific groups of people. This makes it easier to reach particular segments of the market.

Similarly, *geographic selectivity* refers to the ability to reach a particular part of the country, state, or town. Many magazines run regional editions while small townships put out local papers. Source credibility considers how believable the medium is viewed to be by the reader or listener. Certain media offer better-quality visuals than others. Generally speaking, the quality of visuals in newspapers is poor.

When an advertisement competes with other activities for a person's attention, the noise level is said to be high. If the tendency is to give total attention to the message, the noise level is said to be low.

Life span and pass-along rate are closely related. A newspaper has a life span of one day. One person reads it and usually discards it. A magazine, on the other hand, is kept around longer and may be read by someone other than the person who purchased it. A radio advertisement has an even shorter life span than that of a newspaper, as the message cannot be referred to again. Among other things, this means that radio advertisements have to be repeated a number of times to have any kind of impact.

Finally, *timing flexibility* refers to the lead time needed to run or change an advertisement.

## Newspapers

**Effectiveness.**   Newspapers, as noted previously, are the primary advertising medium for table-service restaurants. They generally offer the most cost-effective means of reaching potential consumers, both in terms of total cost and cost per contact. Market selectivity is low, and geographic selectivity is average. It is possible, for example, to zero in on specific towns. The trust factor appears to be low and the visual quality less than average. To counteract a high noise level, low life span, and low pass-along rate, newspapers offer a great deal of flexibility in the timing of advertisements.

**Copy/Layout.**   When using a newspaper advertisement copy, layout and photographs/sketches must be considered. The copy consists of the headline and body. The headline of the ad must catch the reader's attention while the body includes the details. A good advertisement starts with a headline that is enticing, provocative, and attention grabbing. A clever, punch headline with few words is preferable to one that attempts to tell the entire story.

**Size/Shape.**   Choosing a different size and shape is one way to make an ad stand out. If most other ads are 1/4-page vertical, a 1/4-page horizontal space may attract more attention.

Suppress the urge to crowd as much information as possible into an ad. The most successful ads tell a simple story in clear, concise language. Ads jammed with too many facts and figures are least likely to be read. All ads create certain types of impressions. A simple test can determine what stands out most in an ad. The ad is turned upside down to see what is most noticeable. People are used to reading left to right, top to bottom. Once a page is turned upside down, the viewer's mind's eye becomes disoriented and he or she cannot read according to learned methods. At first, an ad may look like a big blur, but later the viewer will be able to detect the most outstanding element in the ad, the one that will have the most impact on readers. If that element is not the one intended, the ad needs to redesigned. If the big blur remains and the viewer finds it difficult to determine any outstanding elements, the ad needs to be redesigned. A catchy headline, a strong graphic, a bold price, or any other single element should be prominent.

## Radio

Radio is an immediate medium for quick news and information. Advertising time can readily be bought and commercials produced quickly for relatively low cost. It is selective for broad market segments and has a high geographic selectivity. Credibility is low and noise level high, while timing flexibility is better than average.

**Station Formats.**   In seeking a share of the market, radio stations have created many individual formats that reach different target audiences efficiently. Radio station formats include talk, Spanish, easy listening, Top 40, R&B, classical, contemporary, religious, adult contemporary, nostalgia/big band, news/talk, oldies, disco, educational, jazz, progressive rock, blues/soft, and gospel music. Individual stations claim that their listeners are loyal and selective because of their strong preferences for a station's format and their personal identification with the particular interests reflected by the station.

**Effectiveness.**   Radio uses words and sounds to describe products and services and special occasions. Radio plays on the imagination of the listeners and attempts to sell the sizzle rather than the steak.

Many radio stations in a market result in fragmented audiences. Radio advertising can therefore be costly and inefficient when many stations are needed to reach a broad cross section of target audiences. Radio cannot show or demonstrate products or services. The advertising message usually must remind people of things they know. New, unique, or complicated ideas may be difficult to express. Radio is a transient medium. Messages cannot be kept for later reference. Listeners, for example, must remember addresses and telephone numbers. Coupon offers are out.

The Federal Trade Commission (FTC) regulates the percentage of total air time that can be devoted to commercials. Many listeners, however, believe that some radio stations are overcommercialized, particularly at peak periods.

Advertising messages therefore need strong creative treatment to be noticed and remembered.

**Commercial Formats.** Commercials generally come in two formats: 30 and 60 seconds. The half-minute spots do not cost half the cost of full-minute spots. The expense is so close that many advertisers use 60-second commercial spots for the greatest cost efficiency. Also, 30-second commercials are very brief. A 30-second spot involves 65 to 70 words of copy, while a 60-second commercial generally accommodates 125 to 135 words of copy.

## Television

Unquestionably, television is the powerhouse medium. It combines most of the advantages of sight, sound, immediacy, dramatization, and emotional involvement of the viewers in a way that no other medium can match. It is also expensive. It can make customers aware of what there is to offer, at a price that requires considerable planning and budgeting.

**Effectiveness.** Television is the dominant medium. It reaches people of every type and is of average market selectivity while covering large areas of geography quite efficiently. However, television is inefficient when advertisers need to reach a highly selected group of people. It cannot isolate distinctively differing groups of people, as does radio with its highly categorized formats.

Television can also show how a product or service works, and it provides strong name identification. It builds awareness rapidly and, by its intensity, increases audience perception of commercial message. As a medium it is not credible, the noise level is high, and the timing flexibility is low.

Television ads cannot be saved for later reference or couponing. In addition, commercial time is generally short and, like radio spots, television messages must have an immediate impact on viewers. Television cannot be used for long, complicated explanations.

## Magazines

**Effectiveness.** There are almost as many different kinds of magazines as there are different kinds of restaurants. Therefore, a magazine will pinpoint the market by the type of publication chosen. However, any bona fide publication seeking advertisers should provide information concerning its readership, circulation, and advertising costs to permit a restaurateur to determine where it should fit into the advertising program.

Some magazines devote special sections to restaurant advertising. Frequently, the readership of such columns is high and comparable to an editorial feature of the same length. Most magazines are read by the same people, issue after issue. An eating establishment whose advertisement is noted regularly becomes a part of the readers' subconscious mind. An acceptance is established because of the familiarity of name or message.

Another option is menu-only magazines. There has been an increase in the number of third-party services that promote the menus of affiliated restaurants both in magazines and on Web sites. The service takes the order, forwards it to the restaurant, and picks up and delivers the meal. One survey indicates that over 80 percent of families with children under age 5 order food to go several times monthly.[7] Takeout Taxi began delivering meals in 1987. Others have followed. They agree that printed menu magazines are the best way to market both the restaurants and the meal delivery. Menu-only magazines are distributed at the restaurants themselves as well as at apartment buildings, universities, businesses, and hotels.

The industry standard discount on meals sold to delivery services ranges from 20 to 30 percent of the total food bill. The third-party service uses the difference between the full menu price it collects from the customer and the discount price it pays the restaurant to print the menu-only magazine, maintain its Web site, and deliver the meals.

This is an expensive way for restaurants to build sales. Before committing to this strategy the operator should be convinced that sufficient incremental business is being brought to offset the discount being given.

---

### quick quiz

Can you name the companies who used the following slogans?

a. "Where's the Beef?"
b. "Have It Your Way"
c. "Finger Lickin' Good"
d. "You Deserve a Break Today"
e. "Pizza! Pizza!

---

## Yellow Pages

**Effectiveness.** Yellow Pages advertisements are important in every promotional campaign. They provide good value for the investment. It is important to have the advertisement draw in the reader. However, to compete with all the listings in the Yellow Pages, many restaurants find it advantageous to place an ad close to their listing or to have their business name set in bold type.

In Yellow Pages advertising the name, address, and phone number of the restaurant are highlighted for people who have sought out the restaurant section for a specific interest. If a person is scanning the pages to decide on a place to dine, an advertisement has an opportunity to direct him or her to the establishment.

**Layout.** Advertising space in the Yellow Pages is sold in standard-size units. The sizes are usually 1/4 page, 1/8 page, and 1/16 page. The rates vary according to the number of phone books printed. Based on a cost per thousand impressions, it is not an expensive medium. The total bill, a combination of rate and production costs, can be paid in advance or prorated to coincide with the restaurant's regular service billing.

## Signs and Billboards

Signs and billboards can be found on location, on highways, or on buildings. The message should be brief yet eye-catching. Gigantic signs are now being constructed that swing and shimmer at the slightest touch of wind. Changeable copy panels make it possible to advertise daily menu changes and even provide public service messages from time to time. Generally, a contract for painted display advertising runs for one, two, or three years. The contract specifies the number of times that copy will be renewed or changed during the contract period. It is a rule of thumb in the outdoor advertising business that the message should be renewed or changed every four months. Many advertisers consider outdoor reminder advertising to be supportive rather than primary in nature. Outdoor posters must be brief, with just a few bold, easy-to-read words to tell a story or theme.

## Direct Mail

Direct mail marketers send mailings that include letters, glossy advertisement, samples, and foldouts to prospects on their mailing list.

**Advantages.**   Direct mail offers a number of advantages to the restaurateur. This form of advertising has a high degree of control as the manager decides to whom the message is to be sent. The number of pieces mailed can be tailored to the size of the budget available. It is highly audience selective in that the mailing lists are developed from customer lists or from lists obtained from mailing-list houses, which can provide lists of names broken down into a variety of specific segments. Direct mail is increasing in popularity because it permits high target-market selectivity.

Direct mail is also highly flexible in that the message can be personalized to different market segments. There is some question as to whether or not it is cluttered. Certainly, people are unlikely to be doing anything else when they read their mail. On the other hand, so much mail is now regarded as "junk mail" that any and all nonpersonal mail stands a good chance of being thrown out unopened unless the piece is carefully designed. The ability to assess responses from a mailing by enclosing a coupon or a phone number allows easy measurement of the results of a campaign.

**Disadvantages.**   Direct mailings tend to have a high discard rate, high total cost, and long lead time. A rule of thumb is that a direct mailing gets a 1 to 3 percent response rate. This means that for every 100 letters sent out, the operator will receive only an average 2 percent response rate to a mailing. To get 100 customers with a response rate of 2 percent would require a mailing of 5000 pieces. The response rate can be improved by having a high-quality list and a mailing that is targeted to the needs of the potential customers being sought.

It is estimated that between 15 and 30 percent of mailing lists change each year. The cost of updating lists, in addition to the low response rate, can result in a relatively high cost to conduct a campaign. Implementing direct mail through a list house can furnish a lengthy list. If you were to send a mailing to each name, it could develop into a high-priced expenditure.

**Mailing Lists.** A properly conducted campaign requires preparing up-to-date mailing lists, designing the piece, processing the bulk mailing, and responding to inquiries. This can involve a long lead time, ultimately resulting in higher costs.

Commercial lists can be purchased or rented from companies specializing in the development of such items. They can also be obtained from general lists through business directories or membership rosters of associations, or from house lists developed by the restaurant itself. The best source for a mailing list is the property's own customers. The major problem is that such a list takes time to develop. To "prime the pump" a general list tied to the zip codes within a three- to five-mile radius of the operation is probably the second-best alternative.

**Types of Mailings.** The most appropriate options for restaurants are letters, newsletters, and menus. Letters are very simple to prepare and can be used for such things as announcements, invitations, and so on. Newsletters to regular customers can be sent monthly, bimonthly, or quarterly, to keep the property in the customer's awareness. As with all direct mail, newsletters should be filled with information that is interesting and important to customers. Seasonal messages and recipes and informative tips regarding food and wine are some of the items to consider. Many people select a restaurant based on the type of menu. For them, mailing the menu itself may induce people to try the operation, particularly a new facility.

Mailing can be either first class, suitable for letters and postcards; third-class single piece, best for booklets and brochures; and third-class bulk, for newsletters or other items mailed in bulk. The latter is the least expensive but takes longer than first class to be delivered. A variety of restrictions and regulations must be met for the use of third-class mailing.

**Success Factors.** To be successful a mailing piece should follow the five P's.[8] First, it should form a picture in the mind of the customer. We think in terms of pictures, not letters or words. Second, it must offer a promise and show how the promise will be fulfilled. The promise should be something that is important to the customer.

Next, the message must prove to the reader that what is being promised is true. "Proof" might come in the form of testimonials, success stories, or statistics. Fourth, the message should push the customer to action—ask for the sale. This might involve making a reservation, sending in a coupon, or showing up for dinner.

Finally, there should be a postscript. In reading a direct mail piece, most people first read the letterhead, then check to look at the signature and to see if there is a P.S. Interest can be generated by means of a clever postscript.

The effectiveness of a direct mail campaign is measured by the number of responses generated. As noted earlier, one of the advantages of direct mail is that the results are readily measurable against the costs involved.

## quick bite 4.5
### Wild Wings on TV

**Learning Objectives:** Compare and contrast the effectiveness of various media. Identify the criteria used in selecting which media should be used.

Buffalo Wild Wings Grill & Bar promoted their Finger Foods menu for the first time in 2004. The 200-chain unit uses the agency Periscope Marketing Communications of Minneapolis and plans to break two TV spots later in the year 2004 as a part of their $8 million advertising program.

TV offers many advantages, including the ability to reach a wide audience simultaneously. Buffalo Wild Wings Grill & Bar will place their ads during the NCAA "March Madness" basketball playoffs and the NBA's playoff games. "Strategically, it's always been one of our busiest times," said Kathy Alberga, who is senior vice president of marketing, advertising and brand development for the sports-themed chain. "We really feel that this is a fantastic opportunity to look at additional sales."

*Source:* Cebrzynski, Gregg, "Buffalo Wild Wings Puts the Finger on New Promo, Preps TV Spots," *Nation's Restaurant News*, March 10, 2004, p. 14

**Discussion Questions:** Why is placing advertisements for Wild Wings during sporting events a good choice? What led Buffalo Wild Wings Grill & Bar to make this decision?

## INTERNET

Use of the Internet as a source of information as well as an advertising vehicle is expected to increase rapidly in the next decade. To get the most out of a Web page,[9] it is important to downplay the advertising aspect of the page and play up the information aspect. Viewers tend to get turned off by pages they consider too "advertising aggressive." The objective is to get prospective customers to add the restaurant page to their electronic address book and return often. The Web page has to be integrated into other marketing efforts. Use the page to refer people to newspaper advertisements, which, in turn, should list the electronic address of the restaurant. The initial impression is important—browsers may stay for as little as five seconds before moving on. Emphasizing a customer benefit may get them to stay. Lead with a banner that will teach browsers something, such as information on wine and food pairings.

The site should be simple to navigate around and downloading pages should be easy and fast. Like other advertisements, the information should be updated on a regular basis to encourage repeat visits. Including links to other related sites is regarded as good "Netiquette" and professional. Finally, the Web page by itself will be of little use. As noted previously, the Web page should be mentioned in all other promotions and advertisements as well as on menus and business cards.

Restaurants are upgrading their sites and moving away from bare-bones information to educate and entertain customers. McDonald's allows site visitors to determine the nutritional and fat content of a meal by filling a virtual bag with menu items and getting a running tally of fat grams and calories.

To help determine the effectiveness of a Web site, some operators include a toll-free number that is only available online. By tracking the responses from that number, it is possible to quantify the Web site investment. It is estimated, for example, that a Web presence requires a minimum investment of $4000 to $5000.[10]

The Internet is also the tool being used to build traffic during off-hours through price discounting. Visa's Dining Privileges program allows its high-end Signature card users to get off-peak meal discounts, make reservations online, and get access to tables during prime dining times.[11] Restaurants use flexible or dynamic pricing to change menu prices by hour or daypart to attract business during nonpeak times. Since it is impractical to print menus for different times during the day, the reduction in menu prices comes in the form of a percentage discount that varies by time of day. Discounts tend to range from 15 to 30 percent of the total bill (excluding tax and tip). Participating restaurants pay a monthly fee and a small amount for each off-peak reservation taken by the third-party service.

More restaurants are using e-mail to communicate with customers. Fishbowl is an e-mail services firm that sends over 2 million e-mail messages a month on behalf of 60 restaurant chains. Participating chains pay a one-time setup fee and a monthly retainer tied to the size of their database. The company claims measurable positive results.

## PERSONAL SELLING

Personal selling consists of oral conversations, either by telephone or face to face, between salespersons and prospective customers. In a restaurant situation, personal selling occurs outside the operation as staff attempt to book business and inside as employees try to "sell up," get customers to increase the amount spent. The latter topic is dealt with in Chapter 6.

## SALES PROMOTION

### Incentives

Sales promotion consists of short-term incentives to encourage the purchase of a product or service. Consumer promotions may include coupons, frequent-diner programs, premiums, patronage rewards, contests, sweepstakes, and games.

Promotions may be open or contingent. Open offers do not require the customer to do anything other than buy the product. Special meals and discounts are examples of open offers. The advantage to the restaurant is that the promotion will have broad customer appeal since no effort to redeem a coupon, for example, is required. On the other hand, the restaurateur has no idea how many people will take advantage of the promotion. More people may show up than was anticipated, creating bad will if items being promoted are not available or high costs if they are.

A contingent offer requires the customer to do something: clip a coupon, eat out three times within a month, or make a specific purchase. The redemption rate is more easily controlled, although fewer customers will be attracted. The latter method is preferred for cost-control reasons.

Because of their short-term nature—good promotions have an expiration date—they can have the benefit of stimulating sales during the period of the promotion. Promotions cannot be used as the sole or even most important part of the marketing effort. If the business makes too much use of promotions, there is a danger that customers will wait for the next promotion before they buy. This, in essence, is what has happened in the pizza business. Many, if not most, households will simply not buy pizza unless they have a coupon for a discount or two-for-one.

**Coupons.** Coupons are certificates that give customers a savings when they purchase a product, as in a two-for-one meal purchase. This is the most widely used special offer, surpassing such things as restaurant specials, combination offers, or senior discounts. A 15 to 20 percent discount is needed to induce customers to buy. Pizza chains are responsible for most couponing. It is estimated that over half of all pizza purchases are driven by coupon deals.[12]

Jay Solomon suggests using coupons for bringing in business on slow nights.

Coupons offering free products are used to generate customer trial. Thus the measure of success is whether or not the customer count increased. A successful trial promotion would attempt to get customers to buy something they would not ordinarily order. For this reason, a free beverage with a sandwich is not a good idea, as most people will order a beverage anyway. It might be better in this situation to offer free onion rings. Restrictions can and should be placed on when the coupons can be used to bring in customers when business is slow.

The most popular strategies for distributing coupons are freestanding inserts in newspapers and direct mail. However, a growing number of restaurants are using the chain's Web site, the back of register tapes in local supermarkets, data-encoded plastic swipe cards.[13] Many full-service restaurants avoid coupons for fear coupons will tarnish their image. However, research has shown that the higher the level of education and income of a customer, the higher the redemption rate of coupons.[14]

When Lettuce Entertain You Enterprises (LEYE) introduced a loyalty card program in the earlier 1990s, it partnered with a local bank that collected the program's data. The first card was both a loyalty card and a credit card. Since then LEYE has outsourced the information collection and discontinued the credit card function. LEYE admits it made a mistake by not charging for participation in the program. Now LEYE charges $25 for its loyalty card. Customers receive one point for each dollar spent. They redeem points for prizes. To encourage customers to try other LEYE restaurants—there are 40—the program gives double points to customers who visits a restaurant they had not previously dined at.[15]

A McDonald's franchisee in Kansas City pays 19 cents for a discount card and sells it to customers for 25 cents. The card gives a 15 percent discount on orders over $5.00. It has the effect of increasing the average check.

**Premiums.**   Premiums consist of items given away free or at reduced cost. The best and most successful premium has been glasses. The reasons? Glasses break, so households continually need them and it is easy to tie them into popular movies or sports teams. Premiums should be structured to sell higher-priced items—a larger drink, for example—and to encourage repeat visits—collecting all six glasses in the set.

**Patronage Rewards.**   Patronage rewards are cash or other awards for regular use. Restaurants might start a VIP club and establish an awards system based on how many times customers come in or how much they spend. Punching a customer card means that the card is carried around in the customer's purse or wallet, thereby acting as an advertising reminder.

**Contests, Sweepstakes, Games.**   Contests, sweepstakes, and games give customers the chance to win something. A contest calls for the customer to submit an entry, a jingle, a guess, or a suggestion, to be judged by a panel that will select the best entries. A sweepstake calls for names to be entered into a drawing. A game presents customers with something every time they buy that may or may not help win them a prize.

Other companies are selling systems that allow operators to create advertisements on their own television monitors. One test site features a "cell-phone shootout" that showed a countdown on the television screen. The first person to call in at the end of the countdown gets a free beer. Within a few days customers began putting the restaurant's phone number on their speed dial. The restaurant claims a direct result of a 20 percent increase in lunch sales.[16]

One of the tools on the horizon is a machine that electronically blends and sends out aromas. Used by theme parks since 1995, the system can be installed for about $2500.

---

**q u i c k   q u i z**

In 1888, an English doctor prescribed three hamburger meals a day as a cure for various ailments. His name is remembered today as the name of a seasoned ground beef patty served with gravy. What is his name?

*Source:* Allan F. and Lana E. Lazarus, *Restaurant Industry Review,* U.S. Bancorp Piper Jaffray Equity Research, March 2003, pp. 54–55.

---

## Key Steps

In setting up a promotion the objective needs to be determined, the target market selected, a strategy for implementing the promotion outlined, ways to promote the promotion identified, and evaluation methods set up.

**Objective.**   The purpose or objective of the promotion needs to be determined up front. The objective can be thought of as the problem to be solved. Typically, promotions are used to attract new customers, keep existing customers happy, speed up slow periods, or spotlight specials. The implementation of the promotion will differ depending on what the objective is.

**Target Market.**   As part of the objective it is necessary to identify the market segment to whom the promotion is to be directed. As stated previously, the promotion will be to either existing or potential customers. Existing customers have already tried the restaurant and know what to expect. They will require less information on the facility than will new customers, who will have to be sold on trying out the facility.

The promotions used must be compatible with the set of objectives. Slow periods can be offset by coupons, contests, packages, gift certificates, or discounts. Low check averages are best dealt with through coupons, product samples, contests, or premiums. Contests and product samples can help if existing customers are bored and want something new and different. The point is that the promotion selected will depend on the objective or problem to be solved.

**Strategy.** The success of a promotion will depend on how it is promoted. The concept of vertical integration is important here. Vertical integration means that the same message is given to the target market through a variety of interconnected means. For example, a Halloween-themed evening could be promoted through radio spots announcing the promotion, newspaper ads with cut-out coupons for specials, local promotions inviting kids to wear costumes, and in-house activities with posters in the restaurant and an employee costume contest. The important point is that all methods are coordinated to complement each other in promoting the event.

**Promotion.** Restaurants may split the cost of a promotion by hooking up with a supplier interested in moving his or her product. Similarly, cross-promotions can occur with a noncompeting business. A restaurant close to a theater may offer a discount to theater patrons upon presentation of the theater ticket.

Disclaimers and disclosures are often overlooked in putting together a promotion. The following guidelines are important:[17]

- *Product size and specifications.* Clearly identify the menu item and size being promoted.
- *Price/discount.* Highlight the price savings by stating the regular price and the promotional price.
- *Where to find the offer.* In smaller markets, identify your location; in larger markets, stating that the offer is good at participating restaurants will suffice.
- *Expiration date.* Make this date clear and easily readable.
- *What to do.* Let the customers know precisely what is expected of them— for example, whether they must bring in the coupon or buy two meals within a certain period of time.
- *Avoid double hits.* State that the offer is not good with any other promotional offer.
- *Limitation.* If the offer is limited to a number, state the number. It may be one per customer or one per household, for example.
- *Time and day restrictions.* Since one of the purposes of a promotion is to stimulate sales during slow periods, it may be necessary to note the times when the promotion is in effect.

**Evaluation.** It is important to determine whether the promotion has been effective. The true measure of a promotion is whether or not there was an increase in sales activity. This requires a comparison of sales activity—number of customers, sales in dollars, average check, and so on—before and after the promotion. If a promotion were being targeted for the month of August, the July sales figures would serve as the base. This year's August figure would have to be adjusted in light of sales trends to give an accurate picture. Suppose, for example, that sales revenue in July of this year were up 6 percent over those of the

```
 ··  quick  bite  4.6
 🐒  Marketing Creatures
```

**Learning Objective:** Identify the key parts of a successful sales promotion: merchandising effort and public relations campaign.

What is a spongemonkey? The sandwich chain Quiznos had these creatures created for their new advertising campaign and television commercials in 2004. Don't worry, no genetic engineering took place. Spongemonkeys are puppets that appear in Quiznos advertisements singing, "We love the subs!" The commercials were created for Quiznos by The Martin Agency of Richmond, Virginia. Spongemonkeys resemble rats or gerbils, and have ratty fur and high-pitched voices. Perhaps the most logical question to ask is who would want rats representing their food? It turns out that Quiznos isn't aiming the campaign at all of their customers. They're hoping to bring in young teens, who might think that the new Spongemonkey ads are edgy and hip.

Does this mean that Quiznos will have to make up for the loss of older customers who will be put off by the ads? Will the restaurant chain have to hope that they can make up for this loss by relying on younger customers? Possibly. When a campaign appeals to one customer group while ignoring or alienating another, restaurants take the risk that the increase in sales will not compensate for the lost customers.

*Source:* Cebrzynski, Gregg, "Love 'Em or Hate 'Em, Creatures Sing for Quizno's Subs," *Nation's Restaurant News,* vol. 38, no. 9, March 1, 2004, p. 14.

**Discussion Questions:** Who are these ads aimed toward? What are the risks of targeting a specific audience?

---

preceding year. A reasonable expectation would be that even without a promotion, sales figures for this August would be up 6 percent over sales in the preceding year. Any increase above 6 percent in this August's sales figures would then be attributed to the promotion.

A target for increased sales that will be necessary to cover the cost of a promotion can be determined if the restaurateur knows the promotional costs and his or her cost structure. As identified in preceding chapters, costs can be either fixed or variable. The variable costs—food or beverage, labor, discounts, and supplies—should be determined as a percentage of sales and totaled. This total is subtracted from 100 and the resulting percentage figure divided into the promotional cost in dollars to determine the sales necessary to cover the promotional costs.

For example, if a sandwich that normally sells for $9 costs $3.50, the food cost percentage is 39 percent. If it is being discounted by 15 percent, and extra employee costs and extra supplies are estimated at 5 and 1 percent of sales, respectively, total variable expenses for the promotion are 39 plus 15 plus 5 plus 1, or 60 percent. Subtracting this from 100 leaves 40. If the cost of the promotion is estimated at $350, the sales necessary to break even on the promotion are $350 divided by 40 percent, or $875.

Working backward, $875 in increased sales will result in $525 of extra costs ($875 multiplied by 60 percent). The remaining $350 ($875 minus $525) represents the cost of the promotion. Anything more than an increase in sales of $875 will result in increased profit; anything less will result in a loss. For example, sales of $1200 will result in $720 in costs (60 percent of $1200). When the cost of the promotion—$350—is subtracted, the resulting profit is $370.

## MERCHANDISING

Merchandising consists of materials used in-house to stimulate sales. The difference between merchandising and promotions is that promotions are used to get customers in the door, whereas merchandising occurs once the customer is inside the restaurant. Merchandising includes brochures on display, signs, posters, tent cards, and other point-of-purchase promotional items. Some suggest that operators spend at least 60 percent of their marketing dollar within the restaurant itself.[18]

Visual Deal is a technological tool that attempts to increase the average check in quick-service restaurants by targeting the estimated $30 million in change that is handed back to customers each year.[19] A point-of-purchase screen facing the customer displays two menu items the customer can buy at a discount based on the amount of change owed. In this case the "personal" selling comes from a digital voice that asks which item the customer would prefer. Operators also use the displays to push sales of slow-moving menu items. The system costs up to $17,000 per restaurant for the hardware and a three-year software agreement. Some operators claim a payback is as little as nine months.

### Purpose

The purpose of merchandising is twofold: to retain a store's loyal customer base, and to increase the percentage of total business generated by these loyal customers. In the former case, this means developing ways to prevent core customers from becoming bored with the restaurant. In the latter situation, it involves ways to increase the visitation and/or average check of existing customers.

### Effectiveness

One of the primary merchandising tools available is the menu itself. By changing the menu periodically, or through the development of daily or holiday specials, a restaurant can continually offer something new and different to its customers.

Effective merchandising can also come from displays and samples of food. It is said that we eat with our eyes rather than our mouths. Nowhere is this as true as in the way in which desserts are sold. The presence of a dessert tray can be very effective in increasing sales. Similar displays for wine, entrées, and salads as well as table-side preparation can be equally effective.

Care must be taken that the number of tent cards and promotional materials not overwhelm the customer. The intent is to prevent boredom, not create confusion because of all the choices available.

Many operators with limited advertising/promotional budgets will learn to develop ongoing and ever-changing activities for their guests and personnel to enjoy. The element of surprise and fun can be one of a restaurant's major strong points.

New themes, catchy ideas, and fresh gimmicks require careful planning and follow-through. Meals will, as always, be the star attraction, but the presentation may need serious rehearsal and trial runs. Customers enjoy being invited to dress rehearsals. The wrinkles can be ironed out for unveiling in such a way that competition will pale in comparison.

## Merchandising of Beverages

Beverages can be merchandised in a variety of ways. Easy access can be made by having portable bars in the lobby while customers are waiting for a table. Once seated, the drink order should be taken and delivered right away. Some restaurants promote a happy hour with free hors d'oeuvres to attract cocktail business. The price and quality of hors d'oeuvres must be kept in mind. The price of the hors d'oeuvres must be absorbed by the price of the drink, and the quality must be indicative of the facility.

Another area to expand into is wine sales. Wine merchandising must be realistic and uncomplicated for the consumer. Many people find wine intimidating and will not order for fear of the unknown or fear of looking foolish. An awareness can be generated through wine displays, lists, and verbal reminders from waitstaff. The ability of employees to sell is a major merchandising tool.

---

q u i c k   q u i z

What was Burger King's original name?

a. Insta-Burger-King
b. Burgers Your Way
c. Burgers on the Go

*Source:* Hickok, Allan F. and Lana E. Lazarus, *Restaurant Industry Review,* U.S. Bancorp Piper Jaffray Equity Research, March 2003, pp. 54–55.

---

# PUBLIC RELATIONS AND PUBLICITY

Public relations includes everything that a restaurant does to maintain or improve its relationship with other organizations. Publicity is the use of nonpaid communications such as press releases and press conferences.[20]

Businesses have a number of different "publics": individuals and organizations with whom and with which it interacts. These range from employees and their families, unions, and owners to customers, competitors, government, hospitality schools, and the media. It is the job of public relations to represent the operation favorably to these publics.

On the day that the Dallas Cowboys introduced Bill Parcells as their new football coach, a local restaurant featured the "Big Tuna" (Parcells's nickname) on the menu. The item, a 16-ounce piece of tuna and a 22-ounce steak, was prominently featured in a variety of media outlets. When Krispy Kreme opens a new store, it sends several dozen doughnuts, together with a representative to answer any questions, to local TV stations and newspaper offices.

The key is to get attention. It is easier to get the attention of the media on a slow news day. Public relations consultants advise restaurants to keep a calendar of days when government offices, schools, and courts are closed because, on these days "There goes half our news out the window."[21]

A number of restaurants are packaging leftovers in a way that attracts attention. More than 60 percent of restaurant diners leave with a doggie bag. Women are more likely than men to take home leftovers.[22] Operators are packaging leftovers in unique ways that makes the doggie bag a walking advertisement for the restaurant while creating positive word of mouth. Gladstone's Malibu, an upscale seafood restaurant, wraps leftovers in made-to-order gold foil that costs $120 a roll. Front-of-the-house staff must master 40 designs—mermaid, crab, handbag, and so on—before they are allowed on to the floor. The Fork Restaurant in Philadelphia packages leftovers in a round tin with an aluminum cover placed in a plastic drawstring bag decorated with the restaurant's logo.

It is vital that the doggie bag is made from a material that is acceptable for food storage. Certain materials are not compatible with food and can leak into food. Polystyrene foam or paper, which is designed to keep hot foods hot and cold foods cold until they can be refrigerated, are good choices. Placing menus and holiday reminders inside each bag further promotes the restaurant.

## Word of Mouth

The value of public relations is that although the organization gives up total control of the message, the resulting message is very persuasive because it is perceived as being more objective than a commercial advertisement. Word-of-mouth publicity is by far the most desirable form of advertising. It means that someone was sufficiently impressed with your establishment to discuss it with others. An endorsement by a friend is usually enough to cause a person to try a place. Potential customers are bombarded with every sort of advertising every day. Advertisers are always proclaiming how great their places, foods, quality, service, and prices are. Customers can get tired of all the exaggerated promises, especially when a few places do not measure up to what was promised. Understandably, people tend to be skeptical and often discount an advertiser's claims. In short, there is a gap between what advertisers say and what customers believe. There is, however, little or no gap when a friend recommends an eating place to another friend. The friend has no motive for profit or gain; therefore, the suggestion is appreciated and believed.

While the power of word of mouth has been demonstrated time after time, it takes too long to develop positive word of mouth into sufficient numbers of customers to ensure the financial success of the establishment. It has been argued that the role of advertising is primarily to expose people to the fact that the facility is out there but that it will take word of mouth to induce actual patronage. This is probably true of more expensive purchases, such as weddings or anniversary parties, but is less true for an individual or family decision to eat out.

Similarly, editorial and commentary reviews in the media are not suspect. Readers, listeners, and viewers have more trust in these reviews than in advertising messages. The idea, then, is to get the media to write or talk about a business without the suggestion that they are in it for personal profit. Newsworthy events, for example, are not considered as being commercial. If it is news, it is fact.

## Implementation

Implementing a program of public relations requires care. Objectives need to be set that tie into the overall marketing plan. Public relations activities can be continuous, preplanned short-term activities, or unpredictable, short-term activities.[23]

**Continuous Activities.** Continuous activities can include such things as

- Being involved in the local community by donating food for local charity events
- Being involved in industry organizations, serving as an officer, and/or giving seminars
- Communicating to various publics through newsletters
- Engaging in a variety of employee relations programs, such as employee-of-the-month awards, sending birthday cards, or employee incentive programs
- Keeping in regular touch with the media by offering yourself as an industry spokesperson
- Continually updating media kits and photographs to meet editorial deadlines
- Preparing annual or periodic reports to owners
- Acting as guest lecturer at hospitality and/or local schools
- Becoming involved with government agencies in a proactive rather than a reactive way
- Developing a format for keeping in touch with customers through newsletters or other means

**Preplanned Short-Term Activities.** Preplanned short-term activities revolve around something of interest such as an opening, a prestigious award, or a special employee. This type of information is typically communicated through a press release—an announcement or short article written in an attempt to attract the attention of the media. If something is to be printed or viewed, it must, in the opinion of the editor or director, be of interest to readers or viewers. For press releases, this should be kept in mind. An item of "major" importance to a restaurateur may be of little or no interest to the average reader or viewer.

**Press Release.**   A good press release should answer the questions "who, what, when, where, why, and how." Ideally, this information will be summarized in the opening paragraph. In addition to being newsworthy, the press release should be dated, list a contact person and phone number, indicate when the information can be released (usually, the indication is that the information is "for immediate release"), be typed double spaced, have an eye-catching headline, be printed on specially designated paper, be no more than two pages in length, and be factual.

As a restaurateur with many things going on, there is the opportunity to make news with virtually everything. Consider these new possibilities even before the restaurant doors are opened:

- Releases to the press on the signing of a lease or the construction of a building to house a restaurant
- Advance announcement of the number of local people who will be employed
- Notices of the grand opening
- Arrangements with public figures to appear at a fundraising opening

Press conferences can be held when there is something really important to announce to the media. The press should be given a summary in writing of the news story in addition to being given the opportunity to ask questions.

Ceremonies and openings offer yet another opportunity for a planned event. Remember, the event will probably be more important to the company than to the media. The task is to make it equally important to readers or viewers.

**Unpredictable Events.**   The third type of activity involves events that are unpredictable. These usually involve some type of activity wherein the purpose for the restaurant is to avoid negative publicity. It may be that patrons became ill after eating at the restaurant or that an employee is a suspect in a crime. The rules of thumb are as follows:

- Tell the truth.
- Do not cover things up.
- Collect the facts and communicate these to the media.
- Take action to correct the situation.

The best measure of a public relations plan is, Did it meet its objective? When people are asked if they have frequented a particular business and reply "No, but it has a good name," the goal of public relations has been reached.

## quick bite 4.7
**Road to the Top: Koren Grieveson**

Salami and wine? They go great together, says Koren Grieveson. Her restaurant Avec is a recent addition to the Mediterranean wine bar scene in Chicago. In addition to fine wine, Avec specializes in delicacies such as sausages, salamis, prosciutto, and other cured meats. Koren Grieveson oversees the kitchen as well as the salami production, which is a time-consuming process involving the curing and aging of meats.

"We were trying to make an inexpensive place to dine with true, simple food and no fuss," says Grieveson. She knows what she's talking about; she spent four years as sous chef under Paul Kahan. Kahan is the chef-owner of Blackbird, a popular fine dining destination in Chicago. Grieveson came out of the experience with a clear idea of what she wanted to offer: "we wanted a rustic food that wasn't going to break the bank."

Presentation is not the most important part of a meal, Grieveson insists. Food is the paramount concern. Half of Avec's customers order the salami, the preparation and curing of which is actually a complicated process. "Every recipe turns out different, and you have no way to guarantee it will turn out the way you want," Grieveson says. "You have to wait two to three months to know if the salami is even edible. If the humidity is too high or too low, it really affects it."

*Source:* Garber, Amy, "Avec, Chicago," *Nation's Restaurant News,* vol. 38, no. 15, April 12, 2004, p. 38.

**Discussion Question:** How can unique, in-house prepared foods help make a name for a restaurant?

## ENDNOTES

1. T. F. Chiffriller, *Successful Restaurant Operation* (Boston: CBI Publishing Company, 1982), p. 278.
2. National Restaurant Association, *Restaurant Industry Operations Report,* 2004 (Washington, DC: Deloitte & Touche and the National Restaurant Association, 2005), pp. 29, 57, 85, 113.
3. National Restaurant Association, "Drawing Diners to Your Door," *Restaurants USA,* May 1998, pp. 41–43.
4. Robert D. Reid, *Hospitality Marketing Management,* 2nd ed. (New York: Van Nostrand Reinhold, 1989), pp. 284–286.
5. Ibid., p. 233.
6. Sherri van Saxon, *How to Market Your Restaurant* (Washington, D.C., National Restaurant Association, undated), p. 11.
7. Amy Spector, "Menu Marketers Deliver Dinner, Incremental Sales," *Nation's Restaurant News,* vol. 37, no. 20, May 19, 2003, p. 154.
8. James R. Abbey, *Hospitality Sales and Advertising* (East Lansing, MI: Educational Institute of the American Hotel and Motel Association, 1989), pp. 336–337.
9. Phillip M. Perry, "Honing Your Home Page," *Restaurants USA,* September 1997, pp. 21–25.

10. Lori Loymeyer, "Feeding Stories To Press Creates Feast Of Free Publicity," *Nation's Restaurant News,* vol. 37, no. 20, May 19, 2003, p. 160.

11. Alan J. Liddle, "Using Web for Discounting Clicks with Digital Diners," *Nation's Restaurant News,* vol. 37, no. 20, May 19, 2003, p. 172.

12. Amy Garber, "Redeeming Factor: Coupons Shout 'Value,' Boost Traffic," *Nation's Restaurant News,* vol. 37, no. 20, May 19, 2003, p. 138.

13. Ibid., p. 138.

14. Ibid., p. 138.

15. Paul Frumkin, "Frequent-Guest Clubs Multiply Sales with Loyal-Diner Rewards," *Nation's Restaurant News,* vol. 37, no. 20, May 19, 2003, p. 142.

16. Amy Spector, "Menu Marketers Deliver Dinner, Incremental Sales," *Nation's Restaurant News,* vol. 37, no. 20, May 19, 2003, p. 132.

17. Tom Feltenstein, *Foodservice Marketing for the '90s* (New York: John Wiley & Sons, 1992), pp. 101–102.

18. Mark Hanstra, "War College Drills Operators in 'Underdog Marketing,'" *Nation's Restaurant News,* October 13, 1997.

19. Spector, "Menu Marketers Deliver Dinner, Incremental Sales."

20. Alastair M. Morrison, *Hospitality and Travel Marketing* (Albany, NY: Delmar Publishers, 1989), p. 420.

21. Lori Loymeyer, "Operators Drive Traffic Via Information Superhighway," *Nation's Restaurant News,* vol. 37, no. 20, May 19, 2003, p. 137.

22. Marnie Roberts, "The Art of Packaging Leftovers," *Restaurants USA,* August 2001, www.restaurant.org/rusa.

23. Alastair M. Morrison, *Hospitality and Travel Marketing* (Albany, NY: Delmar Publishers, 1989), pp. 429–440.

## INTERNET RESOURCES

| | |
|---|---|
| Quantified Marketing Group | *http://www.restaurant-public-relations.com/* |
| | *http://www.quantifiedmarketing.com/* |
| Takeout Taxi Meal Delivery | *http://www.takeout-taxi.com/* |
| Restaurant Loyalty Program | *http://www.edining.us/restaurant_loyalty_programs.html* |
| Hard Rock Cafe | *http://www.hardrock.com/* |

## QUICK QUIZ ANSWER KEY

p. 88—Wimpy burgers.

p. 93—a. Wendys; b. Burger King; c. Kentucky Fried Chicken; d. McDonald's; e. Little Caesar's Pizza.

p. 100—Salisbury (as in Salisbury steak).

p. 104—a. Insta-Burger-King (changed in 1957).

# CHAPTER FIVE

# PRICING AND DESIGNING THE MENU

"I went to a restaurant that serves 'breakfast at any time.' So I
ordered French toast during the Renaissance."
Steven Wright, Canadian comedian

## learning objectives

*By the end of this chapter you should be able to*

1. Identify the functions of the menu.

2. Identify trends in menu content.

3. Compare the three different philosophies of pricing the menu.

4. Compare and contrast the various methods of menu pricing.

5. Describe the different methods of listing prices on a menu.

6. Compare and contrast the different methods for measuring the strength
   of a menu.

7. Give specific guidelines on the design, layout, and pricing of a menu to
   increase the average check while boosting the sales of specialty items.

## Hot Concepts: Menu Styling

The two basic types of menus include table d'hôte, a menu that includes one price for complete dinners, and à la carte, which has separate prices for every item on the menu. One advantage of table d'hôte menu is price change. Changing the prices is relatively simple, for example, if you have 20 items on the menu then you only have 20 prices to work with and balance. In the case of an à la carte menu pricing is more complex; there could be as many as 60 prices included on the menu. With the classic table d'hôte menu [customers' decisions are] made easier since they only have to pick an entrée from the menu, and all other selections are made for them.

Now it is more common for customers to have some choice of the accompanying items with their entrées. Nevertheless, selections are made easier for the consumer using the table d'hôte menu. Since combinations are limited, orders are easier to put together in the kitchen, making simplification another advantage for this type of menu.

The disadvantages of table d'hôte menu include pricing inflexibility and food waste. Restaurant operators lose some of the ability to influence selection decisions with reduced price combinations due to prix-fixe entrées. Also some customers may feel that the prices of the entrées are too expensive and may not want to select items when they know they will not eat a part of the dish. Some entrées may include items the customer may not want and therefore does not eat, making . . . customer[s] feel disappointed because they had to pay for and waste food that they did not want. This creates a negative price/value perception in the customer's mind. Restaurants that operate with a table d'hôte menu generally have a hard time increasing check averages.

One of the biggest advantages to an à la carte menu is its ability to build up check averages. It is much easier to increase the check average using an à la carte menu since every item on the menu is priced individually, especially when the server attempts to get the guests to order a separate vegetable, salad, beverage, appetizer, etc. The total check cost tends to "sneak up" on the customer as they are not fully aware of how much they are spending. With a table d'hôte menu, if the customer does not wish to spend $17.00 on an entrée they can order a $12.00 dinner; whereas with an à la carte menu they may spend $17.00 without even knowing it. Food waste is not a problem since guests order exactly what they want. If they only want an entrée and a salad then that is all they order.

One disadvantage and a real danger with à la carte menus is the customer's ability to perceive the method of pricing as an attempt to raise prices. Predicting sales is far more difficult since customers may eat light or heavy depending on how they feel.

Today, menus that combine both concepts are probably the most common. The advantages and disadvantages are the same as noted previously depending

*(continued)*

on which style the menu favors. For example, the operator may have a table d'hôte menu but decide to remove coffee and price it separately, figuring it is a good way to increase the check average by a dollar or more per person since nearly everyone will have coffee after dinner. This type of menu is known as semi à la carte, where some items are priced separately while others are incorporated with entrées at a set price. In some cases the menu may have several full dinners in addition to a few specialties/sides that are priced separately. Another technique that some operations use is to offer entrées as à la carte and as full dinners complete with salad, soup, dessert, and beverage. But no matter which style an operation chooses to use, the ultimate goal is to increase the average check by displaying items on the menu that are most appealing to the customer.

*Source:* "Types of Menus," Food Service Operations Fundamentals, *http://www.unlv.edu/depts/foodbeverage/fsofmenutypes.html* (May 15, 2004).

**Discussion Question:** When designing a table d'hôte menu, what concepts need to be considered?

## IMPORTANCE OF THE MENU

A menu lists the various product offerings of a restaurant. However, it does much more than that. First, it is a contract with the customer, an indication that what is described on the menu is what will be delivered to the customer. At a minimum the menu should identify the name of each dish, the major ingredients, and how the dish is prepared. Second, it is an essential part of the marketing effort. As a merchandising tool the menu seeks to do certain things. Properly priced, designed, and presented, the menu can increase the average check, boosting sales of specialty items while complementing the overall atmosphere of the facility.

## MENU CONTENT

The 2005 Forecast report from the NRA indicates a number of menu trends:[1]

- Consumer concerns about health and wellness are leading more restaurants to add items that appeal to diet- and nutrition-conscious customers as well as adjusting preparation methods of existing menu items.
- More low-carb items are being added to the menu.
- Healthier choices specifically targeted to children are finding their way onto menus.
- There is increasing demand for locally produced foods and organic items.
- Wine, bottled water, specialty coffees, and iced tea all continue to grow in popularity.

- Full-service operators report increasing orders for the following:

  - Entrée salads
  - Vegetarian salads
  - Side salads
  - Side vegetables
  - Side fruit

- As an illustration that consumers are becoming more adventurous in their food choices, the National Restaurant Association reports the following percentages of diners who have never tried these items but who say they are interested in trying them:

  | | |
  |---|---|
  | Ciabatta | 44% |
  | Naan | 40% |
  | Empanadas | 28% |
  | Tandoori | 27% |
  | Falafel | 26% |
  | Goose | 25% |

 quick bite 5.2
**Menu Labeling**

**Learning Objectives:** Identify the functions of the menu. Compare and contrast the different methods for measuring the strength of a menu.

In 2001 the U.S. Surgeon General reported that obesity could be responsible for as many deaths in America as cigarettes. The food industry is battling highly skilled lawyers who insist that the restaurant business is solely responsible for encouraging Americans to become obese. Some lawyers have even called it "corporate irresponsibility."

One way federal and state lawmakers have decided to deal with the issue of obesity is through new regulations calling for nutritional menu labeling. This new regulation has been introduced to the U.S. House of Representatives as the Menu Education and Labeling Act. This act would require all foodservice chains with 20 or more units to post calories, sodium, saturated-fat and trans-fat content for each item on hand-held menus. Those chains without individual menus would have to list the number of calories for each item on their menu boards. While some of the other regulations have not yet been stated in the Act, this is not the first time a bill such as this one has reached the federal level. In 1990 Congress received a similar bill which endorsed the same concepts as the Menu Education and Labeling Act. The bill was known as the Nutritional Labeling and Education Act, but the bill did not

*(continued)*

pass. Currently, New York, California, Washington, D.C., New Hampshire, Maine, and Texas are all currently considering the nutritional-labeling bill.

Many restaurant operators believe the contents of the bill to be impractical. In their opinion it is close to impossible to calculate the calories in every meal served, especially with the different possible combinations. For example, a deli shop that makes sandwiches has a hundred or so different possibilities from which their customers could decide on when making their own sandwich. Figuring the different nutritional value for every possible variation of sandwiches would account for a lot of space lost on the menu, especially if the foodservice operation displays [its] menu on a sign board. Another concern that restaurant operators are facing is portion control. In the instance of the deli shop, measuring out all the condiments put on a sandwich, or weighing every slice of meat so each one is proportional to the standard, is extremely time consuming.

Representative DeLauro says she is aware that the restaurant industry has its share of problems and that she is not looking to complicate matters, but wants consumers to be educated about the food they eat in restaurants. Some foodservice operators believe that if an operation has the ability to produce such information [it] should flaunt it as a marketing tool and a point of differentiation, as some restaurants are just unable to manage such a task.

*Source:* Koteff, Ellen, "Too Much Information: Mandated Menu Labeling Not Healthful for Consumers or the Food Industry," *Nation's Restaurant News,* vol. 37, no. 46, November 17, 2003, p. 21.

**Discussion Question:** Name other ways restaurants could make nutritional labeling more practical so that menus are not just a list of nutritional labeling.

## MENU PRICING

The pricing of items on the menu requires a knowledge of both marketing and accounting. From the marketing side, this means setting a price that will appeal to the market while being competitive; from the accounting side, it involves establishing a price that will contribute to the profitability of the operation.

### Pricing Philosophies

Before setting the prices of individual menu items, management should have determined what the pricing philosophy is to be. Three common approaches to pricing involve the following:[2]

1. Demand-oriented/perceived-value pricing
2. Competitive pricing
3. Cost-oriented pricing

**Demand-Oriented/Perceived-Value Pricing** Demand-oriented or perceived-value pricing looks at the menu from the viewpoint of the customer and prices relative to what the item is worth to the customer—its perceived value. It is important to realize that it is the customer's reaction that is being sought rather than the manager's or employee's. Although an employee may consider the price charged exorbitant, a customer may perceive that the value gained is greater than the price charged.

The items being served are only part of the experience of the meal. The attention gained from having a special dessert flambéed tableside may be worth much to the customer in terms of prestige, and the value thus gained can offset the price charged. This approach prices menu items on the basis of what the customer will pay.

The perceived value in the mind of the customer has to do with more things than the items on the plate. Certainly, customers might be willing to pay extra for menu items advertised as prepared daily from scratch. People expect to pay more for dinner than for lunch; for more service than for self-service; for an inviting atmosphere rather than an austere environment. A brand-name fast-food chain may be perceived as delivering more value than an independently owned operation, whereas the reverse may be true of a fine-dining establishment. A number of things can be done to increase the perceived value of the meal experience (see Chapter 4), although, as we will see later, prices can be set in such a way that they appear less than they are.

Two common approaches in demand-oriented pricing are market skimming and market penetration.[3] Conventional economics indicates that as prices rise, demand for the product falls. Total revenue is a combination of price charged and number of items purchased.

*Market Skimming.*  In the market skimming approach to pricing, operators use a relatively high price to attract or skim a small segment of the market. This philosophy works best when there is a small percentage of a large potential market who can and will pay the higher prices, when the competition is unlikely to undercut the prices set for similar product offerings, and when customers perceive that the value given in the form of the restaurant experience is greater than the prices charged.

*Market Penetration.*  Market penetration, on the other hand, involves setting prices as low as possible while still contributing to profits. This approach sets out to attract as large a market as possible. Ideally, lower prices will create a loyal following, which will translate into greater sales volume and long-term profitability. This philosophy works best when demand is price elastic: that is, when changes in price result in a greater change in demand, and when lower prices will deter competition from invading the market.

Care must be taken when reducing prices in an attempt to increase sales revenue. An item priced at $12 and selling 120 portions produces $1440 in revenue. A reduction in price of 10 percent will bring the selling price down to $10.80. This will require that 134 portions be sold to produce a revenue of $1447.20. This is an 11.7 percent increase in the number of portions sold. In other words, a reduction in price requires a greater percentage increase in portions sold just to maintain total revenue.

**Competitive Pricing.**  Competitive pricing establishes prices according to those set by the competition. Prices set are typically slightly below or above those of the competition. The major drawback to this pricing method is that it allows the competition to "control" the pricing of the operation. The competition may have a cost structure that is different and can afford to advertise lower prices.

It is not advisable to compete principally on the basis of price because price is a factor that can readily be met by a strong competitor. In such a situation the customer gains in the short run from the lower price until the weaker operation, unable to sustain profits based on the price charges, goes out of business.

However, the prices set must take the competition into account. It is unwise to offer essentially the same product as the competition but at a higher price. An increasingly value-conscious and educated consuming public will buy from the competition.

**Cost-Oriented Pricing.**   Cost-oriented pricing is the oldest, and still the most commonly used, method of pricing in the industry. Prices are set on the basis of the costs incurred by the operation.

---

q u i c k   f a c t

According to the Organic Trade Association, the $14 billion organic foods market is the fastest growing food segment in the industry. Studies indicate that 39 percent of the U.S. population buys organic products. The global market for organic food and drink reached $23 billion in 2002, according to *Organic Monitor.*

*Source:* Organic Trade Association, *http://www.ota.com/organic/mt.html*. Accessed November 2, 2005.

---

## PRICING METHODS

A variety of quantitative or rational pricing methods are available to the restaurateur. In reality the vast majority of operations use the true mark-up system or cost-multiplier method described in this section.

### Factor, Cost-Multiplier, or Mark-Up System

The factor, cost-multiplier, or mark-up system is very popular because of its simplicity. In it, the raw food cost is multiplied by a pricing factor or divided by the desired food cost percentage to arrive at a selling price:

$$\text{selling price} = \text{raw food cost} \times \text{factor}$$

where

$$\text{factor} = \frac{100}{\text{desired food cost}}$$

or

$$\text{selling price} = \frac{\text{raw food cost}}{\text{desired food cost percentage}}$$

The raw food cost is obtained easily enough. This is the cost to the restaurant for the items in the dish. Standardized recipes and recipe cost sheets are essential to determine the actual food cost of every item served.

The factor is obtained by dividing the desired food cost into 100. For example, if a 30 percent food cost is desired (industry averages range from 28 to 34 percent of sales), the factor to be used will be

$$\frac{100}{30} = 3.33$$

The raw food cost is then multiplied by this factor to obtain the selling price. If the raw food cost on an item is $5.25, the selling price will be

$$\$5.25 \times 3.33 = \$17.50$$

The selling price can also be obtained by dividing the raw food cost by the desired food cost percentage. With a raw food cost of $5.25 and a desired food cost percentage of 30 percent, the selling price is

$$\frac{\$5.25}{30\%} = \$17.50$$

This method is simple to use. However, it should be noted that it is inexact because no costs other than food costs are used. When a combination of items prepared from scratch and convenience foods is being used, a high convenience food cost may be offset by a low labor cost to produce the item. Conversely, a low food cost for an item prepared from scratch may require costly amounts of time to prepare. Consider, for example, stew as a convenience product compared to stew prepared from scratch:

|  | Raw Cost | Labor Cost | Total Cost | Factor | Selling Price |
|---|---|---|---|---|---|
| Convenience | $2.25 | $0.75 | $3.00 | 3.333 | $7.50 |
| Scratch | 1.10 | 1.90 | $3.00 | 3.333 | 3.67 |

While the total cost of preparing the dish is the same ($3), the higher food cost for the convenience item means that it would be priced higher than the stew made from scratch. Additionally, it disregards the fact that customers may be willing to pay extra for the perceived value of the item.

## Prime Cost

The prime cost of a menu item is defined as its raw food cost plus the labor cost involved in preparing the item. The raw food cost of a dish is added to its labor cost.

The desired prime cost percentage is then divided into 100 (as previously) to determine the factor. The prime cost is then multiplied by this factor to determine the desired selling price. For example, the prime cost of the beef stews above is $3. Assuming a prime cost percentage of 50 percent, the factor is

100/50 = 2

and the selling price is

$3 × 2 = $6

The cost of producing the item can be determined by means of a time-and-motion study. The actual time involved in preparing 100 portions of beef stew can be multiplied by the hourly rate of the person preparing the dish and divided by 100 to get a preparation cost per serving.

A variation breaks labor cost into unskilled, semiskilled, and skilled and assigns a dollar cost for each. A beef stew, 30 portions, might take 15 minutes of skilled time, 20 minutes of semiskilled time, and 30 minutes of unskilled time to prepare. If the pay rates for skilled, semiskilled, and unskilled labor were $12, $8, and $5, respectively, the labor cost to prepare the stew would be

$12/4 + $8/4 + $5/3 = $8.67

The labor cost per portion would be 28.9 cents ($8.67 divided by 30 portions).

A second method assigns an average labor cost to each item produced by dividing the number of meals prepared by the actual production labor cost. The drawback here is that the method assumes that all items take the same amount of time to prepare. Labor-intensive items will be underpriced, and vice versa.

Third, menu items can be designated as involving low, medium, and high labor costs and a dollar value can be assigned to each. It might be that low-cost items are defined as those requiring less than 10 minutes to prepare, medium-cost items those taking from 11 to 20 minutes, and high-cost dishes those requiring more than 20 minutes of labor time. A unit production cost can be determined by dividing labor cost by the number of low-, medium-, and high-cost meals produced. For example, assume that during a given period when production costs were $3145, 2000 meals were produced, of which 700 were low-cost meals, 800 were medium-cost meals, and 500 were high-cost meals. If we further assume that the medium-cost meal takes twice as long and the high-cost meal takes three times as long to prepare as the low-cost meal, the unit labor cost is

$$700(x) + 2(800x) + 3(500x) = \$3145$$
$$700x + 160x + 1500x = \$3145$$
$$3800x = \$3145$$
$$x = 0.83$$

The cost of preparing a low-cost meal would be 83 cents; a medium-cost meal, $1.66; and a high-cost meal, $2.49.

The major drawbacks to this pricing method are that it ignores the other costs of preparing and serving the item in addition to the profit desired by management. The assumption is that desired profits will ensue as long as the prime cost percentage is not exceeded.

## Actual Pricing or All Costs Plus Profit

The actual pricing or all-costs-plus-profit method takes into account all the costs involved in running the business. In addition, the percentage of profit desired from each menu item is added before establishing a selling price.

Previously, we established a methodology for determining both raw food cost and preparation cost. Service and other costs can be divided by the number of covers served to get a cost per cover. This cost would then be added to the raw food and production costs to obtain the total costs for the dish. The desired profit percentage is subtracted from 100 and divided into the total costs to obtain the selling price.

If total costs are $9.50 and management wants a 15 percent profit,

$$\text{selling price} = \frac{9.5}{(100 - 15)\%}$$
$$= \$11.18$$

In this method all costs are accounted for, then profit is planned for and built into the price. The price of higher-cost entrées is reduced when compared to using other methods of pricing. In previous methods the factor used had to take into account both high- and low-cost items. The factor used is higher than reality for high-cost items and lower than reality for low-cost items. Thus high-cost items tend to be priced higher than they should be while low-cost items tend to be priced lower than they should be. Reducing the price of higher-cost entrées should lead to increased sales (and profits).

This method is more complicated than either of the first two, tends to increase the prices of lower-cost items (for the reverse of the reason cited previously), and the determination of average cost may not be totally accurate. In addition, the desired profit percentage tends to be determined arbitrarily.

## Gross Mark-up or Gross Profit

The gross mark-up or gross profit pricing method assumes that every customer should pay a specific amount to cover nonfood costs and profit. It can be used in situations where there is to be a narrow range of prices on the menu. The gross mark-up is determined by subtracting the cost of food sold from projected sales and dividing the result by the projected number of meals or covers.

For example, if $800,000 in annual sales is projected with a food cost of 30 percent, or $240,000, and an anticipated customer count of 120,000,

$$\text{gross mark-up} = \frac{\text{gross sales} - \text{cost of food sold}}{\text{forecasted customer count}}$$

$$= \frac{\$800,000 - 240,000}{120,000}$$

$$= \$4.67$$

This mark-up is then added to the raw food cost of each item to determine the selling price. This method is easy to use and, like the previous method, tends to reduce the price of higher-cost items. It is best used in operations that are not susceptible to changes and that have enough history to accurately forecast sales, costs, and customers. Any change in any of these items makes this method inaccurate.

## Base Price

The base price method identifies the desired selling price and works backward from that to determine how much can be spent for the raw food cost. Analyzing guest checks can identify the price range preferred by customers. It is necessary to know what the labor and other costs are in addition to the desired profit percentage. If the operator wants 15 percent profit and has a labor cost of 30 percent and a fixed cost per item of 20 percent, total costs will be 65 percent (15 + 30 + 20). This leaves 35 percent (100 − 65) for the raw food cost. If the customer is willing to pay $12 for a menu item, the amount that can be spent on the raw food cost for that item is $4.20 ($12 × 35%).

Alternatively, the selling price of the item can be multiplied by the desired food cost to identify the maximum amount that can be spent on the item. If, in the preceding example, a food cost of 33 percent is desired, the maximum that can be spent on food cost would be $3.96 ($12 × 33%). Some way would have to be found to produce the menu item for that amount. This method has the advantage of taking the customer's willingness to pay into account.

## Texas Restaurant Association

The Texas Restaurant Association pricing method identifies actual costs incurred over a period of time and the sales associated with these costs, and adds the desired profit percentage to get the ideal or optimal food cost. If, over the course of a year, a restaurant has sales of $600,000, labor costs of $180,000 (30 percent of sales), other costs (excluding food costs) of $150,000 (25 percent of sales), and the owners want a 15 percent profit, the ideal food cost percentage is

$$600,000 - (180,000 + 50,000 + 90,000) = 180,000$$

$$100 - (30 + 25 + 15)\% = 30\%$$

This ideal food cost is divided into 100 to obtain a multiplier or factor, in this case 3.33. The raw food cost of the menu item is then multiplied by this factor to obtain the recommended selling price.

Recommended profit percentages will vary depending on the item. The common ranges are as follows:[4]

| Menu Category | Profit Mark-up Range (%) |
|---|---|
| Appetizers | 20–50 |
| Salads | 10–40 |
| Soups | 100–500 |
| Entrées | 10–25 |
| Vegetables | 25–50 |
| Beverages | 10–20 |
| Breads | 10–20 |
| à la carte | 10–40 |
| Desserts | 15–35 |

## Marginal Pricing

An operation's costs are either fixed or variable. Fixed costs do not vary as volume varies; variable costs vary proportionately with volume. After a restaurant has reached its break-even point, the fixed costs have been covered. At this point the only costs incurred by the restaurant are the variable or marginal costs, those extra costs incurred in serving another customer. Marginal pricing covers the marginal costs. Any revenue beyond this is profit. In this way, a facility, if it is sure that break-even will be reached, can offer special prices on slow nights.

Marginal pricing can be successful if it brings in business at the reduced price that would not come in at the full price. However, the operation must, at some point, account for covering fixed costs in pricing menu offerings.

## Daily Pricing

When the cost of items varies from day to day (for example, fresh seafood) a menu offering may be listed as having a market price. This indicates that the price varies depending on the cost that day.

In Table 5.1, a comparison of menu prices using different methods, but assuming the same cost structure and desired profit level, is shown. Note that different selling prices and profit margins are obtained depending on the method used. Selection of an appropriate method should take costs, competition, and the desires of the customers into account.

## Handling Price Increases

There is both a practical and a psychological side to handling an increase in prices. From the practical side, as costs increase, profits decline. Cost increase

**Table 5.1  Comparison of Menu Prices Using Various Methods**

|  | Roast Rib of Beef Dinner | | Stuffed Flounder Dinner | |
| --- | --- | --- | --- | --- |
|  | Menu Price | Profit Margin | Menu Price | Profit Margin |
| Factor method | $10.04 | $6.53 | $6.95 | $4.52 |
| Prime cost method | 10.67 | 7.16 | 8.79 | 6.36 |
| All-cost-plus-profit method | 8.28 | 4.77 | 7.96 | 5.53 |
| Gross mark-up method | 8.16 | 4.65 | 7.08 | 4.65 |
| Texas Restaurant Association method | 9.86 | 6.35 | 6.83 | 4.40 |

*Source:* Robert D. Reid, *Foodservice and Restaurant Marketing* (Boston: CBI Publishing Company, 1983), p. 229.

can come from such things as an increase in the minimum wage, in the cost of borrowing money, or higher wholesale prices charged for food and beverage items. Typically, an increase in costs is passed on to the customer in the form of higher prices. The key is to increase prices while maintaining customer counts such that sales volume is maintained.

Several strategies can be effective. Generally speaking, for minimum negative impact, price increases should be limited to 2 to 5 percent. Prices should also be kept stable during four to six customer visits. If an increase in the wholesale price of food is announced, the time to increase menu prices is when the announcement is made public rather than when the increase in prices is passed on to the operator. The reason for this is psychological—the public is aware of increased prices and, as such, is more likely to accept it at that time rather than later, when the memory of the price increase has vanished from customers' minds.

Another approach, used by the fast-food chains, is to price the items à la carte, that is, individually. The price of the hamburger seems very economical to the customer. Most people will add french fries and a drink. This increases the average check, but in the mind of the customer, the meal price is acceptable because the price of the main item in the meal seems reasonable.

The key in keeping sales volume up is to ensure that the perceived value received by the customer is equal to or greater than the price charged. When prices are increased, one answer is to increase the value. Perhaps an additional accompaniment can be added to the entrée at the time of the price increase to increase the value to the customer.

## Listing Prices

Menu prices can be listed in a variety of ways.[5] The way the prices are presented should be part of the overall marketing plan for the operation. In the one-price or prix fixe method, a fixed price is set for all meals. Pricing is simplified. However, since the gross profit varies depending on the item chosen, the total gross

## Which Is the Better Approach?

**Learning Objectives:** Describe the different methods of listing prices on a menu. Compare and contrast the various methods of menu pricing.

Listed are two different ways for displaying items on the menu:

### Appetizers
1. Vegetable Tempura ..............................................................................6.95
   House fried assorted vegetable & fried tofu served with Chef's choice sauce
2. Samosas ..............................................................................................4.25
   Deep-fried, vegetable-filled pastry
3. Korean Hearty Scallion Pie ..................................................................6.95
   Korean pizza, with chopped scallion, chives, and seasonings, lightly pan fried
4. Fried Wonton ......................................................................................4.95
   Served with Malaysian curry dipping sauce (vegetable or pork filled)

### Soups and Salads
1. Miso Soup............................................................................................2.25
   Tofu and seaweed with soybean paste
2. Mulligatawney ....................................................................................4.25
   Made with lentils, herbs, and mild Indian spices
3. Thai Hot and Sour Soup ......................................................................3.25
   With baby shrimp
4. Larb Kai .............................................................................................6.95
   Minced chicken with Chinese greens and ginger dressing

### Seafood and Signature
1. Ginger Scallion Duck ........................................................................10.95
   Roasted duck with fresh ginger and lite oyster sauce
2. Pan Seared Salmon Fillet ..................................................................14.95
   Served on a bed of fresh greens and Chinese black beans
3. Shrimp or Scallop Choo-Chi .............................................................12.95
   Served in Choo-Chi curry and green beans
4. Grilled Eel Rice Bowl ........................................................................11.95
   Traditional Japanese tangy and sweet eel on a bed of rice, garnished with daikon Radish

The $20.03, three-course Prix Fixe lunch menu is your choice of one appetizer, entrée, and dessert from the following daily menu:

**Monday**

*Appetizers*
Vegetable Soup with Sorrel and Watercrees
Asparagus Vinaigrette with Mimosa

*Entrées*
Herb-Crusted Fillet of Sea Bass
"Pot-Roasted" Pork Loin, Eggplant Sauce

*Desserts*
French-Style Cheesecake
Passion Fruit Soffle
Lavender Crème Brulée (Provence)
Assortiment du Patissier du Jour

**Tuesday**

*Appetizers*
Baked Whiting Filets with Herbed Butter Sauce

*Entrées*
Poached Skate Wing in a Lemongrass Broth
Daube of Beef in the Style of Arles

*Desserts*
Panna Cotta with Strawberry-Rhubarb Compote
Mango and Apple Tart with Puff Pastry Leaves
Warm Almond Brioche with Strawberry Compote
Assortiment du Patissier du Jour

*Sources:* All Asia Asian Cuisine & Bar, *http://web.mit.edu/afs/athena/user/w/c/wchuang/www/ menus/menus/All_Asia.txt* (September 10, 2001). L'Ecole-Prix Fixe Lunch Menu, *http://www .frenchculinary.com/subpages/ecole/prix_fixe.html* (May 15, 2004).

**Discussion Question:** Which is a better pricing method? Why?

profit may be reduced if too many higher-cost entrées are chosen. This can be avoided by having items on the menu that cost approximately the same to produce. Low-price operations offering few choices often choose this method of listing prices.

The à la carte menu was mentioned earlier. It is associated with upscale restaurants. The initial perception is that prices are low. "Sticker shock" may set in when the final bill is presented unless the perceived value is greater than the amount of the check. This approach appeals to customers who like to individualize their meal. It does complicate the pricing of checks for the employees. A version of the à la carte menu prices the entrées separately but includes potatoes and vegetables in the entrée price.

A table d'hôte meal consists of a set number of courses at a set price. The price of the meal is determined by the price of the entrée. It is assumed that all other courses cost about the same. Additional charges may be made for a special appetizer and/or dessert.

Finally, customers can be offered the choice of a platter or a complete dinner. Platters may appeal to those who wish to have a smaller meal. A modification involves serving a smaller portion of the entrée at a lower price.

In selecting a method for listing menu prices, management should consider the overall impression they are seeking to give while attempting to produce satisfied customers and maximum revenue.

## MEASURING MENU STRENGTH

A variety of ways exist to quantify the strength of the overall menu or of one item relative to another.

### Average Check

Operators will have determined that a specific average check—total sales divided by the number of customers—is necessary to ensure a particular level of profitability. The simplest method of evaluating menu prices is to compare the average check desired with the actual average check.

This method assumes that there will be a normal distribution of customers around the average, something that rarely occurs. For this reason, the average check method is not very useful.

### Range

A better method is to establish menu ranges based on price—for example, $6 to $8; $8 to $10; $10 to $12—and track the number of actual sales in each of the ranges. The result is a frequency distribution graph. This will show the range of prices that customers are willing to pay. In addition, the graph can spotlight potential problem or opportunity areas. If the graph is skewed around the low-price end of the menu, it indicates that the items offered are outside the prices that customers are able or willing to pay. On the other hand, clustering toward the high end of the menu indicates that patrons are willing to spend more.

## Menu Scoring

Menu scoring combines the profitability and popularity of menu items to arrive at a consensus score. The higher the score, the better the menu. An existing menu can be scored, then compared with a proposed new menu, after sales for the new menu have been estimated. Table 5.2 illustrates a menu scoring comparison for several items on a menu.

The menu score is the product of the gross profit average per meal and the popularity of the meals analyzed. In this example four items are scored—chicken, beef, turkey, and filet. The popularity of the meals is found by dividing the number of menu items sold (285) by the total number of meals served (450). The popularity of the meals analyzed in thus 63 percent.

Determining the gross profit average per meal is more complicated. Total sales in dollars is found by multiplying, for each menu item, the number sold and the sales price. Seventy-five beef items were sold at a price of $11.95 for sales of $896.25. Adding up the sales for all four items gives total sales of $3177.75 for 285 items. The gross profit average per meal is a product of the meal average check (total sales divided by the number of menu items sold) and the gross profit percentage. The average meal check is $3177.75 divided by 285 items or $11.15.

To determine the gross profit percentage, it is necessary to identify the gross profit. The gross profit is found by subtracting total food cost from total sales. Total sales has already been identified as $3177.75. The food cost for each menu

### Table 5.2  Menu Scoring

| (1) Menu Item | (2) Number Sold | (3) Item Sales Price | (4) Food Cost Percentages | (5) Total Sales (2) × (3) | (6) Total Food Cost (4) × (5) |
|---|---|---|---|---|---|
| Chicken | 65 | $9.95 | 30 | $646.75 | $194.03 |
| Beef | 75 | 11.95 | 38 | 896.25 | 340.58 |
| Turkey | 90 | 10.25 | 31 | 922.50 | 285.98 |
| Filet | 55 | 12.95 | 45 | 712.25 | 320.51 |
| Total | 285 | | | $3177.75 | $1141.10 |

(7) Meal check average:              (5) ÷ (2)   =   $11.15
(8) Gross profit:                    (5) − (6)   = $2036.65
(9) Gross profit percentage:         (8) ÷ (5)   =   64%
(10) Gross profit average per meal:  (7) × (9)   =   $7.15
(11) Total meals served                          =   450
(12) Popularity of meals analyzed:   (2) ÷ (11)  =   63%
(13) Menu score:                     (10) × (12) =   4.5

*Source:* Adapted from James Keiser, *Controlling and Analyzing Costs in Foodservice Operations,* 2nd ed. (New York: Macmillan Publishing Company, 1989), pp. 61–62.

item is found by multiplying the sales by the food cost percentage. Chicken sales are $646.75 with a food cost for this dish of 30 percent. Food cost is $194.03. Adding up food costs for the four dishes brings a total food cost of $1141.10. Gross profit is found by subtracting total food cost ($1141.10) from total sales ($3177.75). Gross profit is $2036.41. The gross profit percentage is found by dividing this figure by total sales of $3177.75 and is 64 percent. The gross profit average per meal is 64 percent of the meal average check of $11.15 or $7.14.

The menu score is the gross profit average per meal ($7.14) multiplied by the popularity of the meals analyzed (63 percent) or 4.5. After the initial menu score of 4.5 is developed, one or two items could be substituted for items on the list and another score developed. By comparing the two scores, a determination can be made as to which menu listing is better.

---

**quick quiz**

Which salad is most often on fine dining menus?

a. Cobb salad

b. Spinach salad

c. Caesar salad

*Source:* Hickok, Allan F. and Lana E. Lazarus, *Restaurant Industry Review,* U.S. Bancorp Piper Jaffray Equity Research, March 2003, pp. 54–55.

---

## Menu Engineering

Menu engineering combines the concepts of menu mix percentage and dollar contribution margin to determine the relative strength of menu items. An item with a relatively low contribution margin percentage may still deliver a healthy dollar margin.

Table 5.3 and Figure 5.1 illustrate an analysis of a menu using menu engineering. The contribution margin of each menu item is determined and compared with the contribution margin for the menu as a whole. Similarly, the popularity of each item on the menu is compared with the average popularity of the items assuming an even distribution of purchases. Various authors have said that sales are acceptable if an item achieves anywhere from 70 to 90 percent of the average item sales per entrée. If, for example, there were 10 items on a menu and sales were distributed evenly, each item would account for 10 percent of sales. Thus a sales percentage of 7 to 9 percent would be acceptable. This example uses 80 percent of sales as the acceptable figure.

The scores on both dimensions are combined and placed on a graph (Figure 5.1). Plowhorses are items that are relatively popular but have a low contribution margin. Items falling into this category can have their menu prices increased or the portion size cut in an attempt to increase the contribution margin. If the market does not resist the price increase, this action will move a plowhorse into the star category. If the market is price resistant, the items can be buried in an incon-

**Table 5.3    Menu Engineering**

| (1) Menu Item | (2) Number Sold | (3) Item Sales Price | (4) Food Cost Percentages | (5) Total Sales (2) × (3) | (6) Total Food Cost (4) × (5) |
|---|---|---|---|---|---|
| Chicken | 65 | $9.95 | 35 | $646.75 | $226.36 |
| Beef | 75 | 11.95 | 38 | 896.25 | 340.58 |
| Turkey | 90 | 10.25 | 31 | 922.50 | 285.98 |
| Filet | 55 | 12.95 | 45 | 712.25 | 320.51 |
| Total | 285 | | | $3177.75 | $1173.43 |

(7) Food cost percentage:                    (6) ÷ (5)   =        36.93%

(8) Total contribution margin:               (5) − (6)   =    $2004.32

(9) Average contribution margin/customer:  (8) ÷ (2)   =        $7.03

(10) Contribution margin per menu item:    $\dfrac{(5) - (6)}{(2)}$

Chicken:   $\dfrac{\$646.75 - 226.36}{65} = \$6.47$

Beef:   $\dfrac{\$896.25 - 340.58}{75} = \$7.41$

Turkey:   $\dfrac{\$922.50 - 285.98}{90} = \$7.07$

Filet:

$\dfrac{\$712.75 - 320.51}{55} = \$7.13$

(11) Average popularity:

80 percent of the average item sales per entrée: 100 divided by 4 × 80% = 20%

(12) Popularity of each menu item:

number of portions sold ÷ total number of meals sold

Chicken:   65 ÷ 285 = 22.8%

Beef:   75 ÷ 285 = 26.3%

Turkey:   90 ÷ 285 = 31.6%

Filet:   55 ÷ 285 = 19.3%

*Source:* Adapted from James Keiser, *Controlling and Analyzing Costs in Foodservice Operations,* 2nd ed. (New York: Macmillan Publishing Company, 1989), pp. 61–62.

spicuous place on the menu in the knowledge that people will find these relative bargains anyway. Stars have both high popularity and high contribution margins. It may be possible to increase menu price and/or cut portion size to increase profits while maintaining volume. Puzzles have relatively low popularity and high margins. They need to be promoted more to stimulate sales. Dogs are low in popularity and contribution margin. They are prime candidates to be dropped

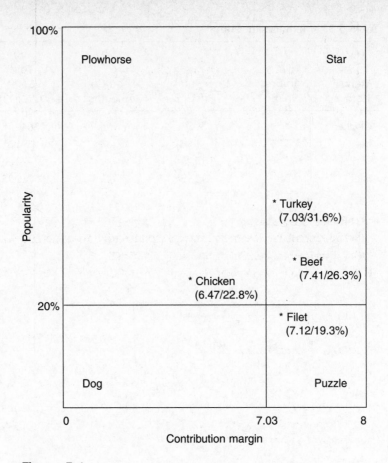

**Figure 5.1** Menu engineering analysis.

from the menu. In the example used, chicken would be dropped from the menu, while the filet would be promoted more heavily. The prices on the beef and the turkey might be raised a little and these items featured visibly on the menu.

Menu engineering has been criticized because it uses the mean as the basis of comparison.[6] Using the mean will always put some menu items above the mean and some below. Thus, an item that was producing adequate sales and/or contribution margins becomes a problem if the sales and/or contribution margin of another menu item changes. It is suggested that a marginal analysis approach is better. Such an approach evaluates menu items individually based on the marginal, or extra, contribution gained from selling an additional menu item.

## MENU DESIGN

The menu, to a large extent, determines what customers will order and how much they will spend.[7] It is estimated that customers spend less than two minutes examining the menu. A properly designed menu helps achieve the objectives of increasing the average check and promoting the sale of specialty items and can improve sales by anywhere from 2 to 10 percent.[8] This is done by presenting the product offerings of the restaurant in an attractive manner, describing them in a way that paints an attractive picture, and pricing them to give the impression of value. The menu should tell customers what the operators want them to buy.

## Cover

The menu cover should be designed to complement the overall theme of the restaurant. Line graphics or photographs are often used to present an attractive first impression. Black-and-white photographs are easy to reproduce and less expensive than color.

The name of the restaurant is the only copy required on the cover. Additional information regarding the address, phone number, acceptance of credit cards, and so on is best left to the inside or the back cover.

## Size

The size of the menu will vary depending on the number of items being featured and the amount of copy used to describe them. Traditionally, one menu listed appetizers, soups, salads, side dishes, entrées, desserts, and beverages. A separate menu was common for breakfast, lunch, and dinner. Today, many of the rules have been broken. Separate menus can be created for children, wine, desserts, cocktails, and so on. The key is to design the menu in such a way that it effectively communicates with the customers. For example, many think that a separate dessert menu is more effective than listing them on the entrée menu. They argue that this helps create the feeling that this is another separate occasion. Customers, in selecting an entrée, may notice the price of desserts, add it to the price of the entrée, and decide at that point not to order dessert because of the combined cost of entrée and dessert. A separate dessert menu means that the decision to order dessert is more likely to be made on the basis of desire than of cost.

When presented with the entrée menu for a dessert selection, diners may cast their eyes back to an item not ordered and wish that they had taken the chicken rather than the sole. A dessert menu says, "forget the entrée; this is different; this is separate; let's have dessert." As has been pointed out previously, a person can still have an appetite for dessert even though the taste for the entrée has been satisfied. Presenting a separate menu reinforces that thought. The favored method of promoting desserts is to have the wait staff describe the desserts to customers.

## Materials

The weight and quality of the paper on which the menu is printed adds to the impact. Heavier paper gives a feeling of quality. It also adds to the life of the menu. This has to be weighed against the menu price change cycle. When price changes are listed by stickers covering the previous price, the impression is not a good one. Similarly, menus that are torn or dirty give a very poor impression of the operation.

The life of the menu can be increased through the use of water-resistant paper or lamination. The latter is more appropriate for lower-priced operations. A compromise might be to have an expensive cover, which would not change, with a less expensive insert.

## Placement

**Menu Sequence.**   There are two schools of thought regarding the placement of items on a menu. Some believe that the sequence of dishes on the menu should follow the progression of a meal. Just as a meal moves from appetizers and soups through entrées to desserts, with side orders, salads, sandwiches, and beverages interspersed, so should the layout of the menu.

**Focal Points.**   Others believe various focal points should be used on a menu. Customers' eyes are naturally drawn to specific points—focal points—when pre-

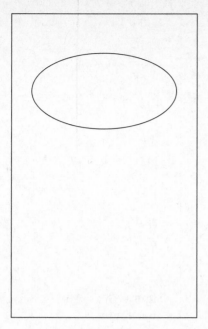

**Figure 5.2** Prime location on a single-sheet menu.

sented with a menu. The restaurateur should place menu items that he or she wants to push in the focal points of a menu.

The focal point varies with the type of menu. On a single-sheet menu, the eye initially focuses on the area just above the centerline (Figure 5.2). With a twofold menu the upper right part of the right inside cover is the focal point (Figure 5.3).

On a threefold menu, the eye moves from the center to the upper right-hand corner, then to the upper left-hand corner, bottom left-hand corner, through the center to the upper right-hand corner, bottom right-hand corner, and back to the center (Figure 5.4). In all, the center is crossed three times. It makes sense to place in the center items that the restaurant wishes to push. In this regard it is not necessary to use the focal point to highlight items for which the restaurant is famous. Customers will search the menu for these items. Focal points are to be used to highlight items that the restaurateur wants to sell and that customers would not ordinarily search for.

A typical threefold menu lists appetizers in the left-hand column, entrées in the middle column, and desserts at the bottom of the right-hand column. However, the items that increase the average check are appetizers and desserts. One enterprising restaurant in Scotland features its appetizers in the center of the menu. Customers will not necessarily order an appetizer. However, they do see a listing of items that they might not generally search for.

One restaurant that primarily sold lower-profit burgers and sandwiches increased the average check by listing high-end specialties on the inside right cover toward the middle and moving the burgers and sandwiches from that spot to the back page. In addition, management increased the font size of the specialties and

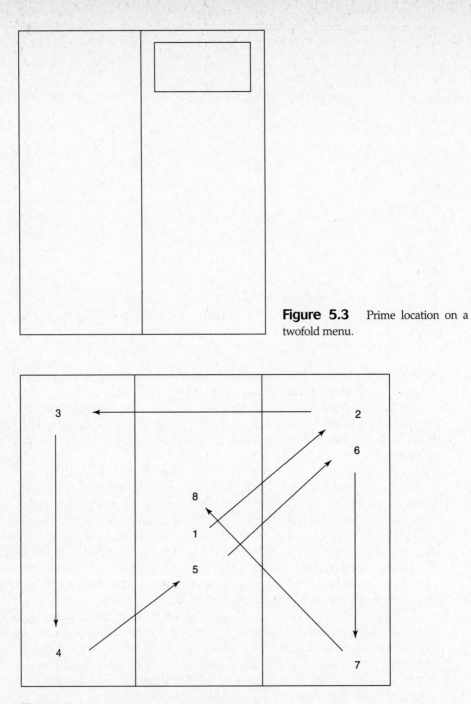

**Figure 5.3** Prime location on a twofold menu.

**Figure 5.4** Focal points of a threefold menu.

reduced the font size of burgers. In one week the average check went from $16.00 to $21.00.[9] If customers really wanted a burger, they had to search for it. In the meantime many were drawn to the higher-profit items.

The key is to place not the *higher-priced* items in prominent positions. It is to place the *highest-profit* items in those positions.

## Specials

There are various ways to draw attention to particular menu items. Specials can be listed in larger and bolder type than that used on the rest of the menu. They can also be given a longer description. The concept of closure indicates that people's eyes are drawn to whatever is enclosed by a box. By drawing a box around a menu description, attention is drawn to what is inside the box. In addition, color, illustration, and/or pictures can be used to draw attention to the restaurant's signature items.

## Menu Descriptions

The objective in describing menu items is to present them in a way that will give customers an accurate picture of the dish while increasing the likelihood of their sale.

**Accuracy.** Municipalities are becoming more vigilant about prosecuting restaurants for false statements on the menu. Typical errors deal with the grade, point of origin, size, weight, prepared form, preparation method, picture, price, or dietary or nutritional content of the product. Government grades can and should be used accurately to describe fish. A USDA Choice piece of meat should be just that. Listing where the item came from can help sales. However, Lake Superior whitefish must come from Lake Superior. The precooked weight of menu offerings should be listed, as shrinkage during cooking can reduce the size and/or weight of an item. A great deal of controversy has arisen over the use of fresh or frozen on a menu. Fish that is frozen on the boat minutes after it is caught may actually taste fresher than "fresh" fish consumed two days after being caught. However, customers still seem to believe that fresh is better than frozen. The word *fresh* cannot be used to describe fish that has been frozen. A number of operations use pictures on the menu to help sell items. The dish being served should look like the one in the picture.

Managers must balance their right to advertise menu items in a manner that makes them sound attractive with their duty not to misrepresent the product being advertised. To do so violates truth in menu or accuracy in menu laws.

Many operations automatically include a 15 percent service charge on parties of six or more. If this is the case, it should be stated prominently on the menu. Additionally, it should be clear to the reader what is, and is not, included in the price of a meal. Finally, there is a great deal of confusion about the dietary and/or nutritional claims of certain dishes. A term such as *low calorie* is too vague and should not be used. What does it mean? Low-calorie compared to what? Increased concern for health on the part of consumers is causing a number of operations to list nutritional information on the menu or, as in the case of the major fast-food chains, in prominent positions in stores. Organizations such as Healthmark certify certain menu items as being healthy choices.

Menu items should be described in such a way that customers can see them in their minds. This is important because we think in pictures, not in words.

As a whole there are ten words or phrases that, in the words of NRA, "add a lot of interest" to a menu choice for the majority of diners. These words are as follows:[10]

- Fresh, farm fresh
- Homemade
- Grilled, charcoal-grilled
- Roasted
- Charbroiled, broiled
- Baked
- Barbecued
- Marinated
- Sautéed
- Hearty

At the same time there are certain words or phrases that turn off many people:

- Raw
- Deep-fried, fried, flash-fried
- Blackened
- Infused
- Pureed
- Flan
- Jambalaya
- Poached

As noted in Chapter 2, the NRA has identified four broad "attitude segments" based on sense of adventure and concern about nutrition. They are adventurous diners, health-conscious diners, carefree diners, and traditional diners. Certain menu descriptions appeal more to individuals in certain segments. Words from the preceding list that turn some people off will appeal to others.

Adventurous diners like "spicy, organic, herb-crusted, aged, free-range, wild, infused, sun-dried." Health-conscious diners like "broiled, baked, natural, stir-fried, pesticide-free, organic, delicate, hormone-free, stewed, raw, pureed." Carefree diners are turned on by "grilled, charbroiled, hearty, seasonal, mashed, mesquite, au gratin, fried, sauced, breaded." Finally, traditional diners like "fresh/farm fresh, homemade, roasted, broiled, baked, farm-raised, crispy/crunchy, pesticide-free, mashed, deep fried, shredded, ground."

## Typeface

The typeface used must be large enough and legible enough to allow customers to read the descriptions. Type sizes are listed by point size, with 72 points to the inch. A type size of 12 or larger is recommended for menus.

The main typeface styles used on menus are Roman, modern, and script. Most books and magazines are set in some version of a Roman typeface. Modern typefaces are newer, clean looking, and do not have the serifs or flourishes of the Roman typeface. Script imitates handwriting and should be used primarily for headings and subheadings, as it is difficult to read. Some upscale restaurants, however, use script for the entire menu, to give a handwritten look.

Typefaces can be set in uppercase or lowercase, regular or italics. It is easier to read letters that are set in regular lowercase. Italics and uppercase letters are tiring on the eyes and should be used sparingly for maximum impact.

Many feel that operators should stay away from unusual type styles, as they clutter a menu. This is an individual decision based on the image that is being portrayed.

Leading refers to the space between the lines of type. Three points of leading between lines is regarded as a minimum for a menu to ensure easier reading.

Type that is black and printed on white or light-tinted paper, such as tan, cream, ivory, or gray, is easy to read. Where colored inks are used, it is important that the shade be dark, to make it readable. Reverse type—white type on a black background—is very difficult to read and should be avoided.

## Verbal Pictures

The words used to describe items on the menu should be chosen carefully to add to the sales appeal of the dish. The following questions can be used as a guide to writing compelling copy:[11]

1. What is it?
2. How is it prepared?
3. How is it served?
4. Does it have unusual taste and quality properties?
5. Where do the ingredients come from?

Menu descriptions should aim to excite the senses. People think in pictures. Consider the image given by the following:

new     moist     crisp     succulent

Certain words have been overused and have lost their effectiveness. These words do not excite the senses:

excellent     classic     special     the     best

Consider the following:

BEEF TENDERLOIN

or

GOURMET SLICES OF BEEF TENDERLOIN

Generous slices of tenderloin, sauteed in butter and served with a sauce made with a delicate Madeira wine, shallots, and mushrooms.

The key is to praise the virtues of the dish while avoiding hyperbole; say it in words that are understandable to, and that will move, the customer while avoiding cutesy topical references that have a short shelf life.

## Menu Pricing

In a previous section we considered menu pricing in terms of profitability. In this section we deal with pricing as a marketing tool.

**Odd-Cents Pricing.**   The vast majority of menu prices end in either a 5 or a 9. There is psychology involved here. The real difference between $12.99 and $13.00 is one penny. However, psychologically, the former seems less expensive than the latter. The customer perceives that she or he is getting a "discount" from the higher price. This method of odd-cents pricing was actually instituted as a control method by R. H. Macy. By pricing items at $2.99, when a customer paid with three $1 bills, cashiers had to ring the item up on the cash register to give the penny change. This guaranteed that the sale was recorded.

**First-Figure Dominance.**   A price change from 25 cents to 29 cents seems less than one from 29 cents to 33 cents. The reason is that, in the first case, the dominant first figure remains at 2, whereas in the second situation, it increased from 2 to 3.

**Length of the Price.**   The length of the price is also important. A price increase from $9.95 to $10.25 is perceived as being more than an increase from

quick bite 5.6
**Designing Menus That Sell**

**Learning Objectives:** Compare the three different philosophies of pricing the menu. Give specific guidelines on the design, layout, and pricing of a menu to increase the average check while boosting the sales of specialty items.

Since customers take only a few minutes to look through the menu, it is important that restaurants not only inform customers of what items are on the menu, but also what menu items they want their customers to buy. If a restaurant understands the proper procedure for pricing items on the menu, this technique can be used to increase the operation's sales. When displaying the price of an item on the menu, it should come as the last bit of information the customer receives about the item. There should be no difference in the format of the prices, font, font style, or size. It should all be the same format as the description of the item.

Another principle widely accepted by most foodservice operations is the "rounding strategy." Often times, instead of rounding up to the next dollar, it is better to use numbers that end in 50 or 95 cents. Most consumers do not perceive $11.95 as close to $12.00, although they are nearly the same price. This method of pricing is all a part of the psychology restaurateurs use to lure customers into buying more expensive items on the menu, which in turn allows [restaurateurs] to maximize their profits. Tom Feltenstein, CEO of Feltenstein Partners, explains that the proper pricing must always be based on the value perception of the guest, not a pre-established formula. Concluding that, restaurants must choose the best method based on what they feel their customers will see as the best price value.

*Source:* Arnoult, Emily, "Designing Menus That Sell," *Restaurants USA,* May 1998.

**Discussion Question:** Design a menu consisting of three items that matches the table d'hôte structure.

$9.25 to $9.55. In the former case the length of the price has increased from three to four digits.

**Price Rounding.**   Price rounding also goes on in the mind of the customer. Within certain price bands, price increases have little negative impact on customers.

**Price Spreads.**   The price spread of a menu refers to the difference in price between the least expensive and most expensive item on a menu within a specific category. Excessive price spreads encourage the sale of lower-priced menu items. In general, the highest-priced item on the menu should be no more than twice the price of the lowest-priced menu item.

People tend to buy in the middle price range of a menu. By pricing new items slightly higher than the average guest check while lowering the price of the most expensive items and raising the prices of the lower-priced items, it may be possible to increase the size of the average check.

**Placement.** Many customers read a menu from right to left. They look at the price first before considering the description of the dish. Consider the following:

| | |
|---|---|
| Baked Chicken | $12.99 |
| Lemon Sole | $15.99 |
| Lamb Steak | $17.99 |
| Swordfish Steak | $16.99 |

By using the same typeface for the prices as the menu items and listing them to the right in a straight line, attention is drawn to the price rather than to the dish. Compare that method with the following:

BAKED CHICKEN
Tender pieces of boneless breast of chicken served with stuffing   $12.99

LEMON SOLE
Fresh filets of sole sauteed in a sweet lemon caper sauce   $15.99

LAMB STEAK
Center cut of lamb steak served on a bed of rice with mint sauce   $17.99

SWORDFISH STEAK
Charcoal grilled and served with a beurre blanc sauce   $16.99

## Packaging

One way to increase the sale of items not usually ordered is to include them with the entrée and charge more for the package. If it is found that customers are not ordering appetizers, including an appetizer with the meal can increase the average check size. Similar strategies have been adopted by restaurants to sell soup-and-sandwich combinations.

## Wine Menus

Wines can be described in a variety of formats. Some operations list suggested wines next to the entrées. If this approach is taken, two suggestions should be given for each entrée: one in the low-to-moderate price range, the other in the moderate-to-high range. This gives customers a choice without the feeling that higher-priced wines are being pushed exclusively.

The most common thing for table-service restaurants, however, is to have a separate wine list. A list of the more popular wines can be given to customers with a note that a more extensive list is available to the "connoisseur." This approach appeals to a customer seeking to impress a companion, be it a date or a business client. A short description is appropriate, indicating the relative sweetness or dryness of the wine and the types of dishes it will complement.

Restaurants commonly offer a house wine by the glass, half-liter, or liter. This offers good value, especially to the wine novice, who might be intimidated by the thought of ordering a bottle of wine.

To appeal to the discriminating diner, an increasing number of restaurants are offering better-quality wines by the glass. Improvements in storage techniques allow them to keep opened bottles of wine fresher longer. Few half-bottles of wine are found on menus. It may well be that customers could be enticed to "trade up" from having a glass by effective merchandising of half-bottles of wine. Adults who drink alcoholic beverages away from home are more likely to order wine by the glass than wine by the carafe.

Wine should always have a bin number listed on the menu. This saves the guest from the embarrassment of mispronouncing the name. Most consumers feel comfortable ordering from a wine list although many do not feel well informed about wines. Wine glasses on the table are a subtle reminder that wine is appropriate.

A sommelier or wine steward can offer specialized knowledge to the customer while adding to the ambience of the occasion. Care should be taken not to intimidate the customer with the mystique of wine: choosing the wine, feeling the cork, and tasting. The purpose is to sell the wine, not to impress the guest with one's wine knowledge. Whatever format is used, the wines offered should be those that appeal to the segments of the market being served.

## Menu Alternatives

Restaurants can present their product offerings in a variety of ways. In keeping with the theme of the operation, some use chalkboards to announce the dishes. Items and prices can be changed with the swipe of an eraser. Menu cards placed strategically throughout is another alternative.

A hand-held menu is not practical for some segments of the industry, such as fast-food operations and institutional feeding. In facilities where the menu changes several times a day, it may be feasible to have an electronic menu that, in addition to listing the menu items, could display graphics, messages, and digitalized photographs.

As mentioned earlier, waitstaff are used when selling desserts. The use of the menu as a primary merchandising tool has eclipsed the traditional role of the employee in performing this function. It is a way for management to standardize the merchandising message—to have the menu "say" what management wants in a way that does not depend on the ability of the server. It also means that servers do not need the knowledge previously expected of someone required to recite the choices, methods of preparation, and ingredients of everything on the menu. A few operations do not present the customer with a menu but rely totally on employees to describe the items for sale. This can only be used when attempting to present an upscale image and where relatively few items are offered. Many table-service restaurants use employees to describe the daily specials.

Having said all of this, items will not sell if they do not taste good. In addition, while menus help draw customers to specific items, it is the server who closes the sale.[12]

---

quick bite 5.7
## Road to the Top: Designing the Menu

Foodservice operators not satisfied with the sales of their restaurants should examine their menus. Does the restaurant's menu appeal to customers or does it turn customers away? At Chi-Chi, the old, standard menu was replaced by a menu that features a jagged edge, warm earth tones and vibrant drawings of fresh fruits and vegetables. The structure of the menu was developed so that the 25 new menu items could be better arranged on the menu. With the design of their new menu, Chi-Chi hopes to get a new message across to their customer base emphasizing that they are no longer serving the same old food.

Many other operations are now realizing that the appearance of their menus relay signals that affect how customers view their operation. "The menu is part of your brand identity," says Bill Main, founder of California-based Bill Main and Associates, a foodservice management and training company. "It's a reflection of who you are in the marketplace. If you have a dirty menu, it sends out a message that you probably have a dirty kitchen. If it's a bright, clean, sharp menu, it looks like you're a bright, clean operation." It has also been shown that a well-kept menu encourages customers to order higher-priced items.

Most customers do not make up their minds by themselves when ordering. The menu advises them on what to buy. The way items are positioned on the menu could very well determine the point of sales. If an operation has items such as hamburgers and sandwiches at the focal point, then customers are more likely to order those menu items. Alternately, a focal point incorporating the most popular and highest-priced dishes will help sell those items. According to Steve Miller, the president of the Miller Resource Group in Grafton, Massachusetts, it is all about the placement of items on menu. Miller states that the "power position" on a menu is on the inside right page above the middle. He also says that people have the tendency of remembering the top two items on a list and the bottom item.

There are several different ways that foodservice operations can design a menu so that it brings attention to certain items. The font size, print size, boxes, and shading can all help draw attention to an item. Photos can also help enhance the appearance of a menu. Allowing customers to preview their order before actually ordering is highly recommended.

Descriptions can also have a surprising effect on which items customers choose. For instance, today's customers are more knowledgeable about the

---

food that is being served to them than in the past, and some items on the menu do not need a written description. Most restaurants provide a description of the ingredients of their more unusual dishes. The most profitable items should receive the most descriptive word association and come across as most appealing to the customer. Isidore Kharasch, president of Chicago-based Hospitality Works, says that certain words have more selling power than others. For example, "marinated," "roasted" or "cooked in our wood-fire oven" often have more allure than words such as "fried" or "pan fried." Kharasch suggest that if an item is fried you can say that it is hand-battered. In that way you have told the customers the item is fried without really saying it. Permitting some items to be more descriptive than others is part of the psychology operators use on customers in order to sell higher profit items. "If you want to sell something, make it sound as delicious as possible," says Andy Lansing, president and chief operating officer of Levy Restaurants. "Even the ones you don't want to sell should sound good and taste great—they just shouldn't sound as good as your signature dishes."

The placement of price is also important to the effectiveness of a menu. Most foodservice operations place the price at the end of the item description in order that it might appear less important. Stating the price without a dollar sign, in the same style and typeface, allows the customer to focus more on the menu item rather than the price.

According to Feltenstein, an effectively designed menu will entice guests to buy the items you want them to buy. The most influential menus are those that subtly weave those important factors such as price and item description into a pleasing presentation that drives home the restaurant's message in just minutes.

*Source:* Panitz, Beth, "Reading Between the Lines: The Psychology of Menu Design," *Restaurants USA,* August 2000. Arnoult, Emily, "Designing Menus That Sell," *Restaurants USA,* May 1998.

**Discussion Question:** How does the customer's perception of the menu affect a foodservice operation?

## ENDNOTES

1. National Restaurant Association, *2005 Restaurant Industry Forecast* (Washington, DC: National Restaurant Association, 2005).
2. Robert D. Reid, *Foodservice and Restaurant Marketing* (Boston: CBI Publishing Company, 1983), pp. 207–209.
3. Ibid., pp. 204–206.
4. James Keiser, *Controlling and Analyzing Costs in Foodservice Operations,* 2nd ed. (New York: Macmillan Publishing Company, 1989), p. 56; Reid, *Foodservice and Restaurant Marketing,* p. 228.
5. Keiser, pp. 49–50.
6. Bradley Beran, "Menu Sales Mix Analysis Revisited: An Economic Approach," *Hospitality Research Journal,* vol. 18, no.3/vol. 19, no. 1, 1995, pp. 125–142.

7. Albin G. Seaberg, *Menu Design: Merchandising and Marketing,* 4th ed. (New York: Van Nostrand Reinhold, 1991), p. vii.
8. Beth Panitz, "Reading Between the Lines: The Psychology of Menu Design," *Restaurants USA,* August 2000, www.restaurant.org/rusa.
9. Ibid.
10. National Restaurant Association, *2005 Restaurant Industry Forecast* (Washington, DC: National Restaurant Association, 2005), p. 2.
11. Seaberg, *Menu Design,* p. 207.
12. Panitz, "Reading Between the Lines: The Psychology of Menu Design."

## INTERNET RESOURCES

Boxer Brand Menu Covers       *http://www.boxerbrand.com/*
Restaurant Costing Software   *http://www.restaurantcosting.com/*

## QUICK QUIZ ANSWERS

p. 128—a. Cobb salad.
p. 137—c. 1983.

# CHAPTER SIX

# DELIVERING HIGH-QUALITY SERVICE

"We agreed that of all virtues a waiter can display, that of a
retiring disposition is quite the least desirable."
Lewis Carroll [Charles Lutwidge Dodgson] (1832–1898),
British author, mathematician, clergyman

## learning objectives

*By the end of this chapter you should be able to*

1. Identify the various features that make the service encounter unique.

2. Identify ways to determine service problems.

3. Specify the gaps that explain customer dissatisfaction with service and suggest ways to close these gaps.

4. Identify the various procedural and convivial dimensions of service.

5. Describe the principles of waiting.

6. Describe the duties and responsibilities of captain, server, and busperson in providing quality service.

Brazil is beginning to make a mark on the culinary environment in the United States. When two pairs of brothers from a small farm town in southern Brazil took jobs in local restaurants to help their fathers pay off bank loans, they never expected to end up in the United States. The Coser and Ongaratto brothers saved money earned from tips, which in 1979 allowed them to open their first restaurant in Brazil: Fogo de Chão.

Fogo de Chão's innovative concept is modeled after traditional South Brazilian "churrascaria" dining. Guests pay a set price for the meal, which includes a salad bar that offers more than 30 dishes. All the food is authentic Brazilian fare made from ingredients found within the country. After helping themselves to the salad bar, guests sit down to enjoy what Brazilians call "espeto corrido" or "continuous service."

Patrons let their servers know when they are ready for the main course by turning a disk at the table to the green side. A server dressed as a gaucho (cowboy) brings a platter of meats to the table. After the guest makes his selection, the server roasts and carves the meat right in front of the patron. Servers keep bringing meats to the table until the guest flips the disk to the red side.

In 1996, the brothers moved to Texas. It was here that Fogo de Chão was established in America. Critics attributed the restaurant's success to the food and the idea. No one has seen a concept like Fogo de Chão. Authenticity, alone, is enough to keep people curious and coming back.

The brothers have continued to expand. They now have locations in Atlanta, Chicago, and Houston as well as a new location in Brazil. Because of the success at existing locations, the Cosers and Ongarattos hope to spread the taste of Brazil by opening one new restaurant in the United States every year. The concept is bringing Brazil to our hometowns and taste buds.

*Source:* Thorn, Bret, "Fogo de Chão: Brazilian Churrascaria Records Beefy Sales with Style, Consistency, and Service," *www.nrnhotconcepts.com/2003_winners/fogo.cfm*, April 14, 2004.

**Discussion Question:** Why is an idea like "continuous service" considered innovative?

## THE SERVICE ENCOUNTER

During restaurant service there is an encounter between customers and employees. It should not simply "occur." Management is responsible for ensuring that the encounter is planned, organized, and, to the extent that it can be, controlled to ensure customer satisfaction.

## Enduring Insights

Hollander has noted that a review of the historical literature on service uncovers certain features of the service encounter that persist.[1] Service encounters and purchases are considered important to the customer and routine to the service provider. Employees serve scores of customers a day. For the customer that meal out may be a once-a-week occurrence. It is difficult for the employee to generate the same level of enthusiasm for every customer that each customer has for the occasion.

Second, many service employees resent some or all of their customers. This may be because of one of a number of factors. For some employees there is the feeling that customers do not appreciate all the work that is necessary to provide good service. Others feel lower in status because they are serving the customer and may resent their job because of it. In some cases the difficult or rude behavior of customers generates negative feelings on the part of the employee.

Third, many customers want special treatment in a service situation. Perhaps they feel the need to throw their weight around or they feel that by demanding special treatment, they are accorded more status. This places the employees in a difficult situation. They probably resent the fact that everyone pays for equally good service, but some expect to receive more than what everyone else is getting.

Fourth, customers have differing needs and wants regarding service. Some prefer an unobtrusive manner of service, while others revel in a fawning, attentive

Maggiano's Little Italy.

style. It is up to the employee to match the level of service expected to the service delivered.

Related to customer expectations is evidence that factors such as the age, gender, and dress of the employee affect customer perceptions of whether or not the service to be provided will be satisfactory. A customer in a first-class restaurant may feel that "proper" service in such a setting would come from an older, male waiter. A younger, female waitress—no matter how skilled—may well set up negative initial reactions from the customer.

Finally, Hollander notes that many service encounters appear successful—or at least tolerable—because customers bring lowered expectations to the service encounter and employees develop coping strategies to deal with potential problems arising from the points just discussed.

## Service Problems

What kinds of things can go wrong? A study by the National Restaurant Association[2] indicates that in the restaurant industry, complaints about service far exceed complaints about food or atmosphere. When customers are asked to name their biggest complaint about table-service restaurants, speed of service and inattentive waitstaff are mentioned most often. The former is noted by about one out

---

**quick bite 6.2**
**Napkins**

**Learning Objective:** Identify the various features that make the service encounter unique.

Who would think that the color of a napkin could result in a customer complaint? Well, black pants and white napkins do not go together. In an upscale dining establishment where attire matters and guests dress in their finest, white lint is noticeable and irritating.

Giving guests the option of a black napkin in place of a white one will make the customer feel more cared for, more valued. As a server or manager of any dining establishment, one has to pay attention to the customers' preferences, even about napkins. Asking about small, personal preferences such as napkin color makes for a unique service encounter.

Every guest is different and requires special psychological as well as physiological needs. Accommodating the guest as an individual and not a number will increase the chances of a pleasurable experience within the establishment.

*Source:* Ruggless, Ron, "Operators See the Light, Offer Diners Black-Napkin Option," *Nation's Restaurant News*, vol. 36, no. 39, p. 206, September 30, 2002.

**Discussion Question:** What are other ways to make the service encounter unique?

---

of every four customers while the latter is noted by one in six patrons. The level of customer satisfaction has not changed since the beginning of the 1990s even as the number of restaurants has increased. Customers indicate that servers are excellent or good at providing friendly service (81%), answering menu questions (80%), delivering an accurately totaled check (80%), providing timely service (70%), handling complaints (62%), and recommending appropriate menu items (61%). It might be argued, however, that these percentages are not very good.

A study of airline, hotel, and restaurant interactions between customers and employees by Nyquist and colleagues[3] indicated two major problem areas. Difficult interactions were caused when customer expectations were greater than could be delivered by the service system or when the performance of company or employee did not match up to the potential of the system.

In their study, difficulties regarding the former accounted for three out of every four problem encounters. Difficulties occurred for a variety of reasons:

- Demands by the customer that the industry typically does not or cannot offer
- Demands against company policies that are difficult or impossible to fulfill
- Unacceptable treatment of employees by customers
- Drunkenness of customers
- Breaking of societal norms by customers
- Customers with special needs

When performance did not match the capacity of the system, problems arose when services or products were unavailable, performance was slow, or where the service or product was unacceptable.

## Assessing Customer Satisfaction

There are a number of ways in which restaurateurs can determine the extent to which customers are satisfied with the level of service they are being provided.[4] Probably the most commonly used method for collecting this information is through the use of comment cards. A card may be available on the table or it can be brought by the server at the conclusion of the meal. In either case, customers are asked to evaluate various aspects of the meal experience. The concern with comment cards is that they tend to be filled out either by people who have had a wonderful time or by those who have major complaints about the meal and/or the service. In either case those who respond are not typical of most customers. As such, this is a biased sample on which to make decisions about changing the service.

A similar comment can be made about customers who verbally complain or compliment the operation. Most people, if they have a mild complaint, will say nothing within the restaurant but will not return. Management does not hear from them and has no idea what caused the problem. Neither will management hear about experiences that were just "OK." The meal may have been adequate, but who wants to be "adequate"? In both situations management is unaware of potential problems.

One indirect measure of customer satisfaction is the percentage of repeat customers. If it is correct to assume that customers will not return to a place they are not satisfied with, this indicates potential problems with the operation.

Similarly, increasing sales indicate satisfied customers, while decreasing sales are a sign of problems. Care must be taken to measure sales changes in real terms, discounting sales increases by any change in menu prices. In addition to looking at sales trends, management can consider changes in market share. If the size of a market decreases but a restaurant's share of that market increases, sales overall may be down but the operation is more than holding its own. It is much more difficult to get a handle on the size of a particular market segment than on individual sales.

Finally, many companies use "mystery shoppers" to evaluate an operation anonymously. Since employees are unaware of the identity of the shopper, the report is a true indication of the physical and service aspects of the meal. Properly trained evaluators, oriented toward the unique aspects of a particular operation, can give very valuable feedback on potential problems.

One example of a mystery shopping report[5] allocates 350 points as follows:

| | |
|---|---|
| Facility/environment | 125 |
| Service/personnel | 175 |
| Food and beverage | 50 |

The mystery shopper gives the restaurant a score on each of these criteria and determines the percentage for each. For example, if an operation scored 100 on facility/environment, it would score 80 percent (100 divided by 125). The relative weights would have to be adjusted taking into account which factors are most important to the particular customers of a specific restaurant.

Additionally, in this example, the shopper indicates the top three items in which the restaurant did very well and the top three items that could be improved.

## SERVICE GAPS

Customers develop certain expectations about the service they are to receive based on such things as their own past experience, word of mouth from friends who have tried the restaurant, the advertisements of the restaurant itself, and their own needs and wants. During the restaurant visit they compare what they expected to get with what they perceive they got. The key word is *perceive*. The portion on the plate may be large. However, if the customer perceives the portion to be skimpy, it is skimpy. Perception, for the customer, is reality. The problem for the restaurant may be to change the image or perception of the customer rather than to increase portion size. However, a problem does exist.

If the perception of the service received is less than expected, the customer is dissatisfied; if the service received is perceived to be equal to or more than

**Learning Objective:** Identify ways to determine service problems.

Operators must offer customers an opportunity to provide feedback as a way of opening the communication lines with their customers. Comment cards and surveys are two tools that can be used to obtain opinions in order to learn about and resolve problems.

College foodservice operators are testing the effectiveness of the online survey. Food Insights, based in Memphis, Tennessee, has developed a program allowing college food service operators to measure student satisfaction. The system lets students voice their opinions when changes are made or new items are introduced.

The survey is found on the dining service Web site, a location that makes it easily accessible to the student. The survey enables operators to make changes quickly in order to respond to the needs of the students. This online survey, like any feedback medium, is an excellent way to gain insight into how expectations can be met.

Food Insight's survey shows how one segment of the foodservice industry is making an effort to identify problems in service. All operators must be aware of the discrepancies that can occur between the guest and their expectations. Developing a system to obtain feedback will positively affect customer relations—and the operation itself.

*Source:* King, Paul, "Colleges Use Online-Survey Method to Tap into Students' Opinions," *Nation's Restaurant News,* vol. 36, no. 37, p. 20, September 16, 2002.

**Discussion Question:** Why is it important to give customers a way to express opinions or problems?

expected, the customer is satisfied. One Denver restaurant—now out of business—would advertise, "Warm Beer, Lousy Food." By producing low expectations that are easily met, one would think that customers would be satisfied. However, expectations have to be raised to a level high enough that customers will want to eat out. The problem then becomes how to produce service good enough that customers' (raised) expectations are met.[6]

Service problems occur because of the following:[6]

- Management does not know what is important to customers.
- Management knows what is important to customers but does not translate that knowledge into service standards.
- Service standards are in place but employees do not practice them.
- Customers are promised a level of service that is not delivered.

## Lack of Knowledge

The first gap in delivering service occurs when management's perceptions about what customers expect are different from the customer's expectations. Management may not be aware of what is really important to the customer for one or more of several reasons.

**Market Research Orientation.**   The best way to find out what is important to customers is to ask the customer! As obvious as this seems, many people think that they know best when it comes to satisfying customers. Research should be conducted on an ongoing basis, both formally and informally, to understand the needs, motives, and expectations of existing and potential customers.

---

### quick fact

55% of consumers say that at least once in the past 12 months a bad food-service experience led them to vow never to return. Among families with children, the figure is 60%.

*Source:* Foodservice 411 (*R&I* 2004 Tastes of America Survey), November 5, 2005, *http://www.foodservice411.com/rimag/archives/2005/10a/consumer-loyalty.asp?dt=1*

---

**Upward Communication.**   Too often, communication is primarily downward from management to employee. Managers may think that they should know the answers to operational problems without having to ask employees. For others it is beneath them to seek guidance from their subordinates. Yet front-of-the-house employees have much more contact with customers than does management. They are in the best position to identify which features of the operation and menu please customers and which turn them off. To put such a system in place requires overt action on the part of the manager. Suggestions have to be encouraged from customer-contact employees. A system put in place to reward any idea about improving service will produce more ideas than a system to reward only good (in the eyes of management) ideas. Good ideas have to be rewarded and implemented if management wants the flow of ideas to continue.

The success of such a system will depend, to a large extent, on how management handles bad news—feedback about service problems. If the orientation is to find out who messed up and to punish the offender, employees will be reluctant to report bad news to management. On the other hand, if the emphasis is to find out why the mistake happened and improving procedures to ensure that it does not happen again, employees will be more willing to share with management.

**Levels of Management.**   The farther that decision makers are from the customer, the greater is the likelihood that they will be out of touch with what is important to the customer. Many companies are flattening their organizational structure, getting rid of middle management, in a dual attempt to cut costs and get closer to the customer.

## Lack of Standards

Appropriate service standards may not be set if management does not believe service quality to be a strategic goal, if management thinks that customer expectations cannot be met, if service cannot be standardized, or if standards are set based on management, rather than customer, expectations.

**Management Commitment.** As noted earlier, J. C. Penney has been credited with saying, "If you satisfy the customers but fail to get the profit, you'll soon be out of business; if you get the profit but fail to satisfy the customers, you'll soon be out of customers." The question is, Which comes first—profits or customers? Restaurants are in business to make money. Will the provision of quality service result in profitability? In their book, *In Search of Excellence,* Peters and Waterman[7] compared the bottom-line profitability of companies that stressed financial goals—return on investment, net profit, and so on—with those that stressed nonfinancial goals—cleanliness, quality, and service, for example. They found that the companies that stressed nonfinancial goals actually produced better bottom-line results than companies that stressed financial goals. A major reason, they argued, was that employees could relate more to such things as quality and service than to return on investment and were more likely to support a program to improve these things than to get behind an effort to improve profit.

First, then, management has to set quality service as an important strategic goal. According to Zeithaml and colleagues, there are five dimensions of service:[8]

1. **Tangibles:** Appearance of physical facilities, equipment, personnel, and communication materials
2. **Reliability:** Ability to perform the promised service dependably and accurately
3. **Responsiveness:** Willingness to help customers and provide prompt service
4. **Assurance:** Knowledge and courtesy of employees and their ability to convey trust and confidence
5. **Empathy:** Caring, individualized attention provided to customers

Tangibles in a restaurant setting might refer to the cleanliness of the restrooms, the personal hygiene of employees, and the ease with which the bill can be understood. Reliability covers such things as a table being available at the time the customer was told it would be available, a steak being cooked as ordered, and the bill being free of errors. When employees correct problems immediately or when they show a willingness to answer customer questions about the menu, the company is demonstrating its responsiveness to the customer. Assurance comes from such things as employees demonstrating their knowledge and competence, being polite and friendly, and offering guarantees of satisfaction. Empathy is shown by employees being approachable, talking to customers in

**Learning Objective:** Specify the gaps that explain customer dissatisfaction with service and suggest ways to close these gaps.

Brian Sill is the president of Deterministics, a restaurant consulting and design firm. Interested in how design affects service, he researched and developed the Ten Commandments of Service Design. The Commandments outline ways to construct service effectively while closing the gaps among management, server, and the guest.

A summarized version of The Ten Commandments of Service Design follows:

1. **Create a schedule.** Knowing the number of courses ordered and cooking time per menu item enables a smooth and timely deliverance of service.
2. **Timing is key.** Each aspect of service from greeting to dropping the check should be methodical without leaving the guest looking or waiting for the server's attention.
3. **Read the guest.** Looking for certain body language or being aware of special occasions improves the chances of delivering the type of service the guest expects.
4. **Give them control.** Making suggestions and providing alternatives and the guest will feel in control when making the final decision.
5. **Service should be seamless.** Understanding the needs and expectations of the guest helps build a relationship that enhances the flow of service.
6. **Capabilities ought to be considered.** Management must know the potential of every server in order to avoid poor service and upset customers.
7. **Be consistent.** A reliable server will ensure a satisfied customer.
8. **Communication must not be underestimated.** Front-of-the-house to back-of-the-house, guest to server, everyone must know what is going on at all times or the chance of chaos increases.
9. **Gratuities are not included.** However, successful service delivery will come back in the form of a financial reward.
10. **A guest will not forget.** A request for a specific server is directly related to an exceptional service experience.

*Source:* Sill, Brian, "Ten Commandments of Service Will Spare You from Sins of Overpromising, Underdelivering." *Nation's Restaurant News*, vol. 38, no. 15, pp. 26, 84, April 12, 2004.

**Discussion Question:** In what ways do The Ten Commandments of Service Design close the gaps associated with service?

language they can understand, and making an effort to understand the needs of the customer.

Surveys of customers of various service companies (which did not include the restaurant industry) indicated that of the five factors just mentioned, reliability was the most important factor, followed by responsiveness; tangibles was regarded as the least important of the five factors, although all five are regarded by customers as being critical. In another study of tourism industries,[9] the two most important expectations concerning service were (on a scale of 1 to 7):

Restaurants—assurance (6.33) and reliability (6.18)

For performance, the highest ratings were

Restaurants—tangibles (5.69) and assurance (5.43)

## Setting Service Standards

Martin suggests that service standards need to be developed in two areas: procedural and convivial.[10]

**Procedural Aspects.**  The procedural part of service consists of what is involved in getting the products and services to the customer and consists of

- Incremental flow of service
- Timeliness
- Accommodation
- Anticipation
- Communication
- Customer feedback
- Supervision

*Incremental Flow of Service.*  This first aspect of the procedural dimension of service is concerned with ensuring that there are no bottlenecks in any part of the restaurant. A slowdown in service can occur because one part of the service system is overloaded. An inexperienced bartender may result in drink orders arriving long after the food has been served; overloading one server with too many tables in too short a time may mean slow service for his or her customers while other servers are underworked; it might also mean that in one station, all the tables are ready for their entrées at the same time. The result of any or all of these is poor service.

Standards can be set to help ensure that a breakdown in service does not occur. Customers can be seated in alternate sections, thereby ensuring an even spread of people throughout the restaurant. Within a particular section this will help ensure that each party is at a different stage of the meal: some being seated, others having appetizers, others enjoying entrées, with some relaxing over coffee.

## A Day in the Life: Emile Blau

After 20 years at Atlanta's original steak and lobster house Bones, Emile Blau decided to join the Buckhead Life Restaurant Group. He acts as general manager of Chops and The Lobster Bar as well as The Club at Chops, a members-only cigar bar and restaurant. The three luxury dining establishments are located in the same building and operate within 6,000 square feet of each other. All of the restaurants combined have the capacity to serve 300 guests between 400 and 700 meals a day. Blau is committed to providing his clientele with quality service and food characteristic of an average dinner check of $70.00.

In order to maintain the standards of Chops and The Lobster Bar, Blau has a lot to accomplish in a single day. He begins his routine at 9 A.M. by greeting the lunch sous chef and unlocking his office. Blau verifies the steak inventory and proceeds to make any necessary orders. He checks the reservations for lunch and dinner and reviews any notes made during previous service periods. Blau then follows up on any previous problems and makes phone calls to customers and associates.

At 11:30 A.M., Blau addresses the staff during line-up before each shift. During line-up, questions are asked and answered, "corrective and positive feedback" is given, and words of motivation and relevant service points are exchanged. During service, Blau can be found on the floor welcoming new guests and greeting regulars. When business slows for a bit, he goes back to his office to take care of any other business.

During his 12 hour day, Emile Blau writes personalized letters to new customers, returns customer calls, and replies to emails regarding any requests or problems. The layout of his day emphasizes his dedication to two goals: quality food service and profit maximization. Blau agrees that some would call this hard work; however, he has a passion for his work at Chops and The Lobster House.

*Source:* Hayes, Jack, "Emile Blau: Raising the Stakes at Chops with Polished Hospitality," *Nation's Restaurant News,* vol. 37, no. 16, pp 46–48, April 21, 2003.

**Discussion Question:** What are some things that general managers can do to ensure customer satisfaction?

***Timeliness.*** Timeliness means giving customers the service they want when they are ready for it. This involves setting standards as relative to how long a customer should wait before being greeted, before being seated, and before a food and a beverage order is taken and delivered. Notations of the time made on the order pad can serve as a way of measuring whether or not standards are being met.

*Accommodation.*  Accommodation implies that procedures are designed around the customer rather than around the restaurant or its employees. Often a customer will have a drink in the bar before dinner. The customer is then told that the bar charge cannot be transferred onto the dinner bill. It would be easier for the customer to pay one bill at the end of the night. The reason typically given is that the bar's computer system is different from that of the dining room. The obvious response from the customer's viewpoint might be, "Buy a system that is compatible and that makes it easy for the guest."

In many cases the real reason for this policy is to ensure that the bar server receives the tip for providing service in the bar. Here we have an example of a policy that is designed to accommodate the property and/or the employees rather than to serve the guest.

Another example is that of menu substitutions. Substitutions may either not be allowed or be actively discouraged because they make things more confusing for the server and cooks. The question needs to be asked, Who is most important—the customer or the employee?

An accommodating policy standard would be one that allows bar tabs to be transferred to the dining room, that allows menu substitutions, and that makes every effort to meet the needs of the customer.

*Anticipation.*  Anticipation ensures that customers never have to ask for something—that service is provided before customers request it. Whenever customers have to ask for something, service is less than perfect. When customers arrive with little children, booster chairs should appear automatically. Servers should come by with something to keep the child occupied while the meal is being prepared. Customers should be asked about water and/or wine refills before a request is made, typically when the glass is one-fourth full. When a customer has to ask for something, the server has failed to anticipate the needs of the guest.

*Communication.*  The provision of top-notch service requires effort on the parts of many people: servers, bussers, chefs, and management. Accurate, complete, and timely information is required among all parties to ensure customer satisfaction. Standards must be set to ensure, among other things, that customers understand servers, that cooks can read the written orders of servers, and that customers receive exactly what they ordered.

*Customer Feedback.*  To determine whether or not customers are satisfied with the level of service provided, it is necessary to get a reaction from them. At some point in the meal, every customer should be asked how it is and management should be made aware of any and every complaint. Often this is done in a perfunctory way. The first mouthful of food has barely been chewed when someone arrives to inquire about the food. A typical customer response is "fine" or "OK" and the employee leaves. This is not enough if the true intent of the question is to get customer feedback.

The natural tendency when there is a minor problem is to mumble "fine," continue with the meal, and never return. Don Smith of Washington State University suggests that employees should ask, "Is everything *fantastic?*" This question would probably elicit fewer noncommittal responses. A more subtle method would be for the employee to take note of the tone of voice and body language used by the customer in responding. A person given minimal training in nonverbal communication can tell whether or not an honest response is being given.

The truth is, however, that many employees do not want to hear about problems. If something is wrong, the employee will be expected to take care of it. This will slow down service for the other tables. Worse still, the manager may find out about the problem and blame the employee. This point is explored in more detail later in this chapter.

*Supervision.* The six elements of service noted previously will not happen smoothly unless the efforts of the staff are coordinated and monitored. This is the task of the dining room supervisor.

While an increasing number of companies are "empowering" their employees to handle any problems that arise, customers appreciate seeing and hearing from a "manager type" in the dining room. It is a mark of status to have a manager rather than an employee available. Where this is important to the level of service being provided or the type of customer being catered to, it may be desirable to have a supervisor check with each table at least once during the service.

As with all of the convivial elements of service, quantifiable standards are more difficult to develop than are procedural dimensions. The key is to identify, preferably with the help of employees and customers, the visible, measurable behaviors that are examples of the various factors.

**Convivial Aspects.** The convivial dimension of service is comprised of

- Attitude
- Body language
- Tone of voice
- Tact
- Naming names
- Attentiveness
- Guidance
- Suggestive selling
- Problem solving

*Attitude.* Attitude, the first element of the convivial dimension of service, refers to the way people act, think, and/or feel and is expressed through the way they act and the things they say. A smile is a visible manifestation of a positive attitude. Thus a standard could be set that in all interactions with customers, employees should exhibit a smile before talking.

*Body Language.* People communicate much more through nonverbal communication than through the words that are used. Entire books have been written on the subject of body language. One point that is usually made is the desirability to maintain eye contact with the person being spoken to. This can be yet another standard of quality service.

*Tone of Voice.*   The second most important way in which people communicate is through the inflections used in speaking. Although difficult to measure, standards can be set to ensure that servers communicate in an enthusiastic, friendly, and/or upbeat way, depending on the type of atmosphere desired by management.

*Tact.*   Tact involves saying the correct thing at the right time. Standards can be set regarding proper etiquette for various situations. This will include the terms used to address people, how to respond to complaints and special orders, the avoidance of restaurant slang in front of customers, how to handle unruly customers, and so on.

*Naming Names.*   We all like to think of ourselves as individuals. One way that service people can communicate individuality to customers is to call them by name. Standards can be set such that an individual is called by name when being seated by the host or hostess as well as when a credit card or check is being used to pay for the meal.

*Attentiveness.*   Attentiveness implies that people are treated as individuals, not just numbers. It goes beyond calling people by name but means that service is adjusted to the special needs of the individual patron. Servers can be told to inquire, at the beginning of the meal, whether there are any particular restrictions on the party, such as requiring quick service to make the opening curtain of a play, or whether this is a special occasion. The latter situation is often self-evident, as when a large family group enters the restaurant with presents for the guest of honor. Management would want the server to follow up on the inquiry to make whatever adjustments were necessary to provide individualized treatment. In the former case, service would be speeded up; in the latter situation, a birthday treat might be provided on the house.

*Guidance.*   When customers are perplexed about what to do or to order, the convivial server offers appropriate suggestions. To offer guidance, service personnel would have to be familiar with all the dishes on the menu, including the ingredients and the method of preparation and suggest items appropriate to the various perceived needs of the customers. This effort is hindered by management that refuses to allow servers to taste-test items—both food and wine—on the menu. The server, when asked what is good, is left to respond rather weakly, "Everything is" or (more truthfully) "I don't know; I haven't tasted anything."

*Suggestive Selling.*   Some people think of selling as pushing unwanted choices on someone. The servers' job is, in part, to expose customers to items that might enhance the experience of the meal. Effective suggestive selling results in a higher check. What should be set as a standard, however, is that servers ask all customers if they would like appetizers, drinks, desserts, and other specialty items. Further, servers should describe the benefits of these choices in ways that paint a verbal picture of them. Not everyone who is asked will buy dessert. But no one will buy if they are not invited to. Servers might ask, "Can I get you a glass of Pinot Grigio this evening or maybe you'd like to try one of our other award-winning wines?"

At the same time some customers are turned off by an approach that can be too flowery. Attentive servers look to the host/hostess for cues. A frown probably indicates that the host/hostess wants to make the decisions based on what he or she considers the rest of the party will like. At that point the server should present the menus and let the customer take charge.

Finally, the importance of showing the menu item can be the best type of selling. Bringing a dessert tray to the table so customers can see the choices will increase the likelihood of a sale. It's a lot harder to refuse "Tempura Fried Apples with Cinnamon Ice Cream and California Raisin-Pistachio Compote" once it is seen up close.

*Problem Solving.* Finally, service providers are there to solve any problems that might arise. Rather than taking the attitude, "I don't want to hear

---

## quick bite 6.6
### Dimensions of Service

**Learning Objective:** Identify the various procedural and convivial dimensions of service.

Casual restaurants constantly look for ways to offer a unique experience to the customer. Owners and managers strive to reinvent aspects of the restaurant to make them distinct from the competition. Becoming increasingly popular within the industry is tableside service.

What exactly makes service tableside? While interaction between server and guest is a large portion of the guest experience, preparing simple menu items tableside adds entertainment to the typical appetizer or entrée. Tableside service promotes suggestive selling, guest and server interaction, and individual guest attention.

The Mexican Shrimp Martini is the number one seller on the menu of Rockfish Seafood Grill, a casual-dining restaurant based in Dallas. The appetizer's popularity stems from its tableside preparation. After the server brings all of the ingredients to the table, customers specify what they want included in the dish. All of the ingredients are shaken in a shaker and poured into a martini glass. Customers also have the option of adding a shot of tequila for extra zing.

Tableside service is a good service concept because customers are involved in the preparation from the beginning to the end. They receive individual attention from their server as well as positive attention from neighboring tables. This type of service allows servers extra time to get to know their customers and offer them suggestions and/or recommendations. Tableside service, by its interactive nature, offers a whole new dimension to the concept of service.

*Source:* Duecy, Erica, "Tableside Trends in Tip-Top Shape: Operators Add Upscale 'Wow Factor' to Menus," *www.nrn.com/foodtrends/index.cfm?ID=794540492*, April 14, 2004.

**Discussion Question:** How does tableside service enable a server to shape the guest experience?

---

about any problems you are having with the meal," employees have an obligation to identify any problems that customers are having. This provides them with the opportunity to solve these problems and ensure a satisfied customer.

Problems will occur in any setting. The measure of excellent service is what happens after the problem is noted. Earlier we noted the desirability of identifying problems. At this point attention turns to the resolution of these problems. Standards can be set such that within the boundaries of reason and the law, every problem brought to the attention of an employee and/or management is dealt with to the satisfaction of the customer. Will this result in some customers taking advantage of the situation to get a discount or a free meal? Undoubtedly, yes. However, the cost involved will be small compared to the goodwill gained from attending to the real concerns of the restaurant patrons.

***Feasibility.*** One reason that goals are not set is management's perception that customer expectations cannot be met. While customer expectations are seen as limitless, the resources of the company are not. Certainly, businesses have to make money. They do so by satisfying the customer. Too many managers use the idea of unlimited customer expectations as an excuse to maintain the status quo. If, in fact, satisfaction equals perception minus expectations,[11] satisfaction is increased if expectations are lowered or perceptions are heightened.

The problem of attracting customers if expectations are lowered was noted earlier. It may, however, be possible to change the perception of the customers to increase satisfaction. Take as an example the problem of waiting. Given the fact that in a restaurant, supply is fixed in the short run and demand is variable, there will be times when there are more customers than tables available and a wait ensues. Management may take the view that nothing can be done to alleviate the situation.

Yet there are various principles of waiting that management can utilize to improve customer perceptions of service. Maister has identified eight such principles.[12] First, unoccupied time feels longer than occupied time. To reduce the perception of the wait, various strategies can be used. Menus can be handed out while customers are waiting for a table; the waiting area can be the bar, typically a scene of activity; and/or entertainment can be provided to occupy the time of the waiting patrons. The activity provided, according to Maister, should offer intrinsic benefit as well as being somehow related to the meal experience.

Second, the same amount of time after service has ended seems longer than that before service has begun, which, in turn, seems longer than that endured during service. In other words, a five-minute wait after the meal has ended and customers are waiting for the bill seems longer than a five-minute wait for a table, which seems longer than a five-minute wait between courses.

Handing out menus as soon as people arrive gives the impression that the meal service has begun. Consequently, the wait appears shorter than it really is. Even when customers are seated, it is wise to bring water, menus, or, at least, acknowledge the customers' presence to let them know that they have not been forgotten.

Air travelers flying to an international destination are typically instructed to report to the airport two to three hours before takeoff. A series of activities helps to convince them that the "flight experience" has begun. Baggage is checked; they go through passport control; they are told to report to the international departure lounge; they go to shop duty free; they report to the gate. Each activity piece divides up a large block of time while attempting to give the impression that the "flight" has begun.

Third, anxiety makes the wait seem longer. Customers worry about such things as whether or not they have been forgotten, whether others are being seated out of turn before them, or whether they will still be able to eat and make the opening curtain of a play they intend to see after the meal. The idea is to be aware of the fact that customers have worries that are both rational and irrational, to identify them, and to seek to reassure the customer. Checking with people by name and giving them progress reports on the wait indicates that they have not been forgotten; asking if they have a deadline and indicating that they will have plenty of time to make it (if, in fact, that is the case) can also alleviate tension.

Fourth, uncertain waits are longer than known waits. When a customer makes a reservation for 7:30 P.M., the expectation is that a table will be ready at that time. The customer may arrive 30 minutes early, wait contentedly for the 30 minutes, but get very agitated at having to wait 10 minutes beyond the deadline. Yet restaurants may have parties who linger over a meal. They cannot be eased out. Some operations choose to handle this situation by refusing to take reservations. On the surface this seems fair. Yet the absence of a reservation system will be a turnoff for many, particularly if they travel a significant distance to the restaurant.

Another problem occurs when people who have made reservations do not show up, but the table is kept for them even as others wait. In taking reservations, a small number of operations ask for a credit card number and charge $10 per person against the card. The amount charged is credited to the bill for the meal. If the party does not show up, the $10 per person goes on their bill.

One thing that can be done is to let the customer know specifically how long the delay will be. "Your table will be ready in 10 minutes" is better than "Your table will be ready in a few minutes."

Fifth, closely related to the aforementioned principle is the idea that unexplained waits are longer than explained waits. Not knowing why there is a delay creates a feeling of powerlessness. Customers are angry because employees do not share the reason for the delay. Respect the customer by sharing this information.

Sixth, unfair waits seem longer than equitable waits. In a restaurant situation there are two typical problem areas. The first occurs because restaurants have a limited number of tables for two, four, or more people. Customers are seated by matching the number in the party to the size of the table. From an operational viewpoint it does not make sense to seat a party of two at a table for six. Thus, even if the larger party came in later than the party of two, they would be seated before them. This seems unfair to the smaller group.

The second situation arises when a host or hostess is responsible for answering the phone in addition to seating people. Who has priority when the phone rings just as a table is about to be seated? The people who are there may resent the fact that a potential customer on the other end of the phone is receiving a higher priority than they—the actual customers—are receiving.

The point is that customers have a sense of equity that may be different from that of management. This must be recognized and managed. In general, this means matching the policy to the customer's feeling of equity or persuading the customer that the rules are fitting. In the preceding examples, the policy regarding seating can be explained to the customer. In the latter case the customer who is present should be given preference. This might involve having another employee who is nearby seat the customer while the host or hostess responds to the call or by putting the person phoning on hold or transferring the call while the party is seated.

The seventh principle indicates that the more valuable the service, the longer people will wait. Airlines segregate lines based on those with simple transactions—seat selection—and those who have more complex arrangements to make—ticket purchase. Supermarkets also have express checkout lines for people buying a limited number of items. In a restaurant situation a bar area may be set aside for snacks and light meals. Those wishing to spend a little can be seated immediately in the bar, while those desiring a larger meal will be willing to wait for a seat in the dining area.

Finally, solo waits are longer than group waits. Although there is little that an operation can do in this regard, it is wise to note that people waiting alone will experience the wait to be longer than will those in groups, so more attention should be paid to alleviating their concerns.

*Standardization.* Some argue that because service is intangible and delivered individually, it cannot be standardized. Standards can be developed for a recipe, but how, it is argued, can a smile or a tone of voice be standardized?

Service standardization can occur with the use of hard or soft technology or with a combination.[13] Pizza Hut uses hard technology to improve its service. Instead of having order taking, baking, and delivery in all its stores, order taking is centralized and computerized in a customer-service center. With a database that shows what has been ordered in the past, an operator can take an order and verify directions to the house of the customer in an average of 17 seconds. The order is then delivered electronically to the store nearest the customer's house,

## quick bite 6.7
### Accommodating the Waiting

**Learning Objective:** Describe the principles of waiting.

Dining out has always been a social event. Unfortunately, after the hostess asks for the number in the party, smoking preference, and a name, a wait is certain. For the guest, waiting for a table can be a time filled with uncertainty and anxiety. However, restaurants are making an effort to make waiting a pleasurable and entertaining part of the dining experience.

Perry's, a steak and seafood restaurant in Dallas, understands the frustration that is associated with waiting. Because the owners of Perry's sympathize with the feelings of their guests, they have designed the restaurant to accommodate waiting. The bar area has a 27-seat bar that caters to long waits and those who prefer the option of dining at the bar instead of putting a name on the list.

If the restaurant provides a comfortable place to pass time, it benefits the guest tremendously. Waiting guests can alleviate their boredom and tension by ordering drinks, finding a comfortable place to sit or stand, and enjoying some light conversation with others. This takes their attention off waiting and facilitates the social side of the dining experience.

For the restaurant, inviting the guest to enjoy a drink at the bar is another form of suggestive selling. Waiting guests will be increasing sales in the bar and having a good time instead of continually asking where their name is on the list. Also, having a place specifically for waiting reduces crowding and confusion by the host stand.

Ideally, all dining experiences should be pleasurable. The restaurant should provide guests who are waiting with options other than standing by the host stand or staring at a watch. Instead of watching the minutes pass by, guests should enjoy the amenities offered by the restaurant.

*Source:* Ruggless, Ron, "Perry's Dishes Up Helping of Service, Variety and Ambience." *Nation's Restaurant News,* vol. 36, no. 35, p. 22, September 2, 2002.

**Discussion Question:** What problems can be avoided by providing the guest with a place to pass time during a wait?

from where it is baked and delivered usually in less than a half-hour from the order being phoned in.

Self-service salad bars exemplify the use of soft technology. By passing some of the service tasks to the customer, management diverts some of the responsibility for service from the operation and its employees to the customer.

***Customer Requirements.*** The concept of a perceptual map was developed in Chapter 3. A perceptual map is drawn indicating what customers consider important when dining out and how they perceive the job the restaurant does in meeting these expectations. This approach ensures a focus on what the customers think is important rather than on what management thinks is important.

Goals should be set that are as follows:[14]

- Designed to meet customer expectations
- Specific
- Accepted by employees
- Designed to cover the important dimensions of the job
- Measured and reviewed with appropriate feedback to the employee
- Challenging but realistic

Who should set the goals? In a customer-oriented operation, customers would be asked what they consider to be the main features of excellent service. They can then give examples of specific behaviors that employees would exhibit when giving excellent service. These behaviors can serve as the basis for setting standards for employee service.

Employee acceptance can come from involving them in setting quality service standards. Employees can also be asked to give examples of specific behaviors that would indicate, for example, that employees were displaying a positive service attitude toward customers. These behaviors, as identified by the employees themselves, become the standards by which quality service is provided.

## Lack of Performance

Even when service standards have been determined, they may not be carried out by the employees whose task it is to deliver them. In fine dining establishments, service work is handled by one of four people: captain, front server, back server, or busser.[15] The positions of front and back servers are commonly combined into one job. Various operations will, in addition, combine the functions of their employees such that, for example, servers also bus tables or act as their own captains. This designation is useful, as it focuses attention on what has to be done in providing the highest level of service. Management can then tailor these functions to the level of service provided in their operations.

**Busser.** The busser is responsible for:[16]

- Setup of the station
- Water, coffee, and tea service
- Bread and butter service
- Clearing of soiled dishes, glassware, and flatware from tables
- Resetting of tables

**Server.**   A server is responsible for three things:[17]

- Representing the operation to the customer
- Selling the dining experience, including food and beverage items, to the customer
- Delivering on that promise

**Captain.**   In an upscale restaurant the captain is in charge of a serving team consisting of several servers and bussers and a specific station consisting of a number of tables. The captain is responsible for ensuring that customers receive the level of service that is proper for the establishment. Captains coordinate the efforts of servers and bussers in providing the desired service.

The captain will

- Take the order for food and beverages
- Use suggestive selling to increase the average check
- Perform any tableside cooking necessary
- Stagger seating within the section to ensure that no server is overloaded

There are a number of potential reasons why employees will not produce the service expected by management.[18] Employees may lack the information and/or training to do the job; they may feel they cannot possibly satisfy all the demands placed on them by the variety of people they must please; the skills of the employee may be wrong for the job that he or she is in; employees may not have the tools to perform up to the standards set; the supervisory control system may reward actions inconsistent with the provision of excellent service; employees may feel that they have insufficient control over their ability to deliver service; and employees and management may not be pulling, as a team, in the same direction.

**Information and Training.**   When employees do not know what management expects from them or how to go about satisfying management's expectations, they experience role ambiguity. Ambiguity is a result of the employees being given insufficient information and/or training to perform their jobs. Employees need to know what they are supposed to do, what parts of the job to focus on, how and for what they will be rewarded, and how well or how poorly they are performing. If skills are lacking, it is management's responsibility to train employees so that they can provide the level of service expected by management.

In the restaurant business there is a heavy reliance on on-the-job training. Many think this means following an experienced server around for a few days to observe what they do. Yet on-the-job training requires as much care in the planning as do more formal training methods. The design and implementation of an on-the-job training program are described in Chapter 13.

**Satisfying Demands.** The job of customer-contact employees is made more difficult by the fact that they have, at minimum, two bosses: the manager, who hired and can fire them; and the customer, who they are expected to please and who probably accounts for most of the employee's pay through tips.

When employees feel they cannot satisfy all the demands placed on them by the people—management and customers—they are responsible to, they experience role conflict. The expectations of management and customers may be very different (but they should not be!). Customers want service; management wants a higher average check. Customers want leisurely service; management wants turnover. Customers want more service; management, in an attempt to save money, has increased server station size to a point where personal attention is reduced.

Customers themselves are very different in their needs and wants. The term *contact overload* has been coined to refer to the emotional "work" that comes from having to deal with too many customers over a prolonged period of time. The result can be emotional burnout, resulting in emotionless employees. The problem is compounded by the fact that servers have to rely on other employees to provide excellent service. When items are held up in the kitchen or are cooked improperly, the result is a less than satisfactory experience for the customer through no fault of the employee.

Role conflict can be reduced by setting employee standards and behavior based on the expectations of customers rather than those of management. If employees know that given a conflict between what management wants and what customers want, the customer prevails, they can go about their work with less confusion. Take, for example, the customer who complains that a steak is not cooked to his or her satisfaction. If employees know that the customer is always right, neither server nor cook will attempt to argue with the customer. Servers will know that they can go back to the kitchen without getting an argument from the cook. Similarly, if in this situation, the server decides to make an adjustment in the customer's bill, the server will know that he or she will be backed up by management rather than chided for "giving away something" and thus increasing costs.

By actually involving employees in the setting of service standards, some believe that standards will be set that are higher than would have been set by management alone. In addition, employees are more committed to achieving these standards because they were involved in their setting. This point is made in Chapter 14 in a discussion of management by objectives (MBO). The basic premise behind MBO is that employees will work toward meeting objectives to which they are committed. The way to get that commitment is to involve employees in the setting of objectives.

**Employee–Job Fit.** The basic skills used in any restaurant service are as follows:[19]

- Loading and carrying a tray with food and/or beverages
- Loading and carrying a bus box or tray with soiled wares
- Handling serviceware
- Clearing a table during service

Ruth's Chris Steak House.

In more upscale settings, restaurant personnel will also be called upon to perform Russian or French service and to reset a table during service. Russian service consists of using a spoon and fork to serve from a platter, while in French service, a serving spoon and fork are used to serve a plate from a cart. Resetting a table during service includes changing the tablecloth with minimum disturbance.

In addition to the technical skills of service, dealing with the public requires certain skills not needed for employees in back-of-the-house positions.[20] Successful service providers possess interpersonal skills, demonstrate behavioral flexibility and adaptability, and show empathy.

Education in college programs and training on the job tend to focus more on providing technical skills than interpersonal skills. Yet successful service depends more on the latter than the former. Such skills can either be "bought" by hiring people who possess these skills or developed through training.

Servers who are successful are able to adapt their behavior to that of the guest and respond accordingly. So-called "flexible-focus" employees can be found through their scores on the Central Life Interest Measure.[21] Adaptable people would be low in dogmatism, high in tolerance for ambiguity, and/or high on self-monitoring. Simulations, assessment center techniques, and situational interviews are ways to determine the existence of all of these.

Finally, employees should demonstrate empathy—a temporary merging— with customers. Employees can demonstrate empathy through such techniques as repeating back to customers what they have heard and giving feedback that indicates an understanding of customer concerns.

Minor and Cichy suggest a number of open-ended questions suitable for identifying servers with service potential.[22]

| Question | Intent |
|---|---|
| How do you feel about working here? | How does the applicant feel about the company? |
| What is the most important responsibility of a server? Why? | What is the person's attitude about the job? |
| Who has more responsibility: a server or a cook? | Does the applicant appreciate the cook's job? |
| What are the most important qualifications of a server? | Does the applicant understand the responsibilities of the job? |
| Are servers usually fair to each other? | Can the applicant get along with people? |
| What would you do if a guest made insulting remarks to you? | Is the applicant easily upset? |
| Suppose the manager insists that you do a job a certain way when you know there is a better way to do it: What would you do? | What is the applicant's attitude toward authority? Toward supervisors? Is this person stubborn? |
| What do you think about servers who change jobs often? | Is this person a job hopper? |
| What is more important: courteous service or prompt service? | What is the applicant's attitude toward both? |
| What would you do if your tips were falling off? | Can you admit mistakes? |

## quick fact

The masterpiece of Russian cuisine is the "zakuski," or hors d'oeuvre, ceremony. Limited to the role of an overture in other cuisines, "zakuski" are the equivalent of a whole first movement in a formal dinner.

Depending upon the occasion and the financial position of the hosts, the "zakuski" menu may include:

one or more fish hors d'oeuvre
one or more meat hors d'oeuvre
one or more salads and vegetable hors d'oeuvre
one or more egg hors d'oeuvre
marinated and/or salt-pickled vegetables and mushrooms and marinated fruits (plums, apples, and others)
condiments: mustard, horseradish, and freshly ground pepper
fresh white and dark breads

*Source:* Anne Volokh, *The Art of Russian Cuisine* (New York: Collier Books, 1983), pp. 11–13.

Personal hygiene for service people is also critical. This involves the following:[23]

- A daily bath or shower
- Daily use of an effective deodorant or antiperspirant
- Clean hair restrained above the shoulders
- Clear or natural nail polish
- Clean fingernails
- No more than one ring per hand
- No ornate jewelry
- Avoid excessive cologne or perfume
- No gum chewing
- Moderate use of natural-looking makeup
- Clean uniform and well-polished shoes

Jobs that require customer contact tend to be rather low paying. This severely limits management in attracting highly skilled employees. Companies argue that because of low margins, they are unable to pay wages high enough to attract high-caliber employees. The result is that companies have to compromise in their hiring. For the customer, that often means less than desirable service.

Companies are beginning to learn that they get, in employees, what they pay for. There is anecdotal evidence that paying premium wages will result in employees with better skills and lower turnover and absenteeism. Whether or not the bottom line improves is a matter open to debate.

**Technology–Job Fit.**   Similarly, employees need the tools necessary to perform their jobs. Advances in technology have enabled servers to send customer orders to the kitchen by means of hand-held computers. As a result, servers are able to stay on the floor attending to customer needs and make fewer trips to the kitchen.

**Supervisory Control.**   If companies wish to improve service, they need to set up a supervisory system that rewards employees who exhibit behaviors that are regarded as providing quality service. Employees are expected to engage in suggestive selling, describing a dish in such a way that the likelihood of the customer ordering that dish increases. An employee may engage in suggestive selling, painting a verbal picture of that dish while accurately describing its contents.

Suppose the customer is full and does not order the dish. Should the employee be rewarded? In many operations employees are rewarded solely on the basis of results, such as the number of desserts sold. Yet this employee has engaged in high-quality service behaviors. The employee who sells the dessert may have used tactics to get the order that leave the customer unhappy.

To be successful, employee recognition programs must set challenging standards, be accepted by employees, have the right number of rewards, and be long lasting.[24] British Airways has identified for its middle managers 60 statements of behavior necessary for providing good-quality service. Their bonuses—worth 20 percent of their base pay—are determined half by their achievements and half by the behaviors used to get results.

**Employee Control.**   Employees experience less stress in their jobs when they feel that they have control over situations that occur in their work. Customer satisfaction with the service depends on the efforts of several people: the host or

---

## quick bite 6.8
### Serving and Marketing

**Learning Objective:** Describe the duties and responsibilities of captain, server, and busperson in providing quality service.

Getting people to walk into the restaurant is the first of the many challenges that operators face. The next challenge is giving customers a reason to come back. Restaurant operators must optimize atmosphere, food, and most importantly the staff to gain customer loyalty and repeat business.

Servers must be empowered by management. They must feel as though it is up to them to satisfy the guest with whatever it takes. Managers should emphasize marketing internally. In other words, the server is the best form of advertisement. The server should strive to exceed guest expectations; it is the best way of retaining customers.

Giving guests the "star treatment" no matter who they are is another way of creating guest loyalty. If you remember their names, chances are they will remember to come back. Servers can check the reservation book, credit card, or simply ask, "I'm sorry, what is your name?" Asking for a name is a great way of expressing interest in the guest and makes customer feel like their business matters.

The saying "eyes are often bigger than the stomach" holds true for customers, especially if they are hungry. Displaying the restaurant's dessert selection in plain sight of hungry guests is a great way to upsell. Informed staff members can effectively promote menu items or specials, make suggestions and provide quality service.

Restaurant operators should view the restaurant's staff as an asset. Servers have the ability to keep customers coming back—but they can also ensure that a guest will never return. Understanding the importance of the server's role in representing the dining establishment is key to creating the best customer experience possible.

*Source:* Asbury, Bill, and Jim Matorin, "Basic Training: Independents Must Teach Staffs Marketing, Customer Service Tactics to Survive," *Nation's Restaurant News,* vol. 36, no. 35, pp. 26, 28, September 2, 2002.

**Discussion Question:** How can the server combine service with marketing?

---

hostess who receives the reservation and has a table ready at the appointed time, the busser who has set the table in the proper manner, the cook who prepares the order, and the server who delivers it. Yet if there is a problem, it is the server who is the recipient of the complaint. Giving the server—or, for that matter, any employee—the authority to resolve the complaint is an example of employee empowerment. Employee empowerment entails pushing authority down to the lowest level possible. Instead of getting a manager to hear a complaint and to make a decision on how it should be resolved, the employee who gets the complaint owns that complaint and is responsible for solving it to the satisfaction of the customer. The result is a faster response to complaints and motivated employees who feel that they can control the delivery of high-quality service.

**Teamwork.**   In the restaurant business there are a number of traditional rivalries: management and employees; kitchen staff and waitstaff as a whole; dishwasher and busser as a specific. Quality service requires that everyone works together for the goal of good-quality service. Cooks may feel that their job is done when they cook the food even if the timing means that it is ready either before or after the customer is ready for it. Problems of timing? That is the concern of the server. Or consider the dining room that never seems to have enough silverware. Servers take to stashing a supply to take care of their individual stations.

The result of such practices is that employees feel they are working against one another instead of being united in a common goal. Management's task is to provide the climate for this unity to happen. Tom Peters has said that if employees are not serving the customer, they had better be serving someone who is. This type of attitude ensures that everyone realizes the importance of working together to serve the customer.

## Promising Too Much

It was noted earlier that customer expectations must be raised to a level high enough to motivate people to leave home and come to the restaurant. It is more difficult to sell a meal than a part for a car because if the part does not work, it can be returned and replaced. This is not true of a restaurant meal, which is consumed before the customer can determine whether or not it is all right.

This means that expectations have to be raised even higher for an intangible product such as food plus service than for a tangible good. This can lead to a tendency to promise too much in an attempt to get customers in the door. When customers come in with unrealistic expectations, employees may not be able to deliver, no matter how well they perform.

A second problem arises because of a lack of communication between those who sell the experience and those who are expected to deliver it. Employees who cook and serve the food must be involved in marketing decisions to provide a reality check on those who plan the advertising.

By the same token, employees should see what customers are being told in advertisements for the restaurant in order that they know what customers are being promised—promises they will be expected to deliver on.

## Plan of Attack

Where is the manager to begin? Closing all four gaps (lack of knowledge, lack of standards, lack of performance, and promising too much) may require time, money, and effort. If all four gaps exist, management would be wise to begin with the fourth gap, the tendency to promise too much.

It may not be possible to improve service immediately. In such a situation, the one thing that management can influence is customer expectations. It may, initially, be necessary to lower customer expectations to a level closer to the service provided. Care must be taken to ensure that the lowered expectations are high enough to induce patronage.

The other three gaps must be closed in order. Customer expectations have to be identified before standards can be set; appropriate standards must be set before they can be implemented.

---

### quick bite 6.9
### Road to the Top: Heather Coin

Heather Coin began her career in the restaurant industry as a sophomore at the University of California, Santa Barbara. By the time she graduated in 1994, Coin was in charge of four of the University's dining units: a coffee shop, a convenience store, a campus pub, and a deli. After graduation, the Chevys Fresh Mex Restaurant chain in Encino, California immediately hired her as kitchen manager. She was later promoted to general manager.

At the beginning of 2001, a headhunter visiting Chevys recruited Coin to the Cheesecake Factory's new location in Sherman Oaks. She accepted the offer as general manager of the 345-seat dining establishment. Two years after opening, Coin's restaurant was servicing 16,000 customers per week with sales exceeding $12 million annually.

The Cheesecake Factory quickly took notice of Coin's personal standards of quality, her drive, and her dedication to her staff. Her employee turnover rate had gone from 25 percent to 10 percent. Coin's ability to delegate earned her recognition as well as another promotion.

Heather Coin is currently the Cheesecake Factory's area manager. The restaurants she manages include three locations in California and three in Colorado. For eight years, Coin's emphasis on communication and staff development has helped her reach the top.

*Source:* Spielberg, Susan, "Heather Coin: Brain Food: Newly Promoted Area Manager Stresses the Importance of Working 'Smarter'," *Nation's Restaurant News,* vol. 38, no. 4, pp. 38–40, January 26, 2004.

**Discussion Question:** What are the qualities of a good manager that Heather Coin embodies?

# ENDNOTES

1. Stanley C. Hollander, "A Historical Perspective on the Service Encounter," in John A. Czepiel, Michael R. Solomon, and Carol F. Surprenant (eds.), *The Service Encounter: Managing Employee/Customer Interaction in Service Businesses* (Lexington, MA: DC Heath and Company, 1985), pp. 48–53.
2. "Rolling Out the Red Carpet: Restaurant Service Rates High with Diners," *Restaurants USA*, August 1997, pp. 39–41.
3. Jody D. Nyquist, Mary J. Bitner, and Bernard H. Booms, "Identifying Communication Difficulties in the Service Encounter: A Critical Incident Approach," in Czepiel et al., *The Service Encounter*, pp. 113–123.
4. Robert Reid, *Foodservice and Restaurant Marketing* (Boston: CBI Publishing Company, 1983), pp. 129–130.
5. *http://www.restauruantowner.com/public/295print.cfm*, accessed September 19, 2005.
6. Valarie A. Zeithaml, A. Parasuraman, and Leonard L. Berry, *Delivering Quality Service: Balancing Customer Perceptions and Expectations* (New York: Free Press, 1990), pp. 36–45.
7. Thomas J. Peters and Robert H. Waterman, Jr., *In Search of Excellence: Lessons from America's Best-Run Companies,* Harper Collins Publishers, New York, NY, 1982.
8. Zeithaml et al., *Delivering Quality Service*, pp. 21–22, 26.
9. Gavin R. Fick and J. R. Brent Ritchie, "Measuring Service Quality in the Travel and Tourism Industry," *Journal of Travel Research*, vol. 30, no. 2, 1991, pp. 2–9.
10. William B. Martin, *Quality Service: The Restaurant Manager's Bible* (Ithaca, NY: Cornell University Press, 1986), pp. 79–81.
11. David H. Maister, "The Psychology of Waiting Lines," in Czepiel et al., *The Service Encounter*, p. 114.
12. Ibid., pp. 113–123.
13. Zeithaml et al., *Delivering Quality Service*, pp. 80–82.
14. Ibid., pp. 84–86.
15. Bruce H. Axler and Carol A. Litrides, *Food and Beverage Service* (New York: John Wiley & Sons, 1990), p. xiii.
16. Ibid., p. 1.
17. Ibid., p. 59.
18. David H. Maister, "The Psychology of Waiting Lines," in Czepiel et al., *The Service Encounter*, pp. 89–113.
19. Axler and Litrides, *Food and Beverage Service*, p. xv.
20. David E. Bowen and Benjamin Schneider, "Boundary-Spanning-Role Employees and the Service Encounter: Some Guidelines for Management and Research," in Czepiel et al., *The Service Encounter*, pp. 137–139.
21. Ibid., pp. 144–147.
22. Lewis J. Minor and Ronald Cichy, *Foodservice Systems Management* (Westport, CT: AVI Publishing Company, 1984), p. 148.
23. Ibid., p. 150.
24. Zeithaml et al., *Delivering Quality Service*, p. 103.

# INTERNET RESOURCES

| | |
|---|---|
| Mystery Shopper Services | *http://www.mysteryshopperservices.com/* |
| TopServe Consulting | *http://www.topserveconsulting.com/training.html* |
| SuperServer Food Server Tips | *http://www.foodservertips.com/* |

# CHAPTER SEVEN

# THE PHYSICAL FACILITY

"I never eat in a restaurant that's over a hundred feet off the
ground and won't stand still."
Calvin Trillin, American journalist and novelist

## learning objectives

*By the end of this chapter you should be able to*

1. Identify the various elements of the immediate package and the external environment.

2. Show how elements of the immediate package can affect the psychological needs and behavior of customers.

3. Give examples of the ways that the size and shape of the room, seating arrangements, light, and color combine to influence customers.

4. Suggest procedures to improve existing layouts.

5. Develop more productive procedures for completing individual jobs.

# FRONT OF THE HOUSE: LAYOUT

The size of an operation will vary depending on the type of service to be provided and the extent of menu offerings: The more extensive the menu, the larger the operation tends to be. In the following estimates, the higher-range figures refer to facilities with more extensive menus and that allow for more room. It is recommended that the dining room space allowance per seat is as follows:[1]

| Service Type | Square Feet Required per Seat |
|---|---|
| Banquet (minimum) | 10 to 11 |
| Buffet | 12 to 18 |
| Family Style | 13 to 16 |
| Fast Food | 10 to 14 |
| Tableside (minimum) | 11 to 14 |
| Tableside (upscale) | 15 to 18 |
| Counter | 18 to 20 |

Additional recommended standard spacing allowances include the following:[2]

- At least 18 inches between backs of chairs
- 36 inches for service aisles
- At least 48 inches for main aisles
- At least 18 inches from the chair back to the table edge
- About 12 inches from the seat cushion to the underside of the table for leg room
- Wheelchair access requires at least 32 inches of aisle space and a table height of 27 inches high by 30 inches wide by 19 inches deep

The amount of space required for the dining area depends on the number of people to be seated at any one time and the square feet of space per seat. The former is, in turn, a function of the total number of people to be served within a given period of time and the turnover. Turnover is a measure of how many times a seat will be occupied during a given meal period and is usually expressed on a per-hour basis. It is, in essence, the average time a seat will be occupied during a particular time or meal period. If, for example, people stay an average of 30 minutes during lunch, the turnover is two times per hour. Turnover rates will vary depending on the time of day and the type of meal service. A dinner crowd will stay longer than a group of lunch people on a schedule. While turnover for the former might range from 1/2 to 1 (indicating an average stay of between 2 and 1 hours), regular table service tends to have an average turnover of 1 to 2 1/2.

Cafeterias average higher turnover, anywhere from 1 1/2 to 2 1/2 for commercial cafeterias to 2 to 3 for industrial or school cafeterias.

Where a high turnover is desired, the concept can be built into the design by[3]

- Using items that do not take long to prepare
- Using preprocessed items
- Using a high level of lighting and light colors in the serving area
- Arranging the tables close to each other
- Designing chairs that become uncomfortable after a short period of time
- Having enough employees to provide prompt service

The square feet per table is a function of the type of seating to be provided (the relative proportion of tables to booths to counters to banquettes), the table sizes and shapes that are preferred, how the tables will be arranged, the aisle space desired, and the number of serving stations required.

# FRONT OF THE HOUSE: ATMOSPHERE

Atmosphere is the general mood or tone set by the restaurant. While excellent food and beverage items are crucial to the success of any operation, the surrounding atmosphere can significantly add to or detract from the diner's enjoyment of the experience of the meal. Research studies have consistently identified the top four reasons influencing a decision to return to a restaurant:

- Quality of food
- Service
- Price
- Atmosphere

While food and beverage items are the basic product of a restaurant, they are "surrounded" by an immediate package that includes the table arrangements, furniture, and the provision of entertainment. This, in turn, is presented within an environment made up of the space, seating arrangements, lighting level, and the colors used. All elements have to come together to form a complete picture.

There is a difference between eating and dining. When customers go out to eat, their principal concern is the food and beverage items served, and their principal need is physiological. On the other hand, when people go out to dine, they want a complete meal experience and their needs are both physical and psychological. It is up to the atmosphere to cater to the psychological needs of the customer. This can be done in a variety of ways, by appealing to the guest through sight, touch, hearing, smell, temperature, and movement.[4] How people perceive and are affected by these elements make up, in their minds, the atmosphere of the restaurant.

It is also important that the elements that make up the atmosphere be designed in accordance with each other and that they bear in mind that customers will be present. The story is told of the modern Dutch painter, Mondrian, who was asked to design a stage set. Upon completing his work, he reportedly said, "The actors must read their lines from the wings: otherwise, they will spoil the set." An appropriately designed interior must include the presence of the customer as part of the final package.

Several elements of the immediate package are explored here: table arrangements, furniture, surface materials, and entertainment.

## Table Arrangements

The tabletop has been described as the center of the selling action—the silent sales promoter. The first impression for customers is visual and the first thing they see is the table setting. It is important to coordinate table settings to the mood of the restaurant: formal or informal; expensive or economical. The table arrangement should be an attractive blend of dinnerware, glassware, flatware, linens, and accessories.

**Dinnerware.**   Many operators stick with simpler dinnerware patterns in order that they not detract from the food. There are four basic shapes for china: rolled edge, narrow rim, coupe, and scalloped edge. It is difficult to set specific rules for choosing china because of the variety of available colors and patterns. However, it is important that the china chosen fit the mood of the restaurant. For example, the narrow rim or coupe is preferable for a contemporary setting. Similarly, a formal atmosphere deserves softer, more delicate shades and a lighter weight than a family-style restaurant. On the other hand, heavier plates give customers the impression that they are getting a lot of food. This is the same rationale that bars have when they serve beer in heavy-bottomed beer mugs.

The average piece of restaurant china is used approximately 7000 times and lasts about three years if handled properly. Operators should expect to replace 25 percent of their china every year due to breakage. In this regard, stock patterns of commercially made designs can be least expensive.

It is important to consider the total effect of the food item and the plate. Overfilled plates look cluttered and are messy; sparsely filled plates give an impression of poor value. Perceptually, the size of the item compared to the size of the plate can make the item appear to be a better or worse value. Consider Figure 7.1. In reality, both inner circles are the same size. However, the inner circle on the right appears to be larger because it is surrounded by a smaller setting. Similarly, the same food item placed on a smaller plate will appear to be larger. A strip steak placed on an oval-shaped plate with mashed potatoes piped the length of the steak will tend to accentuate the length of the steak.

Specialty dishes for specialty items add value to the item. For example, soups can be served in small crockpots, fish on a fish-shaped platter, and desserts in a variety of differently shaped glasses.

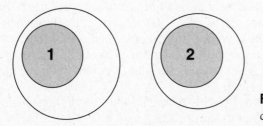

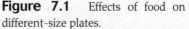

**Figure  7.1**   Effects of food on different-size plates.

Restaurants that cater to families with small children—for example, fast-food operations—will clear the table of most items, preferring to achieve the desired atmosphere through other means.

**Glassware.** Glassware is typically lime, or plain glass, and lead, or crystal glass. In selecting glassware, two things should be considered: design and color. Design encompasses such things as heavy or light, simple or ornate, stemmed or unstemmed. Rustic or family operations might call for a heavier weight or heavy-bottomed glass; fine dining establishments would select a finer, light-weight stemmed glass. Unusually shaped glasses are ways to add interest to the table. However, the more different types of glasses used, the greater the storage space needed.

Wine glasses can suggest that this is the type of facility where wine with the meal is appropriate. Favorite colors for glasses in restaurants are red, green, gold, and smoke blue. Colored glasses can help give a totally coordinated look to the table.

**Flatware.** In selecting flatware—knives, forks, and spoons—the basic decision comes down to a choice of silverplate or stainless steel. The latter is less expensive, although fine dining establishments may feel that silverplate is more in keeping with the atmosphere provided. In this case, consideration will have to be given to periodic burnishing or polishing. This can be done by machine, in a soaking bin, or by hand, but it must be planned for in the warewashing area.

Today's stainless pieces can be delicately embossed and carved to give the look and feel of silverplate. The important consideration is to select the best-quality flatware consistent with the type of restaurant. Some experts suggest that a stainless steel mix with 18 percent chrome and 8 percent nickel (18-8 stainless steel) gives excellent resistance to corrosion while giving off maximum luster.

**Linen.** Linens add to the feeling of quality within an operation. They come in a variety of colors that can be chosen to blend with the mood of the operation. Special attention should be given to flame retardancy, resistance to stains, color-fastness, and texture. Linen, polyester, cotton, or cotton–polyester blended napkins all feel different. Operators must determine what feels right for their facility. Resistance to stains is important because of the constant wear and tear inflicted on napkins. Linked to this is the colorfastness of the napery. If linens start out deep red and, after a few washings, the color fades, the combination of deep-red new napkins and faded-red older napkins will create a negative impression.

The cost of laundering can be greatly reduced by having a full table covering that remains during the meal period and a smaller piece overlaying this that can be changed after each party on an as needed basis. Inexpensive or family restaurants prefer no table covering, utilizing placemats for a touch of color.

The use of warm and inviting colors for place settings in institutions can take the edge off the sterile dining environment. A cloth or doily lining on a tray can also create a warm feeling.

In cafeteria dining it is possible to use Formica tops, such as imitation marble patterns, which tend not to show stains.

## quick bite 7.2
### Aesthetics and Appeal

**Learning Objective:** Show how elements of the immediate package can affect the psychological needs and behavior of customers.

At Ohio's Wild Ginger China Bistro, the design encompasses all aspects of the restaurant. The space is 4,000 square feet of casual yet sophisticated Asian-American décor. Close attention was paid to every detail, providing Wild Ginger with a "comfortable, inviting, and aesthetically appealing atmosphere."

The architecture of Wild Ginger is sleek and contemporary with windows and bi-level seating. The high, wide windows invite guests into the restaurant while creating a sense of openness and space for those inside. The bi-level seating is characterized by stairs and a low wall separating the seating areas.

Serving Chinese cuisine, Wild Ginger is adorned with traditional Chinese décor from finishes to fabrics kept minimal and spread throughout the restaurant. Materials like bamboo and ceramic floor tiles enhance the theme and the food. The color theme is muted and earthy with extensive use of the terra-cotta color palette, giving the customer a feeling of warmth and comfort. Lighting in the restaurant compliments the interior by giving off hues of orange and yellow.

Space, color, and design have been thought out carefully in order to obtain the desired effect for Wild Ginger's China Bistro. The architecture utilizes space in a manner that is both inviting and functional. Décor goes hand-in-hand with the cuisine and color, which both compliment the comfortable environment. Guests leave Wild Ginger with both stomachs and senses pleasantly filled.

*Source:* Wilson, Marianne, "Wild Ginger's Casual Sophistication," *Nation's Restaurant News,* vol. 2, no. 2, pp. 8–9, May 2003.

**Discussion Question:** Why is it important for the design of the restaurant to be carefully thought out?

**Accessories.** Many restaurants insist on covering the table with a variety of table tents advertising special menu items. Operators need to consider carefully whether or not these items produce increased sales or a cluttered image in the minds of the guest. Most texts advise against having too many table decorations. According to them, a flower vase, a candle or lamp, and an ashtray (if the table is in a smoking section) are the only "decorations" that should be on the table. On the other hand, a small bowl of nuts on the table can be a useful way of getting people to order drinks before a meal.

In addition, small touches to the table can add to the mood of the meal. Bringing a hot loaf of bread on a cutting board to the table accomplishes several things: It allows guests to participate in the meal; it keeps them busy during waits before the meal or between courses; and by allowing them to cut slices as thin or as thick as they wish, it gives some degree of freedom over part of the meal. At the same time, the smell of hot bread can act as a stimulant to the appetite.

## Furniture

The selection and placement of chairs, tables, and banquettes has a physical and a psychological dimension. The physical dimension involves having enough room to be comfortable; the psychological dimension involves the feeling the furniture gives the customer.

**Chairs.** Chair or banquette seats of breathable vinyl are practical, durable, and allow for easy maintenance. Placing fabric on the inside and outside back where there is less wear adds an attractive touch. Fabrics can be treated with either vinyl or acrylic coatings to make them more soil resistant and longer lasting.

Particular attention should be paid to firm construction in the legs and backs of chairs, as these factors influence how comfortable it feels to customers. Some restaurants specialize in the "15-minute chair"—so named because after 15 minutes it becomes uncomfortable and the customer is "reminded" that it is time to go. The idea for this chair came from Henning Larsen, who built it after consultation with Copenhagen cafe owners who determined that their customers loitered too long over their coffee. Conrad Hilton noticed that in the lobby of the Waldorf-Astoria, the comfortable divans were utilized every day by the same people. Although well dressed and well mannered, they were not spending money in the hotel. His solution was to move the comfortable divans into the nearest food and drink area of the hotel.

Chairs with arms make it easier to rise from the table. People can get up from a sitting position by pushing upward and outward until the body's center of gravity is moved forward to a position over the feet. This takes the strain off the leg muscles.

Traditional seating will appeal to a discerning clientele. Business travelers, who may walk on hard floors or pavements all day, will appreciate big plush chairs; hard plastic chairs and Formica tables will move people in and out very quickly.

Chairs should be selected in combination with the tables chosen. It is important, for example, that if armchairs are purchased, the arms fit under the tabletop. Although more comfortable, armchairs take up more space.

**Tables.** The most important characteristic of a table is that it should be sturdy. Tops should be a minimum of 1 inch thick. Most tables are made of flakeboard with a topping of a material such as Formica. While durable and practical, it tends to look "cheap" if left uncovered. If linens are not to be used, the only alternative is a solid wood top.

The shape of the table is also important. Round tables, because they offer more opportunity for eye contact with others around the table, promote more communication. This tends to slow down turnover but increases the check average. Rectangular tables do the opposite.

Many people prefer booths as seating. A booth will offer a feeling of privacy, something that may be important for sensitive business meetings or romantic meals. By extending the back of each booth to come behind the customer's head, the guest, when seated, cannot see into the other booths. A feeling of privacy is created.

## Surface Materials

The material used for surfaces can dramatically add to the atmosphere. The durability and characteristics of various surface materials are as follows:[5]

| Material | Life (Years) | Characteristics |
| --- | --- | --- |
| Concrete | 10+ | Can simulate more expensive materials after painting and sealing. Loud and hard walking surface; some consider it too stark; may crack. |
| Vinyl, tile squares | 8–10 | Comfortable to walk on; available in a number of colors and designs. Dirt collects where tiles meet; shows wear; not resistant to grease; requires frequent maintenance. |
| Vinyl, sheet | 10–15 | Available in a number of colors and designs; not grease resistant; shows traffic wear; seams are hard to clean. |
| Cork | 15+ | Excellent for high-moisture areas; deadens sound; resilient; limited U.S. history. |
| Bamboo | 5–15 | Variety of stain and sealer finishes; durable and resilient; can be refinished like wood; limited U.S. history. |
| Ceramic tile | 20+ | Adds color and elegance; doesn't easily wear out; slippery; loud, hard walking surface; easily chipped and broken; grout can discolor. |
| Slate | 10+ | Looks natural and elegant; never wears out; very porous; limited colors; loud, hard walking surface. |
| Carpet, olefin | 2 | Least expensive carpet choice; soft walking surface; quickly visually unattractive; absorbs grease. |
| Carpet, nylon | 3–7 | Good variety of colors, textures, and thicknesses; durable and easy to clean; deadens sound; variety of quality levels. |
| Carpet, wool | 7–10 | Longest-lasting carpet; elegant choice of designs and colors; harder to maintain; may shrink when wet. |
| Marble | 20+ | Looks elegant; very slippery; porous and stains easily; hard, loud walking surface; requires polishing and refinishing. |
| Granite | 20+ | Looks elegant; less porous than marble; limited colors. |
| Wood | Varies | Hardwoods last longer; warm and upscale look; hides soil; good walking surface; not so noisy; requires periodic refinishing; finish can peel or wear poorly; heels and table legs can cause dents. |
| Wood, simulated (vinyl laminate) | 5–25 | High-end appearance; low maintenance; good variety; needs level subsurface. |

## Entertainment

Providing the right kind of entertainment can influence customer enjoyment and customer behavior. In a dining situation the entertainment should complement the overall atmosphere in the operation. In some types of facilities the entertainment may be a major reason why people come in.

**Cost.** The cost of providing entertainment must be justifiable from a profit standpoint. The objective behind the provision of entertainment is that the cost involved will result in greater profits for the operation. This can come about in one of four ways. Customers who would not come in except for the entertainment can be drawn into the lounge and/or the restaurant; customers stay longer; they eat and/or drink more; or they come back again.

The cost of entertainment must produce a revenue increase greater than that cost. Consider the following example:

Before entertainment:

150 customers buy, on average, three drinks at $1.75 each.

Revenue produced each night = $ 787.50
$$\times \quad 6 \text{ nights}$$
4725.00

| | |
|---|---|
| Subtract cost of goods sold | 1181.25 |
| (assume 25%) | 3543.75 |
| Subtract payroll and related expenses | 350.00 |
| Gross operating profit | $3193.75 |

After entertainment:

182 customers buy, on average, three drinks at $1.75 each.

Revenue produced each night = $955.50
$$\times \quad 6 \text{ nights}$$
5733.00

| | |
|---|---|
| Subtract cost of goods sold | 1433.25 |
| (assume 25%) | 4299.75 |
| Subtract payroll and related expenses | 350.00 |
| Subtract cost of entertainment | 750.00 |
| Gross operating profit | $3199.75 |

Note that approximately $1000 in additional revenue must be generated in order to pay for the $750 in entertainment costs. This can be done by attracting more customers, charging higher drink prices during the entertainment, charging a cover charge to offset the entertainment cost, realizing an increase in beverage revenue because people stay longer and/or drink more, or having an increase in restaurant food sales because of increased business in the lounge.

**Programmed Music.**   In lounge settings offering dancing, proper programming of the entertainment can encourage and control alcohol consumption by alternately encouraging patrons to the dance floor and sending them back to their seats for a thirst-quenching drink.

Programmed music with a disk jockey can cost 50 to 60 percent of the cost of providing live music and, depending on the skill of the disk jockey, can be easier to program relative to the needs of customers. This involves playing a type of music in the first set that will appeal to a majority of the crowd. The second set would have music appropriate to the next largest audience, followed by a set of music that would have limited appeal. This may satisfy a small number of customers while sending the majority back to their seats for rest and refreshment. A fourth set of slow music provides a contrast to the faster earlier sets. The format should be adjusted to changing demographics as the programmer notices what music keeps people on the floor and what sends them back to the bar. In nightclubs, where customers are more homogeneous, the same kind of music tends to be played most of the night.

**Effect on Behavior.**   The provision of background music has been shown to affect customer behavior in restaurants. In one experiment[6] the effects of slow-tempo background music (72 or fewer beats per minute) were contrasted with fast-tempo background music (92 or more beats per minute). It was found that

- Customers eating with slow-tempo background music took longer to finish their meals than did customers eating with fast-tempo background music— 56 compared with 45 minutes.
- When fast-tempo music was being played, the waiting time per group was reduced from the 47 minutes usual when slow-tempo music was played to 34 minutes as a result of the diners eating faster.
- The tempo of the music had no impact on the decision to wait for a table.
- The tempo of the background music did not significantly affect the speed with which customers and orders were handled by employees. (The increased

time came from the time it took the customers to eat rather than the time it took them to be served.)

- While the tempo of the background music had no impact on food sales, it did affect bar sales. Slow-tempo music increased bar sales. (This has been verified in studies that show increased drinking in bars featuring slow country music.) Because the gross margin (the difference between selling price and food or beverage cost) is greater for drinks than for food, this had the effect of significantly increasing gross margins for the restaurant.

## Space

Early concepts of layout have given way to a field of study known as environmental psychology, which looks at the influence of the physical environment on people's behavior. Four concepts are of particular importance: privacy, personal space, territoriality, and overcrowding.[7]

**Privacy.**   The more people are afforded privacy, the more control they feel over their behavior. Little is known of the effects of privacy on such things as turnover, conversation levels, and so on.

**Personal Space.**   There are four zones within the concept of personal space. Intimate distance extends 18 inches around a person. If others enter this space, people back off to establish a more comfortable distance between themselves and others. Personal distance goes from 18 inches to about 4 feet and allows an exchange of conversation. Social distance extends from 4 to 12 feet, while public space involves anything beyond that. The amount of personal space and personal distance that people feel comfortable with varies by culture. The British have a larger comfort zone than that of Americans, who, in turn, feel more comfortable farther apart than the space preferred by Latin Americans.

Forcing people together, as in a nightclub, induces conversation between them. On the other hand, a wide table introduces a more formal space between parties and indicates that more formal behavior is appropriate.

**Territoriality.**   *Territoriality* refers to the need to control a defined space. When space is restricted, people move objects to define boundaries. In British restaurants it is common for two parties of two to be seated at a four-top (a table set for four people). This would not be tolerated in American restaurants, where "having one's own territory" means not sharing a table with others. More work needs to be done to identify how much space people need compared to how much is provided.

**Crowding.**   *Crowding* refers to the feeling of being one of a large number of people in a small space. The perception of crowds, whether real or not, may influence a person's decision to leave one restaurant for another.

The space allocated to diners may range from 8 square feet in a cocktail lounge or bistro to 18 square feet in an upscale establishment.

**Learning Objective:** Give examples of the ways that the size and shape of the room, seating arrangements, light, and color combine to influence customers.

Getting guests to enter an establishment depends largely on the atmosphere. Well-designed environments generally include well-defined space, an attractive seating arrangement, a good lighting level, and pleasing colors.

In Oklahoma City, Lotus is making a splash with its ambience. Lotus is located in the historic warehouse district on the first floor of a 100-year-old building. The building might be historic, but the lighting is an incredible example of what today's technology can do for a business.

The restaurant's lighting designer, Eric Stewart, employed Color Kinetics of Boston to assist with the lighting scheme. Color Kinetics utilizes intelligent light-emitting diode (LED) illumination technology to enhance the space with dynamic lighting. LED technology enables continual change in the lighting level, color, and design.

At Lotus, the designer lit each table with a single track head, a halogen light bulb lit dimly. The remainder of the restaurant is garnished with lighting effects creating waves of harmonious colors throughout the restaurant. Because LED technology is so specialized, programs can be written to create subtle light shows that continually change the atmosphere of the restaurant.

LED technology, while expensive, offers several benefits. The lighting has become an attraction. It gets customers coming back and new customers coming in. The lights have an extended usage life, create little heat and require minimal maintenance and power. LED lighting has gained Lotus a lot of publicity and repeat business.

*Source:* Wilson, Marianne, "Lotus Lights Up: LED Technology Creates One-of-a-Kind Dining Experience," *Nation's Restaurant News,* vol. 2, no. 2, pp. 12–13, May 2003.

**Discussion Question:** How are the guests' perceptions changed by lighting?

## Lighting

The cost of lighting ranges from a low of 10 percent of total energy consumption for a fine dining restaurant to 25 percent of the total for a fast-food operation.

Lighting serves four basic purposes. It helps set the mood of a restaurant; it should make both the food and the customers look good; it has to be bright enough to allow employees to complete their work; and, in certain places, it helps provide for the safety and security for the guests.

Five factors must be considered in selecting the type of lighting in a restaurant: time, size, contrast, brightness, and sound.[8]

**Time.** The lighting level should be selected in accordance with the amount of time a customer has to enjoy a meal. Low lighting levels mean that customers have to take longer to read the menu. It also encourages them to linger over the meal. High levels of lighting help provide an atmosphere that encourages people to leave. Low lighting permits greater intimacy between couples, thereby increasing seating capacity.

**Size.** As with colors, careful selection of lighting systems can affect people's perceptions of the physical facility. A low ceiling, brightly lit, will appear higher; high ceilings, dimly lit, will look lower; a narrow room will appear narrower if the long walls are lit. Bright lights will give an impression of speed, thereby increasing turnover. Similarly, trash cans in white or bright colors will appear lighter weight than those in dark colors.

**Contrast.** Contrast is the perceived difference between the detail of an object and its background. Use can be made of direct, indirect, or spotlighting. Direct lighting is stronger, indirect lighting is softer, and spotlighting can be used to focus attention on particular features or objects.

An important consideration is the reflective difference level of the task at hand and the surrounding area. Strange as it may sound, a brightly lit area against dimly lit surroundings make the former more difficult to see. For example, a cash register keyboard can be made easier for the cashier to read by increasing the lighting of the immediate surrounding area to a point where there is only a 10 percent difference between the reflective level of the cash register—reflecting back 50 to 60 percent of the light—and the immediate surrounding area—reflecting back 40 to 50 percent of the light. In short, the correct levels of lighting can improve employee productivity and reduce errors.

**Brightness.** Of the two types of lighting systems—incandescent lights and mercury vapor lights—mercury vapor or fluorescent lights produce up to 4 1/2 times the light and have 9 to 10 times the life of standard incandescent lamps but have lower aesthetic appeal. Incandescent lights, on the other hand, enhance reds and are easier to control; they can be turned down with a dimmer. In addition, food looks best and more natural under this system of lighting.

Because fluorescent lights pick up most of the color spectrum, blues and greens dominate reds and oranges, causing skin to look pasty and food to look gray. Green fluorescent light makes roast beef appear greenish gray, a red pear becomes purple, shrimp cocktail is grayish pink, and coffee becomes muddy green.

Candlelight, with its reddish flame, gives off a light that is flattering to both food and people. Additionally, it gives a romantic feeling of intimacy.

To be as kind to the customer as possible, lights should be placed at or slightly below eye level. Having high-angle lighting produces glare while enhancing shadows and wrinkles on the face. This effect can be reduced by having light-colored tablecloths that reflect light onto the unlighted portion of people's faces.

In bars there seems to be a connection among lighting, noise level, and duration of stay. As the lighting level increases, so does the noise level, and both reduce the amount of time customers stay. The lighting levels in bars should be 20 to 30 percent brighter than in the dining area.

In dance clubs, lighting and sound are combined to give a total effect. In the early days of discotheque clubs—the 1960s—the sound budget was often 90 percent of the budget. Because people are more visually oriented, today's budgets tend to be closer to 80 to 90 percent on lighting and 10 to 20 percent on sound. The dance floor will take up 50 to 60 percent of the total lighting budget, depending on how important it is in attracting customers.

In selecting the appropriate type of lighting, an order should be maintained: The light must be selected before the bulb and the bulb must be chosen before the fixture. One way to prolong the life of the bulb is to stipulate higher-wattage lamps than required for the space and keep them dimmed by using lower-wattage bulbs. For example, operators might request 150-watt lamps from the designer for a particular location but use only 75-watt bulbs. The bulbs will last much longer. This is particularly important if the location of the lamp makes it difficult to replace the bulb. The ease with which bulbs can be replaced is yet another factor that must be considered.

## Color

Colors are classified as either primary, secondary, or intermediary. The primary colors—so called because other colors are obtained from them—are red, yellow, and blue.

Secondary colors are made by mixing two of the primary colors. Green is made by mixing blue and yellow; orange from red and yellow; violet from blue and red. Intermediary colors are a combination of a primary and a secondary color—such as red-violet and yellow-orange. The color wheel is shown in Figure 7.2.

Colors are referred to as either warm or cool. The warm colors, so called because they give off a feeling of warmth, are red, yellow, and orange. The cool colors, which are relaxing and cooling, are blue, green, and violet.

**Harmony.**   Colors should be selected that are harmonious together. Five harmonic principles are useful in the selection of colors: monochromatic, analogous, complementary, split complementary, and triad.

Monochromatic harmony involves the use of a single color as either the pure color itself, as a tint (that is, mixed with white) of the pure color, as a shade (mixed with black) of the pure color, or as a tone (mixed with both black and white) of the pure color.

Analogous harmony comes from the use of any three or four consecutive colors on the color wheel. Blue-violet, blue, and blue-green would be an example of analogous harmony.

Complementary harmony is obtained by using any two colors directly opposite each other on the color wheel. Blue-violet and yellow-orange or red-violet and yellow-green are examples of this.

Split or near complementary colors come from the use of three colors. One of the two complementary colors is used in combination with the two colors

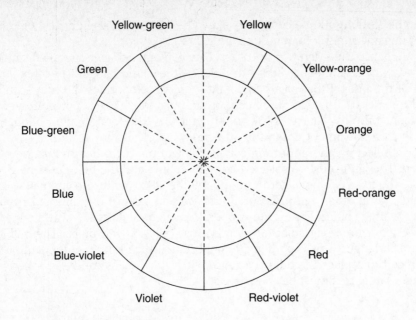

**Figure 7.2**   Color wheel.

adjacent to the other complementary color. For example, blue and orange are complementary colors. A split complementary would be blue, yellow-orange, and red-orange; or orange, blue-green, and blue-violet.

Triad complementarity involves the use of three colors. Every fourth color on the color wheel is selected.

Once the colors are selected, a decision must be made as to the tint, shade, or tone to be used. As noted previously, a color is tinted when white is added to it; a shade comes from the addition of black; and a tone comes from adding both white and black to the color.

**Contrast.**   One of the most important elements in dealing with color is the idea of contrast. One color cannot operate alone. The guidelines for dealing with contrast are as follows:[9]

- Use a light form (pink) with a darker form (red) of the same color.
- Use a weak version (pale blue) with a stronger version (royal blue) of the same color.
- Use a warm color (red) with a cool color (blue).
- Use complementary colors, such as peach and gray-blue.

Contrasts in colors can have a safety effect by making obstructions and exits stand out.

**Effects.**   We can now turn to the overall effect of color on the room, the food, and the customers. Colors should be selected under the type of lighting in which they will be used, as they will look different under fluorescent lighting than under incandescent lighting. Care should be taken in selecting a color from a small sample, as it will appear brighter in a larger area than on the small sample.

Colors can give a feeling of spaciousness or of intimacy. Light colors make a small room look larger, while dark colors make high ceilings appear lower. In general, dark colors will make objects appear smaller; light colors make them appear larger. Similarly, the use of dark colors to emphasize horizontal lines will make the ceiling appear lower, while using dark colors to emphasize vertical lines will make the ceiling appear higher. The ceiling can also be "lowered" by carrying a wall color over to the ceiling.

Long, narrow rooms can be made to feel squarer by using colors on the end walls that are warmer or deeper than those on the other walls.

Another factor to consider is the location of the restaurant. It has been found, for example, that, in the northern states, people will stay longer if warm colors—reds, oranges, yellows—are used, while in the warmer south, greens and blues encourage longer stays.

The location of different rooms in the facility must also be taken into account. Rooms with a northern or eastern exposure will tend to be cool in the afternoon. Muted warm colors will offer a counterbalance. Rooms with a southern exposure will already be pleasantly warm and can benefit from the coolness of green, blue, and turquoise. The natural light in rooms with a western exposure will be tinted by the sun and, in the evening, the sunset. Earth tones—brown, tan, yellow, burnt orange, and copper—will complement the natural light.

Food looks better under warm colors such as red, brown, yellow, gold, and orange. People like food in the red-yellow spectrum: roast beef, brown rolls, french fries, red apples, strawberries, cherries, oranges, and so on. Yellow-greens, apart from the green of salads, peas, broccoli, and spinach, are not highly regarded. Blue, purple, and pink have much less appetite appeal.

Another important consideration is not only how the food looks but how the customers look. Greens and grays tend to make people look pale and are the most unflattering. The combined effect of color and light is important. Green lights tend to show up wrinkles, while pink lighting pales lipstick colors, and amber lights wash out colors.

Some researchers argue that colors affect a person's mood, while others feel that the intensity is the key. Red is perceived as exciting, intense, and stimulating; orange is jovial, exhilarating, and energetic; yellow is cheerful, inspiring, and boosts morale; green is quieting, refreshing, and peaceful; blue is subduing and melancholic; purple is gracious, elegant, and dignified; brown relaxes; white is pure and clean; black is depressing and ominous.

There is some research to indicate that older people have more trouble distinguishing between blues and greens than among the warmer reds and oranges. In general, they prefer brighter primary, secondary, or tertiary colors to pale pastels.

High turnover can be encouraged by having bold colors and high-intensity lighting. The closer to the primary colors of red, yellow, and blue, the bolder the effect. Fast-food operations, in their early development, utilized bright yellows and reds for this reason.

## Accessibility[10]

In 1990 the Americans with Disabilities Act (ADA) was signed into law. The legislation guarantees civil rights protection for persons with disabilities. Employers with 15 or more employees are prohibited from discriminating against any individual with a disability who, with or without reasonable accommodation, can perform the essential functions of a job. Businesses are also prohibited from discriminating against customers with disabilities or perceived disabilities. Businesses must be readily accessible—from parking to entrance-ways to restrooms.

This might mean such things as installing ramps, repositioning paper-towel dispensers, offering Braille menus, and widening doors.

## BACK OF THE HOUSE: SPACE REQUIREMENTS

The following rules of thumb regarding the amount of production space for various foodservice facilities should be taken as general guides only. These recommendations should be adapted to the special needs of particular projects.

The amount of production or back-of-the-house space required will vary depending on the type of service. Table-service restaurants will require 8 to 12 square feet per seat; counter service, 4 to 6 square feet; booth service, 6 to 10 square feet; and cafeteria service, 8 to 12 square feet.[11]

Once the amount of space required has been determined, the amount for each of the functional areas must be calculated. The top-down method allocates certain percentages of the total space to each of the functional areas. One suggestion is as follows:[12]

**Space Allocation**

| Functional Area | Space Allocated (Percent) |
|---|---|
| Receiving | 5 |
| Food storage | 20 |
| Preparation | 14 |
| Cooking | 8 |
| Baking | 10 |
| Warewashing | 5 |
| Traffic aisles | 16 |
| Trash storage | 5 |
| Employee facilities | 15 |
| Miscellaneous | 2 |

## BACK OF THE HOUSE: WORKPLACE DESIGN

A bottom-up approach to determining space requirements involves designing individual workplaces and assembling them into functional areas.

The workplace is where people perform their jobs. The amount of space made available at each workstation and the way it is laid out can aid or hinder employee productivity.

## Systematic Approach

A systematic approach to workplace design begins with an analysis of the menu. Each item on the menu should be identified, together with the portion size, the estimated total number of portions per meal period, the materials, utensils, or hand tools and process required to prepare the item, together with the type of work surface needed.[13] A similar process will determine the area needed for other nonfood functions.

**Work Aisle Space.**   *Work aisle space* is the term used for the floor space needed by an employee to perform a task. Traffic aisles, on the other hand, refer to areas where there is foot traffic. Work aisles and traffic aisles should be kept separate wherever possible to avoid hindrances to employees as they work. A single-person work aisle requires a space of between 24 and 36 inches, depending on the tasks to be done. To allow for employee bending or oven door opening, the larger space is needed. For two employees working back to back a minimum of 42 inches is required; more—6 to 12 inches more—if equipment projects into the workspace.

**Traffic Aisles.**   Traffic aisles are used to move people and materials. They should be kept separate from work aisles. Traffic aisles are not productive space and should be kept to a minimum while allowing easy movement. It may be possible to have one aisle serve two or more functional areas. Traffic aisles should not be placed along perimeters, as this allows access to only one working area. An aisle width of 30 inches will permit one person to walk without a problem. When carts are being pushed or containers carried down an aisle, 24 inches plus the width of the equipment is necessary to allow two people to pass. If a work aisle is combined with a traffic aisle, a minimum of 42 inches is required to allow one person to pass someone who is working. Where two people are working back to back, 48 inches is needed to allow someone else to pass between them. The less movement within the operation, the less aisle space is required.

**Work Surface Space.**   The space required for work surfaces depends on the materials to be used and the hand and arm movements required to perform the task. Normal and maximum hand and arm movements can be identified for the "typical" employee and the work area built to allow employees to perform their jobs within these areas. The normal work area for a work surface is defined as "the space enclosed within the arc scribed by pivoting the forearm in a horizontal plane at the elbow".[14] For most people this is 14 to 16 inches. Cutting, slicing, mixing, and assembling are best done within this area.

To determine the maximum work area, the entire arm is pivoted at the shoulder. When a task has to be performed outside this area, the employee must bend his or her body. The result will be a less productive worker. Most food facility jobs can be performed within an area 2 feet deep by 4 feet wide.

**Workstation Height.**   The height of a workstation depends on the task to be performed there. Lightweight tasks can be done at a surface height 2 inches below the employee's elbow. The larger or heavier the materials used, the lower the work surface should be. For light tasks the preferred height should be 37 to 41 inches; heavy jobs should be 34 to 36 inches off the ground, depending on the height of the employee.

**Storage.**   Tools and utensils should be close to where they will be used and readily accessible to employees.

**Equipment.**   Equipment is either mounted or freestanding. The feeding and working height should be appropriate to the employees who will use them. Freestanding equipment can be moved from one location to another. This makes it easier to clean under and behind the equipment. In addition, changes in layout can be made to accommodate more efficient layout when changes occur in the menu.

**Workplace Environment.**   Productivity is affected by the physical conditions under which employees must work. A temperature between 65 and 70°F in winter or between 69 and 73°F in summer with a relative humidity between 40 and 60 percent is comfortable for most people. The heat and moisture generated in a kitchen can be contained by purchasing equipment that is well insulated.

Despite some research which indicates that kitchen workers are up to 25 percent more productive in the summer if kitchens are air conditioned, most people consider it economically unfeasible to air condition this part of the operation. There are some measures, however, that can be taken to reduce kitchen temperatures.[15]

- Steam and water pipes and equipment that emits heat can be heavily insulated, as can the entire building.
- Hot-water heaters, refrigerator compressors, and condensers can be placed away from the kitchen.
- Equipment can be preheated for the minimum amount of time necessary.
- Sun-reflecting windows can be used to reduce sun heating.
- Whenever feasible, heat-emitting equipment can be covered during preheating and after use.
- Lower temperatures can be used to cook food.
- Gas flames should be adjusted so that they do not come up around the sides of pots.
- The building can be aired out at night.

The amount of lighting required depends on the job to be done. Lighting levels in a kitchen range from 15 to 20 foot-candles in nonwork areas to 30 to 40 foot-candles for most kitchen tasks. General white fluorescent lights tend to distort food color and are not recommended. Incandescent or color-improved fluorescent lighting should be used for work areas. The latter is more expensive to install but cheaper to operate.

There are two other considerations related to lighting: the brightness ratio and glare. The brightness ratio—the relative brightness between a lit and nonlit area—should not exceed 3:1, where the work area is the brighter area. Direct glare occurs when light sources are placed near the line of sight. Both direct and reflected glare tires employees and is an annoyance. The latter tends to come from the large number of stainless steel tables and amount of equipment used in kitchens.

Three aspects of color are important in the workplace: contrast, actual color used, and color coding. Objects are easier to see and the eye is less tired when there is a color contrast between two areas. This can be achieved in one of several ways.[16] A light color can be used with a darker version of the same color; a warm color can be combined with a cool color; a color can be used with its complementary color. The level of contrast in the workplace should be at a moderate level, as too much contrast can be just as bad for the eyes. Warm colors—reds and oranges—tire the eyes easily. Blues and greens are much more restful. In a similar fashion, pure colors, as distinct from tones, strain the eyes after a short period. Pure white is usually not recommended for a work area because it reflects light too much, again tiring the eyes. Colors can be used to color code various pieces of equipment. Green tends to be used for first-aid equipment; red signifies danger; steps coded with yellow can serve as a signal to be careful.

Exposure to noise levels above 50 decibels for a prolonged period can lead to contentious employees. Silencing enclosures can be placed around equipment; acoustical materials can be utilized on ceilings, walls, and floors; and sound-absorbing materials can be used to construct work surfaces.

Music has been shown to boost employee morale. It is particularly useful for workers performing physical tasks. Most workers are productive for the first 2 to 2 1/2 hours after they begin work. Their work performance then declines and holds steady at the lower level until shortly before a meal break, when it improves. Upbeat music during the lull in performance can help a worker perform more productively.

Because of the type of work performed in the kitchen, ventilation is important to remove odors, moisture, and the smell of grease, but air conditioning creates special problems in the kitchen. When food is cooked, the work area becomes hot. Air conditioning aims to cool the work area. The control system used is very important to ensure that the working conditions are comfortable for the employees without causing the cooked food to cool before it is taken into the dining room.

**Safety in the Workplace.**   Unsafe workplaces increase costs for the employer by increasing insurance coverage and reducing productivity. Accidents in the kitchen can occur for a number of reasons.[17] Falling results from slippery floors, floors that are highly polished, and stairways that are too steep. Nonskid flooring or carpeting can help with floors that are wet and/or greasy. Accidents from cuts happen because moving edges are not sufficiently guarded or employees are not using hand tools properly. These can be reduced by guarding cutting edges and ensuring that workers are trained in the safe and proper use of their tools.

Burns can be caused by hot grease, steam, hot water, or hot pipes. Steam and hot-water lines should be insulated and/or placed out of the way of employees, who should be trained in the proper use of equipment.

Electrical shocks in the kitchen are the result of frayed wires, poor insulation on wires, or improper grounding of equipment or machines. Built-in ground wires with three-pronged plugs can be used with portable equipment and grounding outlets provided. Heavy-duty waterproof wiring is recommended.

When hands are sweaty or greasy or when fingers are stiff due to exposure to the cold, there is a tendency to drop things. Keeping hands dry and using gloves when picking up hot or cold items over a long period of time will reduce such accidents.

There are a number of ways to improve indoor air quality:[18]

- Physically separate smoking and nonsmoking dining areas and/or direct the flow of air away from nonsmoking areas.
- Ban employee smoking inside the operation.
- Install a whole-building air cleaner/filtration system.
- Check for radon, mold spores, and biological dangers.
- Use plants to clean the air naturally.
- Check for emissions from carpeting, paint, and cleaning products.

## Layout of Functional Areas

By identifying the functions within the kitchen and the order in which they are undertaken, management gets a feel for the flow of activities within the operation. Boxes of canned goods are received, the boxes are unpacked, the cans are checked for quantity and quality, the boxes are discarded, and the cans are placed on shelves. The order in which activities occur is referred to as *flow*. The idea is to minimize the amount of movement of both people and goods.

**Layout Principles.**   The layout process consists of two steps:[19] arranging individual pieces of equipment into a functional area (for example, salad preparation) and arranging the functional areas into the entire operation. Both steps tend to occur at somewhat the same time in the designer's mind.

Industrial engineers have developed various principles of layout that serve as a guide to this process. The more important of these tend to stress such things as designing the layout to make the production process as easy and as flexible to change as possible, allowing for ease of access for such things as maintenance and the taking of inventory, protecting the equipment from damage, providing a safe and productive environment for employees, and minimizing movement of both materials and employees.

## quick bite 7.5
### Improving the Layout

**Learning Objectives:** Suggest procedures to improve existing layouts. Develop more productive procedures for completing individual jobs.

The layout of any food operation should promote efficiency. Arrangement of equipment and functional areas need to support the flow of traffic for both employees and customers. Kirk Perron, founder of Jamba Juice, prefers the "T-shaped" assembly-line for his smoothie chain.

Before, the production line was rectangular. This resulted in cross-traffic between customers in front of the line and employees behind the line. A large amount of bypassing occurred behind the line, causing collisions and spills. Congestion behind the counter reduced efficiency, causing a longer wait time and a messy work area.

When Perron tested the T-shaped production area in one of his restaurants, the results were remarkable. The new design, although smaller, allowed access to ingredients from two sides and appealed to the customers who could watch the smoothies being made. This moves the customers to opposite sides of the ordering area and eliminates congestion behind and in front of the counter, thereby reducing wait time.

Instead of cleaning the blender cups on the line, the T-shaped design provides Jamba Juice with a designated cleaning area behind the production area. This eliminates the unsightly mess that plagued the rectangular design. The new design reduced movement as well as the number of employees required to operate efficiently. Reducing production time, employee numbers, and wait time has positive implications for the bottom line and the overall atmosphere within the establishment.

*Source:* "Designing for Efficiency: T-Shaped Production Kitchen Drives Productivity at Jamba Juice," *Nation's Restaurant News,* vol. 2, no. 2, p. 7, May 2003.

**Discussion Question:** Why should the flow of traffic for both employees and customers be examined?

**Principles of Flow.** A flow diagram showing the flow of employees, customers, and primary materials helps determine where areas should be relative to one another. For example, after being received, items are separated into either dry or refrigerated storage, from where they go to either baking, meat, or vegetable preparation. From vegetable preparation items go to salad preparation; items from meat preparation go to final cooking and then either to salad preparation or to serving, then to the dining room, and, finally, to dishwashing. Silverware and flatware from the dishwashing area go back into the serving area. The pot wash area receives items from both baking and cooking.

Jamba Juice.

In a station manned by one employee, a flow diagram is best accomplished by surveying the employee's movements among various pieces of equipment and placing pieces involving most movement between them next to each other.

Where employees are engaged in tasks that do not require them to move much, as in dishwashing, where employees scrape dirty dishes prior to loading them into the dishwasher, the most important consideration would be the flow of materials rather than the analysis of employee movements.

Generally speaking, when material flow is minimized, employee movement is minimized. Whichever criterion is used, the following principles are important:[20]

- Flow should be along straight-line paths as much as possible. This principle is particularly important, as it results in minimum movements. Various layouts can be charted and the one giving the best straight-line pattern selected.
- Cross-traffic results in bottlenecks and congestion. The amount of cross-flow or cross-traffic should be minimized. This can be done by locating aisles, passageways, and doors such that traffic flows do not cross.
- When people move back to where a particular activity occurred, they are guilty of backtracking. This should be minimized.
- Bypassing should also be minimized. This occurs when material or people pass one or more pieces of equipment to get to the next part of the process.

As an example, a single counter in a self-service operation leads to a simple customer traffic pattern. In terms of the placement of food and beverage items on the line, desserts should be placed first; hot items and made-to-order foods are placed immediately prior to the beverages; drinks are placed just before the cashier to avoid potential spills.[21]

**Configurations.** Five basic layout patterns are common (see Figure 7.3). The single straight-line arrangement consists of pieces of equipment laid out next to each other in a straight line. They may be laid out along a wall or in an island. It is simple, but the layout options are very limited.

An L-shaped arrangement places equipment on two legs that are perpendicular to each other. It is a useful arrangement where linear space is restricted. Different types of equipment can be separated by using one leg for each type.

U-shaped arrangements are particularly useful for confined areas where only one employee is working. A problem is that this layout does not allow for straight-line movement through the area.

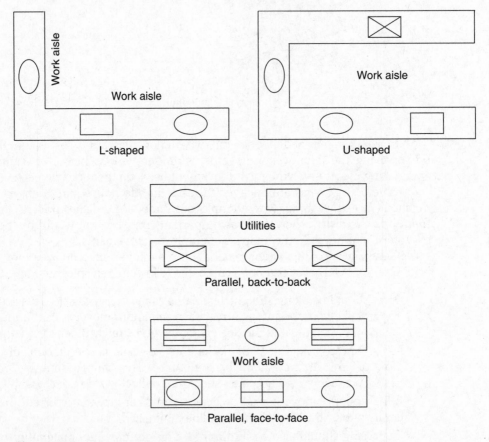

**Figure 7.3** Equipment layout patterns.

Parallel, back-to-back arrangements consist of two parallel lines of equipment placed next to each other back-to-back. In this way the utility line for each line can be centralized between them.

Parallel, face-to-face arrangements utilize two lines of equipment with a work aisle between them. Very commonly used, this arrangement requires separate utility lines for each line of equipment.

## Arranging Functional Areas

As noted previously, the layout process consists of arranging individual pieces of equipment into a functional area and arranging the functional areas into the entire operation. A relationship chart is useful for this second step. A relationship chart shows the desired physical relationship among various functional areas. Such a chart is shown in Figure 7.4. Departments involving a great deal of movement between them are located in relative closeness to each other.

## Comparing Systems

Boger examined four different systems to evaluate their efficiency[22]—the scramble, production line, mall, and airport. In the scramble system, employees "scrambled" to prepare, gather, and deliver the food items to the customer. In the production-line system employees were in stationary positions. The customers traveled from the cashier station to the expediter station, where they received their food items and continued on to the self-service drink station. Under the mall system, employees recorded the orders, then gathered the food items for delivery to the customers. Order and pick-up stations were separated by several feet to allow other orders to be recorded. The airport system allowed customers to travel along the serving line, selecting food items from self-serving units. They paid for these items at the end of the line, preparing their own drinks at a self-service station. The cashier was the only employee to interact with the customers.

Each system is appropriate for different volume levels. The scramble system is designed for high volume, the production line for medium to high volume, and the mall and airport systems for low volume. All but the mall system recorded similar total service times. However, they each use various methods to achieve this. The scramble system makes up for an inefficient design by using more employees. Fewer employees are used in the production-line system through the utilization of customer flow and keeping employees in fixed positions. The mall system, unlike the other three, has a limited and scattered volume of business. Also unlike the other systems, self-service units carried limited inventory to prevent waste. This slows down service time considerably as items are made after the food order is placed.

Each system offers unique advantages and disadvantages. The scramble system can serve up to four customers at the same time and can handle high volumes. However, it is difficult for the production area to catch up if it falls behind during peak periods. The production line utilizes customers as a part of the process by having them prepare their own drink items. This is liable to reduce labor costs. On the other hand, congestion at the drink station can interfere with

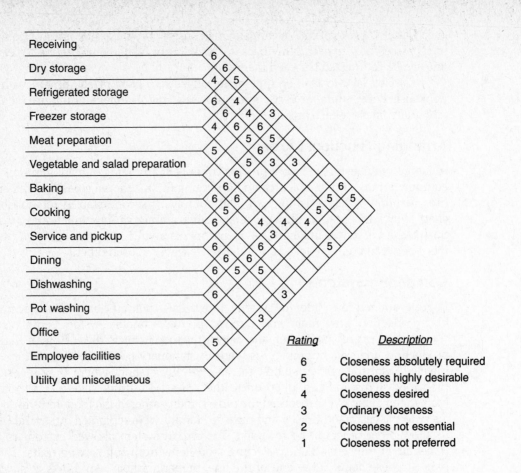

| Rating | Description |
|--------|-------------|
| 6 | Closeness absolutely required |
| 5 | Closeness highly desirable |
| 4 | Closeness desired |
| 3 | Ordinary closeness |
| 2 | Closeness not essential |
| 1 | Closeness not preferred |

**Figure 7.4** Relationship chart with closeness ratings for a typical food-service facility. [*Source:* Edward A. Kazarian, *Foodservice Facilities Planning*, 3rd ed. (New York: Van Nostrand Reinhold, 1989), p. 283.]

customer flow. The airport system allows customers to select items from self-service units while also allowing them to fix their own drinks. The system can only handle low volume and tends to offer only a limited menu selection. The mall system offers food either made from scratch or assembled after the order is placed while being able to serve low volume.

It may be that a hybrid system could be designed utilizing the best features from each of the four systems.

## Ergonomics[23]

The Occupational Safety and Health Administration (OSHA) is a government agency whose mission is to "assure the safety and health of workers by setting standards; providing training, outreach and education; establishing partnerships;

and encouraging continual improvement in workplace safety and health."[24] OSHA has over 2000 inspectors in more than 200 offices throughout the country who establish and enforce standards while offering technical assistance and consultation programs.

One of the areas OSHA is concerned with is ergonomics. According to the Bureau of Labor Statistics, poor ergonomics contributed to repetitive-motion injuries that cost employers over $2 billion a year. OSHA defines *ergonomics* as "the science of fitting the job to the worker." Cutting and chopping are two activities that can lead to the painful condition of the wrist and hand known as carpal tunnel syndrome. Strained backs that can be caused by lifting, excessive standing, or extensive walking is another example of a common workplace injury. These injuries are the result of repetitive motions. Employees who repeat the same motions, perform their work in an awkward position, use a great deal of force on the job, or repeatedly lift heavy objects can be susceptible to these injuries.

The first step is to identify repetitive-motion injuries that workers suffer on the job and take steps to prevent new injuries. Warming up and stretching before the shift begins can help servers avoid back strains from lifting trays. Stretches can include shaking out hands, putting arms over one's head, turning side to side, and bending at the waist and touching toes. Stuart Anderson's Restaurants decreased employees' job strain and sprain injuries 30 percent in one year by instituting a warm-up routine for workers. A reduction in workers'-compensation claims produced a savings companywide of almost $100,000. Another way to reduce repetitive-motion injuries is to rotate jobs so that employees use different motions during the day.

Lower-back strain can occur among employees who lift heavy items. Servers and bussers who lift trays and other heavy equipment are particularly susceptible. Lower-back strains can be reduced when employees are taught how to lift objects correctly. The National Restaurant Association recommends that employees get a solid footing, stand straight and face the load, then bend at the knees—not at the waist—when getting ready to lift a heavy package. Workers are advised to grip the load with their entire hand, not just their fingers, and keep their wrists as straight as possible. To lift the load, employees should first tighten their stomach muscles, straighten their backs, and lift from their legs, smoothly and slowly.

The workplace environment can also be changed to help alleviate repetitive-motion disorders. An employee-friendly workstation includes:[25]

- Antifatigue mats to relieve pressure on feet, legs, and backs
- Footrests to allow employees to change the position of their legs and feet
- Toe space to let employees stand close to the counter

## IMPROVING EXISTING LAYOUTS

The layout of existing operations is improved if the flow among various workplaces can be reduced. Travel charts can be used to evaluate the flow involved in a kitchen layout.

## quick fact

Ergonomics is a relatively new branch of science which celebrated its 50th anniversary in 1999 but relies on research carried out in many other older, established scientific areas, such as engineering, physiology, and psychology.

Ergonomics originated in World War II, when scientists designed advanced new and potentially improved systems without fully considering the people who would be using them. It gradually became clear that systems and products would have to be designed to take account of many human and environmental factors if they were to be used safely and effectively. This awareness of people's requirements resulted in the discipline of ergonomics.

*Source:* The Ergonomics Society, *http://www.ergonomics.org.uk/ergonomics/definition.htm*, November 7, 2005.

Two methods are used. The first looks at the movement of individuals between workplaces; the second considers the flow of materials between workplaces. Whichever method is used, the objective is the same: to minimize movement of both people and materials.

## Individual Movements

When the weight or volume of materials involved in a process is not great, analyzing the movements of individuals is the best method of evaluating equipment layout.

When using individual movements, the most common form of travel charting involves analyzing workplaces that are in a straight line and where workplaces next to each other are equal or can be assumed to be equal. A workplace may be a sink, piece of equipment, worktable, or counter. Watching employees as they work, the sequence and frequency of movements between workplaces can be determined.

A chart can then be constructed showing the number of times an employee moves from workplace to workplace. A travel chart is shown in Figure 7.5. The numbers in each cell represent the number of movements from one workplace to

| To: \ From: | *A* | *B* | *C* | *D* | *E* |
|---|---|---|---|---|---|
| *A* | | 5 | 2 | 3 | 6 |
| *B* | 3 | | 4 | 0 | 2 |
| *C* | 3 | 4 | | 1 | 4 |
| *D* | 1 | 2 | 4 | | 3 |
| *E* | 2 | 4 | 3 | 5 | |

**Figure 7.5** Travel chart for five workstations showing frequency of movements. [*Source:* Idea adapted from Edward A. Kazarian, *Foodservice Facilities Planning,* 3rd ed. (New York: Van Nostrand Reinhold, 1989), p. 298.]

another. For example, the employee moves from C to B twice, while there are four movements from B to C. The cells below the diagonal show forward movements; those above show backward movements. The farther the cells are from the diagonal, the greater will be the number of workplaces that have been bypassed. For example, there are four movements from D to A. This represents backward movement that bypasses three workplaces.

Those movements next to the diagonal—for example, from A to B—indicate that no bypassing takes place.

If it is assumed that the distance between workplaces is equal, the total distance covered can be determined by adding both forward and backward movements and multiplying the totals by a factor of 1 plus the number of workplaces bypassed.

Referring to Figure 7.5, we find the following values:

| | | Total Movements | | Bypass Factor | | |
|---|---|---|---|---|---|---|
| No bypassing: | | | | | | |
| 3 + 4 + 4 + 5 + 3 + 1 + 4 + 5 | = | 29 | × | 1 | = | 29 |
| Bypassing one workplace: | | | | | | |
| 3 + 2 + 3 + 4 + 0 + 2 | = | 14 | × | 2 | = | 28 |
| Bypassing two workplaces: | | | | | | |
| 1 + 4 + 2 + 3 | = | 10 | × | 3 | = | 30 |
| Bypassing three workplaces: | | | | | | |
| 2 + 6 | = | 8 | × | 4 | = | 32 |
| | | | | | | 119 |

This index of 119 provides a base against which other arrangements can be compared. One way of improving the index is to get the larger numbers as close to the diagonal as possible while getting the smaller numbers as far from the diagonal as possible.

Another possibility is to reduce backward movements. The objective would be to get more numbers above the diagonal and fewer numbers below it. The percentage distance moved forward is the index for forward distances divided by the total distance moved. In our example the calculations would be:

| | Forward Movements | | Bypass Factor | | Backward Movements | Bypass Factor |
|---|---|---|---|---|---|---|
| No bypassing | 16 | × | 1 | = | 16:13 | 1 = 13 |
| Bypassing one workplace | 8 | × | 2 | = | 16:6 | 2 = 12 |
| Bypassing two workplaces | 5 | × | 3 | = | 15:5 | 3 = 15 |
| Bypassing three workplaces | 2 | × | 4 | = | 8:6 | 4 = 24 |
| | | | | | 55 | 64 |

So the percentage distance moved forward is:

$$\frac{55}{55 + 64} = 46 \text{ percent}$$

When the distances among various workplaces vary, a simple adjustment can be made to construct a travel chart. In such a case the number of movements from one workplace to another is multiplied by the distance from the midpoint of one to the midpoint of another to give the total distance traveled. For example, if A is 6 feet wide and is placed next to B, which is 2 feet wide, the distance from A to B is 4 feet $(6 + 2 \div 2)$. If there are three movements from A to B, the total distance traveled is 12 feet. In this way a travel chart can be constructed using the same methodology as suggested previously and different configurations tried to reduce the distance that employees move.

## Product Flow

Where large quantities of heavy material are moved, it is better to construct a travel chart based on product movement. The methodology is similar to that described previously except that the amount of weight multiplied by the distance covered is used instead of the number of feet traveled by an employee.

A travel chart is constructed by multiplying the distance traveled between two workplaces by the amount of material moved. If, for example, A and C are 4 feet apart and 300 pounds of material travels from A to C, the travel chart would indicate the index from A to C to be 1200. The amount of product flow for a given arrangement of workplaces is found by totaling the sums of each column. Various workplace arrangements can then be tried to find the one that minimizes product movement. Product movement can be minimized by locating workplaces involving large quantities of material close together.

## TASK PLANNING

Task planning involves the "analysis of specific actions involved in carrying out a job, in order to establish a more productive procedure for completing that job".[26]

The task to be analyzed is chosen and the various factors affecting it determined. The accessibility and storage of the raw materials used in performing the job is one such factor. Since handling materials does not add to their value, such handling should be kept to a minimum. How far an employee has to walk to get the raw food items prior to preparation will affect the amount of time and effort taken to complete the job.

Figures 7.6a and 7.6b illustrate what can be achieved. Prior to analysis a cook had to walk 235 steps to prepare a batch of macaroni. The process involved

- Ten steps to the pot-and-pan rack to get the pan
- Thirty steps to the sink to add the water

- Fifteen steps to the range carrying the pan and the water
- Fifty steps to the storeroom while the water is heating, to get the macaroni
- Fifty steps back to the range
- Ten steps to the drawer in the salad table for a spoon
- Ten steps back to the range
- Fifteen steps to the cabinet for salt
- Fifteen steps back to the range
- Fifteen steps to the sink for a little more water
- Fifteen steps back to the range

Storing the macaroni in the lower cabinet, using the steam-jacketed kettle instead of the range, locating the spoon on a rack above the table, having a hot-water faucet above the kettle, and remembering to get the salt and the macaroni at the same time reduces the procedure to 50 steps. The cook begins at the

---

 **quick bite 7.6**
### Road to the Top: Richard Roberts

In 1995, the Starr Restaurant Organization (SRO) opened the Continental Restaurant and Martini Bar on Market Street in Philadelphia. Richard Roberts has been the general manager there ever since the up-scale dining establishment first opened for business. The restaurant, which seats 127, has been a hot spot from the time the very first martini was shaken there.

The success of the Continental Restaurant and Martini Bar is attributed to the way Roberts directs his servers, kitchen staff, and front-of-the-house management. SRO had initially forecasted sales of $4.3 million for 2003. Roberts surpassed this estimate with sales of $5 million, a 35 percent increase from 2001.

The increase is directly related to Roberts's decision to open the Continental for lunch. Although the numbers provide enough evidence for his dedication, he could not do it alone.

Richard Roberts knows what it takes to make a restaurant run. This includes effective training, well-paid employees, and knowing the restaurant's clientele. All of these factors, along with Roberts's hard work, have put the Continental Restaurant and Martini Bar at the top of Philadelphia's list of places to be.

*Source:* Thorn, Bret, "Richard Roberts: This Restaurant Has More Than One 'Star'; GM Leads Team to 35-Percent Sales Increase," *Nation's Restaurant News*, vol. 38, no. 4, pp. 56–57, January 26, 2004.

**Discussion Question:** What makes Roberts a successful manager?

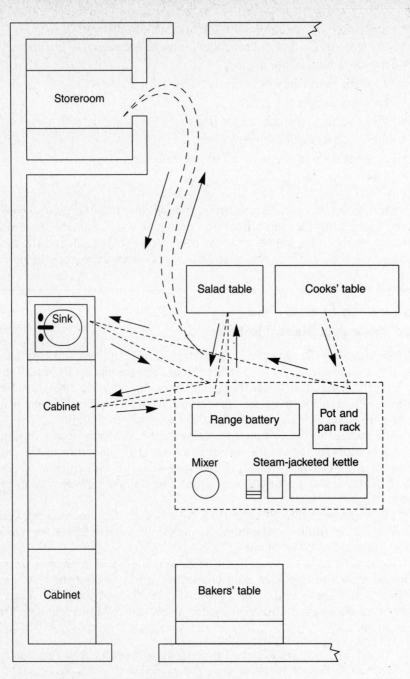

**Figure 7.6a** Steps involved in preparing macaroni.

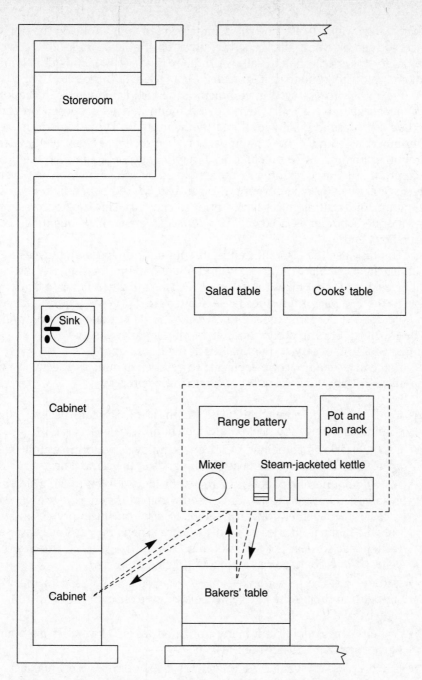

**Figure 7.6b** Steps involved in preparing macaroni—simplified.

baker's table, walks 10 steps to the steam-jacketed table, turns on the hot-water faucet located above it, fills the kettle, turns on the heat, walks 20 steps to the cabinet for the macaroni and salt, walks back to the kettle, and adds the macaroni and salt with a spoon that is located on a rack over the kettle.

Next, the process used in completing the task is identified. In the kitchen this means identifying every item on the menu and its proposed preparation method. The desired quality level and the quantity to be produced must also be determined, as both will have an impact on the process to be used. For example, hamburger patties can be prepared in different ways depending on the quantity to be produced. Large quantities can be readied by spreading the meat evenly in a rectangular baking pan, covering the pan with waxed paper, flattening with a rolling pin, and cutting into squares prior to cooking. This method presupposes that a square burger is acceptable to the customer. Small quantities can be shaped by hand.

The task itself is also affected by the amount of space employees have to work in, the availability of the right kind of equipment, the number and type of employee, how long it takes to perform the task, and when it has to be done relative to the completion of other tasks. Certain menu items require that several tasks be done at the same time. Of necessity, more than one employee will have to be involved. On the other hand, in certain situations, some activities can be completed ahead of service and finished at the last moment.

Procedures can now be established to get the job done as effectively and efficiently as possible. Several questions help in this process.

- Can the task be eliminated? The purchase of a potato-peeling machine eliminates the need to peel potatoes by hand.
- Can the task be combined? Can one employee perform several different jobs? Can employees work with both hands at the same time?
- Are there unnecessary delays? Are insufficient supplies causing slowdowns in service? One bar the author worked with was experiencing service delays because management, in an attempt to save on inventory costs, stocked only 12 highball glasses behind the bar. When the bar got busy, servers would have to clear the tables of glasses and have them washed and dried before drinks could be served to additional customers.
- Is there misdirected effort? Can a conveyor belt be used to move food, supplies, and/or dishes? Can wheels be put on equipment to roll rather than carry it?
- Are employees doing too many unrelated tasks? Have a $5-an-hour employee perform a $5-an-hour task.
- Is work spread evenly? At one hotel, 500 room-service breakfasts were served between 7:00 and 11:00 A.M. In the dining room, service was busiest between 8:30 and 9:00 A.M. Although most of the soiled dishes did not reach the dishwashing area until 10:00 A.M., the entire dishwashing crew was on duty from 7:00 A.M. Upon analysis of the situation, they were brought in at 9:00 A.M.

# ENDNOTES

1. Sharon L. Fullen, *Restaurant Design* (Ocala, FL: Atlantic Publishing Group, Inc., 2003), p. 51.
2. Ibid., p. 50.
3. Edward A. Kazarian, *Foodservice Facilities Planning,* 3rd ed. (New York: Van Nostrand Reinhold, 1989), p. 240.
4. Ibid., pp. 116–119.
5. Sharon L. Fullen, *Restaurant Design* (Ocala, FL: Atlantic Publishing Group, Inc., 2003), pp. 100–101.
6. Ronald E. Millman, "The Hidden Influence," *NRA News,* vol. 6, no. 5, May 1986, pp. 28–29.
7. Carolyn U. Lambert, "Environmental Design," *Cornell Hotel and Restaurant Administration Quarterly,* May 1981, pp. 62–68.
8. Richard E. Hopkins, "Light," *The Consultant,* vol. XVI, no. 4, Fall 1983, pp. 34–37.
9. Marilynn Motto, "Profit by Design," *Cornell Hotel and Restaurant Administration Quarterly,* May 1970, pp. 113–116.
10. Beth Panitz, "The ADA After a Decade: The Industry's Efforts to Provide Accessible Hospitality," *Restaurants USA,* September 2000, www.restaurant.org/rusa.
11. Kazarian, *Foodservice Facilities Planning,* 3rd ed., p. 401.
12. Ibid., pp. 246–247.
13. Ibid., pp. 393–398.
14. Arthur C. Avery, *A Modern Guide to Foodservice Equipment* (Boston: CBI Publishing Company, 1980), pp. 18–19.
15. Ibid., p. 142.
16. Ibid., p. 150.
17. Ibid., pp. 159–161.
18. Fullen, *Restaurant Design,* pp. 57–58.
19. Kazarian, *Foodservice Facilities Planning,* p. 272.
20. Ibid., p. 275.
21. Fullen, *Restaurant Design,* p. 52.
22. Boger, Carl A., "A Comparison Between Different Delivery Systems of Quick Service Food Facilities," *Hospitality Research Journal,* vol. 18, no. 3/vol. 19, no. 1, 1995, pp. 111–124.
23. Ira Apfel, "Taking the Strain Out of Ergonomics," *Restaurants USA,* June/July 2001, www.restaurant.org/rusa.
24. *http://www.osha.gov/oshinfo/mission.html,* accessed October 12, 2005.
25. Adam Blair, "With Ergonomics, Small Steps Equal Big Benefits," Sage, 2003, p.13.
26. Robert Christie Mill, *Managing for Productivity in the Hospitality Industry* (New York: Van Nostrand Reinhold, 1989), p. 65.

# INTERNET RESOURCES

| | |
|---|---|
| National Restaurant Design | *http://www.nationalrd.com/* |
| AMC Industries Restaurant Furniture | *http://restaurantbooths.com/* |
| Food Equipment Unlimited Restaurant Furniture | *http://www.foodequipmentunlimited.com/furniture.html* |
| Golden Age Chandeliers and Lighting | *http://www.goldenageusa.com/hospitality-lighting.asp* |

# CHAPTER EIGHT

# FOOD AND BEVERAGE: FROM SUPPLIER TO CUSTOMER

"Tomatoes and oregano make it Italian; wine and tarragon make it French. Sour cream makes it Russian; lemon and cinnamon make it Greek. Soy sauce makes it Chinese; garlic makes it good."
Alice May Brock, American cookbook author

## learning objectives

*By the end of this chapter you should be able to*

1. Develop procedures for the effective purchasing, receiving, storing, and issuing of items used in the operation.

2. Compare and contrast the various production and service systems.

3. Illustrate the importance and use of purchase specifications, yield, standardized recipes, and portion control in implementing a system of cost control.

## STEPS IN THE PROCESS

The process by which food and beverage items find their way to the customer consists of several steps:

- *Purchasing.* Items are ordered from vendors.
- *Receiving.* Items are delivered by vendors and accepted at the restaurant.
- *Storage.* Items are kept in a secured area until needed by the kitchen staff.
- *Issuing.* Items are released from storage to the kitchen staff.
- *Preparation.* Items are prepared for cooking.
- *Cooking.* Items are prepared for customers.
- *Service.* Items are served to the customer.

After service there is a need to wash dirty dishes, pots, and pans and dispose of waste. At each stage there are specific procedures to be put into place to ensure that costs are controlled while quality is maintained.

## PURCHASING

### Importance

According to Khan, "The primary function of any type of foodservice operation is to convert raw food into cooked products."[1] Profits come from converting and serving the food as efficiently as possible. High-quality dishes come from high-quality ingredients—thus the importance of purchasing. The objective is "to obtain the right quality and quantity at the right time and price and from the right source."[2]

### Process

**Forecast.** Once the menu is set, the number of servings of each item needed for each meal period must be forecast. This serves as the basis for the quantities of each item to be ordered. The easiest forecasting method, and the one used most often, is to use the average number of dishes ordered in the past. Poor forecasting results in too many or too few items ordered. If too many items are ordered, there is increased waste; too few items mean that the restaurant will run out of specific items and customers will be dissatisfied. Restaurants are increasingly using computer systems to improve their forecasts.

**Quantities Needed.** A standard procedure for identifying how much needs to be purchased involves five steps:[3]

1. Determine, from the recipe, the factor to be used to determine the number of servings. If the recipe is for 50 and the number of servings needed is 150, the factor will be 150 divided by 50, or 3.

2. Multiply all the ingredients in the recipe by the factor. This will give the edible portion (EP) weight of each item. The "as purchased" (AP) amount of each item is found by dividing the EP by the percent yield (see p. 218).

3. Select the wholesale purchase unit (case, box, carton, etc.) nearest to the AP weight.

4. Complete the calculations for every item on the menu for that day.

5. Calculate the amounts needed for the delivery. The amount ordered will depend on such things as how much inventory is on hand, the storage space available, seasonal availability, and the time between deliveries. The latter will vary by operation depending on the kind of service given by the suppliers. It is better for an operation to have the supplier maintain inventory rather than having the restaurant keep too many supplies on hand. An order form can then be filled out and the order processed.

## Buying Methods

**Informal.** Purchasing may be done formally or informally. Informal buying usually occurs over the telephone. Several vendors may be called for a price quotation and the order placed with the lowest bidder. This method is ideal for a small operation, as there is little paperwork and the buying can be done quickly. It may be possible to take advantage of lower costs in the marketplace. However, because prices have not been agreed upon ahead of time, price increases will result in higher costs.

Buying can be done on a cash basis at markets or after getting quotations from various vendors. A quotation-and-order sheet would be made out, listing specifications for the various items needed. Several vendors would then be called and asked to quote prices for these items. Space would be available on the form to write down the various prices. The cost of items purchased should be lower because prices are being compared. However, more time is needed to compare the quotes of the vendors.

Under the blank-check method, certain vendors are given authority to deliver various items and bill the restaurant without quoting prices beforehand. This would be done on a very limited basis with vendors who have shown they can be trusted and for items that are in short supply. It is advisable to set a range of prices beyond which the vendor must communicate with the restaurateur.

For items whose price varies erratically, the cost-plus or fixed-mark-up method ensures that the supplier will have a guaranteed profit, negotiated ahead of time and typically 10 to 30 percent over cost.

**Formal.**   There are also a variety of formal buying methods. The most common formal method of buying is the competitive-bid method under which vendors submit written quotes based on specifications sent out by the restaurateur. Bidding is competitive, so a good and fair price can be negotiated. Because everything is done in writing, the process takes longer but provides written safeguards should disputes arise.

In another form, prices may be negotiated with vendors before the formal written bid. Prices are usually set for a relatively long period. Under the standing-order method, vendors send items at predetermined intervals. Milk and bakery items are usually purchased in this way. Once the vendor has been chosen and the quantities set, time savings result because the decision does not have to be revisited every time an order is needed. The quantities ordered should be checked periodically to ensure that the amounts bought are appropriate to the needs of the business.

Prices, but not quantities, are determined under a future-contract method. For a specified amount of time, prices of specific items are guaranteed.

Finally, under the buy-and-hold method, the restaurateur buys large quantities of an item at a good price and the vendor is responsible for storing the item until it is needed by the operation. In this way the restaurateur can take advantage of cost savings even if he or she does not have large storage space.

## Standards

The following items indicate specific guidelines for purchasing food items.

### Fresh Fruits and Vegetables

1. Specific standards can be obtained from the United States Department of Agriculture (USDA).
2. Because these items are perishable, specify the grade desired at the time of delivery rather than the time of shipping.
3. Look for "bright, attractive colors, good shape and appearance, good proportion of weight and size, and absence of any mechanical damage or signs of decay."[4]
4. Specify size, especially for fruit. Smaller sizes tend to have more flavor, while larger sizes are important for display.

### Processed Fruits and Vegetables

1. As specified by the USDA, processed fruits and vegetables come in the following grades:

| Fruits | Vegetables |
|---|---|
| U.S. Grade A or U.S. Fancy | U.S. Grade A or U.S. Fancy |
| U.S. Grade B or U.S. Choice | U.S. Grade B or U.S. Extra-Standard |
| U.S. Grade C or U.S. Standard | U.S. Grade C or U.S. Standard |

U.S. Grade A items are "practically perfect" and score between 85 and 100 points; U.S. Grade B items are "reasonably perfect" and score between 75 and 84 points; U.S. Grade C items are "fairly perfect" and score between 60 and 74 points. For items where there are only two grades, A and B, the specifications for A are as in the preceding table, while for B they must be "fairly perfect" and score between 70 and 84 points.

2. Specify minimum drained weight needed, as this is a better indicator of yield.
3. Syrup density is important because the heavier the syrup, the less chance the product will break up. Also, for dietetic menus, the sugar content of the syrup is important.

**Frozen Vegetables.** The standards are the same as the USDA standards for processed fruit and vegetables, with the following notes:

1. Frozen vegetables may be packed in sugar or syrup.
2. They may be treated with an antioxidant to prevent browning.
3. Salt may have been added as a preservative.

## Meats and Meat Products

1. Meats are graded on the basis of quality and yield.
2. The various grades are U.S. Prime (highest grade), U.S. Choice, U.S. Select (somewhat leaner, lacks juiciness, relatively tender), U.S. Standard (tender), U.S. Commercial (lacks tenderness, more waste), U.S. Utility, U.S. Cutter, and U.S. Canner (for processed meat products).

## Poultry and Eggs

1. Available grades are U.S. Grade A, U.S. Grade B, U.S. Grade C, U.S. Procurement Grade I, and U.S. Procurement Grade II.
2. Order poultry as follows: breasts, breasts with ribs, wishbones, legs, wings, drumsticks, thighs, halves, quarters, and backs.
3. Eggs are graded by size and most are packed in 30-dozen cases. The grades most used in restaurants are large and medium. Medium eggs are a better buy if they are 12 percent or more cheaper than large eggs, while small eggs are a better buy if they are 24 percent or more cheaper than large eggs.[5]

| Size | Weight (oz) per Dozen | Weight (lb) per 30-Dozen Case |
|------|------------------------|-------------------------------|
| Jumbo | 30 | 56 |
| Extra large | 27 | 50.5 |
| Large | 24 | 45 |
| Medium | 21 | 39.5 |
| Small | 18 | 34 |
| Peewee | 15 | 28 |

## Milk and Milk Products

1. Specify the type of product, grade, milk fat content, and type of packaging.
2. Pasteurization is done to destroy bacteria; homogenization is done to prevent the formation of cream and results in an enhanced flavor.

## Fish and Shellfish

1. Items are available as U.S. Grade A (top quality), U.S. Grade B (good quality), and U.S. Grade C (fairly good quality).
2. Specify whether or not the skin should be left on and whether the item should be fresh, chilled, or frozen.
3. Fish may be whole (just as they came from the water), drawn (entrails removed), dressed (cleaned with head on), chunks, steaks, or fillets.

## Control

Within the purchase function two important aspects of control are the need for purchase specifications and an understanding of yield.

**Purchase Specifications.** Specifications are "the description of a particular commodity in terms of its size, quality, or condition."[6] Using specifications lets the vendors know exactly what is required. Specifications ("specs") should be detailed, in writing, and cover the following:[7]

1. Common, trade, or brand name of the product
2. Amount to be purchased in the most commonly used units
3. Recognized trade, federal, or local grade
4. Name and size of the basic container
5. Count and size of the items or units within the basic container
6. Ranges in weight, thickness, or size
7. Minimum and maximum trims, or fat content percentages
8. Degree of maturity or stage of ripening
9. Type of processing required (for example, freeze-dried)
10. Type of packaging desired

**Yields.** The yield percentage must be known before ordering. The yield percentage indicates how much usable food will be obtained from a particular purchased item. Standardized recipes will indicate the number of portions from a specific item. The number should take waste and shrinkage into account. If this has not been done, the yield can be calculated as follows:[8]

$$\text{percentage of yield} = \frac{\text{weight after cooking}}{\text{weight before cooking}} \times 100$$

The yield percentage will vary depending on such things as the cooking temperature and type of oven and percentage of fat in the item. Cooking at lower temperatures, for example, will result in less shrinkage or waste.

Food can be purchased in one of two ways. Food as purchased (AP) refers to items bought without prepreparation. Edible portion (EP) indicates that the item has been processed and is ready for cooking. The EP to be ordered is calculated as follows:[9]

$$\text{EP} = \text{AP shrinkage (or preparation losses)}$$

$$\text{percentage shrinkage or preparation losses} = \frac{\text{losses due to shrinkage or preparation (wt)}}{\text{AP (wt)}} \times 100$$

$$= \frac{\text{AP (wt)} - \text{EP (wt)}}{\text{AP (wt)}}$$

# RECEIVING

The objective in the receiving function is to ensure that the items delivered are exactly what was ordered. Ideally, for quantity and quality verification, the person who ordered the item should receive it. In large operations this is not feasible.

## Methods

There are three methods that can be set up for receiving goods: invoice, blind, and partially blind.[10] Under the invoice method, the delivery is accompanied by an invoice prepared by the supplier and listing the quantities, prices, and specifications for the order. The order is compared against the invoice by someone at the restaurant. This method is simple and fast. It works only if the person receiving the delivery takes the time to thoroughly compare the physical order to the invoice.

Under a blind receiving method, the invoice accompanying the order is blank or, at most, lists only the items being delivered. The receiving clerk is forced to physically count the number of items being delivered and judge their quality to complete the invoice. A separate and fully completed invoice is sent directly from the supplier to the person in charge of purchasing. This supplier-supplied invoice is compared to the one filled out by the receiving clerk and any discrepancies reported to the vendor. While this method is very accurate, it is also very time consuming.

The partially blind receiving method attempts to combine the primary advantages of the previous methods. The delivery comes with an invoice that contains all relevant information about the order except the quantities delivered. The receiving clerk is forced to physically count the number of items received and input those data on the invoice that comes with the order. This invoice is then compared with the order and a later invoice sent by the vendor.

One of the reviewers of this book provided an example from when he was the general manager of a steakhouse. The restaurant had just received 15 cases of prime rib and the prep cook was in the process of weighing them. The cook would place the case of three ribs on the scale and check the weight on the case side with that on the scale and then the invoice. The general manager observed for a while before asking the cook why the ribs were being weighed while still in the box. The vendor had been weighing the box and delivering them as is. With the boxes weighing just over 3 pounds per box, the restaurant had been consistently overcharged more than 50 pounds per delivery.

## Space Requirements

The following tasks are involved in receiving:[11] examining, moving, receiving, unpacking, and verifying. The amount of space required for receiving depends on the number, type, and size of deliveries. If deliveries are accepted only between certain restricted hours, for example, the receiving area will be larger than if deliveries are spread out over a longer period.

Large deliveries might require specialized equipment for handling the goods as they come in. This might range from a cart to a moving conveyor belt system.

Getting the distributor to make smaller, more frequent deliveries will mean that the restaurant will require less moving equipment and storage space for both perishable and nonperishable items. If moving equipment is required, some provision will have to be made for its storage. In addition, space must be available to verify the order and dispose of packing materials.

## Practices

Good receiving practices involve several steps:[12]

1. An invoice or delivery sheet should be used to verify each delivery.
2. All deliveries should be checked in the following ways:
   - Each container should be inspected for signs of external damage.
   - Each item should be weighed and/or counted, checked, and noted on the receiving invoice.
   - When appropriate (as for eggs), convert the weight of the item into the relevant quantity. Conversion tables should be readily available.
   - Remove all packing before weighing items.
   - Tag all wholesale cuts of meat. Meat tags consist of two parts; one stays on the meat while the other goes to accounting. The tag identifies the supplier, cut, weight, and unit price and is used for control purposes as well as to ensure the first in, first out (FIFO) system of inventory control.
3. Verify the quality of the items delivered. This can be done by random inspection using the specification guidelines developed by the restaurant and/or standard USDA criteria. Date all items in order that the operation use a FIFO inventory method. Expiration dates should be identified on cans and packages and cans specifically checked for bulging and leakage. Inspection stamps should be verified on meat items.
4. Checking temperatures is particularly important for frozen or refrigerated items. Recommended standards are as follows:[13]
   - Frozen foods, 0 to 20°F
   - Dairy products, 38 to 46°F
   - Meat and poultry, 33 to 38°F
   - Fish and shellfish, 23 to 30°F

---

q u i c k   f a c t

U.S. food container demand will reach $20.7 billion in 2009, led by plastic containers, bags, and pouches.

*Source:* National Paper Trade Association Alliance, *http://www.gonpta.com/*, October 30, 2005.

---

5. Any shortages or other discrepancies should be noted and the invoice signed, dated, and stamped. One copy is kept at receiving, another sent to management, and a third given to the delivery person.
6. All items should be sent immediately to the appropriate storage area.
7. Invoices should then be filed.

## STORAGE

Storage will be needed for dry, refrigerated, and frozen goods in addition to beverages and nonfood supplies. The objective is to have enough items on hand so that the restaurant does not run out while minimizing loss caused by spoilage and/or theft. Spoilage comes from holding items for too long. Excessive amounts of various food and beverage items tie up money and space.

In storage the following tasks are common:[14] inspecting, inventorying, issuing, rotating, and storing.

### Space Requirements

The number of days of storage to be provided determines how large the storage area must be. An isolated resort community that gets deliveries once a week will require more storage space than a restaurant that can demand daily deliveries. Since buying in bulk costs less, it is desirable to analyze the reduced costs of buying in bulk against the cost of providing additional space.

The following rules of thumb can be used to estimate the storage space required:[15]

- Two to four weeks' supply for dry storage goods
- A weight per meal of 1/4 to 1/2 pound
- An average density of 45 pounds per cubic foot

If an operation plans on serving 400 meals a day and wishes a two-week supply of dry goods, the space requirements can be estimated as follows:

| | |
|---|---|
| Required storage will be for 400 meals × 14 days | = 5600 meals |
| Total weight (1/2 pound per meal) | = 2800 pounds |
| Total volume (45 pounds per cubic foot) | = 62.2 cubic feet |
| Shelving required (at a height of 1.5 feet) (62.2 ÷ 1.5 feet) | = 41.5 square feet |
| Length of shelving required if shelving is 9 inches wide (41.5 ÷ 0.75 foot) | = 53.3 feet |

Convenience and accessibility are the principles upon which storage areas are laid out. They should be designed such that heavy and/or bulky materials are moved as little and as easily as possible. Many operations will find that a central storage area combined with smaller storage spaces scattered throughout the facility will cut down on the movement of people and goods. For example, a hotel with several restaurants will benefit from one major store serving all restaurants, each of which has space for storing small amounts of frequently used products. A combination of one walk-in and several reach-in refrigerators spread throughout the operation can reduce the walking employees would have to do to get required items. A restaurant serving over 300 to 400 meals a day should have a walk-in refrigerator.

It should be noted, however, that more storage areas will lead to increased inventory and greater control challenges. Combination walk-in and reach-in storage facilities greatly assist in increasing access to and within storage areas. Cleaning of walk-in storage areas is made easier by having items stored at least 8 inches off the floor. Mobile bins and containers also achieve this objective. All chemical items and cleaning supplies should be stored separately from foods because of the contamination risk.

**Dry Storage.**  Dry storage for food items requires a temperature between 50 and 70°F and a relative humidity of 50 percent. As such, heat-generating equipment should not be located in these areas. Similarly, pipes carrying hot water should be insulated to prevent temperatures from rising beyond 50 to 70°F.

**Refrigeration.**  Fresh meats, vegetables, fruits, dairy products, beverages, and leftover items require refrigeration at temperatures between 32 and 37°F. Items should not be in direct contact with the floor, walls, and/or ceiling. In addition, air circulation is needed to help eliminate odors and remove moisture.

Calculations similar to those used previously can be made for refrigerator and freezer storage. The weight per meal of refrigerator and freezer items will vary from 0.75 to 1 pound. The average density of refrigerator and freezer items is approximately 30 and 40 pounds per cubic foot, respectively. With refrigerated areas, temperature control is vital. Periodic checks should be made of the temperature at various points in the storage area. As with dry storage areas, items should not be in direct contact with floors, ceilings, and/or walls. Refrigerated areas can also be used to store cooked food items. It is imperative that cooked and raw items not come into contact with each other. Additionally, hot, cooked items should not be placed in the refrigerator as, in cooling down, they will increase the temperature of the surrounding area.

Many refrigeration boxes now have temperature control alarms that warn of high temperatures and/or compressor failure. They can be set up to send an internal alarm to the restaurant office as well as to the security company that protects the restaurant.

**Frozen Foods.**  If frozen foods are used, thawing facilities, sufficient for one day's production, will have to be provided. Frozen foods should be stored at −10 to −15°F. It is possible, and highly desirable, to have a layout wherein walk-in

**Learning Objective:** Develop procedures for the effective purchasing, receiving, storing, and issuing of items used in the operation.

Roger Beaulieu is director of culinary development for Culinart, Inc., which handles foodservice management for corporations, educational institutions, and recreation venues. Culinart is located in New York, where square footage is so expensive that no company will devote more than they have to for employee foodservice. Being able to fit storage space for purchased items while keeping space available for human traffic is quite a challenge in these small dining areas.

Culinart, a $50 million regional foodservice contractor, has met the challenge by using versatile equipment and utilizing little nooks that are commonly overlooked. "Most often, when we go into a corporate account, the client is not willing to give us much space to work with, so we have learned to deal with the small footprints we're given," said Beaulieu. "We will draw on the experience of our managers, and sometimes at the proposal stage we will look at the potential space and brainstorm how that space can be used effectively."

Among the innovative designs they have created are a vertical hot-food display cabinet, a curved glass deli counter with storage space underneath, a counter-top conveyor oven, and counter-top induction burners. The induction burners gave the staff the ability to do more cooking to order and the conveyor oven has expanded menu possibilities. Although these technical remedies can help with a difficult layout, efficiency in purchasing and storage is the most important thing to keep in mind when dealing with tight spaces.

*Source:* Sponsored by Nestle, "Squeezing Money Out of Tight Places," *Nation's Restaurant News,* vol. 38, no. 7, February 62, 2004, p. 28.

**Discussion Question:** Explain why it's especially important in small spaces not to have more supplies and food on hand than necessary.

freezers open into walk-in refrigerators.[16] Thawed food items should never be refrozen. As previously, raw food items should never come into contact with items that have been cooked and then frozen.

## ISSUING

For control purposes it is advisable that as few people as possible have access to the storage and issuing areas. Some type of requisition form, signed by someone in authority, is needed before food and beverage items can be released from storage.

Such forms aid in inventory control and analyzing menu costs. The objective is to ensure that only authorized personnel are allowed to requisition food and beverage items.

## Control

A system of inventory management helps ensure cost control. The inventory refers to the items available in storage. Commonly, two types of inventory are kept: physical and perpetual.[17] A physical inventory refers to the actual number of each item on hand. It is typically taken on the last day of each month.

Perpetual inventories are continuous records of what is bought and issued. While time consuming, especially if manual records are kept, the perpetual inventory will alert management to what must be reordered when, as well as to items that are overstocked. A perceptual inventory is especially appropriate for expensive menu items.

Food and beverage costs are calculated on the basis of the value of the inventory as follows: cost of food (beverage) for a specific period = value of opening inventory + food (beverage) purchases after opening inventory − value of closing inventory.

## PREPARATION

### Function

In the production area, functions tend to be divided into meat/fish/poultry preparation, vegetable preparation, salad preparation, and sandwich preparation. In smaller operations the salad and sandwich and/or the vegetable and salad functions are often combined. The objective is to prepare items to predetermined quality levels in sufficient quantities to meet customer demands while minimizing waste. Care must be taken to ensure that items susceptible to foodborne bacteria should be kept in the preparation area for as little time as possible. Such items can be iced or kept in a cold room to reduce the chance of spoilage.

The preparation area is where items are made ready for final cooking. Operations that purchase preportioned items—a growing trend—will have minimal need of such facilities for the preparation of meat, poultry, and fish. Similarly, using preprocessed and/or frozen vegetables has reduced the need for space to perform the traditional functions of washing, cutting, and chopping.

### Space Requirements

Equipment layout in this area can be arranged in a straight line because the tasks involved in preparing food occur in a logical sequence. Vegetables are trimmed, washed, and reduced in size, in that order. A worktable for trimming can be placed next to a sink for washing and draining, which, in turn, can be placed next to the area where vegetables are cut, diced, or chopped.

Because vegetables come from the storage area and go on to the main cooking or salad preparation area, the trimming table is located close to the storage area and vegetables are chopped near the cooking and salad preparation areas.

Vegetables will have to be stored temporarily prior to processing and a waste disposal area will also have to be included. Similar considerations are necessary for a salad preparation area.

---

## quick bite 8.3
### The New Teamwork of Service

**Learning Objective:** Compare and contrast the various production and service systems.

Employees in restaurants need to have good teamwork, but for a meal to be successful, employees must work well with customers too. This customer/employee teamwork is the successful recipe for great service.

Some new (or reinvented) approaches to service in fine dining include:

- "New American service"—the staff is well-informed and accessible, but very professional and correct in their interactions with customers. No introductions between waiter and table, no overly-intrusive conversation.
- Charming fine-dining service—the atmosphere of the restaurant is very high class, but the staff is open and friendly. Lutece, an upscale restaurant in New York City, combines fine French cuisine with personable service. "Today we sacrifice technical perfection to encourage this [friendly] tradition," said Eberhard Muller, the restaurant's owner.
- Southern hospitality—combines fine dining with friendly, open service. The servers are not overbearing in their conversations with their guests, but they do say hello. The goal is to warm up the chilly formality of fine dining. This approach is related to charming fine-dining service.

All of these styles emphasize server knowledge of the menu and of wines. Waiters must work well with the chefs to understand the daily changes in the menu and to be able to speak intelligently with the customers about any questions they might have.

*Source:* Taylor, Marilou, "Your Table Is Ready," *Restaurants & Institutions,* November 1, 1999, vol. 109, no. 29, p. 97.

**Discussion Question:** What are the pros and cons of discreet, highly professional service?

# COOKING

## Service Systems

Minor and Cichy have identified four major foodservice systems based on the extent to which processed foods are used.[18] Many operations use a combination of systems. The four systems are as follows:

- Convenience systems (maximum use of processed foods)
- Conventional systems
- Ready-food systems
- Commissary systems (minimum use of processed foods)

In convenience or assembly–serve systems, foods are purchased completely prepared and assembly, consisting of heating and/or minor preparation, is done in the operation. Although food cost is high and selections limited, only unskilled, low-cost labor is needed at the service point. Less preparation equip-

---

### quick bite 8.4
### Day in the Life: Richard Hamilton

Sliced Pear fuses Cajun-Creole to classic French to create a memorable fine-dining experience. The restaurant is the result of chef Richard Hamilton's exotic background and his drive to create something special from diverse cuisine. Before starting Sliced Pear, Hamilton studied and worked in a variety of restaurants ranging from France to the Bahamas, looking for innovative ideas and unique dishes. He found that the most important thing for chefs is to have bosses who believe in their vision and allow them to buy the best ingredients.

It's no wonder that Hamilton got into the restaurant business. When he was six years old, Hamilton started working at Hamilton House, his mother's Cajun-Creole restaurant. He also worked at a Southern-style family restaurant called Brandy's, which inspired some of his later choices at Sliced Pear. One thing he knew early on: he wanted to take the best of everything he'd experienced and fuse it to form a greater whole. "The nice thing about seeing all of those cuisines was learning that they're all based on the same techniques, and you need that good technical foundation," said Hamilton. "From there it's really just cooking what's in your imagination and in your heart."

*Source:* Duecy, Erica, "Richard Hamilton: Diversity Sweet Inspiration for Sliced Pear Chef," *Nation's Restaurant News,* vol. 38, no. 12, March 22, 2004, p. 38.

**Discussion Question:** Why could spending a few years working in a variety of restaurants be the ideal training for someone who wants to start his or her own restaurant?

---

ment and energy are required, but more storage space, particularly frozen storage, is needed.

There is some concern over product quality and customer acceptance of various convenience items. Foods are available in bulk, preportioned, and preplated form. Bulk convenience foods are portioned either before or after heating; preportioned items require only assembly and heating, while preplated foods need only be heated before serving.

A conventional system is one in which dishes are prepared from raw ingredients in the restaurant itself. Yet compromises, because of increased labor costs, are being made. Few operations have their own bakery or butcher shop on the premises. More employees, equipment, energy, and space are needed in a conventional system compared to one relying on convenience items.

In a ready-food system the food is prepared on premises, then chilled (cook–chill) or frozen (cook–freeze) for service later. Chilled items are usually held for 1 to 3 days; frozen foods for 30 to 60 days. This system is more complex than the previous two because of the need to package, distribute, and store the food. Management has more control over the handling, quality, and cost of the food because the items are prepared ahead of time. Consequently, there is less of a pressure atmosphere than when cooking items to order. These systems are best suited for large operations such as hospitals, airlines, banquets, and schools.

In a commissary or satellite system, food is prepared in large quantities at a central source and distributed to various service outlets. Economies of scale are possible in purchasing and production, and quality assurance is made easier. Distributing the food to the various satellite units is a major part of the system. Care must be taken to ensure that food safety is assured as the items are moved from the central facility to the outlying units.

## Space Requirements

The design of the cooking area is dependent on the type and amount of items to be prepared. A market analysis should determine what items will go on the menu; a market forecast will predict the amounts to be cooked at any time. From this estimate the type and size of equipment needed and the relationship of one piece to another can be determined.

The amount of space required for baking will depend on whether or not the restaurant prepares its baked goods from scratch. Most operations use either basic mixes or prepared unbaked goods requiring thawing and baking rather than the full line of baking functions.

Goods come into the cooking area from storage and preparation areas; utensils and cooking containers come from the pot-and-pan-washing locations. Food goes out to the service, salad, and sandwich preparation areas.

Equipment that produces heat and/or moisture must either be located under ventilating hoods or have its own ventilating system. Equipment that uses steam to cook the food must be installed carefully using curbs or in depressed areas of the floor.

Vents and grill openings that are required for equipment that needs air for ventilation or cooling must not be blocked. The location of the air conditioning for the main kitchen is extremely important in order that the air be kept reasonably cool while the food and cooking equipment remains reasonably hot.

If a great deal of baking is done, the cooking and baking areas can be placed close together so that they can share kettles, ovens, and mixers. Both should be located close to the pot-washing area.

Where cooks and bakers expect to use the same equipment extensively, employee work times can be staggered to ensure full utilization of equipment without employees getting into each other's way. Bakers, for example, might work at night preparing the following day's pastries and breads.

A well-thought-out layout would have a proof box, an oven, and a landing table next to each other to handle the baking of bread. Baker's tables tend to be centrally located to permit easy access to storage areas and frequently used equipment. Space has to be available for storage of baking supplies and finished items. Perishable items will have to be refrigerated prior to being moved to the serving area.

---

**quick fact**

McDonald's Corp., the world's largest restaurant chain, with more than 30,000 restaurants worldwide, has identified some formerly undisclosed suppliers while launching a graphical feature on its *www.mcdonalds.com* website to give U.S. customers a "virtual tour" of how some of its menu items go "from farm to table."

*Source: Nation's Restaurant News,* "McDonald's Identifies Suppliers to Show That Menu Items Are Nutritional," *http://www.nrn.com/newsletter-sr/story.cfm?ID=8411705304&SEC= QSR%20Newsletter*, November 7, 2005.

---

## Principles of Cooking

**Moist-Heat Cooking.**    Cooking is done by one of two methods: moist-heat or dry-heat cooking. Meat contains collagen, a fibrous matter that makes it tough. A similar tissue in vegetables is cellulose. Moist heat dissolves both to render the meat and vegetable tender. This is the reason that tougher cuts of meat are cooked in liquid.

The liquid used might be water, milk, tomato juice, wine, broth, or stock.[19] The most common cooking methods using liquid are boiling, blanching, braising, poaching, simmering, steaming, and stewing.

Boiling involves immersing the item in water at a temperature of 212°F (100°C). Boiling tends to take valuable nutrients out of the food being cooked. They remain in the water, which can be used for soup, stock, or a sauce. Foods tend to be boiled for a short period of time. Vegetables may be undercooked by boiling and transferred to a steam table, where the cooking process is completed before serving. Meats are simmered rather than boiled, while the process is not recommended for eggs, poultry, or fish because of the harm boiling does to the nutrients contained in these items.

Blanching or scalding involves exposing the food to boiling water for a very short period. Some items are blanched to remove some of their strong flavor, while others are blanched to dislodge external membranes. Blanching makes it easier to remove the skin from some fruits and vegetables. The term *blanching* also refers to the cooking of vegetables in deep oil, almost to the point of doneness, prior to finishing just before service. Parboiling involves keeping the food in the water longer and is used to cook the item partially before finishing it with another form of cooking. Squash, for example, may be parboiled before baking.

The appearance and taste of cooked vegetables and fruits are influenced by the alkalinity or acidity of the liquid in which they are cooked. Thus green vegetables turn drab in an acidic liquid, while the color is intensified in an alkaline medium. The latter type of liquid, however, may negatively affect the structure and presence of vitamins in the vegetables. To maintain as many nutrients as possible, cooking should be kept to a minimum.

In braising, meat is cooked in a small amount of fat in a covered container. Meat may be browned before stewing—called brun—to give it color. Blond braising involves no searing. Searing the food, according to a number of studies, does not help seal in the juices. The juices in which the meat is stewed add to its flavor. Less tender cuts of meat can be made tender by simmering in a liquid for a long time at a low temperature. Stewing is closely related to braising. Whereas braising involves cooking whole or sliced foods, stewing involves chopped or cubed foods. Stewing uses more liquid compared to braising, and the liquid covers the entire item being cooked. A heavy pot is used to ensure even cooking. Dishes may be browned (brun) first or not (blond). Thicker stews result from cooking without a lid over the pot.

*Poaching* is the term given to cooking in a liquid at a temperature below the boiling point of water. It is useful for foods that require gentle handling and low-temperature cooking, such as eggs and fish. Poultry, particularly bigger birds, are moister, more tender, and more flavorful when poached than when roasted.

Simmering involves cooking in a liquid whose temperature is between 185 and 205°F. When meat is placed in cold water and brought to a simmer, it has more flavor than when added to hot water and cooked. Chefs call simmering "let the liquid smile, not laugh out loud."[20]

Steaming food in the vapor of boiling-hot water is an excellent method for retaining nutrients in the food being cooked. Shrinkage is reduced and flavor maintained. Cereal products are typically steamed or boiled. Salt and a little oil can be added to the water for best results.

**Dry-Heat Cooking.**   Dry-heat cooking is used for the more tender foods and includes baking, barbecuing, broiling, grilling, ovenizing, roasting, and frying. Traditional barbecuing means roasting food in a covered pit, usually at a low temperature. The term now includes cooking over a grill or broiler and higher temperatures.

Broiling is usually reserved for the best cuts of meat. Thick pieces of meat will produce uniformly cooked meat with minimum shrinkage. Food is dipped in or brushed with oil to prevent it from sticking to the cooking surface. Meats are cooked on both sides for best results. Oven temperature is best between 300 and 350°F. The internal temperature of the meat should be 140°F for rare, 160°F for medium, and 170°F for well done. Grilling is similar to broiling and is usually reserved for steaks and hamburgers.

In ovenizing, food is placed on greased pans and fat dribbled over it frequently while it bakes in the oven. The finished product resembles fried or sauteed food.

Ideally, roasting is done at lower temperatures (250 to 350°F). In this way, shrinkage is reduced while flavor is enhanced. Because roasts continue to cook after removal from the oven, they should be taken out before the desired internal temperature (the best guide to doneness) is reached. The roast should then "rest" for 15 to 20 minutes before it is sliced. This makes slicing easier.

Foods are fried when they are cooked in fat or oil. The result is a pleasant, nutty flavor. Sauteed items are shallow fried; deep frying involves complete immersion of the food into the fat or oil. In the latter case it is important to ensure that grease does not penetrate the item being cooked. This is accomplished in one of two ways: Either the food is coated with a protective covering or the food is cooked at a temperature high enough that the food emits a barrier of steam to prevent the fat from penetrating the food.

The major ingredients used in baking are as follows:

- *Flour.* All-purpose flour consists of 20 percent soft wheat flour and 80 percent bread flour. Soft, weak, or pastry flour should be used for making pastries; hard-wheat flour is used for making bread.
- *Shortening.* Hydrogenated fats, oils, butter, and lard are used as shortening to produce a tender finished product.
- *Leavening agents.* Air, steam, and baking powder are examples of leavening agents, all used to add texture and volume. Heat helps in the process.
- *Yeast.* Added to water before being stirred with other ingredients, yeast gives off carbon dioxide and alcohol in the baking process.
- *Eggs.* Eggs can be added for flavor, color, or to act as a binding agent.

**Salads.** Salads consist of a base, body, garnishes, and dressings.[21] The base typically consists of salad greens, is used for visual effect, and is usually not eaten. The body of the salad consists of the items that make up the salad. Garnishes are added for eye appeal and include such things as croutons, nuts, and chicken or fish. Garnishes also add flavor and help keep the salad moist. It is difficult to maintain consistent quality because fresh vegetables are used in salads. Salads are labor intensive and difficult to keep for extended periods. However, they are easy to make, the ingredients can be changed at the last minute (depending on what is available), they are nutritious, and they add a different taste and texture to other items on the menu.

Salads should be made up shortly before serving, as they are highly perishable. Stainless steel equipment is required for their preparation. Fruits such as apples and bananas will brown when exposed to the air. This can be prevented by dipping the fruits in lemon juice.

## Control

One important key to controlling costs is to use standardized recipes. Standardized recipes ensure that "when the specified conditions are followed in them, the result is always a product which is similar in all respects."[22] Standardized recipes should contain "(1) the name of the menu item; (2) the pan size; (3) the temperature; (4) the yield; (5) the portion size; (6) the portion utensil; (7) the cooking time; (8) a sequential list of ingredients; (9) the quality of each ingredient; (10) the method; and (11) the special equipment needed."[23]

To prepare a standardized recipe, the following steps are necessary:[24]

1. Prepare the recipe according to the original source and evaluate according to acceptability for the operation.
2. Multiply the recipe to meet the number of portions needed and evaluate again as to acceptability, making any adjustments necessary to improve the dish. For example, the amount of seasonings required is not a simple multiple of the recipe.
3. Prepare the enlarged recipe and have it evaluated by a taste panel for suitability.
4. Prepare the recipe a minimum of three additional times, testing the popularity, preparation cost, and yield.
5. Standardize the recipe relative to ingredients and preparation methods and list all relevant information on a recipe card.

# SERVICE

## Service Styles

Over the years a variety of service styles have evolved, some more formal than others. Good service is more than following various rules of service. Good service is that which pleases the customer, which adds to the customer's enjoyment of the meal. Where the choice is between slavishly following rules and pleasing the customer, the choice should be the latter.

**Family-Style Service.** In family-style service, sometimes called English service, food is brought to the table in bowls or on platters and placed before the host. Traditionally, the host plates the food and, if necessary, carves the meat and hands it to the server, who lays the plate before the guest. Less formally, guests may help themselves from the serving dishes placed on the table. This style of service requires fewer servers and is particularly useful for serving large numbers of people in a short period of time, as at a banquet.

**Plate Service.** Plate or American service involves plating the food in the kitchen and serving it in the dining room. Solids are served from the left and beverages from the right. Designed to be quick and efficient, this service allows for close control of portions.

**Tableside Service.** Tableside or French service requires a *chef de rang* (waiter) and a *commis de rang* (assistant). Food is plated and served in the dining room from a *gueridon* (rolling cart). Final cooking may also be done on the gueridon by means of a small stove warmer or *rechaud.* The waiter takes the order, which is delivered to the kitchen by the assistant. The assistant will bring the food from the kitchen to the *gueridon,* where it is finished and plated by the *chef de rang.* The assistant serves the plates to the customers. The waiter is responsible for serving drinks and presenting the check.

In French service everything is served from the customer's right except for bread, butter, and salads, which are served from the left. Finger bowls, containing warm water with rose petals or lemon slices, are often provided for rinsing fingers.

Because side tables are required for this style of service, fewer dining tables can be located in a given area. This limits the revenue-producing ability of the restaurant. Due to the heavy use of employees and equipment, tableside service is the most costly of all service styles and therefore tends to be used in restaurants that can command a high average check. Tableside service is very dramatic and personal.

**Platter Service.** In platter (sometimes called Russian) service the food is prepared and portioned in the kitchen, where it is placed on platters. Plates are placed in front of each customer from the right of the guest and the food served from the platter to the plate by the server, serving from the customer's left and working counterclockwise around the table. Plates are removed from the right.

**Buffet Service.** In buffet service customers choose their meals from items laid out on a serving table. They either plate their own dishes or are served by employees standing behind the table. Silverware can be provided either on the buffet table or at the individual eating tables.

## Space Requirements

Table-service operations need pickup areas next to the cooking area to hold items prior to service. Salads, beverages, and desserts are picked up separately from cooked items. Rolls, bread, butter, and water are stored at server stations throughout the dining area.

In self-serve operations a variety of serving-line configurations are possible. Straight-line arrangements allow for easy access and a clearly defined flow of traffic. However, this layout limits the number of people who can be served within a set period of time. The greater the amount of linear space available for serving food, the greater the capacity of the system.

For most table-service restaurants, space requirements for serving areas are estimated as part of the main cooking area. Cafeterias, however, are different, in that separate areas are needed for serving. Space is required for the serving counter, for customers, and for servers. The amount of space needed depends on the number of customers to be served and the time allotted for service. Straight-line cafeteria counters can serve anywhere from 2 to 10 people a minute, depending on the number of choices and the number of servers. The more choices and the fewer the servers, the lower the number of customers who can be served per minute.

In recent years the traditional straight-line cafeteria counter has given way to island counters that are accessible to customers from all sides. These so-called shopping-center arrangements can accommodate up to 20 customers per minute.

Straight-line counters require 10 to 15 square feet of floor space for each linear foot of counter. The linear length of the counter depends on the number of items to be displayed. Shopping-center counters require 18 to 20 square feet of floor space per linear foot of counter. In both cases this space takes into account the counters, customer aisles, room for servers, and back-bar equipment.

The size of the serving area for cafeterias should be based on the dining room capacity. Ideally, the rate of people entering the dining room from the serving area—the flow rate—should equal the rate of people leaving the dining room having completed their meals. The number of usable seats needed in the dining room can be determined as follows:

$$N_d = \frac{N_m + N_{sa}}{(T_m/T_d) - 1}$$

where $N_d$ is the number of persons in the dining room or the number of usable seats, $N_m$ the total number of persons to be fed, $N_{sa}$ the number of persons in the serving area, $T_m$ the meal period, and $T_d$ the time a person spends in the dining area.

Cafeteria counters are placed as close to the cooking area as possible. This allows for speedy replacement of food items as they become depleted. Desserts and salads are placed at the beginning of the line; hot foods are located at the end of the line. This minimizes cooling of the hot items while increasing the sales of cold items. Having loaded up with an entrée, a customer may be reluctant to add a dessert. If the dessert is located before the entrée, however, the customer may be more inclined to select it.

The flow of many cafeteria lines breaks down as customers leave the line to pay. Additional cashier stations may be required to take care of this problem.

## Portion Control

The last step in the control process is to ensure effective portion control. The easiest way to ensure this is to use standard utensils when measuring and/or serving food. This can be done using such things as standard-sized pans, ladles, serving spoons, scoops, portion scales, cutting markers, meat slicers, egg slicers, and individually weighed, measured, and packed items (for example, sandwiches).[25]

## DISHWASHING

Dishwashing facilities are typically separated from other functions in an area that requires high levels of ventilation and illumination. Acoustical tile is useful in reducing the high noise level associated with this activity. Machines can be purchased appropriate to the number of dishes to be washed.

Often, separate facilities are used for washing glasses. Satisfactory results can be obtained with the use of additives or by washing glasses shortly after the water has been changed.

Design of this area depends on how much has to be washed and the time available for this function. Some operators carry a large inventory of flatware and store the dirty dishes, washing them over a longer period of time, taking advantage of off-peak energy rates while spreading employee workload. In other situations, management reduces inventory cost but requires that soiled dishes be washed immediately and put right back into service during the course of a meal period.

The sequence of tasks during dishwashing is sorting, scraping or preflushing, stacking, loading, removing, and unloading. Equipment should be arranged accordingly. After changing the water the order of washing would be glassware, utensils, dishes, then pots and pans.

Consideration has to be given to the movement of dishes in and out of the dishwashing area. Commonly, bussers bring dirty dishes into the area in bins. Clean dishes will either go to the kitchen, where the cooked food will be plated, or the dining room, where tables will be reset. Mobile plate and cup racks can be provided to move dishes to these areas.

## Pot and Pan Washing

The amount and type of space required for pot and pan washing will depend on the volume to be washed and when it is to be done. Where the same person washes dishes as well as pots, storage space for the pots will be required, as the dishes will have a higher time priority. Larger facilities may use machines rather than the typical sink for this purpose.

## WASTE DISPOSAL

Waste disposal requirements depend on the total relative amounts of paper, plastic, and cans generated; the cost of removal; and the prevailing laws regarding disposal.

Various disposal options are compaction, incineration, grinding, and pulping.[26] Compactors are useful when handling large amounts of waste. They reduce large volumes of waste into smaller amounts. Both volume and weight are concentrated. Care must be taken that the resulting package can be handled easily. Incineration involves burning the waste. Local pollution regulations may make this option cost prohibitive.

While most municipalities allow grinding as a way of disposing of waste, some communities have experienced problems with non-biodegradable materials and have placed restrictions on the use of this method. In waste-pulping a liquefied waste is produced through the use of heavy-duty rotary grinders using recirculating water. The water is extracted and the resulting semidry pulp is stored in bins prior to removal. This system cannot accommodate glass or metal.

## ENDNOTES

1. Mahmood Khan, *Foodservice Operations* (Westport, CT: AVI Publishing Company, 1987), pp. 254–257.
2. Lewis J. Minor and Ronald F. Cichy, *Foodservice Systems Management* (Westport, CT: AVI Publishing Company, 1984), p. 100.
3. Khan, *Foodservice Operations,* pp. 148–149.
4. Ibid., p. 175.
5. Ibid., p. 197.
6. Ibid., p. 163.
7. Ibid., pp. 164–165.
8. Ibid., p. 148.
9. Ibid., p. 148.
10. Ibid., pp. 209–211.
11. Edward A. Kazarian, *Foodservice Facilities Planning,* 3rd ed. (New York: Van Nostrand Reinhold, 1989), p. 11.
12. Khan, *Foodservice Operations,* pp. 211–215.
13. Ibid., p. 214.
14. Kazarian, *Foodservice Facilities Planning,* p. 12.
15. Ibid., p. 13.
16. Khan, *Foodservice Operations,* p. 218.
17. Ibid., p. 220.
18. Minor and Cichy, *Foodservice Systems Management,* p. 33.

19. John B. Knight and Lendal H. Kotschevar, *Quantity Food Production, Planning, and Management,* 2nd ed. (New York:Van Nostrand Reinhold, 1989), p. 173.
20. Ibid., p. 275.
21. Khan, *Foodservice Operations,* p. 267.
22. Ibid., pp. 252–253.
23. Minor and Cichy, *Foodservice Systems Management,* p. 130.
24. Khan, *Foodservice Operations,* pp. 254–257.
25. Ibid., p. 283.
26. Kazarian, *Foodservice Facilities Planning,* p. 17.

## INTERNET RESOURCES

Cost Guard Foodservice Software    *http://www.costguard.com/*
Food Software/Advanced Analytical, Inc.    *http://www.foodsoftware.com/*
Sysco Corporation    *http://www.sysco.com/*
ARAMARK Corporation    *http://www.aramark.com/*
Canteen Vending Company    *http://www.canteen.com/*

CHAPTER NINE

# KITCHEN EQUIPMENT AND INTERIORS: SELECTION, MAINTENANCE, AND ENERGY MANAGEMENT

"Anybody can make you enjoy the first bite of a dish, but only a
real chef can make you enjoy the last."
François Minot, editor, *Michelin Guide*

## learning objectives

*By the end of this chapter you should be able to*

1. Identify the considerations involved in the selection of kitchen equipment.
2. Identify the basic types of equipment found in kitchens.
3. Compare and contrast the relative advantages of the various materials used in kitchen interiors and equipment construction.
4. Identify the most important concepts in cleaning and maintaining kitchen equipment.
5. Design a comprehensive energy management program.

# EQUIPMENT SELECTION

## Basic Considerations

Several basic considerations are involved in the selection of kitchen equipment.[1] Management should consider capacity, need, cost, functional attributes, and sanitation and safety.

**Capacity.** Determining the capacity of each type of equipment to be used in an operation is critical before deciding how many pieces of which equipment to purchase. If the capacity calculation is too low, bottlenecks and slowdowns occur; if it is too high, the restaurant spends too much money on equipment that will not be used to its capacity.

Required equipment capacity can be determined as follows:[2]

1. Analyze each food item on the menu to estimate the number of portions to be prepared for every meal period. If menus are changed daily, it will be necessary to use a sample of dishes to be served.

2. The portion size for every menu item is then determined.

3. Multiplying the projected number of portions by the portion size will give the total volume of food to be prepared at each meal period.

4. The method of preparation and production is selected next for each item on the menu. Depending on the style of operation, items may be prepared individually to order, in small batches prior to the order, in large batches prior to service, or partially prepared in batches and finished when an order is received. The processing time has to be taken into account, together with when the preparation can be done. It may, for example, be possible to use the same piece of equipment at different times during the day to prepare more than one item.

5. The batch size is then determined for those items to be prepared in batches. The smaller and more frequently prepared the batches, the less equipment capacity is needed and the fresher the end product.

6. For items prepared to order, the number of portions to be prepared at any one time is estimated based on the projected number of customers, which items they are likely to order, and their arrival patterns.

7. Equipment catalogs can then be consulted to determine the number of pieces of equipment to be ordered. Some types of equipment are selected on the basis of the number of pans they can hold. In this case it is necessary to divide the number of portions to be prepared by how many can fit into a standard-size pan to get the capacity of the equipment in "number of pans required." For example, ovens hold bake pans that are 18 by 26 inches. Identifying how many portions can fit into a pan 18 by 26 inches and dividing that into the number of portions required will give the number of pans required and, consequently, an estimate of the size of the oven needed.

**Need.** Equipment should not be bought or leased unless it is needed. But what, exactly, does this mean? A piece of equipment is "needed" if it improves

## quick bite 9.1
### Hot Concepts: Technological Advances in the Restaurant

The restaurant industry is known for being slow to adopt new technologies. Nevertheless, with today's demands, restaurants are being forced to rethink new technology. Nowadays, new equipment is being developed for the kitchen, geared to promote low costs, consistency, efficiency, and safety.

For the fast food industry, new technologies are being developed that will advance the kitchen equipment used currently. New equipment will revolutionize the kitchen by reducing the space required by each piece of equipment, the number of employees needed to run the equipment, and the risk involved with operating current equipment. Such redesigned equipment includes refrigeration units, grills, and fryers.

New refrigeration units will be programmed to notify operators of variations in temperatures that can lead to food contamination. Cooking equipment will become custom-designed to deal with space constraints common in kitchens. These developments will promote the smart kitchen.

The vertical grill will change the way that fast food companies cook burgers. On the vertical grill, the burgers are taken from a freezer unit and put directly onto a conveyor belt. Another technology is the auto fry system. This system is run by a robot which fries, salts, and bags items like French fries. The auto fry will change the old-batch cooking methods and ensure product freshness.

*Source:* Frumpkin, Paul, "Never Fear, New Gear: Brave New World of Interactive Equipment, Robotics Offers Relief for Harried Operators," April 14, 2004, *www.nrn.com/equipment/*

**Discussion Question:** What are the benefits of being attentive to new technological developments?

---

the quality of the food being prepared, produces product and/or labor cost savings-results in increased quantity of finished product, and/or contributes to the profitability of the operation.[3]

The need for a particular piece of equipment should be classified as either essential, high utility, or basic.[4] In this way, priorities can be established in the event of a cash shortage.

**Cost.** Various costs are involved in the purchase of a piece of equipment.[5] In addition to the initial purchase price, the equipment must be installed, insured, maintained and repaired, financed, and operated.

Part of the cost analysis involves inclusion of the labor costs involved in preparation. The cost of buying preprocessed vegetables should be compared with the cost of a vegetable peeler plus the labor cost of peeling the items in-house.

Khan suggests the following formula as a method of calculating the value of a piece of equipment:[6]

$$H = \frac{L(A + B)}{C + L(D + E + F) - G}$$

where $H$ is the calculated value; $L$ the expected life of the equipment in years; $A$ the savings in labor per year; $B$ the savings in material per year; $C$ the cost of the equipment, including installation; $D$ the cost of utilities per year; $E$ the cost of maintenance and repair of the equipment per year; $F$ the annual projected interest on the money in $C$, if invested elsewhere for the life of the equipment; and $G$ the turn-in value at the end of the life of the equipment.

If $H$ is greater than 1.0, the equipment should be purchased. The higher the value of $H$, the more attractive the purchase becomes. This equation requires an estimate of the expected life of the equipment. The normal life of kitchen equipment varies from 9 to 15 years.

**Functional Attributes.**　It is important that equipment do what it is intended to do. Performance relative to cost and compared to the performance of other equipment should be examined carefully. Consideration should also be given to likely changes in the menu that may render an expensive piece of equipment obsolete. Quietness of operation, availability of parts, and ease of maintenance are also important. Finally, the type of energy used must be noted as part of the cost consideration.

The North American Association of Foodservice Equipment Manufacturers (NAFEM) has developed, and is refining, a data protocol that seeks to link restaurant equipment electronically to back-office computers and networks. Equipment that is compliant will alert managers when it needs to be refilled, cleaned, and maintained. Security features can specify which people have access to data on equipment usage.

**Sanitation and Safety.**　The National Sanitation Foundation (NSF) certifies equipment that meets the sanitary standards required for foodservice operations. NSF-approved equipment should be a consideration in making equipment purchases.

Safety is also an important consideration. All materials used should be non-toxic. Parts should be easily disassembled for easy cleaning, moving and sharp parts need to be protected, and safety locks are desirable on all equipment.

A major consideration in restaurants is fire safety. According to the National Fire Protection Association (NFPA), 11,300 fires were reported in eating-and-drinking establishments in 1997 resulting in $172.5 million in property damage Half of those fires started in kitchens and cooking equipment was the major cause. Reliable preparation involves several things:[7]

- Install a reliable fire-suppression system that includes tanks on the wall filled with wet or dry chemicals that are piped to the underside of the stove hood.

- Building codes may require a sprinkler system. While some insurance companies give reduced premiums if a sprinkler system is installed, others do not, arguing that water damage in the event of a fire is expensive and may wipe out any damage savings.
- Have adequate fire and business-interruption insurance.
- Develop an evacuation and recovery plan that shows where the exits are in both the dining room and kitchen.
- Maintain and clean equipment on a daily basis—especially ducts, filters, and hoods—to help guard against fires caused by grease buildup.
- Remove all rubbish before the restaurant closes down for the evening.
- Train busers to make sure cigarettes are out before they dump them in any sort of trash receptacle.
- Check that equipment, such as deep-fat fryers and grills, has been turned off.
- Designate one staff member during each shift as the person in charge of evacuation. This person will be the last to leave in the event of a fire and is responsible of accounting for all personnel once the operation is empty.
- Develop a business-continuity plan that includes names and contact numbers for the companies that supply the restaurant, a list of clients, and names of companies that clean, rebuild, and do fire-restoration work.

## Materials Used

The cost of a piece of equipment is directly related to the type of material used to construct it. The following are the most common materials used in constructing kitchen equipment.

**Wood.** The disadvantages of wood-constructed items outweigh the advantages. Because wood absorbs moisture, it tends to crack, thereby making it unsafe from the viewpoint of sanitation. It is, however, light in weight, can be designed into various shapes, cushions noise, is attractive, and is relatively inexpensive. Today, its use is limited to areas where there will be no contact with food.

**Metals.** Although a variety of metals are used in foodservice equipment, the most common metals in use are alloys. An alloy is a combination of one or more metals, commonly stainless steel (iron and carbon), brass (copper, zinc, and other metals), and Monel (nickel and copper). Pure copper is almost never used because it needs constant polishing, is heavy, and reacts with some food items.

Stainless steel is easily cleaned, is attractive, resists rust and stain formation, and can, because its surfaces show dirt easily, be kept sanitary. Two important considerations in purchasing stainless steel are thickness and finish. Thickness is important because stainless steel is fairly expensive. Selection is done through gauge numbers, which indicate the thickness of the steel. The thicker the steel, the lower the gauge. Gauges 8, 10, and 12 are good supports; 12 and 14 can be used for tabletops. Cost is also a function of the amount of polishing desired. The more polishing required, the higher the cost. The amount of polishing done on the equipment is a function of the finish number; the higher the number, the more polishing was done and the higher the cost. In production areas, finish 4 is common. In serving areas, a higher number would be appropriate.

Nickel is often found on equipment trim, railings, and counters. Aluminum is popular for utensils, equipment both inside and out, and steam-jacketed kettles. It is light, is a good conductor of heat and electricity, does not corrode easily, and is durable.

Cast iron is used in places that do not come into contact with food, such as stands and equipment supports. Iron is used in pots, pans, griddles, and gas burners, while brass is favored in faucets and shutoff valves.

Steel ovens, range interiors, frames, and supports are common. When steel and iron are treated with acid, they are galvanized. Galvanized steel and iron are common in dishwashing machines, sinks, and equipment legs.

**Plastics.**  Various plastics are being used increasingly in foodservice operations. They are very versatile, durable, and capable of being molded into different shapes. Acrylics are used in food covers; melamine can be used for dishes and glassware; fiberglass trays are common; nylons are used for mobile parts; storage bowls and containers are made of polyethylene; dishwashing racks are commonly made of polypropylene; polystyrene is used in cups and covers.

**Coatings.**  Coatings are placed on the interior surfaces of equipment to give the surfaces additional properties. For example, silicone makes a nonsticking surface; Teflon® aids in the release of food from a pan. For surfaces that come into contact with food, the coating should be smooth, corrosion resistant, nonabsorbent, as heat resistant as possible, and easily cleanable. There should be no interaction between the food and the coating such that the taste, color, or smell of the food is changed.

## Energy Sources

Because of the rising cost of energy, the source used to power the equipment is becoming an increasingly important consideration in selecting equipment. Electricity, gas, steam, and oil are all used as energy sources in kitchens.

In foodservice operations the form of energy used most commonly is electricity. Two voltage systems are used: 110–120 volts and 220–240 volts, the latter being more powerful. It is important that the correct voltage be available for a particular piece of equipment.

Fuses are used to prevent the entire electrical system from "blowing." The fuses used must be appropriate to the task. A simple equation is useful in determining the type of fuse required:[8]

$$W = V \times I$$

where $W$ is the measure of electricity in watts, $V$ the force behind the electrical current, and $I$ the amount of electricity flowing.

For 2000 watts of electricity on a 110-volt line, the amount flowing, $I$, is $W$ divided by $V$, or 2000 divided by 110, or 18.2 amperes. Adding in a 25 percent safety factor means that this circuit should be protected by a 25-ampere fuse. Electricity costs are expressed as a certain number of cents per kilowatt-hour, the cost of 1000 watts of electricity running for 1 hour.

## Specifications

It is vital that exact specifications be used when purchasing equipment. These should include the following:[9]

1. The title or name of the piece of equipment
2. The scope or intended use
3. Classification: the type, model, size, and style
4. Specific requirements to include such things as
   - Dimensions and temperature ranges
   - Materials used in construction and finish
   - Electrical requirements
   - Control regulations and displays
   - Performance criteria
   - Certification by various agencies [such as the Underwriters' Laboratories (UL), National Sanitation Foundation (NSF), National Electric Manufacturers Association (NEMA), American Gas Association (AGA), and the American Society of Mechanical Engineers (ASME) for steam equipment]
   - Types of warranties
   - Parts and labor numbers and costs for maintenance and repair
   - Number of manuals required
5. Quality assurance: inspection and performance tests
6. Delivery and installation dates
7. Payment terms and dates
8. Drawings and illustrations
9. The name of the contact

## EQUIPMENT TYPES

### Dry-Heat Cooking Equipment

**Ranges.** Ranges, either gas or electric, are the most basic piece of cooking equipment for most foodservice operations. Generally, they are mounted on the floor, with the cooking done in pots directly on the range top. A heavy frame is preferred because of the heavy use that ranges receive. Ideally, ranges should have reflectors and removable drip pans for ease of cleaning. While the number of ranges required will vary depending on the type of menu served, the following guidelines can be used.[10] For a restaurant serving fewer than 300 meals a day, one range would be sufficient, two ranges would be needed to cook between 300

**Learning Objectives:** Identify the considerations involved in the selection of kitchen equipment. Identify the basic types of equipment found in kitchens.

Restaurant operations are known for producing large daily amounts of waste. Considering the amount of space, time, and money involved in waste management, it is important to consider equipment that would eliminate any excess. The Pack-A-Drum is a manual trash compactor that addresses the problems associated with managing trash such as the number of employee trips to the dumpster, spillage, trash volume, and hauling rates.

The compactor can be wheeled around to various receptacles where the trash bag is placed in the steel drum and compressed to a fourth of the bag's original size. This means that more trash can fit into each bag and that fewer trips to the dumpster are needed. Transferring the compressed trash onto a cart eliminates the "snail trail" or leakage problem which might cause slip and fall accidents as well as contamination.

Because the volume of trash is reduced, the costs associated with hauling fees are reduced. Less trash in the dumpster means fewer visits from the waste company. Waste companies charge fees based on frequency and "weight-to-density."

For operations like McDonald's and Burger King, the Pack-A-Drum provides a sound "trash strategy" because trash bags are often filled with mostly with empty cups, containers, and air. When choosing equipment, capacity, need, functionality, sanitation, and safety should influence the final decision. The Pack-A-Drum has the ability to deal with all these concerns.

*Source:* "Good Trash Goes in Small Packages: A Simple Compacting Procedure Saves Space, Time, Money," *Nation's Restaurant News,* vol. 2, no. 2, p. 19, May 2003.

**Discussion Question:** What factors should be considered when choosing kitchen equipment?

and 400 meals a day, three could handle 400 to 500, while four could cope with 500 to 1000 meals daily.

Hot tops require from 20 to 30 percent more energy than open burners because the heating plate must be heated before the pan is heated. While burners are limited to one pan each, hot tops offer more flexibility by providing an area for several pots and pans.

It is important that grease traps be easily removable for both cleaning and maintenance.

**Conventional Ovens.** Because conventional ovens are used a great deal, durability is important. The ease of cleaning and energy conservation should also be considered. Four to five inches of insulation (fiberglass, rockwool, or vitreous fiber) is desirable to help cut energy losses. Ovens may be stacked one on top of the other to cut down on space needs. The same guidelines for range requirements can be used to estimate oven needs. A more sophisticated formula is as follows:[11]

$$\text{required no. ovens} = \frac{\text{no. servings}}{\dfrac{\text{no. servings}}{\text{per pan}} \times \dfrac{\text{no. pans}}{\text{per oven}} \times \dfrac{\text{no. batches}}{\text{per hour}}}$$

**Convection Ovens.** Placement of the heating element(s) in a conventional oven does not allow for the consistent distribution of heat inside the oven. Convectional ovens are designed to eliminate this problem. The forced-air model uses a fan to distribute heat in a uniform manner, thus allowing more internal space to be used.

In the roll-in type, carts or racks can be rolled into a large oven, thereby allowing heat to reach all the racks equally. Another model, the pulse type, alternates hot and cold air. The hot air cooks the food; the cold air prevents overcooking.

In general, convection ovens require less labor, space, and energy; cook at lower temperatures; and enhance quality by allowing for an even distribution of heat. On the other hand, soft foods or batters may suffer visually from the circulation of air in the oven.

**Infrared Ovens.** The relatively new infrared ovens take up less space than conventional ovens while using less energy because they cook at higher temperatures for relatively short periods.

**Mechanical and Pizza Ovens.** The major differences between conventional and mechanical ovens are that the latter are larger and have mechanical parts inside that help move the food while inside the oven. A reel oven has trays that move vertically in the oven. Glass doors allow for inspection of the food as it is being cooked. Rotary ovens, on the other hand, have circular shelves that rotate horizontally around a central axis. Traveling tray ovens are large ovens that allow food items to travel through the oven on trays. Pizza ovens are deeper than the other types and allow for the horizontal placement of pizzas.

**Microwave Ovens.** Microwave ovens use radiation to cook food. Because of this, food is cooked faster and the surrounding air is not heated. These ovens are particularly useful for reheating items and thawing meats. They cannot handle large quantities of food, nor can they brown food items. To eliminate the latter problem, a combination convection/microwave oven has been developed.

**Deck Ovens.** Deck ovens are decked or stacked to save on floor space. They may be either roasting or baking ovens. Capacity can be estimated by identifying the number of batches per hour that can be handled. Roasting times vary from 15 to 18 minutes per pound for a cooked ham to 30 to 50 minutes per pound for fresh pork. Baking times vary from 15 to 20 minutes for rolls to 50 to 60 minutes for fruit pies.

The two-deck arrangement is the maximum height for safety in a deck oven. In a three-deck arrangement the top oven is too high while the lower deck puts a strain on workers' backs because of the bending that is required for loading and unloading.

**Broilers.**   Broiling produces a charred or smoked flavor to meats by cooking the meat on a grid, which allows the fat to drip down and partially burn, thereby imparting the smoked flavor.

Broilers are commonly included into the range area in one of three ways.[12] Either the broiler is at the same height as the range top, or it is purchased as a central component with an overhead oven heated by the burners in the broiling compartment, or it is mounted on a conventional range-type oven with or without an overhead oven.

A small broiler—a salamander—can be mounted on top of a heavy-duty range for smaller operations that do not require much broiling. Broiler capacity is a function of the size of the broiler grid and the type of food to be cooked. For example, a 1-inch steak will take 15 minutes to be cooked rare, while a half-chicken will require 30 minutes of cooking. The number of portions to be prepared at any one time will determine the number and size of broilers needed.

**Griddles.**   A griddle offers a heated surface particularly useful for short-order cooking. For example, the cooking time for various items on a griddle will range from 1 to 2 minutes for a grilled cheese sandwich to 8 to 10 minutes for a ham steak. Space should be provided near the griddle to hold supplies and other equipment necessary for its operation. Griddle capacity is determined as suggested previously for broilers.

---

### quick  fact

The Raytheon Corporation produced the first commercial microwave oven in 1947. These primitive units were gigantic and enormously expensive, standing 5 1/2 feet tall, weighing over 750 pounds, and costing about $5000 each. The magnetron tube had to be water-cooled, so plumbing installations were also required.

*Source: http://www.gallawa.com/microtech/history.html*, November 7, 2005.

---

## Steam Equipment

**Steam-Jacketed Kettles.**   Steam-jacketed kettles are indispensable in most restaurant kitchens. They are excellent for foods that do not require high temperatures. The steam in the jacket heats the metal, which, in turn, heats the food inside the kettle—the steam does not come into contact with the food, so the nutritional loss is low. If there is no steam supply, a special generator must be purchased, adding to the cost of the equipment. A water faucet over and a drainage line near the bottom of the kettle are important considerations.

The capacity of the kettle needed is calculated as follows:[13]

$$\frac{\text{capacity of kettle}}{\text{(in gallons or liters)}} = \frac{\text{no. servings} \times \text{portion size} \times \% \text{ headspace}}{128 \text{ oz (1 gal)} \times \text{no. batches [or 1000 ml (1 liter)]}}$$

Fifteen percent is usually allowed for the headspace to prevent overflow, spillage, and/or spattering.

**Steamers.** Steamers are capable of cooking large quantities of food quickly while retaining nutrients and maintaining quality. Once food is placed in the steamer, even from a frozen state, it can be left alone. Although useful for vegetables, rice, pasta, and special desserts such as custard, other types of food cannot be successfully steamed. In addition, adjustments are necessary to get the food quality to where it should be.

## Fryers

**Deep-Fat Fryers.** Deep-fat fryers should be made of noncorrosive material, and the temperature controls be placed such that they can be reached safely without exposure to spattered fat. A convenient system should be in place to drain the fat and a mechanism should be in place for removing food particles from the fat.

The capacity of a fryer depends on the pounds of fat in the fry kettle, the heat input, and the cooking time required. Typically, fryers are designed on a fat-to-food ratio of 6:1, indicating that 6 pounds of fat is required in the kettle for each pound of food to be fried. Conventional fryer capacity ranges from 15 to 130 pounds. A useful rule of thumb is that a fryer can prepare 1.5 to 2 times its weight of fat per hour. Thus a 130-pound-capacity fryer can cook from 195 to 260 pounds of food per hour.

Pressure fryers have lids that can be sealed, thus allowing frying under pressure. As a result, cooking time is shorter and at a lower temperature. Because of this the fat does not break down so quickly. In addition, there is less moisture loss, resulting in food that is crispy on the outside and juicy on the inside.

The continuous-type fryer moves food continuously through the fat on a conveyer belt. An automatic basket-lift or a timer bell allows cooks to attend to other tasks while frying food without the danger of it being overcooked.

**Tilting Skillets.** A tilting skillet or tilting fry pan is fastened to the floor by brackets. Its versatility makes it very desirable: It can substitute as a griddle, deep-fat fryer, poacher, or holder of food.

## Small Equipment

**Food Cutters.** Able to handle meats, vegetables, and fruits, food cutters can cut, dice, and shred. Food is placed in a bowl that rotates and exposes the food to high-speed rotating blades.

The capacity of the machine is a function of the size of the bowl and the amount of food that can be processed per minute. Cutters can be either bench or floor models.

**Slicers.** The essential elements of a food slicer are a circular knife blade and a carriage that passes under the blade. These allow for strict control of the thickness of slices of food.

**Mixers.** Every kitchen needs some blenders and mixers. The major purchasing consideration is the horsepower of the motor. It is preferable to purchase a larger model over a smaller one that requires several batches. The variety of attachments available makes mixers very versatile pieces of equipment. A mixer can do much more than mix food. Adapters are available to allow chopping, dicing, shredding, and juice extraction. The smaller bench model comes in sizes from 5 to 20 quarts, while the larger models are sized from 30 to 400 quarts.

**Vertical Cutter/Mixers.** Consisting of a stationary bowl with high-speed horizontal blades, the vertical cutter/mixer has a greater capacity than that of other food cutters.

**Vegetable Peelers.** Vegetable peelers consist of a cylindrical tank that has a revolving disk in the bottom. There is an opening above the disk for loading the vegetables and one below for removing the peels. As the disk revolves, the vegetables are peeled by being thrown against the abrasive-coated walls.

## Dishwashers

Dishwashers come in a variety of types. The most common are the immersion dishwasher, which submerges racks of dishes; the single-tank, stationary-type dishwasher, which wash racks of dishes with jets of water within a single tank; the conveyer-rack machine, which carries racks of dishes on a conveyer belt through the dishwasher; the flight-type dishwasher, which has a continuous rack conveyer on which dishes are placed on pegs or bars for transportation through the machine; and the carousel-type dishwasher, which features a closed-circuit conveyer for loading and unloading dishes.

Dishwasher capacity is stated as the number of pieces that can be washed per hour or the number of meals to be served per meal period. A single-tank dishwasher can handle from 50 to 600 meals per meal period; two-tank machines are capable of handling from 1500 to 2000 meals per meal period; three-tank machines are suitable for 2500 meals per meal period.

## Refrigeration Equipment

Refrigeration equipment may be either mobile or fixed reach-ins, specialized units, or ice-making equipment.[14]

**Reach-Ins.** Reach-in units may be of either refrigerated or low-temperature type. Whether the door opens to the left or right is an important consideration when considering traffic flow throughout the kitchen. Doors, which may be full- or half-length, should have strong catches. Adjustable shelving allows maximum storage flexibility.

Low-temperature reach-ins may be either upright or chest type. The former cost a little more and will lose more refrigerated air than the latter, but they are easier to defrost, require less floor space, and allow for easier storage and removal of items.

**Specialized Equipment.**   Specialized equipment consists of such items as fountains, salad or cold pans, display refrigerators, and walk-ins.

Because fountains must provide for different refrigeration needs, two or more condensing units may be required. For example, drinking and carbonated water, whipped cream, and other foods should be kept at about 40°F, while ice cream must be slightly colder than 10°F for dishing.

Salad pans or cold pans are commonly used in cafeteria counters for display of salads and other cold items. Some are designed to be flooded with water, which is then frozen and the display items placed on the ice.

Walk-ins are used to store large quantities of food in central storage areas. Typically, a large operation uses three walk-ins: one for fruits and vegetables, one for meats, poultry, and fish, and one for dairy products.

**Ice-Making Equipment.**   Electricity, cold water, and drainage facilities are necessary for ice-making equipment. Ice can be made in blocks, cubes, or crushed/flake form. Flake machines produce more ice per day than do cube machines. Block ice can be sculpted into decoration pieces. Cubes can be from 1/4 to 1 inch. Cube ice lasts longer in drinks and is, therefore, used in takeout and for drinks to be held before being consumed. Flake ice, on the other hand, cools the drink faster but melts faster as well. Small cubes or flakes make a drink look larger in the glass than do large cubes.

## INTERIOR SURFACES

### Materials

Selection of materials for interior walls, floors, and ceilings must take into account not only attractiveness to customers, but also such things as ease of cleaning, ease of maintenance, and safety.

**Flooring.**   The most important factors to consider when selecting floor coverings are the resiliency and porosity of the material. *Resiliency* refers to the ability of the material to withstand shock. Asphalt, linoleum, vinyl, and sealed wood are examples of resilient floors.

*Porosity* identifies the extent to which the material can be penetrated by liquids. Absorption of liquids can damage a floor, in addition to making it difficult to get rid of microorganisms on or below the surface.

A variety of materials can be used for floor coverings.[15] Asphalt is tough, inexpensive, and resistant to water and acids. However, it tends to buckle under heavy weight and does not wear well under exposure to grease or soap.

Good carpeting holds its shape. It absorbs both sound and shock and has a good appearance. It should not be used in food preparation areas because of the difficulty in keeping it clean and hygienic in an area where spills are common.

Ceramic tiles are nonabsorbent. They are useful for walls but are much too slippery for use on floors. Concrete, a mixture of cement, sand, and gravel, is inexpensive. However, because it is porous, it should not be used in food preparation areas.

Although it retains its shape, linoleum is nonabsorbent and is unable to withstand weight. Marble has a good appearance, is nonresilient, nonabsorbent, expensive, and slippery. Plastic is the most resilient of all the materials listed. It is, however, nonabsorbent and cannot be exposed to alkalines or solvents.

Rubber helps prevent slips and is resilient. It can be slippery when wet unless an abrasive is added. Although resilient and resistant to water, grease, and oil, water seepage can cause vinyl tiles to lift, causing a safety and sanitation hazard.

Terrazzo, a mixture of marble chips and cement, offers a good appearance if sealed properly. However, it is nonresilient and nonabsorbent, and it is slippery when wet. Additionally, the installed cost is approximately six times that of vinyl. However, because of its longer life span, over a 40-year period the cost of terrazzo is only 12 percent higher than that of vinyl.

Wood is absorbent, can be fairly inexpensive, and offers a good appearance. It should not be used in food preparation areas, as it offers a breeding place for dust and insects. Properly sealed, wood can be used in serving areas.

Kitchen floors need to be nonslip, sanitary, and able to handle spills and constant cleaning. Preferred materials are marble, terrazzo, natural quarry tile, asphalt tile, or sealed wood. Poured seamless concrete can be used if it has been sealed adequately.

Carpeting can only be used in serving areas. Carpets that are closely woven are easier to clean. Medium to dark colors with patterns tend not to show spots. They do, however, require vacuuming on a daily basis in addition to periodic shampooing. Because bar areas suffer from dropped cigarettes and spilled drinks, they can use marble or tile to advantage.

Coving is a useful technique that improves sanitation by providing a curved sealed edge between floor and wall. Sharp corners or gaps that would be difficult to clean are thus eliminated.

**Walls and Ceilings.**   In selecting wall and ceiling materials, four things are particularly important: cleanability, location, noise reduction, and color. Often materials are chosen without regard to future maintenance time and costs. For example, ceramic tile, which is a popular wall covering, should have its grouting smooth, waterproof, and sealed to help in keeping it clean.

Stainless steel is a favorite material for kitchen locations because it is durable and moisture resistant. This is important in an area such as a kitchen, which involves a great deal of traffic and has a high humidity level. On the other hand, painted plaster or cinder-block walls, if selected properly, can be used successfully in dry areas. They would not, however, be suitable in areas where food or grease could splash on the wall.

Older people tend to touch the wall for support, especially on stairs and in corridors. Wall surfaces in these areas should be easy to clean. Smooth sealed plastic, plastic-laminated panels, and plastic-coated tiles are excellent ceiling choices for their ability to spread light and absorb sound.

In food preparation areas it is desirable to have light-colored walls and ceilings to help distribute light and to make dirt easier to see (and, therefore, to clean).

---

quick bite 9.3
## Advantages of Equipment

**Learning Objective:** Compare and contrast the relative advantages of the various materials used in kitchen interiors and equipment construction.

Kitchen-hood controls like the Intelli-Hood provide an efficient ventilation system with several benefits. The Intelli-Hood is an innovative alternative to the noisy ventilation systems characteristic of traditional kitchen hoods.

The Intelli-Hood incorporates "smart technology" which has built-in temperature and optic sensors to reduce energy use. These sensors regulate the fan speeds and monitor the "heat and smoke load" from cooking. When the kitchen is busy, the fans will provide the ventilation necessary. Likewise, if the kitchen is slow, the fans run at a slower speed.

The benefits of the Intelli-Hood include:

- An improved working atmosphere in the kitchen
- Reduced electrical costs
- Reduced noise levels associated with ventilation fans
- Cooler kitchens because cool air from air conditioners is not being exhausted outside
- Less grease accumulation on the roof's grease guards

Not only is the system "fool-proof," the Intelli-Hood can be overridden with the push of a button. Because the fans are not running at 100% all of the time, the operation can reduce electricity costs by one-sixth.

*Source:* "Smart Choices Pay Off: Controls on Kitchen Hoods Provide 'As Needed' Ventilation at TGI Friday's," *Nation's Restaurant News*, vol. 2, no. 1, p. 1, May 2003.

**Discussion Question:** Why is choosing the right equipment necessary for the kitchen?

# EQUIPMENT MAINTENANCE

The cost of equipment maintenance, which is largely a function of labor, should be determined when purchasing equipment. Planning the maintenance function will help assure lower operating costs through reduced maintenance while ensuring continued high sanitation standards throughout the life of the equipment.

The following are the most important concepts involved in cleaning and maintenance:[16]

1. Minimize soil, dirt, and food buildup.
2. Remove buildup immediately.
3. Avoid as many soil-collecting surfaces and recesses as possible.
4. Select smooth, nonporous surfaces.
5. Provide easy access to areas that have to be cleaned frequently.
6. Streamline electrical, gas, and plumbing connections.
7. Use coved corners on equipment and building surfaces.
8. Provide adequate drains and cleanouts.
9. Use automated cleaning and sanitizing systems.

## Stainless Steel Surfaces

Stainless steel surfaces are subject to staining. Stainless steel requires contact with air to keep the layer of oxide that gives it its shine, and thus it must be cleaned regularly. On a routine basis the surface should be cleaned with a hot detergent solution, rinsed, and wiped dry with a soft clean cloth. Periodic deep cleaning consists of a paste of water and a nonabrasive scouring powder. The paste is rubbed in the direction of the polish lines to prevent scratches. The surface is then rinsed and dried.

Stainless steel, wood, or plastic scrapers—but not steel wool, steel scrapers, or knives—can be used to remove heavy deposits of food and/or soil. A vinegar and water solution, followed by rinsing and drying, is appropriate for removing hard-water deposits.

## Equipment

**Broilers.** Broiler grates and other movable parts should be cleaned daily. With gas broilers it is important to check the flame. A yellow-tipped flame indicates insufficient air. The burners can be adjusted to give a blue flame. Gas ports should be kept clean. With electric broilers heating elements can be replaced when they burn out.

An energy management program would ensure that[17]

1. Burner orifices are checked and cleaned.
2. Pilot lights are cleaned and adjusted.
3. Air shutters are checked to ensure that the air–gas mixture is correct.

4. Ceramic and metal radiant units are checked for deterioration and replaced with new chips if blackened or cracked.

**Coffee Urns.**   Two problems with coffee urns can ruin the taste of the coffee. First, minerals in the water can be deposited. Second, deposits will accumulate on surfaces that are exposed to brewed coffee or coffee vapors.

The solution is to clean the urn after making every batch of coffee. This is done by rinsing out the urn to remove any remaining coffee and deposits, adding a gallon or so of hot water, brushing the interior of the urn, then rinsing the urn. Twice a week the urn can be cleaned with a manufacturer-recommended product to remove stubborn deposits.

Thermostats should be checked periodically to ensure that the correct serving temperature is being maintained. Weekly checks for leaks should also be made.

**Dishwashers.**   The power should be turned off before cleaning a dishwasher. Tanks have to be drained and cleaned, wash arms removed, and lime or hard-water deposits eliminated from the rinse jets.

The exterior can be cleaned with a detergent solution, rinsed, and dried. Periodic checks are necessary for leaks, and belts and conveyors are examined for wear and lubricated.

On a regular basis,[18]

1. Spray nozzles, tanks, and heater coils are cleaned with a wire when lime deposits are detected.
2. The temperature of the final rinse is checked to ensure that it is at 180°F on high-temperature machines and at 140°F on low-temperature machines.
3. Feed and drain valves and pumps are checked for water leakage.
4. Speed reducers on conveyor-type washers are examined to ensure proper lubrication.
5. The insulation of water lines in the recirculation loop is noted.
6. The power rinse is examined to ensure that it turns off automatically.
7. Thermometers are checked and adjusted.

**Fryers.**   Fryers should be cleaned daily or at least twice weekly, depending on use. The fat must be removed and the interior wiped out and filled with water and a fryer cleaner solution. The interior is then rinsed and dried after removal of the cleaning solution. Since different temperatures are need for different foods, it may be necessary to maintain two or more fryers to cook various food items—one for seafood, another for vegetables.

Tilting fry pans should be cleaned daily. Food residue is scraped from the surfaces, which are then washed down with warm water and the pan rinsed.

An energy program would ensure that[19]

1. Fat containers are inspected for grease leaks.
2. Thermostats are calibrated.
3. Gas burners and pilot lights are cleaned and adjusted.

## A Day in the Life: Paul Pinnell

Paul Pinnell has been the general manager of Nana for nine years. Located in Dallas, Texas, on the 27th floor of the Wyndham Anatole hotel, Nana is a fine dining establishment that seats 170 and contains five private dining rooms set aside exclusively for dinner. Guests choose Nana because of the incredible food, wine, and service. Paul Pinnell along with his well-trained staff are committed to going above and beyond each individual's expectations.

A day in the life of Paul Pinnell starts around 10 or 11 o'clock in the morning. He begins by checking the average 75 emails and 10 to 12 voice-mails. He attends to the messages, and then proceeds to review private party bookings. From noon to 2 o'clock, Pinnell and the executive chef work to finalize menus for private parties, create menus for upcoming parties, and book future parties. Around 2 P.M., Pinnell ties up any loose ends with regards to special requests and any private party requirements (flowers, table set-up, etc.).

At 4 P.M., Pinnell meets with the rest of the managers to forecast business for the night. They discuss reservations and parties as well as potential walk-ins. This prepares management for the staff line-up at 5 P.M. During the pre-shift meeting, Pinnell mentions any new additions to the wine list and menu. He discusses changes in the restaurant and outlines the flow of service for the night.

Pinnell can be found on the floor for the remainder of the night providing support for the staff and personalizing the dining experience for each of Nana's guests. He approaches guests minutes after food has been brought to the table to inquire after their satisfaction. If there is a problem, Pinnell himself deals with it.

Pinnell's day doesn't end when the kitchen closes. Instead, he prepares for the next type of business at Nana's. The bar, which can hold 300 people, brings in live music seven days a week. Pinnell prepares to go home at around 1 or 2 o'clock in the morning. Yet his day still has not ended. Once at home, Pinnell winds down by reading magazines and books about restaurants with the goal of remaining up-to-date with the trends of the industry.

*Source:* Ruggless, Ron, "Paul Pinnell: Former Theater Major Takes Performance Seriously, Treats Every Night Like Opening Night," *Nation's Restaurant News,* vol. 37, no. 16, pp. 71–72, April 21, 2003.

**Discussion Question:** Why would a general manager want to forecast the flow of service before the doors open?

4. Flues are examined for possible obstructions.
5. Gas valves are lubricated.

Fat is the most costly part of the frying process. During frying the food absorbs fat, which must constantly be replaced. Fat should be strained daily and 15 to 20 percent of the kettle capacity added as fresh fat.

Fat breakdown can be minimized by[20]

1. Switching the fryer to "standby" during slack periods.
2. Never adding seasonings to foods during frying.
3. Keeping all metal components in contact with the fat free of carbon, food crumbs, soap, and moisture.
4. Ensuring that the fat level not be topped up with lard, meat drippings, or other fatty substances.

**Griddles.** At a minimum, griddles should be cleaned once a day. A griddle stone rather than steel wool should be used on the griddle surface, always rubbing with the grain of the surface. The surface is then seasoned prior to the next use.

It is also important that[21]

1. Thermostats are calibrated.
2. Pilot lights are adjusted to the lowest possible flame.
3. The air–gas mixture is checked to ensure a blue flame. Cold spots should be checked for on a periodic basis.

---

q u i c k   f a c t

In 1938, Roy Plunkett capitalized on an accident and invented one of the best known and most widely used polymers of all time: Teflon. Polytetra-fluoroethylene, or PTFE, was first marketed under the DuPont Teflon® trademark in 1945. The molecular weight of Teflon can exceed 30,000,000, making it one of the largest molecules known. The surface is so slippery, virtually nothing sticks to it or is absorbed by it.

*Source: http://inventors.about.com/library/inventors/blteflon.htm,* November 7, 2005.

---

**Ovens.** Similar maintenance procedures for griddles should be evident in the operation of ovens. On a daily basis, burned-on particles of food should be removed from the decks and the interior of the oven brushed out. Hardened food can be removed by sprinkling with salt and running the oven at 500°F for half an hour. The charred food is then removed with a spatula.

Ovens and oven racks need to be level for even cooking. Door crevices need to be kept clean to ensure proper closure, which keeps the heat in.

The interior of convection ovens may be porcelain, stainless steel, aluminized steel, or Teflon® coated and should be cleaned following the recommendations of the manufacturer. Clean doors help ensure minimum heat loss. Fan blades that are dirty reduce airflow and can be cleaned with a detergent solution.

Microwave ovens require less maintenance than do other types. As before, special attention should be paid to the door to ensure a tight fit.

After cleaning ranges a light coating of cooking oil is applied to help prevent rusting.

**Food Cutters, Choppers, and Slicers.** Choppers and cutters should be rinsed after each use. They should be unplugged before cleaning. Special care must be taken with slicer blades, which should be sanitized and allowed to dry after cleaning.

**Mixers.** Mixers should be cleaned right after use.

**Tables.** Tabletops can be scrubbed with a hot detergent solution before being rinsed, sanitized, and allowed to dry. Drawers should be emptied and washed weekly.

**Refrigerators.** The inside of reach-in refrigerators should be cleaned once a week. Shelves are removed and cleaned at the pot sink or run throughout the dishwasher.

Condenser coils need to be watched for dirt buildup, which cuts down on the transfer of heat and causes the unit to run excessively. Coils are dusted or wiped free of dust and dirt.

Walk-ins should be cleaned at most once a month, depending on use, following the procedures outlined previously. A comprehensive program would ensure that[22]

1. Worn or damaged compressor belts are replaced.
2. The refrigerant level is checked if a short cycle or loss of temperature control is noticed.
3. The fan, condenser fins, plates, and blower coils are cleaned.
4. Gaskets, seals, and hinges on doors are checked for a tight fit.
5. Defrosting is done monthly.
6. Thermostats are properly calibrated.
7. Hinges and latches are lubricated with food-grade oil.
8. Outside walls are felt for cold spots that would indicate insulation failure.
9. The defrost cycle is set such that freezers will defrost during off-peak hours.
10. Compressors are checked for leaks and refrigerant levels.
11. The condenser is brush cleaned.
12. Coils are examined to ensure that they are not clogged with dirt or grease.
13. All service motors are inspected regularly.

**Steam Equipment.** Steam-jacketed kettles are cleaned after the steam is turned off and they have been allowed to cool. The kettle is flushed, filled with a detergent solution, and soaked for 30 to 60 minutes. The kettle is then drained, rinsed, and sanitized.

**Ventilating Hoods.** Filters should be cleaned at least once a week. Clogged filters reduce airflow and significantly reduce the efficiency of the ventilation system. As a result, droplets can fall onto food that is being prepared. A more serious danger is that posed by the threat of fire due to grease buildup. Some states require that restaurants have periodic cleaning of hoods by a certified hood cleaning service.

---

## quick bite 9.5
### Are Shiny Floors Clean Floors?

**Learning Objective:** Identify the most important concepts in cleaning and maintaining kitchen equipment.

McDonald's has implemented a program to test the effectiveness of the cleaning products used on the floors. The program tests the "coefficient of friction" or COF as a way of evaluating amounts of dirt and film left behind from cleaners. According to the Occupational Safety and Health Administration a "safe" COF is 0.5 or higher.

After using a chain-approved floor cleaner, McDonald's measured its COF level at 0.47. The floors looked shiny, but were not yet up to standards set by OSHA. Compliance to standards reduces the chances of accidents like slip-and-fall while making the work place safer.

In November of 2002, McDonald's tried ProTile 700. The floor cleaner has a "blend of alkali raw materials" designed to remove film build-up resulting from ineffective cleaning products. When ProTile 700 was tested, the COF showed a major increase to 0.75. This is well above industry standard.

ProTile 700 has become McDonald's official deep cleaner, used monthly. With the new cleaner combination, the chain has seen a significant decrease in the number of slip-and-falls, almost 58 percent.

Problems in maintaining proper COF levels come from poor cleaners and inadequate cleaning techniques. Therefore, operators must become proactive in their approach to floor cleaning and floor safety.

*Source:* "Testing for Safety: McDonald's Measures the Effectiveness of Its Floor-Cleaning Products," *Nation's Restaurant News,* vol. 2, no. 1, p. 16, May 2003.

**Discussion Question:** Why is it necessary to implement cleaning standards in the restaurant operation?

---

# ENERGY MANAGEMENT

It is estimated that a comprehensive energy management program can save the average foodservice company 20 percent of its energy bill. According to the U.S. Environmental Protection Agency (EPA), saving 20 percent a year on energy operating costs can increase a restaurant's profits by as much as one-third.[23] One of the major problems in controlling energy costs is that a significant part of the cost is fixed. Refrigerators and fans are in operation regardless of sales volume, and most appliances are designed for high-volume operation. A reduction in number of meals prepared will not result in a corresponding reduction in energy costs. To get costs under control it might be possible to plan less energy-intensive meals—prepared foods and salad plates—during low-business periods.

## Comprehensive Program

A comprehensive approach to handling energy costs involves several steps:[24]

**Top Management Commitment.** Employees pay attention to what management pays attention to. Getting the support of top management is an essential first step in a successful program. Top management's responsibilities are to define the goals and standards for the program. Basic goals might include the following:[25]

- Reduce the consumption and cost of energy and water utilities by 20 percent per year.
- Improve the quality of the operation such that guest satisfaction is increased.

Standard methods to track and summarize energy consumption must also be developed to monitor the program. A base level should be established to serve as a measure of progress made. Usually, this figure is developed from the 12-month period prior to the implementation of the program.

Base measures should be established for each month. The total water consumption in gallons and water consumption per customer should be noted.

For electricity, gas, and other energy sources the various units of energy, as reported on utility bills, must be converted into a standard measure, usually the British thermal unit (BTU). The following factors are used to convert energy use into a BTU value:[26]

| Source | Measure | BTU |
|--------|---------|-----|
| Electricity | kWh (kilowatt-hour) | 3413 |
| Natural gas | Cubic foot | 1000 |
| Oil | Gallon | 140,000 |
| Steam | Pound | 1000 |

From these sources total annual water and energy use can be determined, broken down by month and per meal served. This will serve as a base for comparing consumption before and after the program is implemented.

**Energy Coordinating Committee.**   Management will not, however, have the time to oversee every detail of the program. Responsibility must be placed in the hands of someone to ensure accountability. The committee should be made up of a representative from each major department. This committee is responsible for tracking energy consumption and implementing improvements.

**Energy Audit.**   Once a base level has been established, the coordinating committee can conduct an audit to determine where energy waste is occurring.

**Revised Operating Procedures.**   The audit should have revealed areas for improvement. Based on the findings of the audit, the committee can develop revised operating procedures for presentation to management. A new procedure might require ovens to be turned on 30 minutes prior to use rather than at the beginning of the shift.

A list of operating procedures can be developed and new policies implemented and explained to employees. Employees may need to be trained in the new procedures, and incentives may have to be developed to ensure compliance.

**Analysis of Alternatives.**   Some energy-saving suggestions will require the modification of existing or the purchase of new equipment. Detailed analysis will be required to determine the costs and benefits of a suggestion.

Significant savings can occur when attention is paid to the following areas:[27]

- Lights
- Gas
- Climate control
- Air control
- Preventative maintenance
- Equipment

**Lights.**   One way to save money on energy bills is to change light bulbs or fixtures. Upgrading lighting, particularly in typically brightly lit restaurants, can be a major source of cost savings. Fluorescent bulbs cost about $15 each but last two to three years compared to incandescent bulbs that last an average of three months. A single fluorescent bulb running 12 hours a day can produce savings of 200 kilowatts or $20 a year.

Light fixtures that don't have screw-in light bulbs can be replaced with energy-efficient track lighting. Many also prefer the quality of the light coming from the new fixtures and describe it as more of a daylight compared to a yellow light.

**Gas.**  Choosing to use gas for some appliances is another way to save money.
While electricity is needed for air, lights, computers, and cash registers, restaurants can use gas for cooking, hot-water heating, and space heating. Chefs overwhelmingly prefer using gas equipment for cooking. It is easier to control the
temperature with a gas-powered stove compared to an electric stove, and gas
costs less than electricity. Gas equipment can cost more to purchase, but the operating costs are lower.

Even taking into account the fact that a gas stove is less efficient because
the open flame allows some of the heat to escape into the hood, power costs are
less than half of a comparable amount of electric power. It may be necessary to
use more ventilation with an all-gas kitchen as gas stoves put off more heat than
electric stoves.

Gas can also be used for dishwashing. A gas burner can be used to heat a
hot-water tank. Because the system can heat the rinse water to as high as 180°F,
the use of a sanitizing chemical is unnecessary.

Electricity has a demand charge based on peak usage. Using gas instead of
electricity lowers peak usage, thereby reducing the demand and energy costs.

**Climate Control.**  It is important to maintain a comfortable climate within the
operation. At the same time, savings in the area of climate control can be found.
Many restaurants, especially quick-service operations, have a lot of windows that
are designed specifically to attract the attention of potential customers. Those
windows gain heat in the summer and lose heat in the winter. A high-tech glaze
for windows called low-e coating is scientifically designed to block out the heat
portion of the spectrum while still letting in the light. This helps prevent the heat
loss and heat gain associated with large windows and glass-walled sections.

Use can be made of the natural light. In a northern climate the gain from the
sun can be maximized by placing the glass to take advantage of a southern exposure. Adding a concrete tile floor means that heat will be absorbed during the
warmer part of the day and then released slowly at night. Restaurants in the South
can benefit from the use of natural shading and good high-tech glass to screen out

solar gain. As with any building, it is important to properly insulate walls, ceilings, and foundations as every degree of cooling uses 4 to 5 percent more energy.

**Air control.** The exhaust ventilation hoods over stoves push the air generated from the stoves out to the roof of the building. These systems also allow hot or cold outside air to be drawn in. Energy is wasted heating or cooling the outside air. Installing a heat exchanger in the air passage allows the restaurant to make use of the heat generated by an exhaust ventilation system. The warm air passing through the heat exchanger warms up some liquid, which is then piped somewhere else.

Problems with air leaks or inadequate insulation can be reduced through the use of weatherstripping or foam.

**Preventative Maintenance.**   A piece of equipment that is not operating properly can use up to 15 percent more energy a year. Servicing the equipment on a regular basis—at least twice a year—can result in dramatic energy savings. Additionally, the life of the equipment is increased. Each piece of equipment has a maintenance-preventative schedule recommended by the manufacturer that every manager should know and follow. Many operators have found that it pays to institute preventative maintenance contracts through a certified contractor rather than performing the functions in-house.

**Equipment.**   As people become more environmentally aware and new technologies become available, it is likely that[28]

- Electric power will become cleaner.
- The use of coal will become less common.
- The use of natural gas will become more common.
- Renewable energy, such as wind-power generation and fuel cells, will become more common.
- More businesses will generate their own power with on-site micro-turbine power generators. Most systems produce hot water as a byproduct of cooling the engine that can be used in a number of ways.

The following recommendations can assist in reducing energy consumption.[29]

## Lighting

1. Wash walls and ceilings to help maximize light reflection.
2. Remove decorative lighting in the dining room.
3. Clean all lamps and light fixtures.
4. Replace several small-wattage light bulbs with one large one.
5. Remove all unnecessary light bulbs.
6. Change extended-life lamps to standard-life lamps; reflector floor lights to parabolic floodlights; and older-model fluorescent lights to high-efficiency fluorescent lights.

**Learning Objective:** Design a comprehensive energy management program.

Saving energy saves money. The kitchen makes up a large portion of any operation's electric and energy costs. If proper care is taken to ensure kitchen equipment operates efficiently and is maintained effectively, kitchen energy consumption can be reduced.

Ramin Faramarzi, manager of Southern California Edison Co.'s Refrigeration and Thermal Test Center, has made a few suggestions for operators looking to improve the energy efficiency of refrigeration systems:

1. Ensure proper loading of products by keeping boxes away from fans and the return-air grill.
2. Maintain optimum space conditions. Pay attention to air distributions as well as temperature and humidity controls.
3. Reduce the amount of cooling needed after opening the door. This can be done with plastic swing doors in addition to the automatic closing door and plastic strip curtains.
4. Install energy efficient equipment. Buy equipment with the Energy Star label.
5. Implement routine maintenance and monitoring programs.
6. Enforce energy management principles.

*Source:* "Electric End Use Cools Off: Proper Refrigeration Improves Energy Efficiency in Quick-Serve Restaurants," *Nation's Restaurant News,* vol. 2, no. 1, p. 18, May 2003.

**Discussion Question:** What steps should be taken to maintain an energy efficiency program?

7. Replace lamps installed more than two years previously because of the decrease in light output.
8. Install skylights to reduce the need for artificial lighting.
9. Timers or motion detectors can be installed on all lighting (e.g., in storerooms and walk-in coolers) that can be shut off after a specified time.

## Water

1. Replace washers immediately in dripping faucets.
2. Drain and flush hot water tanks every three to six months.
3. Check the steam trap on steam water heaters regularly.
4. Check insulation on water heaters by feeling for hot spots.

5. Have burners adjusted if the exhaust is smoky or high in $CO_2$ emissions or if the stack is extremely hot.
6. Insulate all hot-water pipes.
7. Use a lower water temperature for nonsanitizing areas.
8. Reduce water pressure at the intake valve.
9. Replace 3- to 6-gallon urns with an instant hot-water dispenser.
10. Reduce ice machine costs by purchasing a small tube and shell heat exchanger that transfers cold water from the drain cycle of the ice machine and uses it to prechill the incoming water.

## Heating, Ventilation, and Air Conditioning (HVAC) System

1. Turn off the heating and cooling in seldom-used spaces.
2. Remove obstructions from heating and cooling vents.

---

### quick bite 9.7
### Road to the Top: Kelly Marshall

Kelly Marshall began her career in the restaurant industry in the 1980's at an Applebee's location in Atlanta. Later, Marshall joined T.G.I. Friday's as a bartender and server. Three months after accepting the job, she was approached to be a trainer. Marshall traveled from restaurant to restaurant specializing in the training of management until 1989.

A former manager of Marshall heard she was leaving Friday's and asked her to come to the Hard Rock Café in Miami as a kitchen manager. Over the next few years, she moved to different locations, left the Hard Rock Café, and came back as General Manager for the Hard Rock Café in San Francisco.

Marshall is considered an asset for the Hard Rock Café because of the way she handled the relocation of the restaurant. Instead of closing the original location and forcing patrons to wait for the new one to open, Marshall decided to double her staff. This enabled her to train employees in preparation for the new site on Pier 39 and to avoid any discrepancies between the two restaurants.

Kelly Marshall is a manager who has earned the respect of her colleagues and employees. She is willing to do anything to help the restaurant run smoothly, including washing dishes. Many have described her as fair and approachable.

*Source:* Daniels, Wade, "Kelly Marshall: Not Just Another Starstruck Fan, GM Keeps Her Casual Cool at This Celebrity-Focused Restaurant," *Nation's Restaurant News,* vol. 38, no. 4, pp. 86–88, January 26, 2004.

**Discussion Question:** What are some aspects of managing that help to motivate your staff?

---

3. Replace caulking and weatherstripping around doors, windows, and ventilating units.

4. Clean or replace all filters in exhaust hoods and the HVAC system.

5. Check heating and cooling ducts and exhaust hoods for cleanliness, insulation, and leaks.

6. Use natural gas rather than electricity as the energy source for the booster heater for dishwashers.

The five most common conservation methods used by restaurants are[30]

- Installation of low-water heaters and/or toilet fixtures
- Modification of lighting fixtures
- Serving water to customers only upon request
- Sponsoring community conservation activities
- Installing heat recovery equipment on refrigerators and air conditioners

The EPA offers many other energy-conserving suggestions on its Web site, *www.epa.gov/smallbiz/restaurants.html.*

## ENDNOTES

1. Mahmood Khan, *Foodservice Operations* (Westport, CT: AVI Publishing Company, 1987), pp. 112–116.
2. Ibid., pp. 164–166.
3. Ibid., p. 112.
4. Lendal H. Kotschevar and Margaret E. Terrell, *Foodservice Planning: Layout and Equipment,* 3rd ed. (New York: John Wiley & Sons, 1985), p. 330.
5. Khan, *Foodservice Operations*, pp. 112–113.
6. Ibid., p. 113.
7. Madeleine Burka, "Don't Let Your Business Go Up in Flames: How to Prevent Fires and Be Prepared when Disaster Strikes," *Restaurants USA,* May 2000, www.restaurant.org/rusa.
8. Khan, *Foodservice Operations*, p. 119.
9. Ibid., p. 138.
10. Ibid., p. 126.
11. Ibid., p. 126.
12. Edward A. Kazarian, *Foodservice Facilities Planning,* 3rd ed. (New York: Van Nostrand Reinhold, 1989), p. 171.
13. Khan, *Foodservice Operations*, p. 113.
14. Kotschevar and Terrell, *Foodservice Planning: Layout and Equipment,* 3rd ed. (New York: John Wiley & Sons, 1985), p. 447.
15. Kazarian, *Foodservice Facilities Planning,* pp. 112–113.
16. Kazarian, *Foodservice Facilities Planning,* p. 219.
17. Lewis J. Minor and Ronald F. Cichy, *Foodservice Systems Management* (Westport, CT: AVI Publishing Company, 1984), p. 242.
18. Ibid., p. 242.
19. Ibid., p. 241.
20. Kazarian, *Foodservice Facilities Planning,* pp. 223–224.
21. Minor and Cichy, *Foodservice Systems Management,* p. 241.

22. Ibid., p. 242.
23. Madeleine Burka, "You've Got the Power to Cut Energy Costs Through Conservation," *Restaurants USA,* August 2000, www.restaurant.org/rusa.
24. Robert E. Aulbach, *Energy and Water Resource Management,* 2nd ed. (East Lansing, MI: The Educational Institute of the American Hotel and Motel Association, 1988), p. 99.
25. Ibid., p. 101.
26. Judy Ford Stokes, *Cost Effective Quality Food Service: An Institutional Guide* (Rockville, MD: Aspen Systems Corporation, 1985), p. 258.
27. Madeleine Burka, "You've Got the Power to Cut Energy Costs Through Conservation," *Restaurants USA,* August 2000, www.restaurant.org/rusa.
28. Ibid.
29. Minor and Cichy, *Foodservice Systems Management,* pp. 243–244; "Equipment Insights," A Joint Report from FCSI and *Nation's Restaurant News,* vol. 4, no. 1, September 1, 2003.
30. Ira Apfel, "Don't Waste Your Energy," *Restaurants USA,* June 2002, www.restaurant.org/rusa.

## INTERNET RESOURCES

USA Restaurant Equipment *http://www.amer-rest-equip.com/*
Galasource, Inc. *http://www.galasource.com/*
Greenlight Management Corp. *http://www.greenlight-management.com/literature-restaurant-energy-study.html*

# CHAPTER TEN

# SANITATION AND FOOD SAFETY

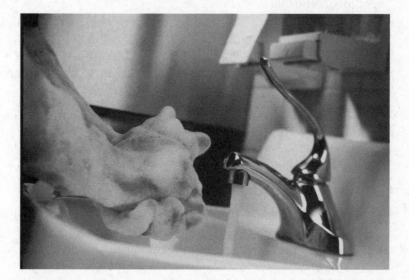

"Contrary to popular notion, truck drivers know nothing about good restaurants. If you want a reliable tip, drive into a town, go to the nearest appliance store and seek out the dishwasher repair man. He spends a lot of time in restaurant kitchens and usually has strong opinions about them."

Bryan Miller, restaurant critic

## learning objectives

*By the end of this chapter you should be able to*

1. Identify the role of the restaurant manager in sanitation.

2. Identify the major sanitation problems in a restaurant.

3. Show how to establish proactive sanitation and safety programs.

4. Develop procedures for preventing foodborne diseases.

5. Build effective employee hygiene habits.

## ROLE OF THE MANAGER

Management is responsible for serving food that is nutritious, appeals to the senses, and is safe to eat.[1] According to the National Assessment Institute, a restaurant manager is responsible for[2]

- Identifying health hazards in the daily operation of the restaurant
- Developing and implementing policies, procedures, and standards to prevent foodborne illnesses
- Coordinating training, supervision, and direction of food handling and preparation while taking corrective action as required to protect the health of customers and employees
- Inspecting the operation periodically to ensure that policies and procedures are being followed correctly

To assist them in taking a proactive stance in assuring sanitary procedures, managers should have some knowledge of the following:[3]

---

quick bite 10.1
**Hot Concepts: Biotech and Modified Foods**

In 2000, Taco Bell was forced by public opinion to stop using taco shells that had been prepared in part with genetically modified corn. Also in 2000, corn genetically modified to repel pests and intended solely for feedlot use found its way into human food, causing voluntary grocery and restaurant recalls of potentially tainted prepared foods. In 2003, the U.S. Department of Agriculture (USDA) quarantined and destroyed 500,000 bushels of soybeans that had been stored with 500 bushels of corn plants that had been genetically modified to create medicinal pharmaceuticals ("biopharm corn").

In contrast, by the end of 2003, more than fifty food products had been developed or augmented using biotech techniques and approved by the U.S. Food and Drug Administration (FDA). These include canola oil, corn, cottonseed oil, papaya, potatoes, soybeans, squash, sugar beets, sweet corn, and tomatoes.

As of 2003, the use of irradiated beef, primarily ground beef found in hamburgers, has been increasingly accepted by consumers. For example, Dairy Queen International is starting regional use of irradiated beef. Irradiating uncooked meat and produce greatly reduces the number of dangerous pathogens like *E. coli* O157:H7 and salmonella.

Although some restaurants are beginning to use irradiated foods, very few are willing to use genetically engineered (GE) foods. GE foods are those produced from crops whose genetic makeup has been altered through a process called gene splicing. Gene splicing gives plants desirable traits that they would otherwise not have, such as pest resistance.

Many groups are arguing for and against using GE foods. For example, chef-restaurateur Charlie Trotter of Chicago has published his opposition to

---

1. **Properties of food:** The amount of available moisture and the pH level that strengthens or represses the growth of bacteria together with a list of potentially dangerous foods.
2. **Food processing/preparation:** Processes the food will undergo.
3. **Volume of food prepared:** The larger the quantity of food to be fixed, the greater the potential danger.
4. **Type of customer:** Acknowledging the fact that certain people (the very old, very young, infirm, and those who are sick) are more susceptible to foodborne illness than the rest of the population.

## Allergies[4]

For some people with food allergies even one bite can lead to serious illness or even death. Most allergy sufferers know what they can and cannot eat. Common allergens include eggs, fish, milk, peanuts, shellfish, tree nuts (including almonds, Brazil nuts, cashews, chestnuts, hazelnuts, hickory nuts, macadamia nuts, pecans, pine nuts, pistachios, and walnuts), and wheat.

---

the use of GE foods. Other chefs are boycotting the use of transgenic salmon that grow twice as fast as natural salmon. On the other hand, biotech industry members and certain foodservice industry lobbyists are continuing to put forth arguments for GE based upon the rigorous review imposed by the FDA, EPA, and USDA, other scientific studies and trials that have found no harm in the use of GE foods including transgenic salmon.

Non-activist consumer public opinion in the United States is apparently split on the acceptability of genetically modified food. According to an ABC News poll, only about half of Americans believe that GE foods are unsafe to eat. However, the European Union has categorically banned the use and import of all GE foods.

At least 92 percent of the public favors mandatory labeling of such foods. But labeling may prove to be prohibitively costly, particularly when only one component of the dish is genetically modified. Those who oppose labeling argue that if GE food items are unsafe they should not be allowed on the market by the FDA at all. They say that if there is no safety question, labeling is unnecessary.

*Sources:* Bren, Linda, "Genetic Engineering: The Future of Foods?," *FDA Consumer*, vol. 37, no. 6, November/December 2003, pp. 28–35. Liddle, Alan J., "Engineering the Future: Interest in Biotech Grows," *Nation's Restaurant News*, vol. 37, no. 38, September 22, 2003, pp. 128–131.

**Discussion Question:** Many agencies have found GE foods safe. Why do you think that half of Americans think they are unsafe to eat?

**Learning Objective:** Identify the role of the restaurant manager in sanitation.

Health department inspections are incredibly important to the life and reputation of a restaurant. In order to avoid inspection problems, onsite management and staff should treat food safety as the top priority. Requiring that employees be ServSafe certified is one way to foster this attitude.

Implementing good safety practices ultimately depends upon higher management, which controls the amount of money available for training and equipment updates. Food safety competes for funding with many other corporate programs.

Ways to get higher management involved include:

- Telling bosses of regional and national "horror" stories of what sanitation and food safety lapses have occurred and of the costs to the offenders.
- Showing family-oriented bosses how adoption of technology will better protect the health of family customers.
- Inviting the bosses to employee meetings that feature ServSafe briefing materials and slides. Highlight the different areas of the restaurant training and operations that need funding.
- Posting the bosses ServSafe certificates at the entrances to the restaurant.
- Distributing press releases that claim that inspection 'perfect scores' are a result of management's support of SafeServ certification throughout the organization.

*Source:* Jacobs, Don, "Strive for a Perfect Health Inspection Score," *Restaurant Hospitality,* vol. 88, no. 3, March 2004, pp. 90–92.

**Discussion Question:** If something goes wrong at a restaurant, it's usually the management that catches the heat. Why should an employee be concerned with safety and with management involvement in sanitation?

When a customer says that he or she has a food allergy, servers must pay close attention. In one case in a Miami restaurant a customer was told that the egg rolls were not fried in peanut oil. However, the server did not mention that peanut butter was used to seal the dough. The customer died from an allergic reaction. Servers must know all of the ingredients in a menu item and be able to describe accurately how they are prepared.

Kitchen staff need to be careful to avoid cross-contaminating foods with potentially allergenic foods. A prep table should be used that has not been ex-

posed to the allergen and cooking utensils need to be cleaned after working with potentially allergenic foods. Chefs can be trained to prepare allergen-free versions of menu items. As chefs become more creative and use nontraditional ingredients—such as nuts in cheesecake—there is an increased chance that customers will eat foods they are allergic to. Problems can be avoided by including all ingredients in the menu item's name or description. Labels must be read carefully as food manufacturers sometimes change ingredients.

When people eat something they are allergic to, they experience an abnormal reaction in which the immune system overreacts. Skin areas become red, itchy, and swollen; blood vessels widen; and internal muscles contract. Employees should be able to recognize the symptoms of an allergic reaction. Symptoms may show up immediately after consuming the food or after a period of hours. They can include[5]

- Itching in and around the mouth
- Tightening of the throat (airway blockage)
- Wheezing and hoarseness
- Shortness of breath
- Appearance of hives
- Swelling of the eyelids, lips, hands, or feet
- Nausea
- Cramping or vomiting
- A sense of impending doom
- A drop in blood pressure
- A loss of consciousness

## MAJOR SANITATION PROBLEMS

### Foodborne Illnesses

According to the Centers for Disease Control (CDC), foodborne illnesses occur because of the following:[6]

1. **Inadequate cooling and cold holding (63 percent).** Storing food in large containers more than 4 inches deep means that the food in the center of the container will not cool fast enough to prevent bacterial growth. Putting tight lids on containers in which hot foods are stored will slow cooling when the product is refrigerated. Similarly, stacking food containers one on top of the other and arranging cooler racks such that air is prevented from flowing freely around all surfaces of the containers will also slow down the cooling process.
2. **Preparing food ahead of planned service (29 percent).** Food should not be prepared more than a day ahead of time.
3. **Inadequate hot holding (27 percent).** Contaminated food will come from holding food at temperatures between 70 and 120°F for more than four hours;

# quick bite 10.3
## Major Sanitation and Food Safety Problems

**Learning Objective:** Identify the major sanitation problems in a restaurant.

After the terrorist attacks on September 11, 2001, many press reports speculated about possible attacks on the food supply of the United States. From 2002 to 2004, there were several widely reported incidences of foodborne illness outbreaks. One such scare that occurred in mid-2003 was due to tainted green onions acquired from outside of the U.S. Then in December of 2003, mad cow disease (bovine spongiform encephalopathy [BSE]) was discovered in the western U.S. Neverless, according to a 2004 survey conducted by the private Reed Research Group, consumer confidence regarding food safety remained high.

The survey indicates that highly publicized illness outbreaks have increased consumer awareness and questions about food safety. However, many consumers remain ignorant of the benefits of food irradiation. Fully 29 percent of consumers believe that irradiation is a cause of foodborne illness, not a preventative measure. At the same time, despite the immense publicity about BSE, over half of the consumers surveyed in early 2004 stated that the chance of contracting BSE is too low to worry about and fully two-thirds of consumers said they would not change their beef consumption habits.

Congress and restaurant owners have not been so complacent. Under the Bioterrorism Preparedness and Response Act of 2002, Congress has stated that food manufacturers and distributors will be legally responsible for maintaining records to trace exactly where every food product comes from. This type of tracing is designed by the Food and Drug Administration (FDA) to account instantly for threats to the food supply of the United States. To the FDA, this type of tracing is fundamental to its mandate to respond to all levels of food safety threats.

In a Reed Research Group survey, 75 percent of all restaurant operators rank foodborne illness as a serious threat to their businesses. Fifty-three percent believe that this threat is more serious than all other business risks. These threat perceptions have resulted in much more staff coaching and training in food safety procedures. Approximately 48 percent of the operators undertake monthly staff training on food safety with another 49 percent undertaking quarterly or annual training.

*Sources:* Perlik, Allison, "Plating it Safe," *Restaurants & Institutions,* vol. 114, no. 5, March 1, 2004, pp. 44–47. Perlik, Allison, "How Now, Mad Cow," Ibid., pp. 50–53. Perkins, Caroline, "FDA to Distributors: Get Ready for Weapons of Mass Consumption," *Nation's Restaurant News,* vol. 38, no. 11, March 15, 2004, p. 18.

**Discussion Questions:** Do you think it would be useful for the FDA to spend money on educating the public about the benefits of irradiation? Do the benefits of irradiating food outweigh the risks?

using hot-holding units for uses other than intended; improper operation of hot-holding units, such as turning the thermostat too low or failing to turn on the fan; and combining new and old food items.

4. **Poor personal hygiene/infected persons (26 percent).** Inadequate hand-washing and food contact with employees who have infectious diseases are major problems in this area.

5. **Inadequate reheating (25 percent).** It is important that temperatures be brought to 165°F and kept there for a time sufficient to kill any microorganisms.

6. **Inadequate cleaning of equipment (9 percent).** It is especially important to sanitize sinks and cutting boards, ensure that water temperature is above the safe level, and that sanitizing agents are strong enough to reduce bacteria.

7. **Cross-contamination (6 percent).** Cross-contamination can come from such things as touching raw foods, then handling cooked foods before washing hands, inadequate cleaning of raw food items, and improper sanitizing of surfaces and utensils between use with cooked and raw food items.

8. **Inadequate cooking or heat processing (5 percent).** Of particular concern would be the undercooking of poultry, pork, and eggs. Checking the internal temperature of food is essential to ensure adequate cooking.

9. **Contaminated raw materials (2 percent).** Serving food raw means that there is no chance to reduce the level of microorganisms once the initial preparation has occurred.

10. **Unsafe sources (1 percent).** It is vital that approved suppliers be used and that fish be certified as having come from clean waters.

(**Note:** Figures add up to more than 100 percent because more than one factor is usually involved in an outbreak.)

Foodborne illnesses occur from one of three sources:[7] biological, chemical, and physical.

---

### quick fact

Each year 76 million Americans suffer from foodborne illness, according to the Centers for Disease Control and Prevention. To learn about ways to prevent foodborne illness, visit the Centers for Disease Control and Prevention at *http://www.cdc.gov/.*

*Source:* Helm, Janet, "Know the ABCs of Food Safety," *www.theledger.com*, September 1, 2005, October 30, 2005, *http://www.nraef.org/nfsem/training.asp*, October 30, 2005.

---

## Biological Sources

**Bacteria.**   Biological contamination can come from bacteria, viruses, and para-sites. Most foodborne illnesses are caused by microorganisms, the most signifi-cant group of which are bacteria. Bacteria are transmitted by wind, moisture, dust, and direct contact with other living things. They reproduce two to three times an hour, depending on the available moisture, pH, temperature, oxygen, and food levels present. Bacteria prefer high-protein food products. Thus items with high protein—poultry, meat, gravy, eggs, salads, fish, and so on—are par-ticularly susceptible to bacterial growth. They also require a certain amount of moisture. Dry products such as cereals, flour, rice, and sugar do not contain enough moisture for bacteria to multiply.

The U.S. Public Health Service defines the temperature danger zone as being between 40° and 140°F. Some states have their own separate requirements. For example, Arizona law indicates a danger zone between 41° and 130°F. Most bacterial growth occurs within this range. The amount of time that food prod-ucts remain within this temperature range should be minimized. Certain bacte-ria actually prefer cold temperatures as low as 19°F and can even reproduce in refrigerated storage. Freezing or drying foods will delay the growth of but not kill organisms.

Some bacteria require oxygen to reproduce, while others can multiply even without it. Neutral pH is 7.0. As the pH value moves closer to zero, food be-comes more acidic and the conditions for bacterial growth lessen. The preferred range for bacterial growth is 6.5 to 7.5.

The best way to limit bacterial growth is to control time and temperature—the time that foods are within the temperature danger zone. It is impossible to eliminate all bacteria; it is only possible to limit the growth of harmful bacteria to levels considered safe.

**Viruses.**   Viruses are spread to food by employees infected with the virus. This can occur through such means as failing to wash hands after going to the bath-room, coughing, sneezing, or wiping a runny nose with a hand. Hepatitis A is one common illness transmitted by a virus. The most likely foods to cause illness through viral transfer are those which are not heated after handling: salads, cold sandwiches, raw or uncooked oysters, and so on.

**Parasites.**   Parasites live within or feed off another organism. Parasites and their eggs can be contained in such foods as pork and fish. Parasites can be de-stroyed by cooking the food to at least 140°F. Trichinosis and dysentery are the result of parasites in pork and water, respectively.

**Fungi.**   Fungi—molds, yeasts, and mushrooms—can be poisonous. Certain molds can produce toxins that have been associated with foodborne illness. Freezing will retard the growth of molds but will have no effect on those already present. Molds will be destroyed by heating to 140°F for 10 minutes, but heat will not get rid of any toxins already present. Cooking at the correct temperature is the best way to prevent fungi growth.

While yeasts are not known to cause illness, they will cause certain foods and beverages to spoil. They can be killed by heating items to 136°F for 15 minutes and controlled with cleaning and sanitizing.

The symptoms of bacterial food infection are nausea, vomiting, diarrhea, and intestinal cramps.

## Chemical Contamination

Chemical contamination occurs when substances such as cleaning compounds or pesticides get into food. Food additives and preservatives are used to enhance food flavor and keep the product fresh longer. Some, however—such as nitrites, sulfites, and MSG—can be harmful. Although the use of sulfites is prohibited by restaurants, it is allowed in food processing under tight regulations.

Pesticides, used to control insect damage on crops, can lead to poisoning if the residue is not removed completely. Chemical contamination can also come from toxic metals such as copper, brass, cadmium, lead, and zinc. Zinc-galvanized containers can make acidic foods such as fruit juice and pickles poisonous. Care should also be taken that items used for cleaning purposes be stored properly in a manner that will not bring them into contact with food.

## Physical Contamination

Physical contamination occurs when hair, dirt, and similar items come into contact with food. Poor ventilation and maintenance can contribute to objects or moisture coming into contact with food.

Cross-contamination occurs when there is contact between safe and contaminated foods: for example, when raw food comes into contact with food that has been cooked. Cleaning and sanitizing of equipment should occur between use with different foods and between the same cooked and raw foods. As an example, raw chicken might be trimmed on a cutting board and then cooked. The cooked chicken should not be placed back on the cutting board until the board has been cleaned and sanitized.

## TAKING A PROACTIVE STANCE: HACCP

The objectives of a food sanitation program are to protect food from contaminating substances and to minimize the effects of any contamination that does occur.[8] The Hazard Analysis Critical Control Points (HACCP) system, developed in the 1960s to ensure the safety of food prepared for astronauts, is set up to maximize food safety. The system combines three elements—principles of food microbiology, quality control, and risk assessment—and emphasizes a movement away from the inspection of facilities to one that centers on the process of preparing and serving safe food.[9]

The HACCP system consists of seven steps:[10]

1. **Identify hazards and assess their severity and risks.** This involves examining the menu and recipes to identify potentially hazardous foods. Reducing

the number of steps involved in preparing menu items will reduce the risk of contamination.[11]

2. **Determine critical control points.** Four important control points are good personal hygiene, avoidance of cross-contamination, cooking, and cooling.[12]

3. **Implement control measures and establish criteria to assure control.** Procedures must be observable and measurable. For example, the directions for fixing a baked chicken breast should include (1) washing hands; (2) washing, rinsing, and sanitizing the cutting board and knife that are used for slicing the chicken breast; and (3) maintaining the actual product temperature of 160°F (73.9°C).[13]

4. **Monitor crucial control points and record data.** After receiving turkey and checking that the temperature is lower than 45°F, it is important to

---

**quick bite 10.4**
**Proactive Sanitation and Safety Programs**

**Learning Objective:** Show how to establish proactive sanitation and safety programs.

The National Restaurant Association Educational Foundation administers ServSafe, a comprehensive training, testing and certification program that teaches all aspects of food safety.

ServSafe is recognized as the leading food safety training program. ServSafe certification is generally accepted in most states as meeting restaurant health and safety requirements.

The traditional training program uses print, video and CD-ROM materials. The course material may now be found online at *www.nraef.org/e_learning/elearn_home.asp*. The online course is offered in English while the traditional material is available in both English and Spanish.

The ServSafe Manager Certification Training online course takes approximately 6–10 hours. Lessons are delivered in short videos with practice exercises. The exercises for each major section are "virtual" environments where users identify food safety problems based on what they've learned. Completed lessons may be reviewed at any time. Throughout the program users assess their knowledge and identify topics that need further review. Final testing is administered separately at controlled and proctored testing locations.

*Sources:* Editors, "NRAEF Introduces Online ServSafe Training," *Foodservice Equipment & Supplies*, vol. 56, no. 10, October 2003, p. 18. NRAEF Web site, *www.nraef.org/e_learning/elearn_home.asp*

**Discussion Question:** What might be the possible disadvantages of a non-personal safety training course that uses print and electronic materials instead of a human instructor?

---

check that after storing it, the temperature in the refrigerator is 40°F or lower and that the raw turkey is not stored above cooked food.

5. **Take appropriate action when control criteria are not met.** You might find, for example, that the chef is preparing turkey breasts all at one time. The turkey is within the temperature danger zone for longer than it should be. Corrective action is required that will reduce the amount of time the turkey is within the danger zone. New procedures have to be developed such that turkey breasts are prepared in smaller batches and returned to the cooler immediately upon completion.

6. **Set up a recordkeeping system.** The system should be audited by checking steps on a daily basis to ensure that they are being done correctly.

7. **Confirm that the system is working as planned.** For each step in the process of receiving through reheating for service, four areas are determined: the critical control point, the potential hazard, appropriate standards, and whatever corrective action is needed if the standards are not met. For example, the first control point is in receiving beef and vegetables. Contamination and spoilage are potential hazards in both cases. Receiving standards should be set such that the temperature of the beef is at 45°F or lower; packaging on both products is intact; there is no odor, stickiness, or cross-contamination from other foods on the truck; and there are no signs of insect or rodent activity. If any of these conditions are present, the proper corrective action is to refuse delivery. A similar procedure is spelled out for each step in the process.

## PREVENTATIVE PROCEDURES

### Purchasing

The key to effective procedures in purchasing is to use reliable suppliers.

### Receiving

Deliveries should be scheduled during slow periods so that time can be devoted to careful inspection. Check the condition of the delivery truck for signs of improper storage during transit. Temperatures should be checked to make sure that refrigerated foods are below 45°F and frozen foods are below 0°F. Cartons that are damaged should be rejected.

Glass thermometers or those filled with mercury should not be used, as they can break. Select thermometers at least 5 inches long and insert at least 2 inches into food when taking a reading. The thermometers should then be cleaned and sanitized after every use.

Meat products must be inspected by a federal or state regulatory program. If they pass the inspection, they are given a circular identification stamp indicating where the meat was processed. Suppliers can be asked for written confirmation that individual cuts have been inspected. Check the appearance and smell—aged meat will be darker in appearance than fresh; slimy, sticky, or dry meat should be rejected, as should products with a sour smell.

The job of the International Food Safety Council (IFSC) is to ensure that the foodservice industry recognizes the dangers of foodborne illnesses and works to prevent the spread of these illnesses. IFSC is one of the leading proponents of the SaveServ training system.

In the U.S. alone, foodborne illnesses kill 5,000 people a year, send 325,000 to the hospital and sicken another 78 million to a minor extent. Restaurant food poisonings lead to high cost lawsuits and overall damage to the industry. As a result, the IFSC believes that food safety is the fundamental responsibility of the foodservice industry to the public. [The IFSC works] to promote safe food handling despite the fact that assuring food safety is neither glamorous nor greatly recognized.

The IFSC's prime advocate is its president, John Farquharson. Farquharson is a former president of Aramark, the nation's leading contract foodservice corporation, as well as the former president and chairman of the National Restaurant Association. Farquharson travels hundreds of days a year to trade shows, company meetings, hospitality schools, and USDA advisory board meetings lobbying for higher food safety standards. He is equally insistent that food safety training be required at every level in a foodservice organization, from the newest hourly hire to the chief executive officer. Between his trips he engages in IFSC letter writing campaigns, writing about all aspects of food safety. He challenges organizations to learn about the necessity of upgrading food safety practices. His work has paid off. Since 1998, the number of certified food safety practitioners has increased by nearly ten-fold.

*Source:* Frumkin, Paul, "John R. Farquharson," *Nation's Restaurant News,* vol. 34, no. 39, September 25, 2000, pp. 189–192.

**Discussion Question:** Why do you think that it's important that Farquharson is a former president of Aramark?

Poultry must also be inspected under a federal or state program. Operators should use only Grade A poultry. Signs of aging are purple or greenish color, bad smell, darkened wing tips, and soft, flabby, and sticky flesh.

Since there is no mandated inspection program for seafood, it is particularly important to buy from suppliers you trust. Fresh fish should be delivered in crushed ice at a temperature between 32 and 45°F. Fish is safe if it has bright skin; moist, red gills; eyes that are clear and bulging; and scales that are firmly attached. The flesh should be firm and elastic to the touch and should not separate easily from the bone.

Fluid or frozen liquids in cartons of frozen foods or large ice crystals in the product itself are indications that it has been thawed and refrozen. Such items are not acceptable.

Carefully check the expiration date on milk and dairy products. All products must be Grade A pasteurized. Once milk has been taken from a container, it should never be returned to that container.

Eggs can be spot-checked by breaking one or two open to check that the temperature is below 45°F, there is no noticeable odor, the yolk is firm, and the white clings to the yolk.

It is now possible to purchase certain items in packaging from which air has been removed. Gases may be added to help preserve the item. Vacuum-packed foods must be kept at temperatures below 45°F, fish below 38°F. *Sous vide* refers to products that are vacuum packed and then fully or partially cooked. Products must be stored at temperatures from 32 to 38°F. Plants that sell sous vide products must be certified by the Federal Drug Administration (FDA).

## Storage

The six most significant reasons for food spoilage are as follows:[14]

1. Incorrect storage temperatures
2. Excessive storage time
3. Inadequate ventilation in storage areas
4. Failure to segregate foods in storage
5. Unacceptable sanitation standards
6. Excessive delays between receiving and storing functions

The National Restaurant Association recommendations for storing food are shown in Table 10.1. Food products should be used in the order in which they have been received. This concept is known as FIFO: first in, first out. Items should be dated and newer stock placed behind older stock to help ensure the integrity of the process. Ideally, purchases will be kept in their original containers.

**Table 10.1   Recommended Conditions for Storage**

| Storage Area | Temperature (°F) | Relative Humidity (%) |
|---|---|---|
| Dry storage | 50–70 | 50–60 |
| Refrigerated storage | | |
|    Dairy products and eggs | 38–40 | 75–85 |
|    Red meats and poultry | 32–40 | 75–85 |
|    Fresh fish | 30–34 | 75–85 |
|    Live shellfish | 35–45 | 75–85 |
|    Fresh vegetables and fruits | 40–45 | 85–95 |
| Frozen storage | < 0 | |

*Source: Applied Foodservice Sanitation,* 4th ed. (New York: John Wiley & Sons, 1992), p. 121.

If not, care must be taken that the items are kept in containers that are clean and nonabsorbent. Metal containers can be dangerous when they come into contact with foods with a high acidic content.

Different types of meat should be kept separate from each other, as should raw and cooked items. Items should be stored at least 6 inches off the floor and away from pipes that might drip onto the food. Allow for air circulation around all surfaces between packages. Before opening cans, wipe them with a clean cloth to prevent contamination from the outside of the cans. Cleaning supplies should be stored separately from food items.

We can see that the potential hazards are due to cross-contamination and bacterial growth and spoilage. Appropriate standards would be to store raw beef on a lower shelf with vegetables above it; label, date, and use FIFO rotation; and ensure that the beef temperature remains under 45°F. Corrective action would involve moving the beef to a lower shelf and discarding either beef or vegetables if they have been kept longer than they should have.

---

### quick quiz

Which bacterium is an intestinal bacterium that is commonly found on raw meats, poultry, and in eggs, or in foods containing raw or undercooked milk or egg products. It can be killed by temperatures of 130°F or higher for 2 hours, or at 165°F for a few seconds.

*Source:* National Restaurant Association, "About Foodborne Illness: Common Pathogens," *http://www.restaurant.org/foodsafety/how_to_pathogens.cfm,* November 6, 2005.

---

## Preparation and Serving

The highest risk for contamination is when food is being prepared and served. There are three concerns:[15] employee hygiene, time and temperature control, and the cleaning and sanitizing of utensils, equipment, and surfaces with which food comes into contact. Employee hygiene is dealt with later. As far as time and temperature are concerned, the major goal is that the time that a product is in the danger zone, between 45° and 140°F, be minimized. One particular problem for operators is the procedure for thawing frozen food. To minimize time in the danger zone, frozen food should never be thawed at room temperature but can, instead, be thawed under refrigeration, by cooking as a continuous process, in a microwave oven, or under water at about 70°F for a maximum of two hours.

Cross-contamination becomes a potential problem during preparation. As noted earlier, cross-contamination occurs when cooked food comes into contact with raw food. Similarly, surfaces that have had contact with raw food must be sanitized before coming into contact with cooked food.

In cooking, it is especially critical that the internal temperature of food items be checked in several places to ensure that cooking is complete. As noted before, thermometers with stainless steel stems should be used. They should be sanitized between uses and allowed to return to room temperature before being used again. The following minimum temperatures are recommended:[16]

- 45°F or below: steak tartare
- 130°F: beef
- 145°F: potentially hazardous foods
- 150°F: pork and pork products
- 155°F: ground beef
- 165°F: poultry and meat containing stuffing
- 165°F: all foods previously served and cooled that are reheated
- 170°F: pork and pork products cooked in a microwave

Holding equipment should never be used to heat food. The equipment itself should be able to maintain a temperature of at least 140°F and hold the food at the required temperature at all times. A food thermometer will be necessary to check that temperatures are maintained. Chances for contamination can be reduced if holding time is kept to a minimum, if foods are stirred periodically, and if covers are used over containers.

Milk, eggs, and egg products should be stored at temperatures below 45°F. After cooking, eggs should be held at a minimum of 140°F.

Ice should be treated and handled with the same care as for food. Using hands, cups, or glasses to handle ice is to be avoided; hands carry germs, and glasses can break in the ice bin.

In self-service areas, customers, who probably have less sanitation background, are the people who come into contact with the food. The key is to set up the system such that contact with food is minimized. This will mean such things as providing individually wrapped portions wherever possible; supplying food or "sneeze" guards; furnishing enough utensils so that each dish has its own utensil and changing utensils periodically for fresh, sanitized items, and constantly monitoring the temperatures of the various items.

## Reheating

If food has been cooked and held under sanitary conditions, it can be reused. Great care must be taken that it has not been exposed to contamination. It is estimated that up to 20 percent of usable food in the United States is thrown out. Various agencies have been set up to collect restaurant leftovers and distribute them to the needy. The major rule of thumb, however, is, If in doubt, throw it out.[17]

If the decision is made to keep leftovers, the food must be chilled to reach an internal temperature of 45°F as quickly as possible. This can be done by dividing large quantities of food into smaller portions prior to chilling, placing food in containers with a depth no greater than 2 inches, stirring the contents of the container, giving the containers an ice-water bath (placing them in larger containers filled with ice), and using specially designed refrigeration units.

Stored leftovers should be covered and sealed, stored above raw foods, and labeled clearly. Reheated foods must reach an internal temperature of 165°F.

## quick bite 10.6
### Disease Prevention Procedures

**Learning Objective:** Develop procedures for preventing foodborne diseases.

The National Restaurant Association Educational Foundation's (NRAEF) International Food Safety Council suggests the following procedures for dealing with the temperature of foods. These guidelines are especially important for meat, poultry, fish and dairy, which are subject to the most health risk if allowed to sit at temperatures between 41° and 140° Fahrenheit.
   NRAEF's guidelines:

- Check temperatures at the time of delivery of meat, poultry, fish, and dairy products. Do not assume that the temperature has been correctly maintained on a truck or delivery dock.
- Store these deliveries immediately upon inspection.
- Store these deliveries in the coldest part of the refrigerators, away from doors.
- Do not overload refrigerators or line shelves with paper. These can restrict refrigerated airflow.
- Sample and record internal temperatures of refrigerated products on a regular time schedule.
- Do not refrigerate hot foods.
- Set refrigeration at least 2° Fahrenheit cooler than targeted temperatures.
- Dry storage items should be kept in 50° to 70° Fahrenheit conditions.
- The receiving dock clock should be kept on time and quality probe thermometers should be constantly cleaned.

NREAF findings indicate that information about these refrigeration principles is not passed on to employees about 40 percent of the time. This training must occur despite high rates of employee turnover. As for managers, the NREAF suggests recertification of managers in food safety more often than the current rate of every three to five years.

*Source:* Hume, Scott, "Telling Time and Temperature," *Restaurants & Institutions,* vol. 114, no. 3, February 1, 2004, pp. 75–77.

**Discussion Question:** How can a restaurant integrate employee food safety training into everyday operation to offset the effects of turnover?

## Bars

The National Restaurant Association has published a list of 12 effective bar sanitation tips:[18]

1. Wash glasses in a high-temperature dishwasher with a chemical sanitizer.
2. Air-dry all glasses.
3. When using the three-sink method, have the first sink filled with a detergent solution at a temperature of at least 110°F; the second sink filled with clean water at a temperature of 120°F; and the third sink filled with water at 170°F, in which the glasses are sanitized for at least 30 seconds.
4. Have employees use racks or baskets when using the three-sink method, to avoid burning themselves.
5. As a sanitizing alternative to hot water, use a chemical sanitizer at a temperature of at least 75°F.
6. Test the sanitizing water with a test kit.
7. Store glasses upside down.
8. Store bar utensils such that they will be picked up by their handles.
9. Check local regulations on the frequency of cleaning of beer lines; it may have to be done once a week.
10. Use different cloths for wiping down bottles and wiping down the bar.
11. Do not use scented or oxygen bleaches as sanitizers. The label will say whether or not it is registered with the Environmental Protection Agency (EPA).
12. Store glasses a minimum of 6 inches from the ground and protect from soil and condensation.

## Equipment

Various equipment manufacturers have developed standards for equipment designed for sanitation. Operators should look on equipment for designations from Underwriters' Laboratories (UL) or NSF International, for assistance in purchasing.

**Cleaning.**   To reduce bacteria to safe levels, kitchen equipment must be sanitized. Sanitizing equipment means going beyond cleaning with detergent and hot water; it means using heat and chemical agents after cleaning.

A variety of factors must be considered before cleaning begins:[19]

- *Type and condition of soil.* Soil can be protein based (for example, blood or egg), grease or oil, dissolved in water (for example, flour), and acid or alkaline. Whether it is fresh, ground-in, soft, dried, or baked-on will influence how easy it is to remove.
- *Type of water.* Hard water makes cleaning more difficult and leaves a scale or lime deposit on equipment.
- *Temperature of water.* The higher the temperature, the faster the cleaning.

- *Surface being cleaned.* Aluminum can darken in highly alkaline or chlorinated cleaners; abrasive cleaners may be needed for hard, baked-on soils.
- *Type of cleaning agent.* Soap can leave a film; abrasives can scratch the surface being cleaned; acid cleaners may be needed from time to time to remove lime buildup from equipment.
- *Agitation or pressure to be applied.* The more agitation, the more effective and faster the cleaning.
- *Length of treatment.* The longer the cleaning agent is exposed to the object, the more effective the cleaning.

There are three main types of cleaning products:[20] detergents, acid cleaners, and abrasive cleaners. Detergents are used with water to loosen dirt. They are very effective, inexpensive, and can be used on food-contact surfaces. Acid cleaners are used on dirt that alkaline-based detergents cannot remove. Used incorrectly, they can damage surfaces and cause chemical burns on the skin. Abrasive cleaners work by using finely ground minerals that scour the surface to remove soil that is crusted on. Soft plastic surfaces can be easily scratched, thereby making them less effective to bacteria prevention. After using abrasive cleaners, care must be taken to rinse away any residue.

Sanitizing occurs after cleaning and rinsing to kill bacteria. It involves the use of hot water or chemical compounds. Sanitizing should occur after every use. To sanitize using hot water, equipment and utensils must remain under water at a minimum temperature of 170°F for at least 30 seconds.

Chemical sanitizers are used more often than hot water for the purpose of destroying microorganisms. They include chlorine, iodine, and quaternary ammonium. Chlorine compounds work well in either hard or soft water and do not irritate when used properly. However, they can cause damage to metal equipment. Water should be used to rinse away any trace of detergents prior to the use of the chlorine compound, which should be at a temperature of 75°F. Iodine compounds work well in hard water and, being less corrosive than chlorine, do not irritate the skin or harm metal or rubber surfaces. Water temperature should be between 75 and 120°F. Quaternary ammonium compounds (quats) are skin safe and do not damage equipment, but their effectiveness can be reduced in very hard water. At a temperature of 75°F they work well in both acid and alkaline solutions.

Combination detergent–sanitizers are available. They must be used twice, once to clean and a second time to sanitize. Equipment and utensils should not be rinsed after sanitizing. The cycle is wash–rinse–sanitize.

## Rodent and Insect Control

The most frequent pest problems in a restaurant come from rats, mice, flies, and cockroaches. A good pest control program uses both environmental sanitation and chemical or blockage control.[21] Control for rats and mice begins with disposing garbage in a sanitary manner. Rodents must have access to food. Removing the trash and keeping storage areas clean will eliminate hiding places. Rodents can be killed with poison—mice are more susceptible—or trapped. Slow-killing poisons are best because they allow rodents to leave the premises before they die. Rodent-proofing the building consists of ensuring that doors are tight-fitting, with the bases flashed with metal; screening all windows less than 3 feet from the ground with hardware cloth screening; having concrete rather than wooden basement and ground floors; and closing all holes in foundations.

Control of flies begins with eliminating potential breeding places. This entails not allowing food to accrue and spoil and removing garbage quickly. Screens help keep flies out. Sprays, insecticides, and poisons eliminate flies, but their use should be monitored carefully to ensure that food is not affected by them. An electric fly catcher draws flies to an electric element, which kills them.

Cockroaches need moisture to survive. Most commonly, they enter an operation from deliveries. Hence crates and boxes should be inspected and disposed of as soon as possible. Frequent cleaning will reduce the number of new cockroaches. Once their hiding places are known, a qualified exterminator can lay poison to kill them.

In general, the following practices will help prevent problems:[22]

- Use a reputable supplier.
- Dispose of garbage properly and promptly.
- Store recycleables as far away from the premises as is allowed.
- Store all foods and supplies properly.
- Dispose of mop and cleaning water properly, and mop up spilled water at once.
- Clean and sanitize the operation thoroughly.

Most states require that restaurants contract with an independent and certified pest control service for all pest control services.

## Crisis Management

Crisis management is "the organized and systematic effort of an operation to prevent, react to, and learn from crises."[23] The development of a crisis management plan is one mark of proactive rather than reactive management. Three steps are involved in such an effort: preparation, management, and evaluation.[24] In the first stage a crisis team is formed. This team develops procedures and policies to be undertaken in case of a crisis. It is important that one and only one spokesperson be appointed to speak for the operation.

To manage the plan, a standardized complaint form should be developed and used to get information from complaining customers. Once it has been determined that the complaint is justified, the company decides whether to deal with the situation internally or whether outside help is needed. If the problem is small—the food was served cold—it can be settled in-house with a refund or small gift. Bigger problems, such as food poisoning, require outside assistance. It is important to communicate effectively with regulators, the public, employees, and the media.

Afterward, evaluation begins. Whatever caused the problem must be identified and corrected. Employees should be involved in giving their reaction to what happened, how it was handled, and how it can be prevented in the future. Finally, a copy of the complaint should be kept.

One example of a well-executed crisis management plan was that of Jack-in-the-Box over a decade ago. Faced with an outbreak of *E. coli* in California, the company immediately accepted blame for most of the deaths and illnesses linked to tainted food. The company settled with about 500 victims for amounts ranging from thousands of dollars to $15.6 million. The company also settled a class-action suit by its franchisees over the bacteria outbreak for about $44.5 million. The chief operating officer of the parent company at the time, Robert Nugent, indicated that the impact was greater and longer than the company expected. Lawyers for many of the victims credit the company for limiting the fallout from bad publicity by admitting fault and having top officials present at some of the mediation hearings. A week after the crisis, the company hired an independent food-safety consultant, who began investigating where the company bought its food, how the food was distributed, and how it was prepared. He later became vice president of quality assurance and product safety for the parent company, Foodmaker. A food-handling program developed by NASA in the 1960s to ensure sterile food for astronauts was adopted. This was the hazard analysis critical control points, or HACCP, program. The success of the program seems to have been based on moving quickly in a proactive manner, admitting fault, dealing equitably with the victims, and putting in a process to ensure outbreaks would not happen again.

---

### quick fact

Any way you slice it, CiCi's Pizza has addressed the complexities of its buffet-style concept with a comprehensive food safety plan. The Coppell, Texas–based concept, whose 565-store system is 95 percent franchised, employs three certified instructors that provide ServSafe certification training to the concept's more than 250 franchisees. In addition, CiCi's district managers visit the stores at least once a month and coach the franchisees on food safety practices using guideline-based documents from the company's internal Web site.

*Source:* Peters, James, *Nation's Restaurant News,* *http://www.nrn.com/story.cfm?ID= 7879605305&SEC=Food%20Safety,* November 2, 2005.

---

## EMPLOYEE HABITS

### Employee Health

Employees who have symptoms that suggest they are susceptible to passing along bacteria should not be allowed near food. If they have a fever or are sneezing, coughing, or have oozing burns or cuts, they are prime candidates for spreading harmful bacteria. Blood contaminates food and any surface with which it comes into contact. If food is exposed to an employee's blood, it must be discarded immediately. Employees who have cuts can continue to work as long as the cut is protected. Water-resistant bandages, changed often and covered with water-resistant material or plastic gloves, will serve as protection. The same procedures should be followed for burns.

The HIV microorganism that causes the AIDS virus is not spread by food. Service workers infected with AIDS can safely work around food unless they are cut or have other infections or illnesses.

**Personal Hygiene.**  The first step to staying healthy is to practice good health habits. This involves

- Bathing daily with soap and water
- Covering one's mouth when coughing or sneezing, then washing hands immediately afterward
- Avoiding such things as scratching the head or touching the mouth or nose
- Not eating, drinking, chewing gum, or smoking when food is being prepared or cleaned
- Avoiding the dropping of sweat onto food or equipment
- Using disposable towels to wipe away sweat and washing the hands before working with food
- Using hair restraints
- Keeping nails short and clean

**Hand Washing.**  Bacterial contamination occurs primarily when microorganisms are spread to food from the hands of employees. For this reason the best way to prevent contamination is effective hand washing. Hand sinks should be readily accessible and be used exclusively for this purpose. Warm water, soap, and disposable towels or an air-drying machine are required for effective hand washing. Hands must be washed after any act that might cause contamination—using the toilet, eating or drinking, handling raw food, and so on. Similarly, hands should not be dried or wiped on aprons.

**Clothing.**  Employee changing rooms should be kept separate from food preparation areas. Uniforms should also be clean and changed when necessary to prevent contamination.

Employee hygiene is important.

## Safety and Accident Prevention

The Industrial Commission of Ohio's Division of Safety and Hygiene identifies six acts that often result in accidents:[25]

1. Failing to look where one is going
2. Failing to observe surroundings
3. Failing to handle knives and tools with care
4. Reaching too high or too low; lifting a weight that is too heavy, or lifting incorrectly
5. Failing to pay attention when using knives, grinders, or other cutting tools
6. Failing to protect hands from hot pans, pots, and plates

Restaurant employees are particularly susceptible to falls, burns, cuts, and improper lifting. Falls can be minimized by keeping floors dry and in good repair,

---

quick bite 10.7
### Effective Employee Hygiene

**Learning Objective:** Build effective employee hygiene habits.

Statistics indicate that the third most common cause of foodborne illness is poor employee hygiene. The term hygiene includes grooming, hair restraints, clean clothes, clean aprons, and overall health. For managers, addressing these topics with employees may be uncomfortable. Nevertheless hygiene must be addressed.

The following techniques may help managers feel more comfortable about talking to their employees about hygiene:

- Have employees wash their hands thoroughly, apply an appropriate chemical, and shine a black (ultra-violet) light that shows how many germs remain.
- Always train a group of workers using light-hearted role playing illustrations that engage everyone in a specific training program, such as ServSafe's Essentials training class for hourly employees. Use this group context to address the hardest issues such as hair and body odor and staying at home when sick.
- Address sick pay benefits when talking about staying at home when ill.

Employees who continuously show poor hygiene should be counseled one-on-one.

According to ServSafe Essentials, managers must restrict food handlers from working with or around food if they show signs of fever, diarrhea, vomit-

---

wiping up spills immediately; rinsing after cleaning to remove any detergent or grease film; using slip-resistant shoes and floor coverings; and using signs indicating when a floor has just been cleaned.

Burns can be prevented by removing lids slowly to let steam escape; by using dry, flameproof potholders; by turning pot handles inward on the range; and by keeping stove tops and hoods free from grease.

Cuts can be avoided by keeping knives sharp, always cutting away from the body, having knives with built-in guards or shaped handles, and storing knives in a rack or knife holder.

Improper lifting accounts for 25 percent of accidents that result in lost work time.[26] Most injuries occur when putting down objects rather than picking things up. People should lift with their feet rather than with their back. This means[27]

- Getting a good footing
- Placing the feet shoulder-width apart

ing, sore throat, or jaundice. In addition, any cuts, burns, boils, sores, skin infections, or infected wounds should be covered with a bandage when the food handler is working with or around food or food-contact surfaces. Bandages should be clean and dry and must prevent leakage from the wound.

ServSafe also requires that employees wash their hands after:

- Using the rest room.
- Handling raw food (before and after).
- Touching the hair, face, or body.
- Sneezing, coughing or using a handkerchief or tissue.
- Smoking, eating, drinking, or chewing gum or tobacco.
- Handling chemicals that might affect the safety of the food.
- Taking out the trash.
- Clearing tables or busing dirty dishes.
- Touching clothing or aprons.
- Touching anything else that might contaminate the hands, such as dirty work surfaces or wash cloths.

*Source:* Riell, Howard, "A Fun—But Serious—Approach: Employee Hygiene," *FoodService Director*, vol. 16, no. 2, February 15, 2003, p. 80.

**Discussion Question:** In what environment would it be best to chat with an employee who exhibits poor hygiene?

- Bending the knees before grasping the weight
- Keeping the back straight
- Getting a firm hold
- Lifting gradually by straightening the legs

The Occupational Safety and Health Act (OSHA) was passed in 1970 to assure safe and healthy conditions in the workplace. It lays out guidelines for the work environment and inspects facilities to ensure that businesses are in compliance. OSHA checklists can be used as a guide to whether or not the restaurant is safe for employees. A comprehensive program involves four things: inspecting all equipment and physical facilities, examining the physical fitness of employees to perform their jobs safely, reviewing operational practices and personnel activities as they do their jobs, and checking compliance with safety and health regulations.

---

### quick bite 10.8
**Road to the Top: Charnette Norton**

Charnette Norton is principal of the Norton Group in Texas and a vice president of Romano Gatland in New York. Together with Ruby Puckett, Norton authored the book *HACCP, The Future Challenge—Practical Application for the Foodservice Administrator.* She is a prolific proponent of the HACCP system, having written on various aspects of control point management in over twenty articles alone since January 2002.

She is a strong proponent of analyzing food production as a process that flows smoothly from farm to fork. Critical control points must be monitored in order to verify the safety of the food as it passes through the process.

Norton graduated with a graduate degree in food systems management from the University of Missouri. Once out of college, she became director of food services and nutrition at the University of Texas' M.D. Anderson Cancer Center. Following that residency, she worked in foodservice consulting. Norton has also coauthored a book on disaster and emergency preparedness for foodservice operations and has received the national leadership award from the Society for Foodservice Management.

*Sources:* Editors, "News Digests," *Nation's Restaurant News,* vol. 36, no. 45, November 11, 2002, p. 20. King, Paul, "Charnette Norton," *Nation's Restaurant News,* vol. 37, no. 39, September 29, 2003, p. 18. Norton, Char, "HACCP Goes with the Flow," vol. 86, no. 8, August 2002, pp. 84–85.

**Discussion Question:** In your opinion, is it more useful to see food production as "a process that flows smoothly from farm to fork" or as a collection of discrete processes like farming, harvesting, transporting, storing, cooking, eating?

# ENDNOTES

1. Lewis J. Minor and Ronald F. Cichy, *Foodservice Systems Management* (Westport, CT: AVI Publishing Company, 1984), p. 161.
2. National Assessment Institute, *Handbook for Safe Food Service Management* (Upper Saddle River, NJ: Regents/Prentice Hall, 1994), p. 8.
3. Ibid., p. 42.
4. NRA staff, "Food Allergy Awareness," *Restaurants USA,* January 2002, www.restaurant.org/rusa.
5. Ibid.
6. National Assessment Institute, *Handbook for Safe Food Service Management* (Upper Saddle River, NJ: Regents/Prentice Hall, 1994), pp. 11, 39–41.
7. Mahmood A. Khan, *Concepts of Foodservice and Management,* 2nd ed. (New York: Van Nostrand Reinhold, 1991), p. 208.
8. Minor and Cichy, *Foodservice Systems Management,* p. 162.
9. National Assessment Institute, *Handbook for Safe Food Service Management,* p. 35.
10. Ibid., p. 37.
11. National Institute for Food Service Industry, *Applied Foodservice Sanitation,* 4th ed. (New York: John Wiley & Sons, 1992), p. 86.
12. Ibid., p. 87.
13. Ibid., p. 89.
14. Minor and Cichy, *Foodservice Systems Management,* p. 181.
15. *Applied Foodservice Sanitation,* p. 67.
16. Ibid., p. 135.
17. Ibid., p. 176.
18. "Top Twelve Bar Sanitation Tips," *F&B Business,* December 1989, p. 55.
19. *Applied Foodservice Sanitation,* pp. 188–189.
20. National Assessment Institute, *Handbook for Safe Food Service Management,* p. 96.
21. John Knight, p. 47.
22. *Applied Foodservice Sanitation,* pp. 228–229.
23. Ibid., p. 279.
24. Ibid., p. 280.
25. Knight, p. 52.
26. Ibid., p. 51.
27. Ibid., p. 53.

# INTERNET RESOURCES

| | |
|---|---|
| Occupational Safety and Health Administration | *http://www.osha.gov/* |
| Centers for Disease Control and Prevention | *http://www.cdc.gov/* |
| National Restaurant Association Educational Foundation | *http://www.nraef.org/servsafe/* |
| Foodhandler, Inc. | *http://www.foodhandler.com/* |
| San Jamar | *http://www.sanjamar.com/* |
| Ecolab, Inc. | *http://www.ecolab.com/* |

# QUICK QUIZ ANSWER KEY

p. 280—Salmonella

# CHAPTER ELEVEN

# CONTROLLING COSTS

"The third and most mysterious piece of nonabsoluteness of all lies in the relationship between the number of items on the bill, the cost of each item, the number of people at the table and what they are each prepared to pay for. (The number of people who have actually brought any money is only a subphenomenon of this field.)"

Douglas Adams, British author,
from *Life, the Universe, and Everything*

## learning objectives

*By the end of this chapter you should be able to*

1. Identify the five types of financial ratios used by management.

2. Describe a systematic way of analyzing an income statement.

3. Identify the appropriate ratios to calculate when analyzing sales, expenses, and profit.

4. Identify the appropriate ratios to calculate when analyzing the balance sheet.

5. Determine the break-even point for a business, given the appropriate sales and expense figures.

## Hot Concept: Profitability through Cost Control

How do you make a small fortune in the restaurant business? Start with a large one. So sad, so true.

When it comes to profitability, not all money is equal. $100 in sales is reduced by expenses. However, $100 is savings in costs is a $100 saved and added to profitability.

What are some sensible cost control mechanisms?

- In the first few pages of a training manual, explain to employees how expenses relate to revenues, how higher costs reduce the amount of money available for training and the amount of money for employees.
- "Smash the trash"—reduce waste.
- Semiannually give seminars that teach employees and their spouses how to manage their personal finances. Stress how the same principles apply at work.
- Post invoices for the costs of utilities, food, beverages, insurance and the lease so that employees see these otherwise invisible costs and how they compare to their home costs.
- Post photos of the commonly tossed, damaged and over-portioned items with captions of the costs per unit. Include costs of glassware, sugar packets, napkins, silver ware, ketchup packets, extra ounces of meat and liquor.
- Keep knives and blades sharp to minimize cuts and accidents.
- Follow and measure recipe ingredients. Disapprove of "by eye" measurements.
- Offer free, preshift meals to eliminate food theft.
- Reinforce attendance, promptness, sales, work safety, cost control and the like each month by posting a list of employees' names, scratching off names of those not complying with the month's stated goal (e.g., no breakage) and enter[ing] survivors' names into a raffle for a substantive prize.

*Source:* Sullivan, Jim, "Let's Get Fiscal: Look at the Other Side of Profitability," *Nation's Restaurant News,* vol. 35, no. 31, July 30, 2001, p. 18.

**Discussion Questions:** Of the above cost control mechanisms, which do you think will generate the greatest savings? Which will be most likely to be followed?

## FINANCIAL STATEMENTS

An understanding of financial statements is necessary for preparing tax forms, negotiating loans, and—the topic of this chapter—determining the financial condition of the business. Management looks at five types of ratios. Liquidity ratios determine the extent to which a business can meet short-term obligations as and when they become due. As we will see later, this includes such ratios as the current ratio and the acid test or quick ratio. Solvency ratios, on the other hand, look at the ability of the operation to meet its long-term obligations. Both types of ratios are generated from the balance sheet.

Activity and profitability ratios take information from both the balance sheet and statement of income. Activity ratios show how well management is using the assets of the operation in generating income. Profitability or rate-of-return ratios show how profitable the business is. Finally, operating ratios deal with the efficiency of management in actually operating a business.

The two fundamental accounting statements are the statement of income and the balance sheet. The former indicates the profitability of the business over a period of time. The various costs of operating the business are subtracted from the revenue generated to show either a profit, if the revenue is greater than the costs, or a loss, if the costs are greater than the revenue. The balance sheet indicates the financial condition or value of the business at a particular point in time. Typically, December 31 is used as that point.

## Statement of Income

A representation of where the average restaurant dollar comes from and goes to is shown in Table 11.1. Following the standard format for an income statement, averages are shown for four types of restaurant: full-service restaurants, average check per person under $15; full-service multiunit, company-operated restaurants, average check per person $15 to $24.99; full-service restaurants, average check per person $25 and over; limited-service fast-food restaurants.

Revenue and other income for the period are listed. All expenses incurred during the period in question are then subtracted from total revenue to determine the profit (if any) before taxes.

The Uniform System of Accounts for Restaurants has been developed by the accounting firm of Laventhol and Horwath and accepted by the National Restaurant Association as a blueprint for categorizing revenues and costs and laying out a statement of income. By following this guide, individual operations can compare their operating figures with those of similar restaurants in the industry. Annual figures and ratios for this purpose are produced by both the National Restaurant Association and Deloitte & Touche. In analyzing statements of income, it is useful to consider not only the dollar figures but also the amounts as a percentage of revenue. Such a procedure allows for a more reliable comparison of, for example, management's effectiveness in controlling labor costs relative to the volume of sales.

**Revenue.** Revenue is primarily from sales of food and sales of beverages. Other revenues—for example, from room rental—would be shown later as other income. The relative proportions of food to beverage revenue is important because the cost of sales for beverages is less than the cost of sales for food. An operation with a high percentage of beverage to food revenue is thus typically good for bottom-line profit.

**Table 11.1    Statement of Income**

|  | A | B | C | D |
|---|---|---|---|---|
| **Sales** | | | | |
| Food sales | 89.6% | 78.9% | 71.4% | 100% |
| Beverage sales | 16.4 | 21.2 | 28.6 | 3.2 |
| Total sales | 100 | 100 | 100 | 100 |
| Cost of sales | | | | |
| Food cost | 32.6 | 36.4 | 34.4 | 31.3 |
| Beverage cost | 30 | 28.4 | 30 | 30 |
| Total cost of sales | 32 | 34.1 | 33 | 30.8 |
| **Gross profit** | 67.3 | 64.9 | 66.9 | 68.2 |
| | | | | |
| **Operating expenses** | | | | |
| Salaries and wages (including employee benefits) | 34 | 34 | 32.4 | 30.8 |
| Direct operating expenses | 6.7 | 6.6 | 6.2 | 4.9 |
| Music and entertainment | 0.3 | 0.5 | 0.5 | 0.2 |
| Marketing | 2 | 1.8 | 1.9 | 1.5 |
| Utility services | 3.4 | 3.1 | 2.5 | 2.8 |
| Restaurant occupancy costs | 5.2 | 5.6 | 6.7 | 7 |
| Repairs and maintenance | 1.5 | 1.5 | 1.4 | 1.4 |
| Depreciation | 2 | 2.2 | 1.4 | 1.9 |
| Other expenses | 0.6 | 0.4 | 0.4 | 2.8 |
| General and administrative | 2.8 | 2.5 | 2.7 | 2 |
| Corporate overhead | 4.8 | 2.7 | 1.5 | 4.4 |
| Total Operating Expenses | 60.8 | 60.6 | 61.8 | 58.6 |
| Interest expense | 0.8 | 0.3 | 0.3 | 1 |
| Other expenses | 1 | 0.9 | · 0.6 | 1.8 |
| Income before income taxes | 5.4 | 4 | 2.9 | 7.3 |

*Source: 2005 Restaurant Industry Operations Report* (Washington, DC: Deloitte & Touche and the National Restaurant Association, 2005), pp. 25, 53, 85, 109.

*Note:* (1) All figures are medians based on 2004 data. (2) All ratios are based on a percentage of total sales except food and beverage costs, which are based on their respective sales. A, full-service restaurants, average check per person under $15; B, full-service multiunit, company-operated restaurants, average check per person $15 to $24.99; C, full-service restaurants, average check per person $25 and over; D, limited-service fast-food restaurants.

**Cost of Sales.**    Cost of sales is the cost of the food and beverage items that have been sold. To determine the food and/or beverage cost for an operation, beginning and ending inventories must be made. The ending inventory for period 1 becomes the beginning inventory for period 2. Because inventories can vary from day to day, a physical inventory should always be taken on the same day of the week. If an operation deliberately avoided ordering food until the day after a physical inventory was taken, the food cost would be uncharacteristically low; similarly, an unusually high inventory would increase the cost of food and a corresponding lower profit. Inventories are normally taken once a month.

The cost of food sales is calculated as follows:

inventory of food at beginning of period (dollars) + purchases
of food during the period
    = total value of available food − inventory of food at end of period
    = value of food used during the period

A similar calculation is made to determine the cost of beverage sales. Food and beverage cost percentages will be different. It is, therefore, desirable to compare the cost of food to food revenue and the cost of beverage to beverage revenue and express them as percentages.

**Gross Profit.**   Gross profit is the profit after taking the cost of sales—food and beverage—from total revenue.

**Other Income.**   As noted previously, the principal sources of revenue for a restaurant will come from sales of food and beverages. Other income would cover any other revenue taken in the sale of nonfood and nonbeverage items, such as candy, room rental, and concessions.

**Controllable Expenses.**   Management has direct responsibility for and can influence controllable expenses, which include such things as

- *Salaries and wages:* Employee payroll
- *Employee benefits:* Employee meals, Social Security taxes, medical insurance costs, workers' compensation insurance, and so on
- *Direct operating expenses:* Costs involved in the operation of the business, such as uniforms, laundry, and decorations
- *Music/entertainment:* Live or canned music
- *Marketing:* Promotion, advertising, and so on
- *Energy and utility service:* Cost of fuel, water, waste removal, and so on
- *Administrative and general:* Overhead costs not directly connected with providing customer service, such as telephone, postage, and office supplies
- *Repairs and maintenance:* Cost of repairing and maintaining the building and equipment

**Total Controllable Expenses.**   Managers have control over both the controllable expenses listed previously and the food and beverage costs noted earlier. Any costs listed later are fixed in the short run and usually cannot be influenced by the unit manager.

**Income before Rent and Other Occupation Costs.** This figure is obtained by subtracting total controllable expenses from total income. Companies often use this figure as the basis for determining management bonuses.

**Rent and Other Occupational Costs.** These costs are those associated with getting the property operating and include rent, real estate taxes, and property insurance. This overhead is fixed and cannot be changed in the short run. These figures depend on the agreement negotiated and will be in effect for the term of the agreement.

**Depreciation.** Depreciation is a noncash, tax-deductible expense. Since the building, equipment, and other assets wear out, an allowance is given to indicate the cost involved as the assets are used. Various methods can be used to depreciate assets in accordance with guidelines as to how long the assets are expected to last. The expense reduces taxes due and is available as positive cash flow to the operation.

**Interest.** When bank loans are used to finance a business, the cost of borrowing the money is charged as interest. Depending on how a building is financed, the operation may have rent costs (if the building is leased) or interest costs (if it is purchased).

**Income Tax.** Businesses pay taxes on their profits just as individuals pay taxes on their income. Net income is what is left after taxes have been subtracted.

## Balance Sheet

The balance sheet shows the financial situation for the business at a particular point in time, usually December 31. The fundamental equation is

assets = liabilities + equity

The assets are what the business owns; the liabilities are what is owed by the business; the difference is the net worth or equity of the business.

**Assets.** Assets are either short term or fixed. Short-term assets are those that can be or are liquidated within a year. This includes cash on hand, accounts receivable (money owed to the operation), inventories of food, beverage, and other items (china, cutlery, etc.), and any expenses that have been prepaid.

Fixed assets are those items that have a life longer than a year. This includes such things as land, building, and equipment and uniforms. If the building is leased and the operator has made improvements, the improvements would be listed here as leasehold improvements. Note that although the value of the building and furniture and fixtures is reduced by the amount depreciated, the value of the land (although it can change in value) is not changed by depreciation.

**Liabilities.** Current liabilities are those payable within the year. Most of this is made up of accounts payable, bills owed by the operation to various people.

Long-term liabilities are those that will be paid off over several years. The total amount of the outstanding mortgage (less the current portion, which is included under current liabilities) tends to be the largest part of this item.

**Shareholders' Equity.**   As noted previously, the difference between assets and liabilities is the equity or what the business is worth. Profits are either distributed to the owners as dividends or kept in the business. The latter are referred to as retained earnings.

---

**q u i c k   t i p**

To save money, serve beverages from a beverage gun or dispenser, buy bar mixes in concentrate form, and buy milk in 5-gallon dispenser boxes.

*Source:* Business Resource Efficiency & Waste Reduction, "Food Service Waste Reduction Tips and Ideas," *http://www.ciwmb.ca.gov/BizWaste/FactSheets/FoodSrvc.htm*, November 5, 2005.

---

## ANALYZING FINANCIAL STATEMENTS: STATEMENT OF INCOME

Financial statements will be analyzed by various people for different reasons.[1] Bankers will look at the numbers in evaluating a loan proposal to determine the likelihood of repayment; an investor will use the statements to estimate a return on the investment; a supplier may look at the books before deciding whether or not to extend credit; management analyzes the numbers to determine the profitability or efficiency of the operation.

The figures mean little unless they are compared to something. Statements of income may be compared to forecasted or budgeted figures, to industry averages, or to previous results of the operation. Similarly, with the income statement, the dollar figures are not as meaningful as when they are expressed as a percentage of sales. A large operation will have food costs, in dollars, much higher than those of a smaller operation. For people evaluating the operation, the key is how well the costs have been controlled compared to sales. Looking at percentages allows an analyst to compare one operation to another.

### Systematic Approach

A systematic way to analyze the statement of income is to begin with the bottom line, working upward in an attempt to zero in on problem areas. In this approach, the first step is to compare net income as a percentage of total revenue to a standard. As noted previously, that standard may be a forecast, the previous year's figures, or an industry average. If the ratio is acceptable, management will presumably be pleased. This is not to say that the way the business is run cannot be improved; it merely indicates that the operation is "on target."

If, however, the bottom-line ratio is not acceptable, the second step is to move to the next major level, total controllable expenses. Here again, the approach is to compare the ratio of total controllable expenses to total revenue. If this figure is "acceptable" but the bottom-line figure is not, the problem lies somewhere in between the two ratios, in this case with the uncontrollable fixed costs, such as rent, interest, and other occupation costs. We have an indication that management is able to keep the controllable expenses in line but is still not having an acceptable bottom line. The problem in this case is that total revenue is not sufficient to produce enough income before rent and other charges to cover the fixed uncontrollable expenses. The task for management is to increase sales volume while continuing to control costs, thereby generating enough income to cover the fixed costs.

If the ratio of total controllable expenses is not acceptable to management, the problem is somewhere above this line on the statement of income.

This, in essence, is the systematic method of analyzing the statement of income:

1. Compare ratios at two levels.
2. If the lower level (closest to the bottom line) is acceptable and the higher one is not, the problem is with some figures in between the two.
3. If the ratio at a particular level is not acceptable, the problem is with one or more of the figures above this level.

Continuing this analysis, let us assume that the ratio of total controllable expenses to total revenue is not acceptable. As noted previously, the problem lies somewhere above this line. We would then go to the next major level on the statement of income—total income—in an attempt to isolate the problem. If this ratio of total income to total revenue is acceptable, the problem lies somewhere in between total income and total controllable expenses. Each line under controllable expenses would be analyzed to determine which figures are over budget or out of line with competing ratios.

The analysis would continue using the method outlined previously. Using this method, management can isolate problem areas systematically.

Jim Laube, creator and publisher of RestaurantOwner.com, a Web site specifically for independent restaurant operators and featuring business management resources, suggests four major issues:[2]

- How much money should we be making? [All figures quoted in this section are taken from the *2005 Restaurant Industry Operations Report* by Deloitte & Touche and the National Restaurant Association (Washington, DC, 2005).]
- Key indicator is sales per square foot
  - Full-service restaurants with an average check per person under $15 have median sales/square foot of $232.
  - Full-service restaurants with an average check between $15 and $24.99 have median sales per square foot of $252.

- Full-service restaurants with an average check of $25 and greater have median sales per square foot of $308.
- Limited-service restaurants have median sales per square foot of $286.
- How well is management making money?
  - Key indicator is income before occupancy costs
    - Income before occupancy costs are gross profit less salaries and wages, direct operating expenses, music and entertainment, marketing, utility services, repairs and maintenance and general and administrative.
    - Income before occupancy costs for full-service restaurants with an average check per person under $15 is 16.6 percent of sales.
    - Income before occupancy costs for full-service restaurants with an average check between $15 and $24.99 is 14.9 percent of sales.
    - Income before occupancy costs for full-service restaurants with an average check of $25 and greater is 19.3 percent of sales.
    - Income before occupancy costs for limited-service restaurants is 24.6 percent of sales.
- Are our most important costs out of line?
  - Key indicator is the prime cost percentage
    - Prime cost is total cost of sales plus total payroll and benefits.
    - Prime cost for full-service restaurants with an average check per person under $15 is 66.4 percent of sales.
    - Prime cost for full-service restaurants with an average check between $15 and $24.99 is 68.6 percent of sales.
    - Prime cost for full-service restaurants with an average check of $25 and greater is 64.2 percent of sales.
    - Prime cost for limited-service restaurants is 61.1 percent of sales.
- Are occupancy costs too high?
  - Key indicator is occupancy cost percentage, per seat and percentage cost per square foot
  - Industry guidelines (average) for full-menu tableservice restaurants are
    - Percentage of sales      7–8 percent
    - $ per square foot      $14–$20
    - $ per seat      $250–$450
  - Industry guidelines (average) for quick service restaurants are
    - Percentage of sales      7–9 percent
    - $ per square foot      $15–$25

## The Three-Part Method

According to Keiser,[3] a statement of income can be divided into three parts: sales, expenses, and profit. He recommends analyzing each part separately.

**quick bite 11.2**
## Relative Importance of Financial Ratios to Management

**Learning Objectives:** Identify the five types of financial ratios used by management. Describe a systematic way of analyzing an income statement. Identify the appropriate ratios to calculate when analyzing sales, expenses, and profit.

Within the restaurant/foodservice industry there has been no major study of which class of financial ratios is most favored or deemed most important by managers. However, an extensive study of lodging financial executives indicates that of liquidity, solvency, activity, profitability, and operating ratios two sets of ratios clearly stand out as the most important for lodging managers—operating and profitability ratios.

Within operating ratios, revenue maximization ratios were deemed most important. For restaurant operations, this would suggest that the revenue maximization ratios—average check (revenue/number of customers) and seat turnover (number of customers/number of seats)—would be of great importance. Additional operating ratios that would also be important would be: labor cost percentage (total labor cost/total revenue), food profit percentage (food department profit/food department revenues), beverage profit percentage (beverage department profit/beverage department revenues), food cost percentage (cost of food sales/food revenues) and beverage cost percentage (cost of beverage sales/beverage revenue).

Within the profitability ratios, profit margin (net income/total revenue) and operating efficiency (income after undistributed operating expenses/total revenues) were deemed most important.

The study concludes that as operations become larger and more dependent upon external financing and as company structures become more complex (as with the larger, segmented chain foodservice companies such as McDonald's or Burger King), managers will need to focus more on balance sheet ratios, solvency ratios, and return on assets ratios.

*Source:* Singh, A. J., and Schmidgall, Raymond S., "Analysis of Financial Ratios Commonly Used by US Lodging Financial Executives," *Journal of Leisure Property*, vol. 2, no. 3, August 2002, pp. 201–204.

**Discussion Question:** What are examples of revenue maximization ratios that would be considered important?

**Sales.**   In looking at sales, management basically wants to know three things:

1. Are sales increasing or decreasing?
2. Why is this happening?
3. Is the level of sales appropriate to the value of the business, the size of the operation, and/or the amount invested in it?

To answer these questions it may be necessary to break down sales figures by product category and/or by meal period. The former is germane to profitability, as the profit potential on beverages is greater than that on food. In making comparisons it is important to ensure that the comparison base is the same. Figures can be compared for the same month or week of the year compared to previous years as well as year-to-date.

Since revenue is a product of the number of covers (customers) times the average price of a meal, an increase in sales is due to one or both of these factors. A sales increase might reflect an increase in menu prices. This may, in fact, camouflage a reduction in the number of covers served. It is important that the average cost of a meal cover, at a minimum, any cost increase the business incurs. If the cost of doing business increases by 8 percent, for example, the average price of a meal should be at least 8 percent more.

The laws of supply and demand indicate that, other things being equal, as price goes up, the number of customers will go down. A price increase that results in fewer customers may actually generate less revenue than previously. This concept is known as elasticity of demand. A menu item is price elastic if an increase in price produces less revenue because of reduced demand. Similarly, a price reduction will result in more demand and more revenue. Price elasticity means that the demand is sensitive to changes in price.

The item is price inelastic if the price increase generates more revenue. In this case the market is less sensitive to changes in price. An increase in price has not caused sufficient customers to stop ordering the item such that total revenue—the product of price times number of customers—increases. Similarly, a price cut will not generate enough additional customers to generate more total revenue in a price-inelastic situation.

To fully understand the reasons for a decrease in sales, each meal period and each menu item should be analyzed separately. It is only by doing this that management can pinpoint the meal period and/or menu item(s) causing the problem.

Several ratios are important when analyzing sales:

$$1.\ \text{Average check} = \frac{\text{revenue}}{\text{number of customers}}$$

If the average check is less than "normal," prices may have to be increased or promotions put into effect to "push" the sale of more expensive items or to package appetizers and/or desserts with entree items to increase the average amount spent.

$$2.\ \text{Seat turnover} = \frac{\text{number of customers}}{\text{number of seats}}$$

This ratio demonstrates how well the facility is being utilized. A low turnover indicates poor utilization—more customers can be accommodated; a high turnover may be a sign to expand.

Average daily seat turnover for full-service restaurants with an average check under $15.00 is 2.0. [All figures quoted in this section are taken from *2005 Restaurant Industry Operations Report* by Deloitte & Touche and the National Restaurant Association (Washington, DC, 2005).] This figure ranges from 1.2 in restaurants with sales volume less than $500,000 to 2.7 in places with over $2 million in sales volume.

The median daily seat turnover for full-service restaurants with an average check of $15.00 to $24.99 above is 1.2 and is greater for establishments with over $2 million in annual sales volume. The median daily seat turnover for full-service restaurants with an average check of $25.00 or over is 0.7.

For limited-service fast food restaurants the median figure of 4.0 is greatest when operations are the sole occupant of a location.

$$3. \text{ Sales per square foot} = \frac{\text{sales}}{\text{number of square feet}}$$

This ratio is useful when comparing alternative uses for a particular space. What, for example, would the sales per square foot be for sit-down versus take-out service?

Full-service restaurants with an average check of less than $15 report average sales per square foot of $232. This figure is greatest for those located in a shopping center or mall. There is a direct correlation between sales volume and the average sales per square foot. As sales volume increases, so does the average sales per square foot.

The median figure of $252 for full-service operations with an average check between $15.00 and $24.99 is greater for restaurants featuring steak or seafood. As previously, there is a direct correlation between sales volume and the average sales per square foot.

The median figure for full-service restaurants with an average check of $25 or over is $308 and is less for steak/seafood operations. It also is greater for operations with greater annual sales volume.

For limited-service fast-food operations, with a median figure of $286 and the figure is greater for American-themed operations.

**Expenses.** Expenses are either variable, semivariable, or fixed. Variable expenses are those that vary proportionately with volume. Food and beverage costs fall into this category. If selling one hamburger costs 35 cents in product cost, selling two will cost 70 cents.

Semivariable expenses contain both a fixed and a variable component. They will change with volume but not directly. Employee wages are a good example. As volume increases, the number of employees needed will increase and the wage bill will go up. An operation must be staffed in advance of customers coming in, and a certain minimum number of employees must be present. As volume increases, the number of employees can be increased. However, sales forecasting is very difficult and there will be times when there is an imbalance between the number of customers and the number of employees needed to cook for and serve them.

Fixed expenses are those that do not vary as volume varies. The rent must be paid whether one customer or 1000 customers are served. According to Keiser, "The more variable the expense, the more significant its percentage figure as related to sales."[4]

The three most important, because they are the largest, controllable ratios comprise the prime cost. They are

1. $\text{Cost of food sales} = \dfrac{\text{cost of food sold}}{\text{food sales}}$

2. $\text{Cost of beverage sales} = \dfrac{\text{cost of beverage sold}}{\text{beverage sales}}$

3. $\text{Labor cost (\%)} = \dfrac{\text{cost of labor}}{\text{total revenue}}$

It should be noted that an operation can offset a high cost in one area with a low cost in another. For example, a restaurant that uses convenience products will have a higher food cost than one that prepares items from scratch. The latter, however, will have higher labor costs.

For full-service restaurants with an average check of less than $15, the median prime cost is 66.4 percent of sales.

In general, the higher the sales volume generated, the better the food and beverage cost percentages. Labor cost percentages are lowest for operations with more than $2 million annual sales and highest for restaurants with annual sales volume between $500,000 and $999,999.

The median prime cost for full-service restaurants with an average check between $15.00 and $24.99 is 68.6 percent. Food and beverage costs are less for restaurants when sales volume is greater than $2 million a year and greater for steak/seafood-theme restaurants and for operations with annual sales volume less that $500,000.

The median prime cost for full-service restaurants with an average check of $25 or higher is 64.2 percent. For limited-service fast-food restaurants the median prime cost is 61.1 percent of sales. For operations specializing in sandwiches, subs, and deli items, food cost is similar to the median though the labor cost is lower.

Overall, there seems to be an advantage to being a multiunit company-operated restaurant and to have annual sales volume either less than $500,000 or greater than $2 million. It may be that control procedures are better managed in company operations. The lower labor costs in operations with lower sales volume may be because owners and/or managers perform tasks that would be performed by hourly employees. When annual sales volume increase to more than $2 million, there are economies of scale in controlling labor costs.

Although the three items noted previously are the most important—or prime—costs, every controllable expense should be tracked on a regular basis. It is also vital when comparing ratios that the same type of restaurant be used. The ratios for a fast-food unit will be much different from those for a full-service operation. Figures can also be compared on a cost-per-seat or cost-per-meal basis.

**Profit.**   How much is "enough" profit? In the final analysis the profit generated must be sufficient to keep the owner(s) pleased with the investment. A restaurant may produce profit, but if the owners feel they could get a better return on their investment from another investment, the level of profit generated may not be enough to keep the operation open.

Three ratios are particularly important:

$$1. \text{ Operating ratio } = \frac{\text{net income before taxes}}{\text{net sales}}$$

This ratio is also referred to as net profit to net sales, earnings ratio, operating margin, or profit ratio. Obviously, the higher that ratio, the better.

In full-service operations with an average check less than $15, the median income before income taxes is greater for units serving food and beverage (5.5 percent) compared to those serving food only (4.8 percent). Company-operated multiunits produce more (7.3 percent) than independents (4.6 percent). Although the greatest ratio is found in restaurants with annual sales volume under $500,000 (8.0 percent), operating profit typically increases as sales volume increases.

For full-service restaurants with an average check between $15.00 and $24.99, the median income before income taxes is greatest for operations with annual sales volume of less than $500,000 (4 percent) and, thereafter, increases as sales volume increases.

For full-service restaurants with an average check of $25 and up, the median income before income taxes is greatest for operations with annual sales volume of more than $2 million.

For limited-service fast-food operations the operating ratio is slightly more for company-owned chains (7.9 percent) than independents (7.2 percent). Operating ratios increase with increasing sales volume up to $999,000 and decrease slightly thereafter.

$$2. \text{ Net profit to net equity } = \frac{\text{net profit after taxes}}{\text{net equity}}$$

Some businesses—for example, fast-food units—make a relatively small profit on each item sold. However, they rely on a large volume with a relatively small investment compared to sales to produce a modest operating ratio but a good net profit to net equity.

$$3. \text{ Management proficiency ratio } = \frac{\text{net profit after taxes}}{\text{total assets}}$$

This ratio indicates what management does with the assets it has. The higher the ratio, the better job that management is doing.

---

**q u i c k   t i p**

Place rubber mats around bus and dish washing stations to reduce china and glass breakage.

*Source:* Business Resource Efficiency & Waste Reduction, "Food Service Waste Reduction Tips and Ideas," *http://www.ciwmb.ca.gov/BizWaste/FactSheets/FoodSrvc.htm,* November 5, 2005.

---

## ANALYZING FINANCIAL STATEMENTS: BALANCE SHEET

### Current Assets

As noted previously, current assets are those that can easily be liquidated.

**Cash.**   Sufficient cash must be available to meet current expenses. Any remaining cash can generate interest from a bank. Cash is kept on hand for change and petty cash and is also maintained in a bank account to pay expenses.

**Accounts Receivable.**   Accounts receivable are what customers owe. A business that is strictly cash will have no accounts receivable. On the other hand, an operation that has a large banquet business and bills customers after the event may have a substantial accounts receivable.

The time between providing the service and being paid for it represents the restaurant "allowing" the customer use of the restaurant's money. Thus the shorter the average collection period or the greater the turnover, the better for the operation. At the same time, extending credit may be necessary to attract the customer. The important point to note is that there is a cost involved in providing credit.

1. Accounts receivable turnover $= \dfrac{\text{total sales}}{\text{average accounts receivable}}$

2. Average collection period $= \dfrac{365 \text{ days}}{\text{accounts receivable turnover}}$

3. Number of days tied up $= \dfrac{\text{accounts receivable}}{\text{daily sales}}$

The third ratio shows how many days' sales are tied up in accounts receivable. The figure should be as low as possible.

## quick bite 11.3
### Increasing Balance Sheet Cash without Increasing Sales

**Learning Objective:** Identify the appropriate ratios to calculate when analyzing the balance sheet.

Increasing sales is not necessarily the best way to improve cash flow for the balance sheet. Here are several practical suggestions to do just that:

- Concentrate on improving profit margins (1) by passing along limited price increases (for example, supplier increases) that stay aligned with competitor's prices, (2) by removing unprofitable items from the menu, (3) by centralizing the ordering of supplies and food and (4) by changing the menu product mix to pair food offerings with more profitable beverage offerings.
- Take full advantage of trade terms by procrastinating payment until the date a payment is due (but not late which could harm supplier relations).
- Control intangible operating expenses such as personal expenses, utilities, insurance, and telephone service. Shop for competitive rates on insurance and telephone service. Minimize employee downtime and especially overtime.
- Renegotiate with the landlord if leasing in an area with commercial real estate vacancies.
- Renegotiate loan terms with bankers whenever rates permit and take advantage of cash management services including sweep account investment of overnight balances.
- Barter excess capacity by trading meals for services. For example, offer trade dollars where payment for services offered to the restaurant is made to the supplier in so many dollars of meals on days or nights that are not expected to be at full capacity. The use of barter will allow the restaurant to use empty tables, uneaten food and unoccupied staff to its advantage without a cash outlay. It is estimated that 400,000 companies of all sizes nationwide are involved in $9 billion in barter transactions annually. So explore local barter options with all manner of suppliers.

*Sources:* Broome Jr, J. Tol, and Soeder, John, "How to Generate Cash Flow," *Restaurant Hospitality,* vol. 81, no. 3, pp. 32–34. Meharg, Ken, "Boost Cash Flow by Bartering," *Restaurant Hospitality,* vol. 83, no. 8, p. 28.

**Discussion Question:** Why is bartering a good plan?

**Inventories.** Inventory turnover will vary depending on the type of operation and will vary from twice a week for fast-food units to three to five times a month for full-service operations.

The restaurant must balance the need for it to have sufficient supplies on hand so that it will not run out of items with the fact that inventory costs money. The more items on hand for a period of time, the more money the restaurant ties up. Slow turnover indicates that inventory levels are too high. In addition to the money tied up, the longer items are kept, the greater the chance of spoilage.

On the other hand, a particularly high turnover may indicate that the business is, in essence, using the cash from day 1 to purchase supplies for day 2. Some balance must be found.

$$\text{Food inventory turnover} = \frac{\text{value of the food inventory}}{\text{cost of food sold}}$$

$$\text{Beverage inventory turnover} = \frac{\text{value of the beverage inventory}}{\text{cost of beverage sold}}$$

**Current Ratio.** The current ratio measures how strong the business is in its ability to pay off short-term debts. Suppliers need assurance that they will be paid on schedule.

$$\text{Current ratio} = \frac{\text{current assets}}{\text{current liabilities}}$$

Analysts want to see a ratio approaching 2:1 ($2 of assets for every $1 in liabilities), although in the restaurant business, the ratio is closer to 1:1. This is attributed to three factors:[5] a lack of accounts receivable, small inventories, and fast inventory turnover.

$$\text{Quick ratio} = \frac{\text{cash} + \text{marketable securities} + \text{accounts receivable}}{\text{current liabilities}}$$

The quick ratio or acid test is a better measure of bankruptcy risk than is the current ratio because it does not assume that inventory can be sold quickly. A quick ratio below 1 is cause for concern.

The difference between current assets and current liabilities is working capital. There should be enough working capital to allow the business to get through a financial crisis.

## Fixed Assets

Comparing operations on the basis of fixed assets is difficult because of the variety of ways in which operations can be financed. One useful technique is to use a "cost per seat" figure as the basis for determining how much can be spent on the operation.

## Liabilities

The major short-term liabilities are employee wages and payments to suppliers. The average monthly payment to suppliers can be determined by dividing cost of goods sold by 12. An accounts payable figure much higher than this average indicates an operation that is slow to pay.

Liabilities are often looked at relative to the net worth of the operation. Creditors will feel more secure when the ratio of debt to equity is low. Such a ratio indicates that the owners are heavily involved financially in the business compared to the amount of outside or debt financing. Lenders feel that the more owners are involved in the business financially, the greater their commitment to the business. A low ratio will increase the chances that the operation will get more credit.

## Solvency Ratios

Solvency ratios measure the ability to repay debts. The debt-to-equity ratio looks at the proportion of assets financed through debt or, alternatively, the amount financed through owner's equity. A debt-to-equity ratio of less than 1 is regarded as desirable. However, if it is too low, it may indicate that an operation is not taking advantage of its situation to expand the business.

## COST–VOLUME–PROFIT ANALYSIS

Cost–volume–profit or break-even analysis is a graphical representation of the relationship among sales volume, fixed and variable costs, and profit. Management can determine what sales volume is required to show a profit as well as determine the level of costs and profit or loss at specific levels of sales.

### Break-Even Chart

The horizontal axis of a break-even chart (see Figure 11.1) consists of the number of meals sold or customers served; the vertical axis represents both sales volume and costs in dollars.

**Sales.** A sales volume line can be drawn by multiplying the number of meals served by the average price of a meal. Thus if the average check is $9, $6300 in

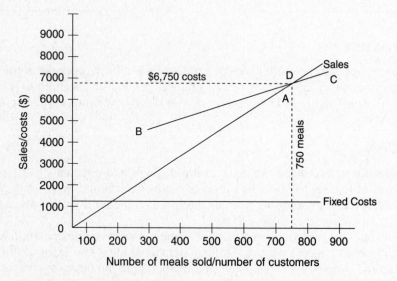

**Figure 11.1**  Break-even chart.

*Source:* Adapted from James Keiser, *Controlling and Analyzing Costs in Foodservice Operations*, 2nd ed. (New York: Macmillan Publishing Company, 1989), pp. 410–411.

## quick bite 11.5
### Find the Break-Even Point

**Learning Objective:** Determine the break-even point for a business, given the appropriate sales and expense figures.

Given the following information, find the daily break-even point for Bubbles restaurant.

1. Forecasted annual sales: $178,500
2. Number of days of operation per year: 255
3. Projected annual costs:

**Fixed**

| | | | |
|---|---|---|---|
| Labor | $36,720 | Advertising | 900 |
| Payroll tax | 3,672 | Dues/subscriptions | 120 |
| Insurance | 700 | Business personal | |
| Rent | 8,400 | property tax | 280 |
| Accounting | 500 | Cleaning expenses | 480 |
| Bank service charge | 180 | Donations | 200 |
| Utilities | 6,000 | Depreciation | 1,800 |
| Telephone | 1,200 | Miscellaneous | 1,000 |
| Interest | 812 | **Variable** | |
| | | Food and paper products | 71,400 |

### Solution

1. Separate fixed and variable costs.
   - Total fixed costs: $62,964
   - Total variable costs: $71,400
2. Divide total variable costs by total sales:
3. Subtract total variable costs as a percent of sales from 1:
   $1 - 0.40 = 0.60$.

Divide the result into total fixed costs:

$$\frac{\$62,964}{0.60} = \$106,940$$

Divide by the number of days the store is open:

$$\frac{\$104,940}{255 \text{ days}} = \$411.52$$

*Source:* Strausser, Michael J., "How to Figure Your Break-Even Point," *Restaurants USA*, vol. 14, no. 2, February 1994, pp. 15–17.

sales volume will result when 700 meals or customers are served. This is represented by point A on the chart.

**Costs.** For the purpose of break-even analysis, costs must be defined as either fixed or variable. Fixed costs are those that do not vary as volume varies. The amount of interest to be paid is the same whether one meal is served or 1000 meals are served.

Thus fixed costs can be represented by a line parallel to the horizontal axis. Variable costs are those that, by definition, vary proportionately with volume. That is, if sales volume doubles, variable costs double. The obvious variable costs are food and beverage costs.

Many costs are semivariable. Labor costs are a good example. A certain number of employees are necessary to open the doors for business. If sales volume increased by 30 percent, the operation would need more employees but labor costs would probably not increase by 30 percent. Existing employees could pick up some of the slack by producing more.

Three methods for breaking costs into their fixed and variable components are[6]

1. Maximum/minimum calculation
2. Multipoint graph
3. Regression analysis

Using the labor cost as an example, it is necessary to identify the sales volume in terms of meals sold or dollar sales volume together with the appropriate labor cost by month. In the maximum/minimum method the months with the lowest and highest labor costs are separated out and the lower labor cost is subtracted from the higher labor cost.

For example, assume that the highest and lowest sales volumes were in July and February, respectively.

|  | Sales Volume | Labor Cost |
| --- | --- | --- |
| July | $40,000 | $12,500 |
| February | 15,000 | 8,000 |
| Differences | 25,000 | 4,500 |

The variable cost per unit is obtained by dividing the wage difference by the difference in sales volume. In the preceding example, $4500 is divided by $25,000 to give 0.18, the variable cost per dollar of revenue. At $40,000 sales volume the labor variable cost is $40,000 divided by 0.18, or $7200. This figure is then subtracted from total costs to obtain the level of fixed costs. Monthly fixed costs are $12,500 minus $7200, or $5300.

The same type of analysis can be plotted on a graph. Assume the following daily figures for a restaurant:[7]

| | | |
|---|---|---|
| Number of meals sold | 300 | 900 |
| Average check | $9.00 | $9.00 |
| Revenue | $2700 | $8100 |
| Fixed costs | $1000 | $1000 |
| (*Determined by dividing the fixed costs of the operation for the year by 365*) | | |
| Administrative and general | $ 850 | $1320 |
| Labor cost | 1750 | 2350 |
| Food costs | 945 | 2835 |
| Profit or (loss) | $(1845) | $ 595 |

It can be seen that if 500 meals are sold a day, the restaurant will lose $1845 per day and will have a profit of $595 if 900 meals are served. Plotting these figures on a chart will show the profit or loss at various levels of sales volume.

The daily fixed costs of $1000 are represented by the horizontal line FC in Figure 11.1. At a volume of 300 meals the remaining costs—administrative and general, labor, and food—of $3545 is added to the fixed costs and charted (point B). At a volume of 900 meals a day, the variable and semivariable costs of $6085 are added to the fixed costs and plotted (point C). A line is then drawn joining points B and C. The break-even point is where total revenue equals total costs (point D). By extending lines to both the horizontal and vertical axes, we can see that this restaurant breaks even when 750 meals are sold. The resulting sales volume of $6750 (750 divided by the average check of $9) will exactly equal the costs incurred. When fewer than 750 meals are served, costs are higher than revenue and a loss will result; when more than 750 meals are served, revenue is greater than costs and the result is a profit.

Similar charts can be prepared to show the impact of changes in price on profit. If, for example, a 5 percent increase in price is being considered, the impact on the number of meals served can be forecast and a new chart prepared to determine the impact on profit. Of course, the analysis is only as good as the impact forecast.

Because this method requires only two sets of figures, it is simple to use. However, these two sets of figures may not be representative of sales volume and labor costs levels.

A multipoint graph improves on this by plotting on a graph monthly figures for an entire year. The horizontal axis would be the sales volume and the vertical axis would be the labor cost. The result is called a scatter graph: "a number of points scattered around a line that has been drawn through them."[8] The resulting line is the one that seems to be the best fit through all the monthly points. The spot at which the line hits the vertical axis represents the level of fixed labor costs.

Regression analysis takes this process one step further by using an equation to determine fixed costs. For each month of the year four figures are listed: the sales volume or number of meals served, the appropriate level of labor cost, the product of these previous columns, and the sales volume or number of meals served squared:

$$\text{Fixed costs} = \frac{(\Sigma Y)(\Sigma X^2) - (\Sigma X)(\Sigma XY)}{n(\Sigma X^2) - (\Sigma X)^2}$$

where $\Sigma Y$ is the sum of the monthly labor costs, $\Sigma X$ is the sum of the monthly sales volumes, $\Sigma XY$ is the sum of the monthly ($X$ times $Y$) columns, and $n$ is the number of periods (12 months).

**Break-Even Point.** The break-even point can also be arrived at arithmetically. When a customer orders a meal for $9, the variable costs associated with producing that meal are subtracted immediately. The remainder contributes toward paying off the fixed costs. When all of the fixed costs have been paid off, the restaurant breaks even. (Remember that variable costs are paid after every sale.) Thus the contribution margin is the selling price of a meal minus the variable costs associated with its production.

Once the break-even point has been reached, the contribution margin becomes profit. Thus if the variable costs associated with the $9 meal are $5.50, each time a meal is served the restaurant takes in $9, pays out $5.50 in variable costs, and "contributes" $3.50 toward paying off the fixed costs. Once these costs have been paid off, the restaurant gets $3.50 profit for each meal sold beyond that point.

The break-even point can be determined by dividing fixed costs by the contribution margin:

$$\text{Break-even point} = \frac{\text{fixed costs}}{\text{contribution margin}}$$

where the contribution margin is the unit selling price minus the unit variable cost, or

$$\text{Break-even point} = \frac{\text{fixed costs}}{\text{contribution margin ratio}}$$

where the contribution margin ratio is contribution margin/sales volume.

Earlier we noted that many costs are semivariable. In calculating the break-even point, some authors recommend that costs be classified as either fixed or variable. If we revisit the preceding example, the drawbacks of allocating costs in this manner can be seen.

The only "true" variable cost in the preceding example is food cost, which is 35 percent of revenue. The contribution margin ratio would, therefore, be 65 percent of revenue. The remaining costs when serving 300 and 900 meals are $3600 and $4670, respectively. If these are classified as fixed costs, it is obvious that different break-even points will result.

Using the cost structure for 300 meals, we find that

$$\text{Break-even point} = \frac{\text{fixed costs}}{\text{contribution margin ratio}}$$

$$= \frac{\$3600}{0.65} = \$5539 \text{ or } 616 \text{ meals}$$

This is the sales volume necessary to break even. The number of meals that must be sold to break even is this figure divided by the average check of $9, or 616. (All figures are rounded up.) Using the cost structure for 900 meals yields

$$\text{Break-even point} = \frac{\text{fixed costs}}{\text{contribution margin ratio}}$$

$$= \frac{\$4670}{0.65} = \$7185 \text{ or } 799 \text{ meals}$$

To get more precise, it is necessary to attempt to classify how much of any one cost is fixed and how much is variable. Working with historical data, it would be possible to derive graphs plotting the various categories of cost against volumes and extrapolate the line back to determine the fixed component of that cost.

Referring to Figure 11.1 and extrapolating line BC back to the vertical axis, it can be seen that at zero volume $3,050 is incurred in costs. This, then, becomes the "true" level of fixed costs. Using the previous example,

| | | |
|---|---|---|
| Number of meals sold | 300 | 900 |
| Average check | $9 | $9 |
| Revenue | $2700 | $8100 |
| Fixed costs | $3050 | $3050 |
| Variable costs (administrative and general and labor) | $550 | $1620 |
| Food costs | $ 945 | $2835 |
| Total variable costs | $1495 | $4455 |
| Contribution margin (revenue minus variable costs) | $1205 | $3645 |
| Contribution margin ratio (contribution margin divided by revenue) | 45% | 45% |
| Break-even point (dollars) (fixed costs divided by contribution margin ratio) | $6778 | $6778 |
| Break-even point in meals [break-even (dollars) divided by average check] | 753 | 753 |

The sales volume necessary to produce a given level of profit can be calculated as follows:

$$\text{Sales revenue required} = \frac{\text{fixed costs plus desired profit}}{\text{contribution margin ratio}}$$

Useful as they are, break-even charts can be only a rough approximation of profit. This is, in part, because assumptions must be made regarding allocation of costs. In Figure 11.1 we assumed that the line CB could be extrapolated back. Cost allocations are good only over short ranges of sales volume. When they are extrapolated beyond that range, the analysis is less exact. In addition, this analysis works best when there is only one product. In a restaurant where there are many items on the menu, mark-ups will vary and an average will have to be used. This limits the accuracy of the analysis.

---

### quick tip

Micros Systems, Inc. recently developed their latest Kitchen Display System. The system offers complete, integrated kitchen automation that synchronizes menu items by course, prep time, and kitchen load to maximize kitchen productivity. "Restaurant owners will benefit most from having the ability to provide a greater guest experience, which will result in repeat business," notes Louise Casamento, director of marketing for Micros, adding that "the ability to coordinate across multiple prep stations and analyze kitchen operations can lead to cost savings in both labor and inventory."

*Source:* National Restaurant Association, "2005 NRA Show Kitchen Innovations Awards," *http://www.restaurant.org/show/exhibitorlist/ki/ki_recipients.cfm*, November 7, 2005.

---

## CAPITAL BUDGETING

Capital budgeting is defined as "the planning of expenditures whose returns are expected to extend beyond one year."[9] Funds can come from depreciation, retained earnings or profit, additional debt, or additional equity from investors and are used for the replacement of existing equipment or facilities or expansion of the operation.

### Determining Priorities

Typically, the amount of funds available is not enough to meet the number of projects available. Some method or methods are necessary to allocate scarce resources (money) to desirable projects. Four methods can be used:[10]

1. **Economy study:** A financial analysis comparing two or more proposals
2. **Rate of return:** A comparison of the savings or additional income generated to the amount invested
3. **Net present value (NPV):** The value in the present of future returns, discounted at the cost of capital less the cost of the investment
4. **Internal rate of return:** A rate of return that equalizes the present value of the return and the investment

**Economy Study.**   An economy study might be used to compare the long-term costs and returns on the purchase of a new piece of equipment compared to keeping and maintaining existing equipment.

Future costs, both fixed and variable, need to be forecast and become part of the analysis. The annual fixed expenses would include such things as interest, depreciation, and taxes and insurance.

There are several methods to calculate depreciation. The simplest method estimates the salvage value of the equipment at the end of its useful life, subtracts this amount from the initial cost of the equipment, and divides this by the number of years the equipment is expected to be in operation. For example, if an oven were to cost $20,000 and have an expected life of eight years, at which time it could be sold for $1000, the annual depreciation expense would be

$$\frac{20{,}000 - 1000}{8} = \$2375$$

Annual operating expenses would include labor, power, supplies, and repairs and maintenance.

Many firms will use the amount of time it will take for the expenditure to pay for itself to judge whether to make the capital expenditure. The shorter the payback period, the better. Payback periods can range from a matter of three years for a small piece of equipment to much longer for a building. The formula for estimating the payback period is[11]

$$\text{payback period} = \frac{\text{cash outlay for project}}{\substack{\text{annual net income or savings before} \\ \text{depreciation but after taxes}}}$$

Although it is fairly easy to estimate future costs, it is much more difficult to calculate changes in sales brought about by capital expenditures. Redecorating the dining room may be justified if the project will bring in more business. A reliable estimate of the new business due entirely to the redecoration is difficult at best.

**Rate of Return.**   The rate of return on a project is the average additional income of savings after taxes and depreciation divided by the average investment in the project.

The rate of return can be determined annually as well as over the lifetime of the equipment. Annual savings of $500 on an investment of $4000 will give an anticipated rate of return of $500/$4000, or 12.5 percent.

The average value of the equipment is the initial investment minus the salvage value divided by 2. If we assume for this example that there is no salvage value and the equipment will last five years, the average value is $2000. The rate of return on the average value of the equipment over its lifetime is $500/$2000, or 25 percent.

**Net Present Value.** One problem with the methods described previously is that they do not take into account the fact that the value of a dollar today is greater than its value in the future.

The desired rate of return on the investment must be determined and an analysis carried out over the life of the project to determine cost savings in present value terms. A piece of equipment might cost $3000 today and will result in annual savings of $1000 for four years.

Net present value calculates the present value of a return in the future. The formula is

$$PV = \frac{FV}{(1 + i)n}$$

where *PV* is the present value of a future return, *FV* the amount received at the end of *n* years, *i* the desired return on the investment, and *n* the number of years before the future return will be received.

Tables have been formulated to indicate the net present value of money at specified interest rates. Using the preceding figures, the cash savings would be calculated as follows:

Year 1    $1000 $\times$ 0.893 = 893
Year 2    $1000 $\times$ 0.797 = 797
Year 3    $1000 $\times$ 0.712 = 712
Year 4    $1000 $\times$ 0.636 = 636
Year 5    $1000 $\times$ 0.567 = 567
Total                    $3605

Thus, over five years, the cash savings in present terms would be $3605. Proceeds from the sale of the piece of equipment to be replaced and any tax advantages resulting from a loss from that sale would also be considered as part of the cash inflow to be compared to the cash outflow of $3000.

**Internal Rate of Return.** The discounted or internal rate of return considers the time value of money and determines the rate of return that would result when the present value of the return equals the initial investment. Management

### Day in the Life: Life Cycle of a Chain Restaurant

The theory of the shelf life of a packaged good such as soup or soap applies equally well to the lifecycle of a chain restaurant.

The first stage of a chain is its start-up introductory phase. During this period, the chain must create a critical mass of locations and establish a smoothly functioning operational formula in order to drive growth.

After its introductory phase, the chain must grow. Growth is usually accomplished by adding even more locations and by using marketing campaigns to develop consumer awareness and increased per store traffic.

As the chain's growth levels off, the chain enters its mature stage where financial management of accumulated assets, shareholder payback, and cost efficiency becomes very important and financial controls crucial.

Once the market limit on the number of stores has topped out and effective marketing has created a loyal customer base and financial management has controlled as much of the bottom line as possible, the chain enters its saturation phase where competition can shove the chain into decline. The average chain restaurant concept has a five-year lifecycle from launch to peak earnings to decline.

Permanent decline and oblivion can be the next phase unless the chain shifts its culinary focus by depending on the chefs and kitchen managers to revitalize the food as heart and focal point of the chain operation. This renewed focus has to be accompanied by new marketing and advertising campaigns that are aimed narrowly at the stores in the chain with the highest potential to benefit from the renewal.

*Sources:* Calkins, John D., et al., "You Want Profits with That," *McKinsey Quarterly,* no. 4, 1999, pp. 134–144. Kruse, Nancy, "Life Studies," *Restaurant Business,* vol. 100, no. 19, October 1, 2001, p. 101.

**Discussion Question:** Explain how to boost a chain's lifespan after it has saturated the market.

could then determine whether or not this rate of return was acceptable in making a decision on the project.

When the cash savings are the same per year, the net investment can be divided by the annual savings to give a factor that can be compared to figures in tables of net present value to give the internal rate of return. Such tables can be found in capital budgeting texts.

Using the preceding figures—a $3000 initial outlay with nothing from the sale of the old equipment and no resulting tax savings—and such a table, the internal rate of return is 19 percent.

## ENDNOTES

1. James Keiser, *Controlling and Analyzing Costs in Foodservice Operations,* 2nd ed. (New York: Macmillan Publishing Company, 1989), p. 335.
2. Laube, Jim, "Restaurant Numbers: Part 1: Introduction—How to Evaluate Your Restaurant's Profitability," *www.RestaurantOwner.com,* accessed September 15, 2005.
3. James Keiser, *Controlling and Analyzing Costs in Foodservice Operations,* 2nd ed. (New York: Macmillan Publishing Company, 1989), pp. 335–347.
4. Ibid., p. 339.
5. Ibid., p. 349.
6. Michael M. Coltman, *Cost Control for the Hospitality Industry* (Boston: CBI Publishing Company, 1980), pp. 16–25.
7. Keiser, *Controlling and Analyzing Costs in Foodservice Operations,* p. 410.
8. Coltman, *Cost Control for the Hospitality Industry,* p. 21.
9. Keiser, *Controlling and Analyzing Costs in Foodservice Operations,* p. 381.
10. Ibid., p. 410.
11. Ibid., p. 385.

## INTERNET RESOURCES

| | |
|---|---|
| Restaurant Resource Group | *http://rrgconsulting.com/operations_consulting.htm* |
| Restaurant Owner | *http://www.restaurantowner.com/* |

# CHAPTER TWELVE

# EMPLOYEE SELECTION

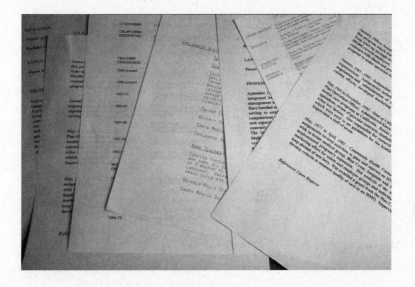

"The haughty sommelier, with his talismanic tasting cup and
sometimes irritating self-assurance, is perceived more as the
high priest of some arcane rite than as a dining room functionary
paid to help you enjoy the evening."
Frank J. Prial, author and wine critic

## learning objectives

*By the end of this chapter you should be able to*

1. Identify the work groups that management will increasingly turn to for
   employees in the next decade.

2. Discuss the major laws and regulations affecting employee hiring.

3. Identify the steps involved in staffing the operation, outlining important
   principles at each stage of the process.

4. Develop guidelines on how to conduct a hiring interview.

# SUPPLY OF LABOR: THE CHANGING PICTURE

The foodservice industry employs approximately 10 percent of the workforce in the United States. At some point, one out of three Americans has worked in the restaurant industry. The industry will increase from 12.2 jobs in 2005 to 14 million by 2015. The projected increase between 2005 and 2015 for various positions is as follows:[1]

| Position | Additional Jobs | Percent Increase |
| --- | --- | --- |
| Food service manager | 45,000 | 11 |
| First-line supervisors | 114,000 | 15 |
| Food preparation and service | 2.6 million | 23 |
| Chefs and head cooks | 163,000 | 16 |
| Servers | 388,000 | 17 |

 quick bite 12.1
## Hot Concepts: Ted's Montana Grill

Ted's Montana Grill, which draws crowds with its casual "bison" dining, has brought media mogul Ted Turner's portfolio back on track. "We've created a unique niche on two fronts: first, the restaurants are refined yet simple," says George McKerrow, Jr. McKerrow, a casual-steakhouse pioneer who teamed up with Turner to create his unique restaurant, concedes that bison is still a significant part of the Grill's success: "[There's also] our totally distinctive menu."

Bison is an incredibly healthy meat. It has 33% the fat of chicken, 26% the fat of beef, and 25% the fat of pork. But the bison-heavy menu of Ted's Montana Grill is not the sole reason for its success.

Ted's Montana Grill utilizes a design similar to that of several classic Old West saloons. Buffalo Bill Cody's tavern was one of the authentic venues that inspired the look of Ted's Montana Grill. Along with replicas of the American West landscapes that decorate Turner's home, each restaurant boasts a variety of architectural highlights such as genuine pressed-tin ceilings, hickory floors, mahogany paneling, pendant lighting, metal crown moldings, ceiling fans and beautiful unpolished brass.

Since the restaurant's debut in January of 2002, the partners have built nineteen restaurants and currently have plans for six more.

"I hear from customers that Ted's is a really good concept," says Augustine Matos, who manages The Boulevard Grille in Columbus. "And I guess they're right because I see a second one under construction here already," he says.

Turner's investment reached $12 million within the first year; the chain averages $14 per check at each restaurant. The partners attribute their success

The profile of a "typical" employee in a foodservice operation has changed little since the second edition of this text. It is[2]

- Female (57 percent)
- Under 30 years of age (57 percent)
- Single (70 percent)
- A part-timer working an average of 25.6 hours per week
- Someone with a relatively short job tenure

The biggest concern for foodservice managers today remains human resources.[3] Specifically, managers are worried about employee skill levels, compensation and benefits, recruiting, motivating, retaining, and training. These problems are not just with hourly employees. Half of the respondents to this national survey identify recruiting skilled managers as a constant concern that is having a negative impact on business.

largely to their employees. McKerrow explains that "we're concentrating on people. We've invested a lot of money because we wanted and executive team capable of moving very quickly."

Each restaurant operates under a team of four managers, overseen by a general manager known as a proprietor. The average staff at a Ted's restaurant consists of 65 people.

Turner's reputation as the largest U.S. landowner is only superseded by his reputation as the largest American bison rancher, owning 10 percent of the nation's bison herd. Since bison make up 70 to 75 percent of the meals served at Ted's restaurants nationwide, controlling the supply is definitely paying off for the partners.

In the end, the success of the restaurant results from the customer's desire for a good, old-fashioned meal. With daily blue-plate specials and an extraordinary smoke-free atmosphere, Ted's delivers.

As Turner explains, "People all over the world are fascinated by the American West—yipee-ki-yo! Get along little bison!"

*Sources:* Hayes, Jack, "Ted's Montana Grill: Media Tycoon Lassos Crowds with Casual 'Bison' Concept," *Nation's Restaurant News,* May 12, 2003, vol. 37, no. 19, pp. 66–67.

Home Page, <*http://www.tedsmontanagrill.com*>, March 19, 2004.

**Discussion Question:** What are the benefits and drawbacks of basing a menu on a nontraditional food?

Beginning in the 1990s, the pool of potential employees restaurants primarily draw on—16- to 24-year-olds—fell 3 percent. At the same time, the number of restaurant locations increased substantially. As a result, there has been a steady decline in the number of qualified applicants for hourly positions in the restaurant industry. Since the mid-1990s, the 16- to 24-year-old segment has bottomed out and is forecast to increase more than 18 percent through 2010. However, during the past 20 years, the proportion of teens age 15 to 17 who are employed has declined and shows no sign of returning to previous levels. Examination of teen demographics and work behavior indicates that more minorities and lower-income teens might be attracted to restaurant jobs. The figures indicate that white teens are more likely to work than minorities, youths from higher-income households are more likely to work than those from lower-income households, and foreign-born youths are less likely to work than native-born youths. It may be that restaurant operators will have to look further into attracting the underutilized labor market of minority, lower-income, and foreign-born teens.[4]

Operators are responding in a variety of ways to cope with the problem of finding enough talented employees:[5]

- *More resources to training.* More than half of quick-service operators and almost a third of table-service restaurant managers report devoting a larger share of the budget to training in an attempt to assist employees move up in the organization.
- *Health benefits.* Two-thirds of table-service restaurants and 96 percent of quick-service operators say that higher health insurance costs are negatively impacting their business. This is a major public policy issue for the National Restaurant Association (NRA).
- *Employee literacy.* Twenty percent of full-service operators and more than half of quick-service restaurant managers say the lack of employee literacy is having a negative impact on business. English-language programs, such as the NRAs Daily Dose English Program, are offered as a way to combat this problem.

## Women

Eating-and-drinking establishments are more likely than other businesses to employ women. Almost 60 percent of those employed in food-preparation and foodservice occupations as well as more than half of those employed in eating-and-drinking places are female.

Approximately two-thirds foodservice supervisors are female. Women are also in the majority as waitstaff, kitchen workers, and food-counter workers. They are less likely than men to be employed full time.[6]

To attract and keep female employees, companies may have to develop more "female-friendly" policies. Flexible work schedules, assistance with day care, and medical benefits aimed at women are some of the ways that companies can demonstrate their interest in attracting and keeping female employees.

A female-friendly atmosphere is one that does not tolerate discrimination or sexual harassment. Discrimination on the grounds of sex has been prohibited since 1968. Sexual harassment—increasingly regarded as a form of sexual discrimination—is an area of increasing importance to employers. The Equal Employment Opportunity Commission defines sexual harassment as follows:

> Unwelcome sexual advances, requests for sexual favors, and other verbal or physical conduct of a sexual nature constitute sexual harassment when (a) submission to such conduct is made either explicitly or implicitly a term or condition of an individual's employment, (b) submission to or rejection of such conduct by an individual is used as the basis for employment decisions affecting such individual, or (c) such conduct has the purpose or effect of unreasonably interfering with an individual's work performance or creating an intimidating, hostile, or offensive working environment.[7]

Management has a duty to create and maintain an atmosphere that does not tolerate sexual harassment on the part of supervisors, employees, customers, and suppliers.

---

### quick fact

Eating-and-drinking places employ more minority managers than any other industry.

*Source:* National Restaurant Association, "Restaurant Industry Facts," *http://www.restaurant .org/research/ind_glance.cfm#employment*, November 7, 2005.

---

## Minorities

Employees in the restaurant industry continue to mirror the population as a whole. Hispanics are also more likely than average to be employed as cooks, waitstaff assistants, and miscellaneous food workers.

Approximately one of every four people living in the United States is a member of a minority group. This is a significant change from past decades.[8] Non-Hispanic whites, who made up 79 percent of the workforce in 1990, will account for a lower 65 percent of entrants into the labor pool between 1990 and 2005. Hispanics will account for 16 percent of entrants, largely attributed to high levels of immigration. Thirteen percent of workforce entrants between 1990 and 2005 will be black, and 6 percent will be Asian.[9]

For Hispanics the cultural and language barriers make their success in the workplace more difficult. Among many Hispanics the tradition of a male-dominated, traditional society can place significant pressures on Hispanic women as they seek the security and independence that working outside the home can bring. This is particularly evident for female managers supervising employees with such an orientation.

Businesses can require that English only be spoken under very narrowly drawn guidelines. Taking a proactive approach and realizing that it is difficult to manage someone if it is impossible to communicate with that person, some companies are teaching English to their employees while supervisors are encouraged to learn Spanish.

To attract and keep employees, it is important to understand what motivates them and to develop an atmosphere that reinforces these things. At the risk of generalizing, it is true that most Hispanics place a high value on the family. Because unemployment rates in Hispanic areas are high, regular work is valued and contributes to the self-esteem and status of adult males.

Urging employees to have families visit the operation can make the employee feel that the family is assimilated into the workplace, thereby heightening the importance of the employee's work.

## Immigrants

It is estimated that a minimum of 450,000 immigrants a year enter the United States legally, while an additional 100,000 to 300,000 come in illegally every year.[10] One in four full-service restaurant managers and half of the quick-service operators report that they are hiring increased numbers of foreign-born employees.[11]

California, Texas, and New York account for more than half of all foreign-born residents; 20 percent of all recent immigrants live in the Los Angeles area.[12]

Under the Immigration Reform and Control Act of 1986, it is unlawful for an employer to knowingly hire any alien not authorized to work in the United States. Irrespective of legal issues, hiring illegal aliens begins the employer–employee relationship with a lie.

"Illegals live in a world of lies. They are not liars, but theirs is a world of lies. They have to live—to eat—and to eat they have to say things that others want to hear. If a boss asks if they are here legally, they say they are. But they know that the boss knows they are lying and the boss is lying when he acts like he believes him."[13]

Restaurateurs have to ask themselves whether or not this is the best way to begin a relationship.

## Older Employees

By 2010 about one in every five persons will be 55 or older—and almost one in three by 2030. Older employees represent a marketing tool for companies faced with increasing numbers of older customers. More than half of all working adults indicate a desire to work beyond the standard retirement age.

Advances in medicine have resulted in greater numbers of healthier older people. Older people tend to be "more dependable, have lower absenteeism, are punctual, . . . show good judgment based on their past experience, interact well with others, and show greater motivation due to increased job satisfaction and less job-related stress."[14] However, they are not as adaptable and creative as younger employees.

An outreach program is necessary to attract older employees. Although most national studies indicate that they tend to prefer part-time employment and flexible work schedules, this finding is not supported by studies in the food-service industry. Older people identify with people younger than themselves. Advertisements showing people about 10 years younger than the age group sought are more likely to be successful.

Seniors are motivated by the desire for social interaction followed by having a purpose in life. Stressing the importance of interacting with customers and other employees and letting them know that their experience is appreciated are important factors in attracting this employee group. The fast-food companies—led by McDonald's and KFC (the former Kentucky Fried Chicken)—have done a particularly good job of reaching out to older employees.

According to the American Association of Retired Persons, to be successful, training should be related directly to the job for which the person is being trained, should be given only for jobs that the employee has a chance of getting, should be active rather than passive, should be self-paced and individualized, and should be a short-term rather than a longer-term program.

## Part-Time Employees

A major reason that many companies like to hire part-timers is that they typically do not pay them benefits. Benefits may add as much as one-third to the labor bill. The importance of benefits was noted in a survey of restaurant operators. The most frequently mentioned changes in benefits mentioned by operators were establishing a 401(K) program, improving health insurance, providing profit sharing, instituting a pension plan, and increasing employees' share of benefit costs. More than half provided meals free of charge, while an additional 12 percent paid partially for them. Ninety percent of the hourly employees at foodservice companies with sales of $1 million or more a year receive meals and paid vacations, while more than 80 percent of the companies offered medical/surgical coverage. Forty-four percent gave Christmas bonuses, while one in eight offered maternity leave.

Part-time employees tend to be less loyal to the company, have higher turnover rates, and must be trained more often and supervised more closely. However, they can be laid off with less risk of lawsuits and/or unemployment compensation claims. They can be more eager to work, as they work fewer hours per day than do full-time employees. They may also be more willing to perform any job given to them. It is important to hire people who really want to work part time. Employees will often say they are happy with part-time hours in order to get a start with a company. If the manager accepts this and continues to give few hours, the employee may become dissatisfied.

The orientation and training programs for part-time employees should be the same as those for full-timers. Although they only work for a few hours a day, those hours tend to be when the business is busiest. They do not have the luxury of slack business periods to get accustomed to the operation. It is therefore important that the training they receive be given during those slack periods and also be sufficiently rigorous to allow them to perform when business is busiest. Finally, they should be treated like full-time employees. People who are treated as second-class employees will act accordingly.

## Employees with Disabilities

In 1990 the Americans with Disabilities Act (ADA) was signed into law. This law guarantees civil rights protection to persons with disabilities. For example, it is illegal to treat an employee with a disability differently from any other employee, refuse to hire or promote qualified individuals because of a disability, put disabled employees into lower-paying jobs, or pay them at a different pay level.[15]

The ADA defines a person with a disability to be one who has "a physical or mental impairment that substantially limits one or more major life activities,"[16] who has a history of such an impairment, and/or who is perceived as having a disability. Individuals with disabilities, who may be customers or employees, are entitled to "reasonable accommodation" from a restaurant. Reasonable accommodations include removing barriers in the workplace, such as rearranging furniture to provide access aisles; providing auxiliary aids and services, such as an adapted computer or occasional assistance; and modifying policies such as dress codes or flex-time and job restructuring. If the operator can show that the accommodation will create an "undue hardship"—it will be a significant hardship or expense—the change is not required.

Barriers present in the operation must be removed if this can be done without much difficulty or expense. This might include such things as[17]

- Providing a minimum of one accessible marked parking space per 25 parking spaces in the lot
- Providing the accessible spaces closest to the accessible entrance
- Ensuring an unobstructed path of travel from the on-site parking to the restaurant entry
- Having continuous handrails at both sides of all stairways
- Having flashing lights and audible signals on all alarms
- Ensuring that pathways to foodservice areas are free of stairs
- Ensuring that service is available at accessible tables or counters within the same area
- Ensuring that the same menu is available in an accessible space as is served in a mezzanine or raised or sunken dining area
- Ensuring that all restrooms, and some telephones and drinking fountains, are fully accessible

Table 12.1 contains reasonable accommodations made by Hardee's in the development of its Creatively Applying People's Abilities (CAP) program.

There may be more than physical barriers to overcome in hiring the handicapped. There may by resentment and apprehension from existing employees. A communications program to orient new and existing employees to each other will help the transition into the workplace.

**Table 12.1    Reasonable Accommodations: Hardee's CAP Program**

| Disability | Job Duty | Accommodation |
|---|---|---|
| Auditory hallucinations | Maintenance | Job coach, flexible schedule, management education on disability |
| Emotional disability | Cashier | Knowledge of medication effect |
| Hearing and speech impairment | Maintenance | Sign language, job restructure |
| | Host/hostess | Job restructure, job reassignment |
| Mental disability | Fried chicken preparation | Job coach, group training, transportation during inclement weather |
| | Host/hostess | Restructured job, additional training time, color-coded bar towels |
| Orthopedic impairment (arms) | Crew | Flexible schedule |
| Alcohol abuse | | Supervisor meetings and counseling, Alcoholics Anonymous |
| Physical disability— paraplegic (legs) | Front-line cashier | No heavy lifting, curb cut, flexible schedule |

*Source:* William F. Jaffe, "Integrating the Disabled Employee into the Quick-Service Restaurant: The Enclave Model," *Hospitality & Tourism Educator,* vol. 6, no. 2, Spring 1994, p. 19.

McDonald's, KFC, Hardee's, Pizza Hut, and Friendly's are just some of the companies that have taken the lead in organizing programs aimed at employing the disabled. The McJobs program at McDonald's, for example, has graduated more than 1000 employees since 1989 from its training program.

About 9 in 10 of these restaurateurs rated the dependability of their employees with disabilities as excellent or good compared to employees who were not disabled. About 7 in 10 rate the productivity of disabled employees as excellent or good compared to those without disabilities.[18]

The Friendly Restaurant Company has a four-step process to help ensure a successful program. This program involves

- Identifying company needs
- Identifying community resources
- Establishing a mutual relationship
- Building the relationship and understanding the pitfalls

Many jobs within the company are routine, repetitive, mechanical, and/or tedious. They are also the jobs that account for much, if not most, of the turnover in the business. The mentally handicapped or person with mental retardation may be perfectly satisfied to handle these types of jobs, which the company has the hardest time keeping filled. Dishwasher, stock clerk, bus help, kitchen help, sorter, janitor, and truck help may be particularly appropriate.

The employment options used most in integrating employees with disabilities into the workplace are individual worksites, enclaves, and work crews.[19] In an individual worksite, a person with a disability works at a community site with a support person. A group of no more than eight people working within a regular industry comprises an enclave, while groups of no more than eight people who perform specialized contract services are termed work crews. There is no consensus as to the most effective method of integration. A Marriott study of the three methods concluded that the individual worksite was most beneficial, while the enclave approach was of marginal benefit and sometimes harmful to the employee. Other studies outside the hospitality field have found the enclave to be the most effective method.

To build the relationship, management must first evaluate the employee to determine the type of work that he or she is best suited to handle. The employee may need the manager's help in overcoming uncertainties in interacting with others. Orientation and training techniques may have to be adapted to the disability of the employee. It is important that the manager, rather than another employee, supervise the training directly. Many employees with disabilities adjust better to a new job situation if they feel they have the full support of the manager. Direct supervision of training is one way to demonstrate this.

A continuous schedule of positive reinforcement may be required to develop a new behavior. Meals, drinks, and verbal praise will, in many cases, be more effective than money in motivating persons with mental disabilities if such people lack a realistic conception of the worth of money.

A variety of community organizations are available to assist in finding and placing employees with disabilities. Contact with one or more specialized agencies to find out what they do will help establish the mutual relationship necessary for a successful hire.

## THE REGULATORY ENVIRONMENT: EQUAL EMPLOYMENT OPPORTUNITY

In hiring employees, managers must operate within an environment of laws and regulations that have been developed by government. In recent decades equal employment opportunity has received more attention than any other in the field of human resource management. Equal employment opportunity involves the "employment of individuals in a fair and unbiased manner."[20]

### Federal Laws

A variety of federal laws have been enacted that affect equal employment opportunity. The major ones are as follows:[21]

- Equal Pay Act of 1963, which requires employers to pay equal pay for equal work regardless of sex. Jobs are considered equal when they entail essentially "the same skill, effort and responsibility under similar working conditions and in the same establishment."[22]

## quick bite 12.2
### Women in the Workplace

**Learning Objective:** Identify the work groups that management will increasingly turn to for employees in the next decade.

Women have become increasingly important to the food service industry. Each year the percentage of female employees climbs as the workforce becomes less and less male-dominated. Yet most of these women remain in low-level positions. What is the key to bringing women into higher-powered positions?

"You have to prove in no uncertain terms that you know how to make money," said Jean Birch. Birch ran restaurants for Pizza Hut and Taco Bell before taking over as the president of Corner Bakery Café in 2003.

The National Association for Female Executives conducted a study to investigate how female employees rose through the ranks to achieve high-level positions. The results of the study? Women need to hold jobs where they are completely responsible for the bottom line before they can move up the corporate ladder. The NAFE study discovered that having experience with profit-and-loss responsibilities along with having support and training from the chief executive were major factors in the advancement of women, regardless of the industry.

The restaurant industry is very good at giving women the opportunity to run stores as managers, but the genders divide when it comes to managing multiple units. As a regional director, a woman would have to travel more, commit more time to her job, and possibly even move. This is a very difficult choice for many women, who juggle their job responsibilities with raising children and managing responsibilities in the home.

Heidi Martin-Gilanfar, former vice president of recruitment for The Cheesecake Factory, explains that the gender gap is not due so much to discrimination as it is to lack of applicants.

"We don't see a lot of women coming to the table, even for the interviewing process; more men come forward," she said.

For restaurants that desire to improve gender equality and diversity within the upper echelon of management, it is exceedingly important that the objective come straight from the top, the NAFE study revealed. Several strategies to improve the number of female managers include mentoring programs, programs that identified possible leaders and put them in fast-track training programs, and training rotation programs in which employees train to perform at multiple levels, including operations.

*Source:* Berta, Dina, "NAFE Survey: Women Must Start at Bottom Line to Reach Top Posts," *Nation's Restaurant News*, February 9, 2004, vol. 38, no. 6, p. 16.

**Discussion Question:** What do women perceive as some of the benefits and drawbacks of upper-management positions?

- Title VII of the Civil Rights Act of 1964 (amended 1972), which prohibits discrimination in employment on the basis of race, color, religion, sex, or national origin.
- Age Discrimination in Employment Act of 1967 (amended 1986), which prohibits discrimination against people 40 years or older in areas of employment because of age.
- Pregnancy Discrimination Act of 1978, which prohibits discrimination against pregnant women in employment if they are capable of performing their job.

These laws cover all private employers engaged in interstate commerce who have a minimum of 15 employees working 20 or more weeks a year.

In addition, companies that are agencies of or contractors with the federal government are subject to various laws and executive orders. Such companies might be foodservice operators who have the contract to provide foodservice at a government facility. The more important regulations are as follows:[23]

- Vocational Rehabilitation Act of 1973 (amended in 1974), which prohibits federal contractors from discriminating against individuals with disabilities and requires them to develop affirmative action plans to hire and promote such people
- Vietnam Era Veterans Readjustment Assistance Act of 1974, which prohibits discrimination against Vietnam era veterans for contractors with government contracts of $10,000 or more and requires affirmative action programs to advance such people

Various other executive orders have been created to extend the same protection to employees of contractors to the federal government.

Because of the restaurant industry's traditional reliance on youth, managers need to be aware of restrictions on how many hours a week teenagers can work. Teens age 15 to 17 work an average of 17 hours a week during the school year and 23 hours per week in the summer months.[24] The average hours worked per week increase with age. Child Labor Laws under the Fair Labor Standards Act place no restrictions on the number of hours, times of day, or days of the week that teenagers 16 or older can work. There are, however, the following restrictions on children 14 or 15 years of age. They can work[25]

- Outside of school hours
- After 7 A.M. and until 7 P.M., except from June 1 through Labor Day, when they can work until 9 P.M.
- No more than 3 hours on a school day
- No more than 18 hours in a school week
- No more than 8 hours on a non–school day
- No more than 40 hours in a non–school week

In addition to federal laws, most states and many other local governments have passed laws prohibiting discrimination in employment. Managers are advised to check with local and state agencies to determine the specific laws applicable to them.

## Bona Fide Occupational Qualification

If an employer can show that discrimination on the basis of age, religion, sex, or national origin is justified by nature of the job itself, he or she can claim a bona fide occupational qualification (BFOQ). Claiming that, for example, hiring a woman instead of a man is a business necessity has been defined very narrowly by the courts. It would be appropriate, for example, to have males only as attendants in a men's bathroom.

---

### quick fact

The number of foodservice employers charged by the Equal Employment Opportunity Commission in connection with allegations of sexual harassment has remained relatively flat for the past four years, at between 1,163 and 1,275 cases annually.

*Source:* Lee Allen, Robin, "A Matter of Education: Workplace-Required Classes a Way to Curb Sexual Harrassment," *Nation's Restaurant News,* January 4, 2005.

---

## Sexual Harassment

Sexual harassment is defined by the Equal Employment Opportunity Commission as "unwelcome advances, requests for sexual favors, and other verbal or physical conduct of a sexual nature." It is illegal when it is determined that such conduct interferes with the work performance of an employee or when it creates a hostile work environment. Although there have been some reported cases of sexual harassment of a male by a female, the vast majority of problems occur when a male supervisor, employee, customer, or supplier is accused of harassing a female.

The employer is held responsible for sexual harassment when he or she knows or should have known about it and did not prevent it or take corrective action. An effective sexual harassment policy should include the following:[26]

1. Develop a comprehensive companywide policy announced to all employees and indicating that sexual harassment will not be tolerated.
2. Provide training sessions for all supervisors to explain the legal requirements and the company policy.
3. Establish a formal complaint system indicating how employees can make charges without fear of retribution and how charges will be investigated and resolved.
4. Take immediate action on receipt of a complaint.
5. Take immediate and consistent disciplinary action once a charge has been substantiated.
6. Follow up on all cases to assure a satisfactory resolution.

## Affirmative Action

Affirmative action programs require employers to institute programs and to correct past discriminatory practices. To comply, employers must make an affirmative effort to find, hire, train, and promote employees of protected groups. Employers who have federal contracts greater than $50,000 are required to have affirmative action programs.

The basic steps in developing an effective affirmative action program are as follows:[27]

1. Develop an equal employment policy and affirmative action program in writing.
2. Assign responsibility and the authority to go with it to a senior manager to implement the program.
3. Publicize the program.
4. Identify the number of minority and female employees by department and job classification.
5. Develop goals and timetables to increase, where necessary, the number of minorities and females.
6. Develop and implement specific programs to meet the set goals.
7. Develop an audit program to monitor and evaluate progress.
8. Develop programs to support the effort.

---

quick bite 12.3
### Hispanics in the Workforce

**Learning Objective:** Discuss the major laws and regulations affecting employee hiring.

Over the last ten years, the Hispanic/Latino population in the United States grew by 58%, or to 12.5% of the population. Hispanic workers are the largest labor force of all the minority groups. Although many Latin American immigrants are highly educated, less-educated Hispanic immigrants have found work in the U.S. as well, especially in the food service industry.

Today's employers face challenges that extend far beyond language differences. Foreign-born Latinos, like every immigrant group, have built-in cultural values that can impede communication in the workplace. Employers who do not actively strive to increase their awareness of these differences risk miscommunication, less productivity and a greater turnover.

The biggest challenge to communication is language. Many companies wisely provide ESL (English as a Second Language) classes on site. Others offer bonuses for employees who complete ESL courses offered in the com-

---

munity. The language barrier can be broken either way; it often benefits the company to have English-speaking employees learn some Spanish. Being able to speak Spanish to Latino employees not only improves comprehension, it establishes comfort and trust. At 380-unit Fazoli's, the fast casual Italian chain, managers take an eight-day program that focuses on the intensive study of Hispanic culture and customs.

Misunderstandings should be avoided at all costs. When translating an employee handbook, make sure that the translator can provide a legally solid Spanish translation that truly conveys the meaning of the English version of the handbook. Understanding employee benefits is essential for Latino employees. Recent immigrants are often unfamiliar with the benefits that U.S. companies provide. Many Hispanics tend not to trust automatic payroll deduction or deposit plans. Often times they don't recognize their benefits until they have a medical emergency. Other times they learn too late that they could have prepared early for their retirement.

The Hispanic culture tends to be more hierarchical than that of the U.S. Latino culture places value on respect for authority. In Latin America, an employee would not dare challenge a boss for fear of causing him to "lose face." This attitude discourages creative thought and taking initiative. For this reason, many American supervisors often incorrectly assume that Latino employees do not have good ideas, or that they can't show initiative. This is an incorrect assumption. The true problem is that Hispanic immigrants are socialized to just carry out orders, no questions asked.

Another possible misunderstanding can occur when it comes to family. An Hispanic employee is more likely to bring his family into the workplace. His supervisor may be across the room and immersed in work, yet the employee would still be pleased for the boss to greet him and to meet his family. Personal interaction between the family and the supervisor will help engender more trust and loyalty from this employee.

Most newly arrived Hispanic workers do not want to admit that they don't understand. Pride or fear of being criticized or fired may make them say that they understand when they do not. Here in the U.S., we try to take professional criticism in stride, with the goal of using it to help improve our performance. Hispanics often do not separate work from personal attitudes. They may take criticism personally, especially if it takes place in front of others.

In short, understanding and a heartfelt desire to interact and learn from Hispanic employees will go a long way to good relations with the workforce of the future.

*Source:* Hastings, Carol, "Going Beyond Translation," *Restaurant Hospitality,* March 2003, vol. 87, no. 3, p. 54.

**Discussion Question:** What are some things restaurants should do to ensure that Hispanics understand their rights and benefits?

# RECRUITING EMPLOYEES

## Job Analysis

A job analysis, a periodic analysis of every distinct job in the operation, is crucial to a successful human resources management program. Figure 12.1 illustrates the relationship and importance of a job analysis to other personnel-related tasks. Before managers can hire an employee, they need to know what they should be looking for. A listing of the knowledge, skills, and abilities required to perform a job is known as a job specification.

The job specification for a particular job comes from a document that lays out the purpose, scope, and major duties and responsibilities of a particular job. This document is called a job description. The job description is developed as a result of a job analysis. The analysis of a job is the basis for developing performance standards for that job. In fact, performance standards for the job cannot be developed until and unless a job analysis has been completed.

Performance standards tell the employees "how well they are expected to perform."[28] They are job descriptions translated into measurable form. The standards of performance expected for the job set the stage for appraising the performance of the employee performing that job. In other words, there is no foundation for firing an employee for not performing the job unless clear performance standards have been developed. These standards can only come from having conducted a job analysis.

An orientation program will include an introduction to the important facets of a job, while training seeks to develop the employee's ability to perform that job. Neither can be done unless the manager can identify the important aspects of the job. This knowledge comes after analyzing the job.

One facet of a motivated workforce is that employees feel they are being treated in a fair and equitable manner relative to their pay. Many suggest that the more important the job to the company, the more someone who performs in that job should be paid. Job evaluation evaluates the relative worth of every job in the operation. Job evaluation typically uses job descriptions as the basis for determining job worth. As noted previously, job descriptions are the outcome of a job analysis program.

## Analysis Process

A job analysis can be carried out in several ways. First, the manager can observe the employee performing the job. While necessary as part of the process, it is not a good idea to rely solely on this method. Employees may adjust the speed of their work if they are aware that they are being watched. The result may distort the number of employees needed. Direct observation does not reveal the mental processes used to perform a job. Some additional input is necessary.

An interview with the person doing the job is usually used as a supplement to direct observation. Employees may be asked to list, in chronological order, everything they do as part of their job. There may also be distortions with this type of review. The worker may exaggerate the importance of the job, or a poor attitude may diminish the importance of the tasks performed. Employees may forget parts of the job or may be performing tasks that should not be part of the job but were inherited from past jobholders.

An interview with the employee's supervisor might take care of any potential problems faced in the aforementioned methods. There is the possibility that the supervisor might be unclear about what should be done, but, generally speaking, supervisory input will round out the picture supplied by personal observation and employee interview.

**Tasks.**  The first step in the job analysis is to develop a job list, an inventory of the tasks associated with the job. These are limited to "how-to" items.

For a garde-manger or cold-meat chef, a job list might indicate that the employee should be able to[29]

1. Plan future meals.
2. Carve cold meats.
3. Prepare various dishes.
4. Prepare sandwiches.

The job list for a food server might read[30] as follows:

1. Greet and seat restaurant guests.
2. Serve water; light candles.
3. Take beverage orders and serve drinks.
4. Present the food menu and beverage list.
5. Assist customers in making food and beverage selections.
6. Place orders in the kitchen.
7. Serve food and beverage items ordered and clear table between courses.
8. Present bill.
9. Perform other duties as assigned.

**Job Breakdown.**  For each item on the job task list, a detailed job breakdown will indicate what is to be done, how it is to be done, and why each step is important. A fast-food operation may need 40 to 60 job breakdowns, each one to three pages in length. The time required initially is well worth the effort.

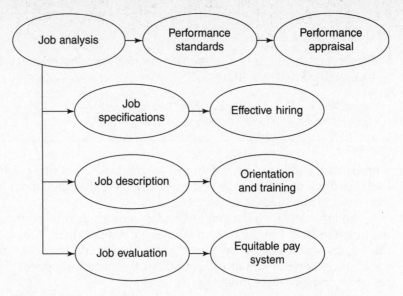

**Figure 12.1** Relationship between job analysis and personnel-related functions.

How many smiling faces does a company need?

The completed job breakdown serves as a listing of standard operating procedures for the restaurant in addition to being the basis for training new employees in how to perform in the way that management wants.

**Job Description.**   As noted previously, the job description lays out the purpose, scope, and major duties and responsibilities of a particular job. Between 68 and 72 percent of table-service restaurants—depending upon average check—report that they have written job descriptions.[31] As a minimum a job description should include the following:[32]

1. Job title .
2. Title of immediate supervisor
3. Job summary: 20 to 30 words identifying the purposes of the job
4. Essential functions: what should be done; percentage of time spent on each; equipment used; types of materials handled
5. Reporting relationships: to whom jobholder reports; who reports to jobholder
6. Qualification standards: personal and professional qualifications; skills, education, and experience required; physical and mental demands; amount of responsibility; personal characteristics for job success

A job analysis should be updated periodically. Often, a restaurant will initiate a change of theme or menu without updating the job descriptions required to perform the work. As the operation changes, so will the jobs and the type of employees needed to perform them.

A job analysis may pave the way for a restructuring of employees. It may turn out that some employees are performing jobs that can be done by others. Some may be performing tasks that have been made redundant. Although this is not the major reason for conducting a job analysis, it is probably the reason many employees are fearful of such an effort—they think management will use the results to eliminate jobs. It is important that whoever conducts the job analysis realize the potential concerns of the employees and the impact they might have on their willingness to participate honestly in the process.

## THE HIRING PROCESS

A television advertisement for oil filters features an auto repairman who examines a car and finds that because the oil filter was not replaced on a regular basis, the car needs a new engine. The tag line is, "You can pay me now, or you can pay me later." The message is that investing a little time and effort up front will save money in the future. The same can be said about hiring employees. Managers who invest little time or effort in selecting employees are likely to have more problems in the future: problems such as absenteeism, high turnover, pilfering, and low productivity. Although restaurant operators cite employee referrals, walk-ins, and newspaper ads as the most effective methods for attracting new employees,[33] additional steps can be taken in the hiring process. Each step taken costs time and money but reveals more information about potential employees. That, in essence, is the cost–benefit decision that each employer must make when determining a hiring process. Will the cost of taking this action result in a better hire that will bring the operation cost savings or increased sales sufficient to justify the cost of hiring? If the answer is yes, take the time and effort to collect the additional information; if the answer is no, forgo that step in the process.

Next we outline a variety of steps in the hiring process. For many operators this list will seem too costly both in terms of time and money. Others willingly spend the time and money up front in the belief that careful hiring will produce better profitability in the future. The steps and the percentage of table-service restaurant operators who say they do them are as follows:[34]

- Preliminary interview
- Completion of application form: 94–97%
- Employment tests
  Personality test: 23–28%
  Skills test: 15–43%
  Job simulation: 18–21%
  Assessment center: 4–8%
- Interview in human resources department
  Structured interview: 91–96%
- Background investigation
  Background check: 53–67%
  Reference check: 85–94%
- Medical examination
  Drug test: 8–20%
- Preliminary selection in human resources department
- Supervisory interview
- Realistic job preview
- Hiring decision

(*Note:* The range varies by average check.)

## Preliminary Interview

Very often, prospective applicants will call or come into the restaurant wishing to know if there are any openings. The preliminary interview might be no more than a first impression as to what job the person is interested in, whether there are openings, and whether the applicant seems like a good fit for such a job.

While it is true that first impressions mean a lot, it is probably wise to err on the side of including rather than excluding candidates. The fact that someone is willing to inquire about jobs shows a certain amount of initiative.

## Completing the Application Form

In reviewing a completed application, certain cues will indicate whether or not a candidate should be considered further. Some of the red flags to consider are as follows:

- Has the candidate had too many jobs in the past? A history of job hopping may indicate someone who cannot be happy at any one thing or someone who cannot keep a job.
- Lack of progress in previous jobs. Employees who have not been promoted and/or who have not received pay increases over time may lack the ambition and/or skills to perform at higher levels.
- The reasons for gaps in employment history need to be explored. The reasons may be legitimate—a return to school—or questionable—spent time in prison.
- Questionable reasons for leaving jobs.
- Inconsistency in career path. People who have worked in a variety of food-service sectors (fast food, fine dining, cafeterias) may not really know what they want to do.
- A messy application with misspellings and erasures can indicate an employee whose work habits are equally messy and undisciplined.
- Illegible handwriting that goes above or below the lines may indicate physical problems.
- Does the handwriting on the application match the signature? Some applicants get friends to complete the application for them if they feel they cannot do it themselves.

## Employment Tests

Selection tests are used to provide an objective means of measuring abilities or characteristics. In the restaurant business, because of ready access to cash and supplies, there are potential problems with employee theft; other customer-contact positions require employees with empathy and an outgoing personality. Many argue that properly constructed tests can identify employees who have the characteristics necessary for specific positions.

Various laws and regulations governing tests used in the United States have been developed at three levels:

- At the federal level most of the laws are embodied in Title VII of the Civil Rights Act of 1964 and related EEOC regulations, in particular the Uniform Guidelines for Employment Selection Procedures.
- Regulations at the state level tend to follow federal guidelines but may add other, more stringent requirements.
- Professional standards are established by the American Psychological Association, American Guidance of Personnel Association, and the National Measurement Association.

The purpose of these regulations is to ensure that job applicants are not subject to discrimination or unfair, arbitrary rejection.

To be useful a test must be

- Sensitive, so that it distinguishes between people who possess the characteristics and those who do not
- Standardized, so that benchmark scores have been identified on a representative and sizable sample of people for whom it is intended and against whom an applicant's scores will be compared
- Reliable, so that it always measures the same thing
- Valid, so that it measures what it is intended to measure

Validity can be either concurrent or predictive. To establish concurrent validity, existing employees are tested and their test scores recorded. Their job performance is also evaluated and noted. The test score of each employee is then compared to how well the person performs on the job to determine whether or not there is a significant relationship between the two. If there is a significant relationship—those who score well on the test perform well on the job, and vice versa—the test is valid and can be used on future applicants as a predictor of future job success.

With predictive validity all applicants are tested and the test scores noted but they are not used to determine whether or not to hire. Applicants are hired on the basis of other methods, such as an interview. After a period of time the performance of each employee is evaluated and the person's job performance is compared to his or her test scores. If there is a significant relationship between test score and job performance, predictive validity exists and the test can be used on future applicants as a predictor of job success.

Although written integrity tests are controversial, the American Psychological Association has given them qualified support, indicating that most of the evidence supports the idea that some of the tests do work. Tests are more likely to work if they meet the four criteria noted previously.

Three companies—London House, Reid Psychological Systems, and Stanton—account for 70 percent of the integrity test market and tend to have the strongest research support. Reid Psychological Systems, for example, claims reliability coefficients of 0.90 on internal consistency and 0.78 on test–retest reliability. Concurrent validity has been measured in four studies at 0.43 (twice), 0.62, and 0.39. This compares favorably with average validity scores over several thousand studies for personality tests of 0.30. Predictive validity scores have also been impressive.

According to Reid, people who possess integrity[35]

- Value their self-concepts and personal reputation as honest persons
- Value integrity in their friends and associates
- Avoid thoughts or situations related to theft, deceit, or inappropriate behavior
- Are willing to discipline other people or themselves for violating socially accepted standards of honest conduct

## quick bite 12.4
### A Day in the Life: Van Eure

Van Eure, the owner of the Angus Barn restaurant in Raleigh, N.C., attributes her success to old-fashioned southern hospitality.

"The main thing we are known for is the hospitality and service," Eure said in an interview with *Nation's Restaurant News.* "People go out to dinner not just because they're hungry. They want to be pampered and waited on and made to feel special.

"Our employees are always willing to go the extra mile to make a dining experience just that much more special."

Eure has definite ideas on how the customer should be treated, and she teaches her employees how to provide great service on an everyday basis. Her 12 Commandments of Customer Service have been presented to the National Restaurant Association and featured in various prestigious publications.

Commandment #1 lays down the Golden Rule of Customer Service: The customer has the Gold, therefore, they make the rules. It's a philosophy that has served Eure well over the years.

Van Eure grew up in the business, spending much of her childhood in Angus Barn, which was started by her late parents. Thad and Alice Eure began the restaurant with the dream of creating a tradition of hospitality and service. Eure is dedicated to continuing that tradition of incredible service by paying attention to all of her customers, old and new. The family's 650-seat Angus Barn is celebrating its 44th anniversary this summer.

Eure also attributes her success to the relationship she has with her employees.

"We hire very carefully and weed out a lot of potential bad hires," Eure said. "We hire people who consider it a profession and try to get a verbal two to five-year commitment up front. We have a 10-week training program with official trainers on staff. I personally teach a three-hour class to every new person about my personal view on service."

Two of the most important commandments laid out by Eure in her 12 Commandments of Customer Service have to do with how employees should be treated. Commandment #3 speaks about how to treat employees, saying that you must treat your employees well if you want them to treat your customers well. Commandment #2 recommends hiring as if you are building a world-class team. Eure remarks that "we don't have a labor crisis, we have a turnover crisis." Fortunately Angus Barn, under Eure's leadership, has managed to avoid such a crisis.

"Our turnover is only 14 percent," said Eure. "We are constantly rewarding years of service at an employee banquet with nice gifts. We give them a lot of authority. They are a major part of all the decisions that are made. We spend a lot of time on positive reinforcement."

Eure says she enjoys pampering her customers on a daily basis.

*(continued)*

"I love having an opportunity to help make such great memories on all the important occasions in people's lives. They treasure those cherished moments that can never be created again."

*Sources:* "Van Eure: Lighting 40 Candles for Venerable Angus Barn," *Nation's Restaurant News,* May 29, 2000, vol. 34, no. 22, p. 27. "Customer Service: ASFSA Key Areas—Operations and Human Resources." *The Outlook,* September 2001, p. 2.

**Discussion Question:** What are some ways to implement positive reinforcement in a restaurant to lower the turnover rate?

In addition to the integrity attitude test, others are available, including

- Substance use attitudes
- Substance use history
- Sales productivity
- Service relations
- Numerical skills
- Social conduct history
- Work/education history

Hire Assist, for example, provides information on an applicant's

- Honesty—attitude toward stealing
- Integrity and work ethics
- Drug and alcohol use
- Willingness to accept and follow directions
- Propensity toward anger/violence

These tests vary in price from $8.50 to $25.00 each, with the unit cost getting progressively smaller as the number used increases. (This section should not be taken as an endorsement of Reid Psychological Systems. It is published as an example of what one company offers in the area of employee testing.)

Batrus Hollweg is piloting the Security Assessment for Employers (SAFE), a 50-item questionnaire to assist managers in identifying job applicants who show counterproductive behaviors. The company developed the test after research that divided employees into three areas—Green Zone employees (25 percent), who almost always were productive and did not take part in negative activities; Red Zone employees (25 percent), who were almost always counterproductive; and Yellow Zone employees (50 percent), who were productive sometimes and unproductive at times. Employees in either the Red or Green Zones could influence those in the Yellow Zone. If a restaurant has too many Red Zone employees, Green Zone employees will leave.[36]

A special form of testing is that done through assessment centers. Over the course of several days candidates go through a variety of tests, case studies, and job simulations. Because of the high cost involved, the use of assessment centers is usually reserved for management positions.

---

## quick bite 12.5
**The Four Stages of Teamwork**

**Learning Objective:** Identify the steps involved in staffing the operation, outlining important principles at each stage of the process.

How can operators put together effective work teams that can improve the staff's efficiency? In his seminar at the National Restaurant Association trade show, Ray Kavanaugh, Ph.D., head of the Department of Hospitality and Tourism Management at Purdue, offered some advice.

"The workplace is growing more complex with each passing day, and it is becoming increasingly competitive," said Kavanaugh. "You are all being asked to do more, to get it done faster and improve the quality of your operations. Oh yes, and you are expected to do this with fewer resources."

"No one person can do it all," he said. "If you think you can, then I don't know if there is any hope for you."

Teams succeed when strong ties are developed between team members, Kavanaugh explained. Emphasizing each individual's strengths, working within the team to resolve personal differences, balancing commitments and improving team communication all help build a strong team. Good teams require striking a balance between doing the work at hand and working on healthy relationships within the team.

Kavanaugh believes that building a strong team is a four-stage process. He advocates the model created by P. R. Scholtes in his book *The Team Handbook*. The stages that Scholtes lays out are forming, storming, norming and performing, Kavanaugh said.

Forming, the first stage, combines opposing feelings of fear and excitement. Kavanaugh said the job of the team leader at this stage is to identify the job, define with the team how they will measure success, decide what acceptable group behavior will be and discuss how differences should be resolved.

Storming, the second stage, is "the most challenging point in the entire process." At this point team members often resist the task at hand, change their attitudes toward the project and/or the team and argue among themselves.

Groups that are able to get past the storming period reach norming, the stage where members become more open to feedback, more accepting of each other and more willing to work together generally succeed.

*(continued)*

Later, as the team becomes a more cohesive unit, it achieves the performing stage, where members feel closely attached to each other. They learn how to work out problems on their own and become more satisfied with the team's progress. Kavanaugh noted that team building is a fluid and sometimes unpredictable process.

"It is possible for teams to jump back and forth between stages until the project is completed," he said.

*Source:* King, Paul, "Teamwork: The Key to Success in Labor-Short Times," *Nation's Restaurant News,* June 12, 2000, vol. 34, no. 24, p.110.

**Discussion Question:** What do you think you could do for a team that seems to be stuck in the storming stage?

## Interview in the Human Resources Department

Where a foodservice company has a corporate human resources department, the individual manager can expect assistance in interviewing employees. The basic breakdown of responsibility is that whoever is better able to do the job should do the job. Human resource professionals have specialized knowledge in the area of selecting qualified applicants within the existing regulatory environment. Managers would do well to utilize that expertise. A typical breakdown of responsibilities regarding interviewing is that the personnel or human resource manager would

- Develop legal, effective interviewing techniques.
- Train managers in selection interviewing.
- Provide interview formats and tests.
- Send qualified employees to managers who want to do the final interview.

The line manager or supervisor, on the other hand, would typically

- Decide whether or not to do the final interview (most will, rightly, want to).
- Do the actual final interviewing and hiring where appropriate.
- Provide feedback to personnel on hiring decisions and reasons for not hiring.

The interview is the most widely used and probably the most subjective method used in selecting employees. It has been demonstrated, for example, that[37]

- Negative information brought out during the interview is weighed too heavily and positive information not weighed heavily enough.
- A favorable–unfavorable information sequence of information resulted in better applicant ratings than did an unfavorable–favorable sequence.

- Interviewers have an "ideal" stereotypical candidate against which they compare candidates. This ideal is a composite of the interviewer's perception of the characteristics of successful jobholders.
- Visual cues are often regarded as more important than verbal cues in reaching conclusions.
- The interviewer's rating of candidates, in part, depends on the quality of the other candidates being interviewed at the same time.

The interview is the best method for determining whether or not candidates possess certain characteristics, such as self-confidence, effectiveness in expressing oneself, and sociability, factors that are especially important in customer-contact positions. For this reason the instances is recommended as part of the hiring process. However, there are ways to improve its effectiveness.

There are three steps in preparing for the interview.[38] The interviewer should be selected, the place where the interview will take place must be identified, and time should be planned to preview the application.

In a corporation, human resource managers may be responsible for an initial screening of candidates. However, line management should have the responsibility for making the final hiring decision. Whoever conducts the interview should have a complete understanding of what the job entails, in addition to the skills, knowledge, and abilities required to perform that job. The former comes from a job description, the latter from a job specification. In addition, the interviewer must be objective, an excellent judge of people, a good listener, and an excellent representative of the operation. The interview is not only an opportunity to select employees; it is a way to represent the restaurant to people in the community. Even if an applicant is not hired, the person interviewed will leave with some kind of an impression about the company based on the type of interview that he or she had. That impression can be positive or negative. Some people have left interviews indicating that, "Not only would I never work for that restaurant; I would never eat there and will tell all my friends to avoid eating there."

Care should be taken in selecting a time and place conducive to making an objective decision on whether or not a candidate is a proper fit for a job. Interviews should be scheduled when the interviewer can devote her or his time exclusively to the task at hand without interruptions. Sitting at a table in the restaurant can be a good idea as long as the manager makes it clear that they are not to be disturbed. This setting gives the interviewee a chance to see part of the operation.

The application form and additional screening information should be reviewed before the interview begins. A list of appropriate questions should also be developed prior to the interview. Many companies have found that a structured interview is most effective. In a structured interview, questions are developed based on the most important and most time-consuming duties of the job, and all candidates are asked those questions. Questions might be situational ("What would you do if . . .?"), cover job knowledge ("How is a 'rusty nail' made?"), consist of a simulation ("Show me how you would clear this table"), or deal with employee requirements for the position. The interview may be part oral, part written, and part physical, and sample answers to the questions to be asked should be developed beforehand.

Developed along the lines suggested, a structured interview is more likely to be objective and nondiscriminatory compared to unplanned interviews. Questions focus on what is important in performing the job. Writing the questions down together with sample answers ensures that everyone is asked the same questions and that the interviewer has thought about the answer that is preferred. Inexperienced interviewers will often ask a question and fail to listen to the candidate's answer, as they have to formulate the next question in their mind while the candidate is answering the first.

One problem with a structured interview is that the structure itself can mean that potentially good candidates can be lost because of the lack of flexibility of the interview itself. Responses that do not conform to the sample answers developed should not be discarded if, in fact, they are good and legitimate.

First impressions are very important. It is often a mistake to judge someone based only on appearances and first impressions. However, someone who comes to an interview late, lights a cigarette without asking for permission, and has dirty shoes and/or messy hair certainly does not seem too interested in the job.

Some small talk is useful to get the interviewee relaxed. The application form should have been reviewed immediately prior to the interview but should not be consulted during the interview, to avoid a stilted question-and-answer session.

During the body of the interview the objective is to get the person being interviewed to do most of the talking. The interviewer has an idea (from the job description and job specification) of what is needed. By listening to the responses of the interviewee, the interviewer is better able to evaluate whether or not that person is the right one for the job.

People can perform a job if they have the skills and the motivation. Many positions in a restaurant are not highly skilled jobs or require skills that can be taught readily on the job. The manager must decide whether it is more important to hire attitude and train skills rather than vice versa. Particularly for front-of-the-house jobs, it is better and easier to hire attitude. It is difficult to identify the basic values, ethics, and motivation of someone rather than the extent to which the person possesses specific skills. Here are some examples that will help:[39]

1. "Tell me about your first job." When a person started work can be a good indication of his or her work values and motivation. It does not matter so much whether or not the job was restaurant related. What is important is the reason he or she went to work and what he or she got out of the experience.
2. "What was your class schedule in school?" The restaurant business is one that is physically demanding. People who had trouble getting up before an 11 o'clock class may not have the energy level needed for your business.
3. "When was the first time you sold anything?" (for server positions).
4. "Tell me about your experience as a customer in our restaurant or in one of our competitors' restaurants." Interviewees' responses will indicate what they think of customer service and what is required to satisfy a guest.

5. "Who are your heroes or best friends? Why?" We tend to look up to people we admire. The answer to this question will indicate what the interviewee's values are.

6. When hiring someone who will take reservations over the phone, interview him or her over the phone. That way you will find out how the candidate really sounds to potential customers. If the candidate passes this test, interview him or her in person.

7. "What were customers like in the last place you worked?" Again, this will indicate true feelings about the importance of customers.

8. "Who was the best (and worst) manager you ever had, and why?" This will give an indication of how well or how poorly this person works with people in positions of authority.

9. "If you could have improved anything about your last job, what would it have been?" Exceptional employees are those who express their interest in the job by continually seeking ways to improve it and others within the operation.

10. "Why should we hire you?" Some employees feel that the world owes them a living. Others, the kind you want, believe that they can contribute something positive to the operation.

Once the interviewer's questions have been exhausted, it is time to ask the applicant if he or she has any questions. It is doubtful that everything could have been covered to the interviewee's satisfaction, so some kind of response should be expected. In fact, if the applicant has no questions, it probably indicates a lack of interest in the job. The number and type of questions asked can also give a clue as to what is important to this person.

Questions can be either direct or indirect. Direct questions are those that require a one- or two-word answer ("When did you leave your last job?"). They are useful for collecting large amounts of information very quickly. However, for a real evaluation, indirect questions (for example, "Why did you leave your last job?") are better because they require that the applicant talk more to answer the question completely. Remember, the objective is to get the applicant to talk.

It may be necessary to probe the answer to a question. A probe is an attempt to elicit more information from the interviewee if the initial answer to a question is considered vague. If it is to work, the probe should seek to confirm, clarify, and/or promote further discussion. Probing can come only if the interviewer actively listens to the initial response to learn that it does not give a complete answer to the question.

There are certain questions that employers cannot lawfully ask. Topics should be avoided that could discriminate against employees on the basis of federally protected categories. Businesses cannot discriminate on the basis of race, ethnic background, origin, color, gender, age (over 40), handicap, military experience, and religion. Additional state and local laws have been enacted to protect additional groups of people. Basically, it comes down to this: Ask questions that deal solely with a person's ability to do the job—and nothing else. A person may be asked whether or not he or she has the legal right to work in the United

States; interviewees cannot be asked whether or not they or their parents are naturalized citizens. They can be asked which high school they attended but not when they went there. They can be asked if they have ever been convicted of a crime but not whether they have ever been arrested for a crime.

---

**quick fact**

The number of foodservice managers is projected to increase 11% from 2005 to 2015.

*Source:* National Restaurant Association, "Restaurant Industry Facts," *http://www.restaurant .org/research/ind_glance.cfm#employment*, November 7, 2005.

---

## Background Investigation

The value of a reference check is the belief that past experience on the job is the best predictor of future job performance. It is, however, increasingly difficult to get worthwhile feedback about prior job experience. Applicants will only give the names of people who might be expected to give glowing references. The best source of past performance is to check with previous supervisors. There are two potential problems. First, because of the high turnover in this business, it may be difficult to locate references from even several months back. Second, previous employers may be reluctant to give detailed information on previous employees. There have been cases where employees who did not get a job have turned around and sued previous employers for giving a negative reference. People who are familiar with the law may be reluctant to do more than give the former employee's date of hire, date of departure, and job title.

Because of the usefulness of a reference from a previous supervisor, it is recommended that managers continue to give honest evaluations of their past employees. This advice is given in the hope that the manager who gives evaluations will receive them from others when requested.

There are some guidelines that, if followed, will help keep managers out of trouble from disgruntled employees.[40]

- Don't volunteer information; respond only to specific requests. Before responding, telephone the inquirer to check on the validity of the request.
- Direct all communications only to persons who have a specific interest in that information.
- State that the information being given is confidential and should be treated as such.
- If possible, obtain written consent from the employee.
- Provide only information that relates to the job and job performance in question.
- Avoid vague statements (such as "She was careless at times").

## quick bite 12.6
### Improvisational Interviewing

**Learning Objective:** Develop guidelines on how to conduct a hiring interview.

| Interview Style | Accuracy in Predicting Performance |
|---|---|
| Standard Interview | |
| The sit-down affair with management or personnel | 7% |
| Resume Analysis | |
| Quasi-scientific resume sifting | 37% |
| Work Sample Test | |
| Pen-and-paper skills tests | 44% |
| Assessment Center | |
| Lengthy, off-site skills/personality workup | 44% |
| Situational Interview | |
| Candidates role-play in mock scenarios | 54% |

*(Data: Handbook of Industrial & Organizational Psychology)*

What's the best interview for evaluating future employee performance? It's called the situational interview, and it's quickly becoming the norm for many companies. Businesses from General Electric Co. to J.P. Morgan Chase are switching to the new methods, along with many food-service companies. After Enron, many corporations are taking more care in their hiring, looking for those who have good ethics and friendly personalities as well as those with great resumes.

The situational interview has the greatest success rate because it can trip up even the most confident of interviewees. Of course, every applicant must prove that they have the knowledge and the skills, but behavior and ethics play a major role. By using a mock situation to gauge the interviewee's qualifications, managers and experts can easily separate the wheat from the chaff. For example, a prospective server at a restaurant might have to face, say, an irate customer. The interviewer, or an outside trained assessor, plays the role of an angry customer who was served the wrong food and delivered the wrong check. It's set up as an obvious mistake on the restaurant's part.

Interviewers watch the candidates' reactions, listening to their voice, how they handle complex information, and how they calm the customer. In this instance, not being honest about the mistake or showing anger or frustration means you're out, no matter how wonderful your resume is.

There are drawbacks to this technique, which can be significant. Most outsourced situational interviews cost more than $500 apiece. Background
*(continued)*

checks and personality tests, which are almost as effective as the situational interview, can cost anywhere from $25 to $245—still expensive, but far less so than the situational interview. Using a situational interview also runs the risk of upsetting prospective employees, who may feel that the line has been crossed into their personal lives. In addition, the interviews must be designed meticulously so as to avoid any race or gender biases. Nevertheless, the situational interview can save millions by avoiding the wrong hire.

*Sources:* Merritt, Jennifer, "Improv at the Interview," *Business Week,* February 3, 2003, no. 3818, p. 63. Tabone, John, "In View of Interviews," *CA Magazine,* March 2004, vol. 137, no. 2, p. 9.

**Discussion Question:** How would you feel if asked to perform in a situational interview?

- Document all released information.
- Clearly label all subjective statements based on personal opinions and feelings.
- When providing information negative to the employee, give the reasons why and specify the incidents.
- Avoid answering questions "off the record."

When requesting a reference, the most important things to check are as follows:[41]

- Employment dates
- Job title
- Primary job duties and responsibilities
- Applicant's performance compared to others
- Attendance and lateness records
- Applicant's ability to get along with fellow employees and managers
- Amount of supervision required
- Quality of applicant's work
- Motivation and enthusiasm toward the job
- Starting and final pay
- Reason for leaving
- Anything else of significance

It would also be useful to find out if the previous employer would rehire the person. It is worth asking this question, although if the person giving the interview knows anything about the law, he or she will probably answer, "It is against company policy to rehire previous employees." In addition to reference checking, employers may wish to check criminal records, driving records, Workers' Compensation records, federal court records, and educational records if it is deemed important.

Specialized companies will check these types of records for a fee, but it is possible to obtain a great deal of information yourself simply by using public records. Criminal records at the county or state level can be checked over the telephone. The state motor vehicle office will provide driving records. Workers' Compensation records, available through the state, will indicate past job injuries together with whether or not an employee has been cleared to return to work. Such records cannot be used to discriminate against an applicant who has made compensation claims at other places. Federal court records can also be accessed, while educational records are checked through the appropriate educational institution. Information from such background checks can be used as part of the selection process only if it is job related and is applied to every candidate.

## Medical Examination

State agencies require medical clearances for all food handlers. An increasing number of companies will test new employees for drug use. Although controversial, drug testing has generally been upheld by the courts as long as it is applied to every job candidate for every position.

## Preliminary Selection in the Human Resources Department

At this point it would be appropriate for the personnel department, having screened prospective employees, to make a preliminary cut of employees deemed inappropriate. The remainder would be cleared for interviews with line managers, who would make the final decision.

## Supervisory Interview

The guidelines given for interviewing with people from the personnel department are equally appropriate for interviewing with line management.

## Realistic Job Preview

Often, the manager will be interviewing an excellent candidate, someone who will really make a difference to the operation. At other times he or she will be in somewhat of a panic to fill a position. In either or both cases, there is a tendency to sell the job to the applicant as something better than it really is. In such a situation the initial job expectations are set too high. The applicant might be told that no more than a 45-hour week will be required and that two days off a week are standard. The job will be viewed as attractive and there will be a high rate of job acceptance.

Once on the job, however, the newly hired employee realizes that all is not as promised. The employee becomes dissatisfied, less motivated, and may quit. In the short run a body has been found; in the long run, there is increased turnover.

A realistic job preview, on the other hand, presents an accurate picture of the job and its conditions as part of the hiring process. The job may or may not be attractive to applicants and there will probably be a lower rate of job acceptance than that described previously. Of the smaller percentage of applicants who do accept the job, however, a greater number will find that the job is, in fact, as represented. They will tend to be more satisfied, more motivated, and will stay longer than the group discussed previously.

---

### quick bite 12.7
### Road to the Top: Manuel Gonzalez

When Manuel Gonzalez was cooking in the back of a family owned restaurant, he never dreamed that one day he would be a general manager for Baja Fresh. But, with a little persistence and hard work, Gonzalez worked his way up from cook to shift manager, then to general manager.

"It's the survival of the fittest," Gonzalez explains. "Only the strong survive."

Gonzalez's commitment to hard work and customer service is only superseded by his determination to encourage and motivate Baja's employees. He sees potential and opportunity within each worker, and tries to help that potential bloom.

"Baja is growing so fast there are so many opportunities for everybody," he clarifies. "You come in as a cashier and work yourself up to management." Gonzalez admits that he considers the way in which he treats his employees his greatest accomplishment. He recently asked a cashier to lunch and explained to her that he thought she had great skills and a lot of potential, and that she would be a fantastic member of the management team. She was flattered, and soon after began the assistant-manager training program. Gonzalez knows that seeing others achieve inspires his employees to do their best.

"People say, 'If Maria did it, I can do it,'" he says.

One of Gonzalez's assistant managers, Israel Vasconcelos, emphasizes how much he enjoys working with Gonzalez.

"It's not easy, but at the same time it's kind of rewarding at times," Vasconcelos explains. "He's a manager who has high expectations of the staff. . . . He tries to push, push, push and develop everybody the most. That is stressful, but at the end it's rewarding. That's why I say it's a good experience."

Steve Heeley, Baja Fresh's senior vice president of operations, explains why Baja recruited Gonzalez.

"He's got an ability to pick people who will work well in a team and be a good fit for the culture. Plus, he doesn't turn a lot of people over."

*Source:* Berger, Liza, "Baja Fresh: Manuel Gonzalez," *Nation's Restaurant News,* January 26, 2004, vol. 38, no. 4, p. 24.

**Discussion Questions:** Why is it a good choice for Gonzalez to promote from within? What does this do for other employees?

## Hiring Decision

It is important that the hiring decision be made in a timely manner and that applicants be made aware of that date. If an applicant is well qualified for the job, any delay in making the decision may mean that the person will find employment elsewhere.

Informing both those who will receive job offers and those who will not makes for good public relations and keeps those who did not get the job interested in applying for other opportunities within the operation for which they might be better suited.

In making a job offer, the following elements should be covered:[42]

- Position title
- Person to whom to report
- Salary or pay
- Shift
- Starting date
- Starting time
- Ending time
- Days off
- Equipment needed
- Clothing required
- Meal arrangements
- Parking
- When to come for processing of personnel forms

The working relationship will be easier if it begins on the right foot. This means making the new employee feel welcome and preparing existing employees for the new arrival. Involving existing employees before a new worker shows up will help ease the difficulties associated with getting to know and work with the new person.

## ENDNOTES

1. *2005 Restaurant Industry Forecast* (Washington, DC: National Restaurant Association, 2005), p. 27.
2. Allan F. Hickok and Lana E. Lazarus, *Restaurant Industry Review,* U.S. Bancorp Piper Jaffray Equity Research, March 2003, p. 32.
3. Cathy A. Enz, "Key Issues of Concern for Food-Service Managers," *CHR Report,* vol. 3, no. 4 (Ithaca, NY: The Center for Hositality Research at Cornell University, 2003).
4. Susan Mills, "Teen Spirit," *Restaurants USA,* March 2001, www.restaurant.org/rusa.
5. *2005 Restaurant Industry Forecast* (Washington, DC: National Restaurant Association, 2005), p. 28.
6. Irina Obenauer, "Who's Who in the Restaurant Industry," *Restaurants USA,* March 2000, www .restaurant.org/rusa.
7. Karen Eich Drummond, *Human Resource Management for the Hospitality Industry* (New York: Van Nostrand Reinhold, 1990), p. 230.

8. Obenauer, "Who's Who in the Restaurant Industry."

9. Johnston and Packer, *Workers for the 21st Century*, p. 89.

10. National Restaurant Association, *Foodservice Manager 2000*, p. 19.

11. *2005 Restaurant Industry Forecast* (Washington, DC: National Restaurant Association, 2005), p. 30.

12. Johnston and Packer, *Workers for the 21st Century*, pp. 92–93.

13. Mill, *Managing for Productivity in the Hospitality Industry*, p. 19.

14. Paul Ehrlich, Loy Bilderback, and Anne H. Ehrlich, *The Golden Door* (New York: Ballantine Books, 1979), p. 242.

15. William F. Jaffe, "Integrating the Disabled Employee into the Quick-Service Restaurant: The Enclave Model," *Hospitality & Tourism Educator*, vol. 6, no. 2, Spring 1994, p. 15.

16. National Restaurant Association, *Americans with Disabilities Act: Answers for Foodservice Operators* (Washington, DC: National Restaurant Association, 1992), p. 2.

17. Ibid., pp. 8–18.

18. Ibid., p. 27.

19. Jaffe, "Integrating the Disabled Employee into the Quick-Service Restaurant," p. 19.

20. Arthur W. Sherman Jr., George W. Bohlander, and Herbert J. Chudren, *Managing Human Resources*, 8th ed. (Cincinnati, OH: South-Western Publishing Co., 1988), p. 63.

21. David Wheelhouse, *Managing Human Resources in the Hospitality Industry* (East Lansing, MI: Educational Institute of the American Hotel and Motel Association, 1989), p. 67.

22. Ibid., p. 66.

23. Ibid., p. 71.

24. Obenauer, "Who's Who in the Restaurant Industry."

25. "Summer Job Prospects Not So Sunny For Teen Workers," *Nation's Restaurant News*, vol. 37, no. 18, May 5, 2003, p. 22.

26. Wheelhouse, *Managing Human Resources in the Hospitality Industry*, p. 79.

27. EEOC, *Affirmative Action and Equal Employment: A Guidebook for Employers*, vol. 1 (Washington, DC: Equal Employment Opportunity Commission, 1974), pp. 16–17.

28. Lewis C. Forrest, *Training for the Hospitality Industry* (East Lansing, MI: Educational Institute of the American Hotel and Motel Association, 1983), p. 56.

29. Donald Lundberg, *The Management of People in Hotels and Restaurants*, 5th ed. (Dubuque, IA: Wm. C. Brown Company, 1992), p. 85.

30. Forrest, *Training for the Hospitality Industry*, p. 41.

31. "Addressing the Needs of a Diverse Work Force," *Restaurants USA*, October 1997, p. 42.

32. Ibid., p. 53.

33. National Restaurant Association, *1998 Restaurant Industry Operations Report* (Washington, DC: National Restaurant Association and Deloitte & Touche LLP, 1998), p. 9.

34. Sherman et al., *Managing Human Resources*, p. 160. Bruce Grindy, "Hooking and Keeping Employees," *Restaurants USA*, October 1998, p. 24.

35. Reid Research Report, unpublished promotional booklet, undated.

36. Dina Berta, "Employee Behavior Study Alarms Operators," *Nation's Restaurant News*, vol. 37, no. 31, p. 99.

37. Sherman et al., *Managing Human Resources*, p. 172.

38. Wheelhouse, *Managing Human Resources in the Hospitality Industry*, pp. 176–183.

39. Bill From and Len Schlesinger, *The Real Heroes of Business* (New York: Doubleday, 1994), pp. 323–333.

40. J. D. Bell, J. Castagnera, and J. P. Young, "Employment References: Do You Know the Law?" *Personnel Journal*, vol. 63, no. 2, February 1984, pp. 32–36.

41. Drummond, *Human Resource Management for the Hospitality Industry*, p. 33.

42. Wheelhouse, *Managing Human Resources in the Hospitality Industry*, p. 119.

## INTERNET RESOURCES

| | |
|---|---|
| U.S Department of Labor | *http://www.dol.gov/* |
| U.S Equal Employment Opportunity Commission | *http://www.eeoc.gov/* |
| Hospitality Careers Online | *http://www.restaurantjobs.hcareers.com/* |
| Global Hospitality | *http://www.globalhospitality.com/* |
| American Association of Retired Persons | *http://www.aarp.org* |

# CHAPTER THIRTEEN

# TRAINING
# AND DEVELOPMENT

"If Broadway shows charge preview prices while the cast is in
dress rehearsal, why should restaurants charge full price when
their dining room and kitchen staffs are still practicing?"
                                        Marian Burros, Food writer

## learning objectives

*By the end of this chapter you should be able to*

1. Design an effective orientation program.

2. Compare and contrast the various training methods.

3. Design, implement, and evaluate an effective training program.

4. Develop the skills necessary to become an effective trainer.

5. List the elements of a strong employee and management development
   program.

## quick bite 13.1
### Hot Concepts: Pei Wei Asian Diner

Pei Wei Asian Diner is designed to offer high-quality fare with the convenience of fast food. This new hot spot is the daughter restaurant of the popular P.F. Chang's China bistro. Now seven years old with more than 64 locations in eleven states (and more planned), Pei Wei has come to satisfy the palettes of Asian cuisine lovers everywhere. It has been called "the platinum standard" for quick casual restaurants. The chain's Pan Asian menu features appetizers, salads, rice and noodle bowls, and entrees, with the average check being $8.50 per person.

The décor of the Pei Wei diner has been described as utilitarian chic. The shiny red floor, walls lined with rich cherry wood, and black ceiling combined with the "happy sound effects" and aromas from the kitchen set the tone for a pleasurable dining experience. By combining friendly and quick service with the high-class ambience of a five-star restaurant, Pei Wei Asian Diner is sure to please every customer.

When diners arrive to Pei Wei, they choose either to dine in or take out. Each option has its own line and cashier. Diners place their orders, get drinks and silverware, and then seat themselves. Servers quickly bring patrons their orders, according to the number pinned to the top of a chopstick container which was given to them by the cashier.

Rick Federico, chairman and chief executive of a PF Chang's in Arizona, says "a lot of the time we can get the food to the table about the time you're putting your rear end in the seat. That's real important in this segment, because we only have 80 seats and relatively high demand. We are very conscious about monitoring the flow of traffic to make sure we can execute with efficiency."

Federico also notes that details are important if you want to exceed the consumers' expectations for the quicker-casual segment. For example, patrons do not have to bus their own tables. Rather than using disposable utensils, Pei Wei uses china and silverware.

The take-out option with Pei Wei is especially successful because the meals carry very well. Guests are presented with the choice of grabbing a quick bite to eat during their lunch hour, sitting down and enjoying a casual dining experience before a movie, or grabbing a quick meal to go. This flexibility, combined with the ambience, character, and quality of food at Pei Wei, is what makes every customer a customer for life.

*Source: National Restaurant News,* "Pei Wei Asian Diner: Quick Casual's 'Platinum Standard' Cuts Delivery Time, But Not Quality of Cuisine," July 22, 2003.

**Discussion Question:** In what ways does Pei Wei Asian Diner accommodate its customers to make them customers for life?

# EMPLOYEE ORIENTATION

Orientation is "the formal process of familiarizing new employees with the organization, their job, and the work unit."[1] Conducted properly, orientation will give employees the knowledge necessary for them to be successful in an operation.

It is generally recognized that a well-run orientation program will help[2]

- Lower turnover.
- Increase productivity.
- Improve employee morale.
- Lower recruiting and training costs.
- Facilitate learning.
- Reduce the level of anxiety of new employees.

As noted previously, a comprehensive orientation program should cover three major areas: the organization, the job, and the work unit. The following elements are typical of a comprehensive program:[3]

### The Organization

1. Description of the operation's history, size, and objectives
2. Company standards regarding job behavior and performance
3. Conditions of employment regarding such things as hours of work and pay periods
4. Key management and the chain of command

The purpose of this segment is to let employees see the "big picture" of what the company stands for. In so doing, employees will get a feeling for how their job fits into the entire operation and realize the history and tradition behind what the operation does.

### The Job

5. Detail the duties and responsibilities of the job and its importance to the entire organization.
6. Explain the training to be given.
7. Explain how performance will be evaluated.
8. Discuss sanitation and safety regulations.

The objective of this segment is to let employees know what a "normal" workday looks like.

### The Work Unit

9. Introduce new employees to fellow employees.
10. Provide the name of the immediate contact person who will assist new employees in dealing with problems.

11. Tour the entire operation.
12. Discuss rules, regulations, and policies.

The Old Spaghetti Factory includes the following items in its orientation program:[4]

- Brief history of the company and store
- Customer philosophy
- Names of managers
- Name of trainer
- Schedule and scheduling
- Where to park
- Attendance and tardiness
- No-solicitation rule (prohibits employees from selling any products or services or from distributing literature on the premises without prior approval from the employer; designed to prevent unions from distributing union literature in the restaurant)
- How to sign in
- Meals
- Wage and raise policy
- Payday and paycheck procedure
- House and safety rules
- Grooming and uniform standards
- Other store rules
- Training schedule
- Hand-washing and sanitizing

It is as important to prepare existing employees for the new hire and vice versa. Employees may be suspicious of new hires and will wonder if and how a new employee will affect them and their job. The goal is to make new employees feel like they belong.

There is a danger in exposing the new hire to too much information over a short period of time. For a new employee, the first day is especially stressful: dealing with a work environment, employees, supervisors, and customers who are different. In such a situation the employee may be unable to absorb much additional information. Nevertheless, the first few days of contact between the employee and the company will set the tone for the longer-term relationship.

To combat potential problems of information overload, employees are given much of the information in writing in the form of an employee handbook. They are then asked to sign a declaration indicating that they have received this information. In this way the company protects itself against future employee claims that they were not told certain information. This is particularly important for those employees who must enforce company rules.

**Orientation Manual**

**Learning Objective:** Design an effective orientation program.

Orientation manuals have become a hot commodity among managers because they ensure that all employees are properly prepared and trained for their job. Here is an outline for what a manual should generally say:

- Operational procedures
  - Clock-in: explain your policy regarding tardiness
  - Smoking: explain where it is acceptable/unacceptable
  - Horseplay: explain whether it is permitted and if it is, where
  - Phone calls: explain policy regarding personal phone calls, cell phones
  - Answering the telephone: explain exactly how employees should answer the phone
  - Solicitations
  - Paychecks: clarify when paydays are
  - Advances
  - Personal property
  - Personal business
  - Age requirements: state the minimum age requirements for each position
  - Accidents
  - Customer complaints: explain policy for handling
  - Employee meals: explain whether employees receive discounted or free meals
  - Break: explain policy regarding employee break times
  - Parking
  - Scheduling: explain the process for scheduling and where the schedule will be posted and when
  - Dress code: be very specific when explaining the dress code
- Personal hygiene
  - Hair should be neatly trimmed
  - Clothing should be clean and neat
  - Hands should be clean and free of cuts and sores
  - Fingernails should be short and free of dirt
  - Employees must wash their hands after using the bathroom, eating food, or using tobacco products
- Employee benefits
  - Insurance: explain employee eligibility

- Promotions: be sure to include a statement about being an equal opportunity employer and all promotions are given on the basis of job performance
- Training: explain training program
- Uniforms: explain policy and expectations regarding uniforms
- Vacations: explain policies regarding paid vacations, terms and eligibility
- Menu breakdown
  - Outline menu briefly with examples. Explain what servers need and expect from the cooks and vice versa.
  - Create a separate handbook for food and drink specifications
- Greeting, seating, and table service
  - Outline ideal procedures for serving a table
  - Explain in detail how to ring up a ticket
  - Illustrate the set-up of the restaurant, include a seating chart
- Abbreviations
- Alcohol awareness
- Employee agreement

*Source:* National Restaurant Association's How-To Series, "How to Write an Employee Manual," October 2000, *http://www.restaurant.org/business/howto/eemanual.cfm*

**Discussion Question:** Why are orientation manuals important? Do you think all restaurants adopt the same outline for their employee manuals? Why or why not?

The final part of an orientation program is the evaluation and follow-up. Too often the assumption is made that because employees have been through the program, they have absorbed the information. The objective is, in fact, to have them absorb certain information deemed important by management. Some companies will test employees several weeks after the orientation to determine whether or not the information has been taken in.

# EMPLOYEE TRAINING AND DEVELOPMENT

## Importance of Training

There are some in the industry who see training as a cost rather than an investment. When sales drop, any training that is currently being done is stopped. The argument is that given the turnover rate in the industry, there is little point in training employees who will invariably leave. These managers argue that they are, in essence, training employees for others.

This argument fails to recognize that employees may be leaving in part because management has not invested the time, money, or energy in them, the employees. A well-trained group of employees should result in a reduction of costs, stress, turnover, and absenteeism and a corresponding increase in efficiency and customer satisfaction.

If training can in fact reduce turnover, the cost of that training is more than justified. Consider the turnover rates in the following table:

| Restaurant Type | Annual Employee Turnover | | | | | |
|---|---|---|---|---|---|---|
| | All Employees | | Salaried Employees | | Hourly Employees | |
| | 2002 | 2004 | 2002 | 2004 | 2002 | 2004 |
| Full-service, average check per person under $15 | 96% | 64% | 50% | 33% | 100% | 67% |
| Full-service, average check per person $15–$24.99 | 72% | 56% | 50% | 33% | 79% | 60% |
| Full-service, average check per person $25 and over | 73% | 45% | 25% | 40% | 80% | 47% |
| Limited-service | 87% | 73% | — | 50% | — | 82% |

*Source: 2002 Restaurant Industry Report* (Washington, DC: National Restaurant Industry and Deloitte & Touche, 2002), pp. 21, 45, 69, 93; *2004 Restaurant Industry Report* (Washington, DC: National Restaurant Industry and Deloitte & Touche, 2005), pp. 22, 50, 78, 106.

The figures in the preceding table indicate that employee turnover is a greater problem for limited-service restaurants compared to other types of operations. The decline (in some case substantial) in turnover rates between 2002 and 2004 is also significant. The National Restaurant Association does not speculate on the reasons for this decline. It may be that the industry is putting more resources into training, and this investment is resulting in employees who are more loyal to the company. It may also be an economic situation wherein employees are more inclined to stay in a position they can count on than to move.

According to the National Restaurant Association, the average cost of losing a minimum-wage hourly employee and a manager is $2494 and $24,000 respectively.[5] Using these figures, assuming a staff of 60 hourly employees and two managers and applying them to the preceding table, the full-service restaurant with an average check per person of less than $15.00 would incur annual costs due to turnover of $173,640.

## Responsibility for Training

The person responsible for training will depend on the size of the organization and how it is structured. For a restaurant that is part of a chain or a unit part of a larger organization, line managers will be supported by staff people in a human resource department with specialized expertise in training.

# quick bite 13.3
## Innovative Training Method

**Learning Objective:** Compare and contrast the various training methods.

Ruth's Chris Steak House has given the phrase "dealt a good hand in cards" a whole new meaning. Bill Hyde joined the Ruth Chris team in 1999 at the request of the company's founder, Ruth Fertel. Hyde brought years of industry experience to the company, as well as a new slant on how to develop and train people.

The S-Mac Learning System is a unique "flash card" learning method designed by DSG Associates in Irvine, California. S-Mac is used for training hourly employees and management. The S-Mac system focuses on core capabilities, such as the company's history and culture. It also focuses on skills related to new products and service standards. The information is condensed onto lightweight cards that are color coded by module. The cards are vest-pocket sized, making them a perfect fit for a chef's coat pocket or a server's maitre d' pad. Additionally, the cards are printed with English on one side and Spanish on the other, which aids Hispanic workers. The system is also available on audiocassette in both languages.

There are seven basic modules within the S-Mac system: Orientation, Product Information, Front of the House Standards, Back of the House Standards, Service Standards, Kitchen Information, and Wine & Spirits. There are also individual modules for the server and cook positions. Each module uses practical examples so that the staff can anticipate and go above and beyond the guests' expectations. For example, in the "Front of the House" module, there are cards focusing on the "Guest Experience" and "Using Guests' Names."

The cards are conveniently stored in racks on the restaurant walls and are available to all staff members at all times. Because the modules for all positions are available on the rack, team members are empowered to advance into higher positions or cross-train into other positions. This also allows employees the options of selecting all cards from a module or just one, if they wish to focus on a specific skill.

The card system is ideal because any module can be easily updated or revised and distributed to keep up with the constant changes within the industry. It is an efficient training and development system combining smart design, technology, and a human touch. Kathryn Harris, director of education and hospitality, says, "Having S-Mac in place when I came to Ruth's Chris made my life a lot easier. . . . It brought to light many of the core competencies needed to run our restaurants."

*Source:* Winning Workforce Ideas, Employer of Choice Awards, "It's All in the Cards," pp. 14–17.

**Discussion Question:** How does having the module help staff members advance into higher positions or cross-train for other positions?

Such staff people can be called upon to[6]

- Assist line managers in developing training programs.
- Conduct general training programs focusing on such general topics as supervisory techniques and time management.
- Coordinate various elements of training, such as the use of outside speakers and seminars and directing programs of succession planning and cross-training.
- Research, monitor, and evaluate training.

Even if there is staff assistance, the unit manager bears the ultimate responsibility for training new employees. At the independent unit level the unit manager does not have the benefit of specialized staff assistance. The general manager of a restaurant will not necessarily carry out the actual training. The training itself is best done by someone who understands the performance standards required for the job and is able to pass those skills on to others. Often, that person is the department manager.

## TRAINING PROCESS

Training can be defined as "any procedure initiated by an organization to foster learning among organizational members."[7] Training is done initially to bring new hires up to the standards required by the company. Beyond this, as the job or the market changes, there will be a need to establish training programs to adjust operations to the new situation.

There are several steps involved in developing a training program:[8]

1. Conduct a needs assessment.
2. Determine learning objectives.
3. Develop the overall training program.
4. Develop individual training lessons.
5. Conduct the training.
6. Evaluate.
7. Follow up.

### Needs Assessment

The purpose of a needs assessment is to determine what types of training are needed. Assessment can be done at three levels:[9] organizational analysis, task analysis, and person analysis.

The organizational analysis looks at the company as a whole and, in light of company goals, resources, and the external environment in which it operates, suggests where the training emphasis should be. For example, the courts have increased their attention on the topic of sexual harassment. In light of this environmental influence, an organizational analysis might suggest supervisory training in this area.

A task analysis involves designing the content of a training program based on the duties involved in a job. A job description is one document that results from having conducted a job analysis. The job description indicates the most important and time-consuming tasks involved in performing that job. Performance standards will then be developed for every important part of the job. These performance standards represent the level of performance required for that job. A person analysis then determines what knowledge, skills, and attitudes are required to perform the job successfully. People hired for that job must either possess these skills or must be trained in them. The need for training can also come from accident records, personal observation, exit interviews, customer complaints, and employee evaluations.

---

**quick bite 13.4**

**Sample Training Method: On-the-Job Training/Testing**

**Learning Objective:** Design, implement, and evaluate an effective training program.

A popular training method is on-the-job training. In this situation, an employee will receive an outline containing the key concepts that will be covered in training. Following the training session, an employee quiz is typically given. Here are a few questions taken from each section of the first of several tests that the servers at Pappadeaux Seafood Kitchen are required to take (servers must score 90% or above on each test to continue with their training):

1. What is our restaurant's phone number? _____
2. What is our restaurant's address? _____

**True/False**

1. Guests are not required to tip. _____
2. Tips may be removed from the table while the Guests are still there. _____

List the name of each type of fish described below:

1. Had a mild taste with very moist and flaky white meat. It is best blackened, pan-broiled, or grilled.
2. Moist, dark meat that has a very distinctive flavor. It is great char-grilled and blackened.

List the type of breading used for each of these menu items:

1. _____ Fried shrimp, stuffed shrimp
2. _____ Oysters and catfish

*(continued)*

---

List the type of cooking procedure next to its appropriate description:

1. Product is dipped in butter, seasoned with 9 Cajun spices and then cooked on a very hot grill to seal in the juices and impart a blackened appearance and taste.
2. Product is broiled over an open flame.

**Fill in the Blanks**

1. All seafood entrees are garnished with _____ and a _____.
2. Beef and grilled chicken entrees are garnished with _____.

Write the approximate preparation times for the following groups of menu items:

1. Soups, beans _____
2. Lobster tail _____

Write the correct abbreviation, prep line time, and cooking times for the following items:

| Menu item | Abbreviation | Prep Line | Time |
|---|---|---|---|
| 1. Fried Crabfinger Appetizer | | | |
| 2. Fried Alligator | | | |
| 3. Boudin | | | |

*Source:* Pappadeaux Seafood Kitchen's Server Test Booklet, Version 2, pp. 1–6, Pappas Restaurants, Inc.

**Discussion Question:** Why is it important for an employee to know the ingredients in every dish?

## Learning Objectives

Learning objectives should be SMART: specific, measurable, achievable, realistic, and time bound. Both manager and employee will then know up front what is to be done, the level of performance that is to be achieved, and when it is to be accomplished.

## Training Program

The complete training program can then be laid out. The training necessary for a specific job comes from an analysis of that job. A job analysis identifies the important tasks that make up that job. This is what people performing the job must be able to do. If an employee is hired without the ability to perform one or more of these tasks, the task must be taught to the employee. The program will identify what is to be taught, when, where, how, and to whom it is to be taught, together with an estimate of the cost involved.

Earlier, the process for conducting a job analysis was identified. The process involves developing[10]

- A job list
- A job breakdown
- A job description
- A job specification

A job list is an inventory of all the tasks that must be performed as part of that job. For example, a job list for a food server might include the following, among others:[11]

- Greeting and seating restaurant guests
- Serving water; lighting candles
- Taking beverage orders and serving drinks
- Presenting the food menu and beverage list
- Assisting guests in making food and beverage selections

A job breakdown is then prepared for each task on the job list. The job breakdown indicates how the task should be performed. It comprises four parts: what is to be done, what materials are needed, how it is to be done, and why that step is important.

The task of "assisting guests in making food and beverage selections" might involve six steps:[12]

1. Approach the table.
2. Take the cocktail order.
3. Serve cocktails.
4. Check back for a second cocktail.
5. Take the food order.
6. Take the wine order.

Each item would then be described in more detail as to the procedures for performing the task, any materials that might be needed, and why the specified procedures are important. The first step might look like this:[13]

WHAT TO DO
Approach the table.

HOW TO DO IT
Stand erect. Look at the guest, smile, and greet them pleasantly. Introduce yourself. If you know their names, use them when you greet them. Be courteous.

### WHY IT IS IMPORTANT

You "win" the table by your first contact when you are pleasant and personable.

From the job breakdown a description of the job can be developed and used to write a job specification: a list of the knowledge, skills, and abilities needed by someone to perform the job. When employees are hired, their existing knowledge, skill, and abilities can be compared to those in the job specification to identify shortcomings. These items form the basis for the tasks that employees have to be trained to perform. The specifics are to be found in the job breakdown. These will also serve later as the performance standards to determine the extent to which employees are performing up to the level required by the restaurant.

## Training Lessons

The entire training program is then divided into segments and a lesson plan developed for each segment. Typically, classroom training sessions should last from 15 to 30 minutes. The training lesson will identify a learning objective for that session and suggest which techniques should be used to meet that objective.

## Conducting the Training

At this point it is necessary to select someone to do the training. Typically, that task is left to the immediate supervisor or a fellow employee. Just because someone knows how to perform a job or has responsibility for seeing that the job is performed well does not mean that the person will be effective in training another person to perform the task effectively.

According to Wheelhouse,[14] effective trainers are

- Good judges of people
- Objective
- Aware of, understand, and accept the differences in people
- Good at listening and communicating
- Good role models for the department
- Optimistic and enthusiastic about the job, the department, and the company

If a fellow employee is asked to take on the role of trainer, that person should be compensated financially and given positive recognition within the operation. A server acting as trainer will be able to serve fewer customers and will have fewer tips. Extra pay and recognition should be given to make up for this shortfall.

## Evaluation

This next step in the process determines the extent to which the training objectives have been met. The success of the training can be measured at various levels.[15] At the first and most basic level the trainees' reactions can be measured: Did they like the program? Next, their knowledge level can be measured: Did they learn the new information? Even better is to evaluate behavior and/or attitude: Do the employees demonstrate new behaviors and/or attitudes on the job that can be traced to the training received? Finally, and most important, was the training cost-effective: Was the cost of the training outweighed by a resulting increase in employee productivity?

## Follow-Up

Follow-up is necessary to ensure that the skills taught are used constantly. Supervisors can follow up through coaching—checking that the results of a training program are improving employee performance and either giving positive feedback when it is happening or correcting that performance, when necessary, in a way that will improve the performance of the employee.

---

### quick fact

Promising hourly employees at Claim Jumper Restaurants are invited to "bridge" into management positions via the Expeditor Program.

Formalized in 2001, the Expeditor Program prepares employees for Claim Jumper's manager-in-training program. After posting management opportunities internally, training personnel evaluate and interview interested employees. Candidates either proceed to the Expeditor Program orientation or work with trainers to identify ways to prepare them for the next opening in the Expeditor Program.

Hourly turnover declined from 70 percent in 2001 to 55 percent in 2004.

*Source:* Donna Hood Crecca, Chain Leader, "Expediting Success at Claim Jumper," April 2005.

---

## PRINCIPLES OF LEARNING

There is a difference between training and learning. Often, it is assumed that because training takes place, the trainees have learned. Learning does not take place until and unless the information that was part of the training program was received, understood, and internalized. Thus for training to be effective, it must be designed such that it helps trainees learn. By identifying how people learn and designing training programs with these principles in mind, trainees will be more likely to learn.

### Intention to Learn

People will not learn unless they want to. The trainer's role is to help supply that motivation by letting the trainee know the importance of the information about to be presented. Employees need to know what's in it for them. It may be that learning how to perform a new task will increase tips, help the employee get a promotion, or give employees more status within the operation. The task is to find out what is important to the employee and to show how actively participating in the training will help the employee satisfy that need.

## Whole Learning

Learning is improved if the entire job or task is shown in relation to other jobs and the task to be taught is then broken down into its constituent parts. Known as whole or Gestalt learning, the idea is that a trainee will better comprehend the task if he or she knows where that task fits into the entire operation. When training a dishwasher, for example, one would first explain how and where the dirty dishes come from, how they are cleaned, and what happens to them once they leave the dishwasher's control. By adding an explanation as to the importance of having clean dishes, the person being taught the job now has a frame of reference for learning the specific steps involved in producing clean dishes.

## Reinforcement

People act in ways that are rewarding to them. Rewards can be external—pay increase, promotion, verbal praise—or internal—a feeling of accomplishment. Trainers should find out what rewards are important to the trainee and reinforce positive behavior using these rewards to get more of the same behavior.

Positive reinforcement—a reward for doing something right—is more effective than punishment—an action to punish the person for doing something wrong. Reinforcement is improved when the reward is given as soon as possible after the action. Praising a hostess immediately after she helps a family calm a child fretting at the dinner table is more effective in reinforcing the behavior than waiting until the end of the shift.

## Practice

The saying goes, "Practice makes perfect." Some would adapt this to say, "Perfect practice makes perfect." The point, however, is that repeating the newly learned skill will improve the performance of that skill. Further, active practice is more effective than reading or listening.

## Spaced versus Massed Practice

Retention is improved when new material is spread out over several sessions rather than being condensed into fewer, longer sessions. If, for example, it is estimated that a new job will require eight hours of training, the trainee will learn better if there are two hours of instruction in the new job each day for four days rather than one eight-hour day of new material.

## Learning Curve

People learn at different rates. There appear to be three patterns by which learning takes place. The learning of most routine jobs follows a decreasing returns pattern, wherein a rapid increase in the skill level is followed by a tapering off in the rate of improvement as the trainee's rate of performance stabilizes at a "normal" rate.

**A Day in the Life: Lisa Chidichimo**

Lisa Chidichimo's day begins at 8 A.M. on a Wednesday in late March. It is the midpoint of a crazy week that included the introduction of a new product and training sessions at two of her store locations. Her first priority this morning is checking the company's website and responding to messages from guests and other visitors. Human interaction is vital to her job; Chidichimo says she'd be lost if she didn't get to interact with people. An extrovert at heart, she admits she's at her best when she's interacting with other people.

About 15 percent of Chidichimo's mornings are committed to store contact and communication with restaurant managers and staff. For about an hour, from 9 A.M. to 10 A.M., Chidichimo tries to maximize her store presence and interact with members of the Monical team. During this time, she is able to track employee and guest satisfaction.

At 10 A.M., Chidichimo returns to her office to follow up on the new product rollout. To do this, she exchanges emails with other managers to evaluate and discuss the product test. She is finally able to take a quick break at noon to eat a sandwich; however, the work continues through lunch.

From 1 P.M. to 3 P.M., Chidichimo talks with guests and responds to Monical's customer service line. Chidichimo deals with complaints just as professionally and courteously as she deals with compliments.

At 3 P.M., Chidichimo plans a promotion with the NFL Chicago Bears, who will be moving their training center to within three miles of two Monical restaurants. She then meets with Jim Hedge, a marketing staff member, who is working on billboard graphics. Staffers continue to connect and interact with Chidichimo throughout the day; for example, an accounting staffer brings sales figures from one of the recent community night events to her when she returns to her office for a brief moment.

Chidichimo spends her remaining hour explaining the new product advertising. The advertising campaign will consist of flyers, a billboard campaign, a direct mail campaign, and television ads. The Monical office closes at 4:30 P.M. However, Chidichimo continues working for another half hour. Chidichimo finally leaves the office around 5 P.M. and heads to her husband's office to pick him up for the commute home.

*Source: National Restaurant News,* "A Day in the Life: Lisa Chidichimo" April 15, 2002. p. 46.

**Discussion Question:** Why does Lisa Chidichimo dedicate the majority of her day to guest interaction, and why is this communication beneficial to her job and business?

When someone is learning a completely unfamiliar job, the increasing returns pattern is common. This learning curve starts out very slowly and increases with more instruction and practice.

The S-shaped curve is one where the trainee's performance starts out slowly, improves rapidly, and then tails off. It is common with difficult tasks that also require the trainee to become familiar with the basics of the job.

With all three patterns, trainees will have periods of growth and times when performance seems to have flattened. This leveling off of performance can be discouraging for many trainees unless they are told that this is normal. Positive encouragement at these times is necessary for long-term growth in job performance.

## Behavior Modeling

One of the most effective ways in which people learn is through behavior modeling: watching other people perform the task and copying their behavior. It is particularly good for situations where trainees have to learn specific information and then apply it in practice.

## TRAINING METHODS

There are three general types of training: learner-controlled, individual, and group instruction.[16]

### Learner-Controlled Instruction

In learner-controlled or self-instruction programs, employees learn individually, at their own pace. It is training without a trainer. Whether a videotape presentation, a programmed instruction manual, or a computer-interactive program, trainees use them at times convenient to them. Because the training message is consistent, learner-controlled instruction is considered to be the best method for training standardized routines to employees.

Depending upon the average check in the restaurants, anywhere from 31 to 47 percent of operations use video-supported training while 28 to 34 percent utilize classroom training. Comparable figures for computer-interactive and CD-ROM-supported methods are 16 to 19 percent and 1 to 5 percent, respectively.[17]

Such programs are particularly appropriate for teaching repetitive tasks, when there are many employees doing the same job, where turnover is high, and/or when there are large numbers of temporary employees who must be trained.[18] There is a downside, however: The initial cost is high in terms of time and dollars to develop the program. When procedures change, the program is out of date and must be redone.

According to Forrest, there are nine characteristics of learner-controlled instruction:[19]

1. Self-direction
2. Performance-based expectations
3. Contract learning

4. Learning environment
5. Printed resource materials
6. Demonstration of mastery
7. Feedback
8. Self-pacing and sequencing
9. Challenge and bypass

**Self-Direction.**   The process of learner-controlled instruction is controlled by the trainee. The objective is to learn the material efficiently and effectively. Some take the view that this type of program can only be effective with trainees who are self-directed. These companies prescreen employees to eliminate any who are not. The advantage to the trainee from this process is that not only are the tasks learned but employees identify how to make solid, responsible decisions while managing their time.

**Performance-Based Expectations.**   In a typical training schedule, trainees spend a period of time on one job before moving on to another. In learner-controlled instruction, trainees move on to other tasks after they have mastered the performance of that task. They need to be told what tasks they will have to perform and what level of competence defines mastery. The performance standards for a particular job could double as the competency level for that job.

**Contract Learning.**   A learning contract serves as an agreement between the employee and the trainer and is a record of employee performance. The trainer, by signing the document, agrees to assist the employee in achieving the competencies defined. Once the trainer is convinced that the competencies have been developed, the contract is signed to that effect. A written contract formalizes the process and helps ensure that both trainer and trainee take it seriously.

A typical contract contains[20]

- *A competency statement:* A learning objective; what the trainee will be able to do
- *Learning activities for developing the competence:* Knowledge that must be developed and skills acquired by the trainee
- *Evaluation guides:* Minimum performance standards for each competency
- *Resources:* Printed information available to the trainee
- *Agreements and certification:* Places for trainer signatures

**Learning Environment.**   Learner-controlled instruction takes place on the job during actual working conditions.

**Printed Resource Materials.**   As noted previously, the trainee must be supplied with written materials indicating the standard operating procedures and company standards for performing the job for which he or she is being trained. In this way, any observed deviations between the way the job is supposed to be done and how it is actually being performed can be noted and corrections made.

**Demonstration of Mastery.**   Trainees show that they have met the expectations laid out earlier when they show that they have mastered the tasks or competencies in the learning contract. Then, and only then, can they move on to learn other parts of the job. In a program where employees spend a certain amount of time in a department, they may have learned the task but must stay in that department until it is time to move to the next stage.

**Feedback.**   When the trainer signs off on a specific competency, the trainee is given specific, timely, and positive feedback on his or her performance. This type of feedback has been shown to aid in learning and performance.

---

 **quick bite 13.6**
**17 Traits of the Most Effective Trainer**

**Learning Objective:** Develop the skills necessary to become an effective trainer.

The following 17 traits have been compiled with the help of trainers from all disciplines and organizations in the restaurant industry. Although it is not only the skills that make the trainer, the following list is a great foundation for any trainer-to-be:

1. Organizational knowledge
2. Management roles and functions
3. Training knowledge
4. Program preparation skills
5. Technological and e-technology skills
6. Sensitivity to program feedback
7. People skills
8. Resilience
9. Commitment
10. Mental agility
11. Creativity
12. Self-development
13. Self-awareness
14. Sharing
15. Credibility
16. Humor
17. Self-confidence

*Source:* Rae, Leslie, *Trainer Assessment: A Guide to Measuring the Performance of Trainers and Facilitators* (Burlington, VT: Gower Publishing Company, 2002), p. 27–40.

**Discussion Question:** In your opinion, what are the three most important traits for a trainer to possess? Why?

---

**Self-Pacing and Sequencing.** Trainees learn at their own speed and construct the training in a way that makes sense to them. Because of this element of control, it is argued, they will learn faster and will remember better what they have learned.

**Challenge and Bypass.** Because employees learn at different speeds, a time-based training program is designed to accommodate slower learners. For employees who have had significant experience or who can learn faster than others, such a program can mean they will spend time on a task that they have already mastered. Learner-controlled instruction allows them to move quickly through tasks they already have experience with and move on to competencies that are new to them. They are thus less likely to be bored by "old" material.

## Individual Training

The most commonly used individual training method is on-the-job training. It is fast, flexible, and inexpensive. Four steps are involved: preparation, presentation, practice, and feedback.

**Preparation.** Preparation includes the development of what is to be taught, how it is to be taught, why it is important, and the standards to be achieved. The job is broken down into its parts, which are then listed in terms of importance. For example, the job of a restaurant cashier might be described as follows:[21]

> Ensures that each guest leaves the restaurant satisfied by being friendly, fast, accurate, and helping other employees if needed, while maintaining a pleasant appearance and a clean work area. Accountable for all cash, guest checks, charges, and related reports for the restaurant during the shift.

The elements or parts of the job are as follows:

- Friendliness
- Appearance
- Teamwork
- Opening duties
- Operating duties
- Closing duties
- Reports
- Equipment

Each element can form the basis for a separate training module.

**Presentation.** A good presentation consists of several steps. The trainee will probably be experiencing some stress as a result of having to learn something new. It would, therefore, be a good idea to say or do something to put the employee at ease. The trainer should introduce himself or herself, giving enough background to justify why he or she is qualified to be doing the training. The trainer would then explain what is to be taught and why it is important. These two items are intended to motivate the employee to learn what is to be taught. Next, the trainer should find out what the trainee already knows about the task at hand in order to communicate at a level appropriate to the trainee.

The entire job would then be explained with a description of how and where it fits into the entire operation. This gives a context for the task to be covered. When people know how their job relates to the overall organization, they are more likely to understand its importance. The job is then demonstrated at a normal pace, then more slowly. As this is happening, the trainer explains what is being done and why it is important that the job be done in this way. The trainee can be asked specific questions as this is going on, to determine whether he or she understands.

**Practice.**   When the trainee practices the new task, the objective is to concentrate first on accuracy, then on speed of completion. The trainee performs the job, explaining what he or she is doing and why each step is important. By having the trainee articulate the steps in this way, the trainer tests that the employee does, in fact, understand the importance of what is being done.

**Feedback.**   Feedback is necessary to ensure that the employee continues to perform the job the way it should be done. People perform better and learn more effectively with positive feedback than with negative feedback. A word of praise works better than a rebuke. When an employee does something wrong, it is important to focus on what went wrong rather than on who did something amiss.

Some trainers will work with an employee to perform a task; then once the employee has demonstrated the job correctly the trainers will move on to work with other employees. When feedback goes from continuous reinforcement to no reinforcement, it is likely that the behavior will stop or that performance will go down. To maintain that performance, periodic reinforcement is required. This will probably be the task of the employee's supervisor. The same principles regarding the importance of positive feedback hold when supervising the employee as when training that person.

## Group Training

Group training is particularly effective for teaching human relations skills. It can be used when a number of employees are to be trained in the same task. A common mistake that trainers make when dealing with groups is to rely on a lecture format. Because this is the format they have been exposed to themselves as students, they feel most comfortable with it as trainers. However, especially when working with adults, participation increases motivation and learning.

A variety of participatory techniques are available to increase both trainee motivation and learning. Brainstorming gets trainees involved in coming up with new ideas or in providing solutions to problems. In small groups, participants attempt to come up with as many ideas as possible. Initially, there is no criticism of ideas. Once a list of ideas has been developed, the ideas are explored as to their feasibility.

Case studies are situations taken from real life. The situation is explained in writing and, through discussion, trainees identify the problem and attempt to come up with a solution. The actual solution is less important than the process the group went through in arriving at it.

In a role-play situation, trainees are given background information and asked to act out a situation. Role-play it may involve such things as responding to a situation where the customer complains about the food.

A simulation is the practice of skills in the work area itself. Prior to the official opening of a new restaurant, the staff may have a preopening in which an invited list of customers eat at the restaurant as a trial run to the actual opening.

---

### quick fact

Nine out of 10 salaried employees at tableservice restaurants started as hourly employees.

*Source:* National Restaurant Association, "Restaurant Industry Facts," *http://www.restaurant.org/research/ind_glance.cfm#employment*, November 7, 2005.

---

## CAREER DEVELOPMENT

### Employee Development

One answer to the problem of employee turnover is a career development program. Such a program involves assisting employees at all levels to determine their career goals and working with them to achieve such goals. To the extent that employees leave an operation because of the lack of opportunities to advance, such a program should help provide opportunities for growth.

A career development program should apply to all employees, not just managers. Too many managers assume that someone who washes dishes for a living has no desire to anything but that for the rest of his or her life. There are people who are good at what they do and have no desire to be moved or promoted to another job. They should not be looked down on but, as long as they are solid contributors to the operation, should be rewarded and appreciated. For those employees at all levels who do want something better or different for themselves, a career development program will help them get there. At the same time, such a program can serve as a motivational device for existing employees that can help increase productivity while reducing turnover.

A career development program consists of[22]

- Identifying the objectives and needs of the business
- Identifying the personal goals and needs of employees
- Developing an action plan to match the employees' needs with those of the organization
- Providing feedback and guidance to carry out the plan

## Management Development

It is important to offer training for management as well as for employees. A recent study points out the need for leadership development at all levels of management in foodservice.[23] Respondents indicate that most leadership development at middle management and above occurs on the job or from general life experiences. Only 14 percent of middle managers received the competencies they needed to advance in their careers from educational and personal training classes. The respondents identify six core competencies as follows:

- Strategic planning
- Interpersonal communication
- Decision making
- Team building
- Financial management
- Creative thinking

These core competencies are supplemented by others for managers at different levels. The top three competencies for various levels of management are as follows:[24]

| Top Management | Senior Management | Middle—Corporate | Middle—Field |
| --- | --- | --- | --- |
| Decision making | Decision making | Creative thinking | Financial management |
| Creative thinking | Financial management | Mentoring others | Decision making |
| Interpersonal communication | Team building | Public speaking | Developing and training others |

A typical management training program revolves around three things:[25]

- Training existing managers
- Promoting people from within
- Developing programs for management trainees

**Succession Planning.**   Many companies use succession planning to identify what type of training is required. Succession planning is "a formal process in which plans are developed to ensure that replacements can be readily identified to fill key positions in your organization."[26]

Such a program involves tracking the key positions with the operation and identifying the feeder jobs for each of these key positions. A feeder job is one from which the jobholder can be promoted into a key position. The short- and long-term staffing needs of the operation are then determined to identify how many managers are needed and when they will be required. Those people in the operation who are potentially capable of being promoted into management are then identified and, for each, an estimate of promotion potential is made. For

**People First, Employees Second**

**Learning Objective:** List the elements of a strong employee and management development program.

Buffets, Inc. has employed a style of training that emphasizes mentoring rather than training. This model encompasses the "People First, Employees Second" philosophy which is the company's creed. Buffet welcomes new employees as a part of a "family environment." This approach is one of the first steps in "People First"; new employees get the message that they as individuals are just as important as established employees.

Training is seen as mentoring right off the bat. For example, rather than running new team members through tedious orientations and setting high and intimidating expectations, Buffet welcomes new team members into the Buffet family. To ensure this, trainers are selected on their ability to be friends and mentors first, thus reinforcing the family concept.

The "People First, Employees Second" philosophy includes programs to retain experienced and successful managers. When Country Buffet and Old Country Buffet merged with HomeTown Buffet in 1996, restaurant turnover reached an all-time high. Manager turnover alone was 36 percent, and turnover as a whole was negatively impacting sales, recruitment, hiring and training costs. Consequently, the new Buffet, Inc. worked on developing programs that would help retain employees and managers, with the focus on the General Manager.

Buffets, Inc. ultimately created eight programs that would help with employee and manager retention: The Founder's Club, The "PRIDE" Program ("Proprietor Retention Incentive Dedication Earnings"), The International Promote Program, The "Managers Bill of Rights," The Senior General Manager Program, The Tenured Manager Program, "Standard Ovation" Recognition, and People First Employee Opinion Survey. Since these programs began, in 1997, there have been considerable improvements in employee management and development. For example, the management turnover has decreased from 38.0 percent to 24.4 percent over a 4-year period. Additionally, the hourly turnover rate has gone from 174.3 percent to 150.7 percent.

Buffets, Inc. continues to improve with the help of their new employee retention programs and their "mentor" approach to training. Their philosophy is simple: "show people a clear path, teach them how to get to the next level, and reward them every step of the way."

*Source:* Winning Workforce Ideas, Employer of Choice Awards, "People First, Employees Second," p. 10–13.

**Discussion Question:** In what ways does Buffets, Inc. create a "family environment" and how has that helped with employee and manager retention?

each person an evaluation is made as to whether or not he or she is promotable and, if so, when. For each key position two or three alternative successors are identified in case of turnover.

For each employee identified as promotable, a list of needed skills is drawn up and a timetable established for the development of these skills. This list, updated every six months, forms the basis for the type and amount of management training to be done. The list also lets management know the extent to which additional management will have to be found outside the organization.

At the same time that the company is evaluating its managers, each individual should be developing a personalized career development plan. The questions to ask are these:[27]

- What are my career goals?
- What are my options for career development?
- What skills and abilities do I need to acquire?
- What plans do I need to make to move toward my goals?
- What will be my implementation steps and timetable?

**Methods.** The methods used to develop managers can be done on or off the job. It is imperative that whichever methods are chosen, they be planned rather than left to chance. The oldest method of development is that of coaching. *Coaching* refers to the ongoing, daily instruction provided by a superior. Some people are better than others at developing subordinates. Managers need training in how to develop their staff effectively. Job rotation is another common tool for developing management talent. This involves moving an employee into different positions in a planned manner to allow the trainee to develop additional skills and knowledge. Larger organizations have the option of giving managers committee assignments or positions as "assistant to," to encourage their development.

---

 **quick bite 13.8**
**Road to the Top: Ted Balestreri**

"I was a very wealthy kid: My father left me in America, and he left me with character. I figure that's about as rich as you want to get."

The above statement, made by Ted Balestreri, encompasses his philosophy on life. Ted Balestreri, chairman and chief executive of The Sardine Factory, Foursome Development, Restaurants Central, and Pacific Hospitality Inc., is a native of Brooklyn. Despite beginning in life as a penniless teenager relocated to the West Coast, Balestreri can put a positive spin on any situation. It has been said that had he been a New York Yankee, Balestreri would be in the same category as Joe DiMaggio or Lou Gehrig. What is the key to his success? Bringing others up the ladder with him; he did it all, not by excluding others, but by including them.

---

Balestreri started his business with a single restaurant and has expanded his assets to include ownership of most of the real estate in Monterey, California, as well as a multi-unit Wendy's franchise.

He first entered the restaurant industry when he was a teenager. His family had just moved from Brooklyn to the West Coast. His family was in desperate need for money, so Balestreri had to work three jobs. To help his struggling family, this young New Yorker needed a business where he could work days and nights, and that business was the restaurant business. Balestreri washed dishes in the morning, bused tables in the afternoon, and worked as a host or waiter at night.

Balestreri continued working in restaurants through high school and college. While taking an economics class, he met his best friend and lifelong business partner, Bert Cutino. According to Cutino, they were the guys in the back row who were always talking. Both were restaurant managers by the time they graduated and after short stints in the military, they decided to rent a building in which they could develop their restaurant.

With the financial help of Balestreri's dentist, Dr. Caselli, the two friends were able to rent and refurbish an old, run-down building. This old, run-down building would soon become the first Sardine Factory. They painted the walls gray, used coffee cans painted black for light fixtures, and borrowed ice plant, a succulent land cover, from the highway for landscaping. They couldn't even afford a walk-in refrigerator. Chef Cutino used a refrigerator trunk rented from a dairy farmer. The Sardine Factory was finally ready for opening on October 2, 1968. It started off serving value conscious Italian food and slowly moved towards more upscale meals. The restaurant was soon known for its slightly avant-garde ambience.

Once established, Balestreri and Cutino were presented with the option of buying the building. They jumped on the opportunity. The two then started buying up the whole neighborhood. Before long, Balestreri and Cutino owned five dinner houses and were soon making a great deal of money in the real-estate business.

*Source: National Restaurant News,* Pioneer of the Year 2003, "Ted Balestreri," September 22, 2003. pp. 51–52.

**Discussion Question:** Balestreri believed that character was all the wealth a man needed. How did this philosophy on life help him get where he is today?

## ENDNOTES

1. Arthur W. Sherman, George W. Bohlande, and Herbert J. Chudren, *Managing Human Resources,* 8th ed. (Cincinnati, OH: South-Western Publishing Co., 1988), p. 194.
2. Ibid., p. 194.
3. Ibid., p. 197.

4.  Vincent H. Eade, *Human Resource Management in the Hospitality Industry* (Scottsdale, AZ: Gorsuch Scarisbrick, Publishers, 1993), p. 180.
5.  Sharon Fullen, *Controlling Restaurant & Food Service Labor Costs* (Ocala, FL: Atlantic Publishing Group, Inc., 2003), p. 86.
6.  David Wheelhouse, *Managing for Human Resources in the Hospitality Industry* (East Lansing, MI: Educational Institute of the American Hotel and Motel Association, 1989), pp. 146–147.
7.  Sherman et al., *Managing Human Resources*, p. 199.
8.  Karen Eich Drummond, *Human Resource Management for the Hospitality Industry* (New York: Van Nostrand Reinhold, 1990), pp. 68–78.
9.  Sherman et al., *Managing Human Resources*, p. 201.
10. Lewis C. Forrest, *Training for the Hospitality Industry* (East Lansing, MI: Educational Institute of the American Hotel and Motel Association, 1983), p. 40.
11. Ibid., p. 41.
12. Ibid., pp. 45–46.
13. Ibid., p. 45.
14. Wheelhouse, *Managing for Human Resources in the Hospitality Industry*, pp. 148–149.
15. Mary L. Tanke, *Human Resources Management for the Hospitality Industry* (Albany, NY: Delmar Publishers, 1990), p. 75.
16. Wheelhouse, *Managing for Human Resources in the Hospitality Industry*, p. 154.
17. Bruce Grindy, "Hooking and Keeping Employees," *Restaurants USA*, October 1998, p. 26.
18. Wheelhouse, *Managing for Human Resources in the Hospitality Industry*, p. 154.
19. Forrest, *Training for the Hospitality Industry*, pp. 112–116.
20. Ibid., pp. 113–114.
21. Wheelhouse, *Managing for Human Resources in the Hospitality Industry*, p. 155.
22. Tanke, *Human Resources Management for the Hospitality Industry*, p. 198.
23. "The Next Generation of Leadership Research," Inserts in *Nation's Restaurant News*, vol. 37, no. 31, August 4, 2003, and vol. 37, no. 47, November 24, 2003.
24. Ibid.
25. Wheelhouse, *Managing for Human Resources in the Hospitality Industry*, p. 176.
26. Tanke, *Human Resources Management for the Hospitality Industry*, p. 80.
27. Ibid., p. 193.

## INTERNET RESOURCES

National Restaurant Association Educational Foundation    *http://www.nraef.org/*
Quality Restaurant Group                                 *http://www.qualityrestaurantgroup.com/*

# CHAPTER FOURTEEN

# MOTIVATING THE EMPLOYEE

"An epicure dining at Crew
Found a rather large mouse in his stew.
Said the waiter, 'Don't shout,
Or wave it about,
Or the rest will be wanting one too.' "

Anonymous

## learning objectives

*By the end of this chapter you should be able to*

1. Suggest what causes employees to behave the way they do.

2. Suggest how management can channel and maintain employee behavior through implementing various process theories of motivation.

3. Identify the six dimensions of organizational climate outlined in this chapter.

4. Describe how to implement successfully the following in a restaurant operation:
   - Management by objectives
   - Job redesign
   - Positive reinforcement
   - A climate of trust

5. Summarize the major theories of leadership, indicating how they can be applied to a restaurant situation.

# EMPLOYEE MOTIVATION

## The Role of Managers

Managers cannot motivate employees—motivation comes from within. However, managers are responsible for providing a climate within which employees are motivated to perform. A recent study indicates that the climate provided by management is not producing the desired employee behaviors. The year-long research study finds the following percentage of respondents who said they committed these acts:[1]

- 44 percent knowingly ignored rules regarding the handling of food.
- 37 percent made fun of their co-workers' or customers' accents.
- 31 percent knowingly served improperly or poorly prepared food.
- 26 percent touched a co-worker in a sexually inappropriate way.
- 24 percent took illegal drugs just before coming to work.
- 22 percent called a co-worker an insulting name.
- 21 percent observed co-workers stealing cash but did not report it to management.
- 13 percent sabotaged the work of other employees.
- 12 percent intentionally contaminated food prepared and/or served to a customer.
- 10 percent knowingly served a customer contaminated or spoiled food.

Many managers do not agree that it is their responsibility to motivate employees. They believe that it is the responsibility of employees to "bend" to the needs of the company. If they do not, they are fired. From a purely economic viewpoint this approach is bad management. Treating employees in an arbitrary, inflexible manner will guarantee that the operation will suffer high turnover as increasing numbers of employees decide that they cannot put up with such treatment. Even if they stay, there is a good chance that productivity will go down and absenteeism and pilfering will rise as employees seek to "get even" with the company for perceived slights.

When an employee joins a company there is an implied, and sometimes an explicit, contract. The employee puts forth time and effort in order to receive pay; the company gives the security of a job in return for that effort.

Although every person is an individual, the operation cannot adapt to each employee. There must be a middle ground wherein management is flexible to

Barbeque is an American classic that appeals to young and old alike. Smokey Bones BBQ Sports Bar, launched in 1999, has already established 38 units in 14 states. The restaurant looks like a hunting lodge, complete with a rustic wood interior, the smell of barbeque sauce, and televisions tuned to sports programs. Darden Restaurants Inc., operator of Smokey Bones BBQ, also manages 672 Red Lobsters, 516 Olive Gardens, and 32 Bahama Breezes. With more than 1,254 restaurants, Darden is one of the largest casual-dinnerhouse operators in the country.

Darden plans to have over 250 Smokey Bones restaurants by the year 2010. Smokey Bones appeals to customers with a combination of good food and a comfortable lodge-like setting. A Smokey Bones experience includes a quick stop for a drink and appetizers, a gathering of friends for the big game, or a nice, relaxed family meal. This is possible because Darden has installed tableside volume controls that allow customers to tune into or out of any of the various televisions in the restaurant.

Darden's success comes from three things. First, they have the right training systems in place to deliver great food and hospitality. Second, they stay connected to consumers by continuing to ask "how can we get better?" Third, they continue to improve the menu and improvise.

Ribs are a specialty at Smokey Bones. However, they also have seafood, chicken, steaks, salads, fish & chips, sandwiches, burgers, pulled pork and appetizers. Their signature drinks include Bacardi Lemonade, Frozen Mountain Margarita, Captain Morgan Frozen and Twisted Timber.

Chip Brown, Smokey Bones' marketing director, believes that having the right people in the front of the house is essential to promoting the brand from within. He says "we primarily just try to open the restaurants in a quality way and let the food and service speak for itself. The intensive training process starts with hiring the right kind of people. It's mostly about the people, not so much about the buildings and the bricks and mortar. We hire friendly [people], train them, and then remind them that they're friendly."

Source: *Nation's Restaurant News*, "Smokey Bones BBQ," May 12, 2003. pp. 60, 64.

**Discussion Question:** How does Smokey Bones BBQ accommodate all types of customers?

employee needs while realizing that the objective is to run a profitable operation. At the same time, employees must sacrifice some of their independence and the satisfaction of their individual needs to the good of the company. An understanding of what motivates employees is critical to getting employees to perform in a productive manner.

We begin this chapter with a survey of the major theories of motivation and propose an inclusive model of organizational climate that builds on these theories. Utilizing this model, managers can implement a comprehensive approach to developing and maintaining a motivated team of employees.

## Theories of Motivation

A complete discussion of motivation must cover the following:

- What causes behavior?
- What channels behavior?
- How is behavior sustained?

**Content Theories.**  Content theories are concerned with what causes behavior. Four such theories that have gained acceptance to one degree or another are Maslow's need-hierarchy theory, Alderfer's ERG theory, Murray's acquired needs theory, and Herzberg's two-factor theory.

---

### quick bite 14.2
**Twenty-somethings: Managing the New Breed of Employee**

**Learning Objective:** Suggest what causes employees to behave the way they do.

Generation X has come to be known by many different names: twenty-somethings, baby-busters, post-boomers, the 13th generation, slackers, etc. This generation typically includes anyone born between 1965 and 1985. Employees in this generation have been stereotyped as employees who don't show up for work or are consistently late. Is it fair that Generation X is labeled so harshly?

Managing employees effectively begins with understanding their values, expectations, and goals. This requires foodservice operators and managers to set aside their systems of values and expectations and opening their minds to the values and expectations of their employees, for example, the Gen-Xers. Several years ago Claire Raines, an organizational consultant and co-author of *Twenty-something: Managing and Motivating Today's New Work Force,* conducted various focus groups in five cities around the United States with employees in the twenty-something category. The following are the results from these focus groups, called "X Requisites:"

1. Appreciate us. Reward-and-recognition programs are great, but if they aren't supported by management's sincere attitude or appreciation, they are meaningless.
2. Be flexible. Effective managers administer policies and schedules with regard for how they affect each individual.

---

*Maslow.* Psychologist Abraham H. Maslow focused on a person's basic needs and the relative order of their importance. He identified a hierarchy of needs as follows:

1. **Physical:** The need for food and shelter.
2. **Safety and belonging:** The need for protection from people and/or the environment. This person would be cautious, avoiding risk and planning for the future.
3. **Social:** The need for love and belonging. This person will have high social needs, like people, wish to be a team player, and want to be accepted.
4. **Esteem:** The need for self-respect and the respect of others. People seeking the respect of others would seek attention and thrive on publicity and praise. They would be aware of status symbols and desire material things.
5. **Self-actualization:** The need to meet one's potential. Such people are interested in making creative contributions and want a challenging work environment.

3. Create a team. Many twenty-something employees did not grow up in close-knit families, so they seek to find family on the job—a group of people who support and encourage each other.
4. Develop us. Baby-busters see themselves as marketable commodities. Effective managers make sure that they are gaining new knowledge and skills to make them more marketable.
5. Involve us. People who tend to do a better job when they feel they have ownership, and when they feel their opinions and ideas are values. This is especially true of twenty-something employees.
6. Lighten up. Twenty-something employees want to have a good time. Fun on the job is a priority for them.
7. Walk your talk. Generation-X employees are keen observers, and they watch to see if managers practice what they preach.

*Source: National Restaurant News,* "Twenty-Somethings: Managing a New Breed of Employee," September 1996.

**Discussion Questions:** Why is it important for managers to understand their employees' values, expectations, and goals? Do you think it would be more appropriate for employees to mold to what their manager is looking for? Why or why not?

Maslow's hierarchy of needs suggests that lower-level needs must be satisfied for the most part before a person can be concerned with the satisfaction of higher-level needs. A corollary of this is that once a need has primarily been satisfied, it ceases to motivate the person.

It is difficult to identify where money comes into this picture. For some, money is necessary to satisfy basic needs and is regarded as crucial to meeting physiological needs. For others, money is seen as a status symbol. The problem for those using this theory to identify needs is that it may be thought that money no longer motivates a person making a considerable salary, as his or her basic needs have been taken care of. For the person who sees money as a way of keeping score with the world, money will continue to be important as a motivator long after basic needs are taken care of.

Managers should attempt to determine what needs employees are seeking to satisfy and create an environment that gives employees opportunities to satisfy them. Consider the restaurant that hired Sarah as a bookkeeper. Sarah had been a stay-at-home wife for 25 years, raising the children. Bored at home, she decided to get a part-time job. After only a few weeks at work, management noticed that Sarah was forever venturing out of the office to visit with the servers and cooks. The result was that the work of the other employees was interrupted while Sarah's job duties were left unfinished. Management could have fired Sarah. Instead, a thoughtful discussion with her indicated that the main reason she took the job was the desire to interact with others. Her husband was doing well financially, so money was not a prime factor in her decision to reenter the job market. Management gave Sarah a job as hostess and now has a personable greeter, a satisfied employee, and customers who are delighted with the service they receive.

*Alderfer.*    Alderfer proposed three need categories: existence, relatedness, and growth. The first—existence—is similar to Maslow's physiological and safety needs; the second—relatedness—involves relationships with others and is similar to the safety, social, and ego-esteem needs of Maslow; and the third—growth—is similar to self-esteem and self-actualization. According to Alderfer, more than one need can operate at a time. He also proposes that in addition to a hierarchy effect, people who are frustrated in their ability to satisfy a higher-level need may regress to become more concerned with the fulfillment of lower-level needs.

*Murray.*    Murray suggests that a large part of performance can be explained by a person's need for achievement. People with a high achievement motivation prefer moderate risk, are persistent, take personal responsibility for their performance, need feedback on how well they are performing, and are innovative.[2] Conversely, people with low achievement needs take high risks.

David McClelland, a student of Murray's, sees motivation as a function of three needs: the need for affiliation, the need for power, and the need for achievement. Those with a high need for power want to control, dominate, or otherwise have an impact on others. Power can be individualized power or socialized power. In the former situation, people want power for its own sake. They desire the emotional feelings they get from applying power. Socialized power comes from using one's influence to attain objectives that will benefit everyone. Obviously, the latter behavior makes for a more effective manager.

These motives are developed through learning. In other words, people learn to behave in ways rewarding to them.

***Herzberg.*** Herzberg identified two aspects affecting the work of an employee: hygiene factors and motivators. The absence of hygiene factors will result in employee dissatisfaction, but their presence will not result in a motivated employee. The most important hygiene factors are[3]

- Company policy and administration
- Supervision
- Salary
- Interpersonal relations
- Working conditions

Motivators are the factors whose presence will act to motivate the employee. The most important motivators are[4]

- Achievement
- Recognition
- The work itself
- Responsibility
- Advancement

Herzberg believes that the key to motivating employees is to enrich jobs such that they provide employees with work that is interesting and meaningful. The content theories described above would indicate that[5]

1. Individuals prioritize needs and act in an attempt to satisfy them.
2. More than one level of need may be operable at any one time. If higher-level needs cannot be satisfied, the satisfaction of lower-level needs takes on greater importance.
3. Much of an employee's performance can be explained by the need for achievement.
4. Certain factors—motivators—motivate people; others—hygiene factors—do not. However, the absence of the latter will result in dissatisfaction.

**Process Theories.** Process theories are concerned with what channels behavior and how that behavior can be sustained. Four theories will be discussed: equity theory, expectancy theory, reinforcement theory, and goal-setting theory.

***Equity Theory.*** Equity theory considers that people look at what they put into the job relative to what they get out of the job and compare both to others. If they perceive that there is an inequitable situation, they will work to reduce the inequity. The greater the inequity, the stronger will be the motivation to reduce it.

There are a number of ways to reduce a perceived inequity. People can[6]

- Reduce what they put into the job.
- Seek more rewards for their effort.
- Delude themselves into believing that the situation is equitable.
- Leave or be absent from a job.
- Get others to lower their efforts.
- Change the basis of comparison.

People will choose the course of action easiest for them.

The key points in this theory are that people make comparisons; that what they perceive or believe (rather than what may actually exist) is what is important; and that their reaction can be one of several.

***Expectancy Theory.*** According to expectancy theory, employees are motivated to produce to the extent that they believe they will receive a reward important to them. They will put forward more effort, leading to greater productivity, for which they will receive a reward important to them. The effort is diminished if

1. The reward is unimportant to them.
2. They do not believe that they will get the reward.

This means that the manager needs to know what is important to the employee and must also convince the employee that he or she can be trusted to provide the reward.

Tying expectancy theory into Herzberg, hygiene factors such as working conditions are seen as less motivating than such things as a promotion. We can speculate, therefore, on the relative impact on performance of employees of promising to improve working conditions compared to the promise of a promotion. The latter, it is suggested, would act as a greater motivating factor.

Expectancy theory can also be examined relative to Maslow. Effort on the part of the employee leads to the employee performing if he or she believes that there will be a reward important to the employee, a reward that will, to some extent, satisfy needs important to the employee.

***Reinforcement Theory.*** Reinforcement theory is based on the idea that performance improves when it is rewarded or reinforced. This idea of modifying people's behavior says that people behave in ways that are rewarding to them. By rewarding existing behavior, that behavior will be encouraged and repeated.

Something in the environment (antecedent) stimulates behavior for which there is a consequence. Behavior can be "managed" by managing antecedents and providing the appropriate consequences. Managing antecedents can be done by removing barriers that hinder the completion of a good job or by providing aids that help employees do a good job.[7] Barriers might be such things as training deficiencies or confusing policies or rules. Factors that help get the job done might include clear plans and instructions and realistic deadlines.

There are four types of consequences to a particular behavior: positive reinforcement, negative reinforcement, extinction (no consequences), and punishment. Positive reinforcement—catching somebody doing something good and rewarding him or her—is generally accepted as the most potent consequence in shaping future behavior.

***Goal-Setting Theory.*** Goal-setting theory states that setting or accepting more difficult goals results in higher performance than the setting or acceptance of easier goals. Employees will set goals for themselves if management does not. Therefore, management should get involved in raising employee goals.

---

## quick bite 14.3
### The Art of Questioning

**Learning Objective:** Suggest how management can channel and maintain employee behavior through implementing various process theories of motivation.

Socrates was an educational reformer and one of the greatest philosophers of his time. He was the master of questioning. He used questions to educate his followers rather than teaching through lecturing or preaching. Sid Feltenstein, the president and CEO of Yorkshire Global Restaurants, believes that many restaurant managers should take note of Socrates' method of leadership and consider applying it within their establishments.

For example, many managers in the food service industry merely tell employees what they want, i.e. "I want these counters spotless." The downside to simply telling employees what you want is that there is no guarantee that they all got or understood the orders. However, by offering employees a question, group interaction is promoted. "Why do you think it is important to keep these counters spotless?" By asking a question, managers will most likely receive direct responses from their employees, ensuring that they understand what needs to be done.

The secret to mastering the art of questioning is to understand the three levels of questions and how to educate employees in a more interactive manner using those questions. The first level of questioning is a question that requires a "yes" or "no" response. A "level two" question is looking for a specific answer. Lastly, a "level three" question asks employees to offer an opinion. Using the Socratic Method, managers are able to teach, train, present, and inspire employees.

*Source:* Winning Workforce Ideas, Employer of Choice Awards, "The Art of Questioning as a Managerial Strategy," pp. 36–37.

**Discussion Question:** How is questioning employees a better form of teaching/managing rather than lecturing? Please provide an example that you've experienced.

The foregoing theories would indicate that[8]

1. People compare what they put into their work and what they get out of it to the inputs and outputs of others.
2. People will expend effort to the extent that they believe they will receive rewards important to them.
3. Behavior can be shaped by a system of rewarding desired behavior and punishing undesirable behavior. Positive reinforcement of desirable behavior is a stronger motivator than is punishment of undesirable behavior.
4. Having a specific goal increases performance; having a difficult (yet attainable) goal results in higher performance than will having an easy goal.

---

**quick tip**

Creating a comfortable break room for your employees is a low-cost perk. Imagine how appreciative your employees will be if they can relax in a lounge chair, listen to some music, catch a bit of TV, or even surf the Internet while on break. You can cost-effectively build morale and create a great employee break area.

*Source:* National Restaurant Association Smart Brief, September 1, 2005.

---

## ORGANIZATIONAL CLIMATE[9]

Bearing in mind the various theories as to what motivates employees, the manager's role is to provide the climate within the organization that will motivate employees to perform. The organizational climate is how it "feels" to work there. The organizational climate

1. Consists of a set of properties of the work environment
2. Is based on the perceptions of the people who work there
3. Influences the motivation and behavior of employees, depending on how they perceive the climate[10]

These points indicate that it is possible to describe and measure the climate within an organization in terms of a number of dimensions. In this chapter we suggest six dimensions of climate. The point is also made that it is the perception of the employees, not management, that is important in defining climate. The employees' perception of what exists within a company may be the same as or different from what is actually occurring in the company. However, it is the employees' perception, right or wrong, that is important. Finally, it is the employees' perception that will influence to what extent employees are motivated as well as how they behave. If, for example, an employee perceives that manage-

**Three Steps to Increased Productivity Levels**

**Learning Objective:** Identify the six dimensions of organizational climate outlined below.

Unfortunately, the restaurant industry is currently being hit with an increase in productivity crimes among hourly employees. These counter-productive employee behaviors range from food violations to product theft and discrimination. This behavior could be attributed to several things, two of which may be insufficient training or errors in the hiring process.

Good restaurant leadership and employee training go a long way to resolving these issues. However, there are additional steps that can be taken to help reduce losses resulting from counter-productive employees:

1. Set a standard for productivity. Although it is not possible to directly measure the exact number of productivity crimes within a restaurant, it is possible to indirectly estimate the extent of the problem. Employee surveys that specifically target productivity are a great way to pinpoint problem areas. The surveys also provide ongoing feedback that can be very effective in rehabilitating underperforming restaurants.

2. Develop an effective hourly employee selection process. By not hiring employees that could potentially be counter-productive, many of the productivity crimes in restaurants will be eliminated. This is best accomplished through a professionally designed interview and testing process.

3. Establish a restaurant culture of productivity. Not only will productivity crimes decrease greatly, but reliability, teamwork, and honesty will also be encouraged with the advent of a culture of productivity.

*Source:* National Restaurant News, "Stopping Crime Does Pay: Correcting Counter-Productive Behaviors Books Profits—Opinion," January 5, 2004.

**Discussion Question:** List three recommendations you would make to a restaurant struggling with counterproductive employees.

ment does not set high service standards (even if the standards actually are high), he or she may decide, "If management does not care about the service, why should I?"

## Dimensions of Climate

Research has resulted in descriptions of climate in anywhere from four to seven dimensions. One well-respected model is that of the Forum Corporation.[11] In this model the climate of an organization is described in terms of six dimensions: three dealing with performance, three with development. The performance dimensions are clarity, commitment, and standards. The development dimensions are responsibility, recognition, and teamwork.

**Performance Dimensions.**   The first performance dimension is that of clarity. Clarity refers to how well employees understand the goals and policies of a company, in addition to how clear they are about their own jobs. It is the feeling that things are organized and run smoothly. For example, when employees are not given a written job description but are told to "watch Joe and learn from him," they are probably unclear about what they should be doing and would give the climate a low score on this dimension.

Many managers do not tell employees enough about the overall goals of the operation. They may feel that employees do not care. However, many employees do care. The result is that these employees do not know what is important to the company. If they do not know what is important, they will not know how to act in certain situations. For example, if a customer complains about the way a steak is cooked, what should the employee do? A restaurant that is concerned primarily with customer satisfaction would want the employee to correct the situation in favor of the customer. A company more concerned with cost control might have the employee try to convince the customer that the steak was prepared the way the customer ordered it.

Commitment, the second performance dimension, is the extent to which employees continually feel committed to achieving the goals of the company, the extent to which they accept goals as being realistic, the extent to which they are involved in the setting of such goals, and the extent to which their performance is continually evaluated against the goals of the organization. Companies have certain goals, such as profitability, return on investment, customer satisfaction, and cleanliness. These goals are achieved (or not achieved) by the efforts of the employees. The goals of the restaurant can be met only if employees are committed to achieving them. The greater the commitment, the more likely it is that the objective will be achieved.

The final performance dimension is standards. Standards measure the degree to which employees feel that management emphasizes the setting of high standards of performance and the extent to which they feel pressure to continually improve their performance. Employees may have higher standards than does the company. For example, in a restaurant that is very bottom-line oriented, concessions may be made in the areas of customer service, equipment maintenance, and employee training. Management may think that their standards—low costs and high profits—are high.

Employees may feel that company standards—cut back on service, maintenance, and training—are low. This influences how they feel toward the company and may well affect their performance. In *In Search of Excellence,* the authors compared the bottom lines of companies that emphasized financial objectives such as profit and return on investment with those that stressed nonfinancial objectives such as customer satisfaction or quality.[12] They found that the latter actually produced better bottom-line results than did the companies that stressed financial objectives. One explanation is that fewer layers of employees can relate to the financial objectives of the operation; they are unlikely to be personally involved in getting a return on investment or participating in a profit-sharing program. Many more layers of employees can relate to something like customer satisfaction: When they go out as customers, they know what it means to be satisfied.

**Development Dimensions.**   Responsibility, the first development dimension, is the feeling employees have that they are personally responsible for the work they do, that supervisors encourage them to take the initiative, and that they have a real sense of autonomy. The employee who has to check with the boss before he or she can do anything does not have this sense.

The second development dimension is recognition, the feeling that employees are rewarded for doing good work rather than receiving criticism and punishment as the predominant form of feedback. In a climate such as this, rewards and recognition outweigh threats and criticism, there is in place a promotion system that helps the best person get promoted, and the restaurant has a reward structure related to excellence of performance. When we hear, "The boss wants to see you," most of us immediately think, "What did I do wrong?" A major reason for this is the idea of management by exception. Under this accounting term, targets are set and, if met, the business is on target and no remedial action need be taken. If sales or cost projections are out of line, however, a red flag goes up to initiate corrective management action. Similarly, in dealing with employees, if employees are performing the way they should, the manager—with many demands on his or her time—will pass over that employee to concentrate on those who are not performing up to standard. The result is that the only time employees hear from management is when things go wrong. Under this type of climate, employees may actually perform negatively in order to receive some feedback, even if it is criticism. An absence of feedback is even more punishing than is punishment.

Teamwork is the third development dimension. This is the perception of belonging to an organization that is cohesive, one where people trust one another, where employees feel personal loyalty and the sense that they belong to the company. It is the feeling of us working together, rather than us versus them, whether that be management versus employees or kitchen versus dining room.

## DEVELOPING A PRODUCTIVE ORGANIZATIONAL CLIMATE

There is a problem within the operation when employees are dissatisfied enough with their jobs that the dissatisfaction affects their job performance. That dissatisfaction comes when there is a gap between what employees want in terms of clarity, commitment, standards, responsibility, recognition, and teamwork and what they perceive they are getting in terms of those dimensions.

Just what do employees want? According to the Industry of Choice report,[13] employees have 20 employment needs called "Deal Breakers"—job characteristics so important that employees would change jobs because of them. They are characterized as human resource practices and elements dealing with the organizational culture.

In order of importance, they are as follows:

**Human Resource Practices Deal Breakers**

1. A regular paycheck
2. A safe place to work
3. A clean place to work
4. Competitive wage or salary
5. The right equipment to do my job
6. Having enough employees to handle the workload
7. Health insurance
8. Working enough hours
9. Paid vacation
10. Worker's-compensation insurance

A recent study of nonsupervisory employees in casual dining restaurants indicates that just over half report low levels of satisfaction especially with pay and the opportunity for advancement.[14] Less than one-quarter report a high level of satisfaction.

**Organizational Culture Deal Breakers**

1. Having a boss who is fair (recognition)
2. Having a boss who doesn't embarrass or make fun of me (recognition)
3. Having a boss who treats others like he/she would like to be treated (recognition)
4. Feeling like the company treats employees fairly (recognition)
5. Feeling like I do my job well (commitment)
6. Having a boss with whom I get along (teamwork)
7. Being treated as an adult, even when I make a mistake (recognition)
8. Feeling like the company is well managed (standards)
9. Feeling like everybody does his/her part to keep things running smoothly (teamwork)

Categorizing these statements in terms of the dimensions of organizational climate, the overwhelming importance of the recognition factor stands out. The same study just referenced finds that other factors contributing to low levels of job satisfaction include inconsistent company policies and practices, managers who did not behave as they want employees to, and not being recognized for performance.

Another study focuses on the retention of general managers in quick-service, casual- and fine dining segments. Recognition and teamwork score big with general managers. The study finds that the key drivers of general managers' commitment to their companies are[15]

### Lifestyle

- Requests for time off or vacation are approved (recognition)
- Schedule enables a balance of work with other interests (recognition)
- Schedule does not require more than seven work days in a row (standards)

### Opportunity

- Supervisor helps to create an individual development plan (recognition)
- Supervisor spends time reviewing personal development plans (recognition)
- Supervisor provides useful feedback (teamwork)
- Personal goals align with opportunities that exist in the company (standards)

### Safe environment

- Restaurants are free from harassment and intimidation (teamwork)
- Hourly employees are respectful (teamwork)
- Managers are respectful (teamwork)

It is suggested that a four-pronged approach to dealing with employees will produce an organizational climate that will motivate employees to perform. The four guiding principles of this system are management by objectives, job re-design, positive reinforcement, and the development of trust. In the following sections we look at how these concepts relate to employee motivation.

---

quick bite 14.5
### A Day in the Life: Steven Johnston

Steven Johnston, general manager of Francesca's on Taylor, speaks Italian, has lived in Rome, drives a car with the license plate "MOLTO" ("much" in Italian), and even pays extra to his satellite cable company to receive Italian stations on his television. Johnston is obviously passionate about everything Italian.

His love and enthusiasm for Italy is evident both in the way with which he lives his life and the way with which he runs his restaurant. Francesca's on Taylor is a casual, Roman-style trattoria with 63 employees. When Johnston first began working at Francesca's on Taylor, he was a server but quickly moved himself through the ranks to No. 3 manager, No. 2 manager, and fi-nally to general manager.

One of Johnston's goals as GM is to keep production and labor costs down. He does this by cutting the front- and back-of-the-house teams early on slow nights and by reducing the hours that hosts work the door. This also keeps the managers on the floor and more involved in day-to-day operations.

*(continued)*

On this particular day, Johnston arrives to work during the middle of a busy lunch shift. He immediately consults with the lunch manager briefly and then jumps right into the action. The phone at the host stand is constantly ringing, so Johnston and the other managers take calls and work the host stand.

As the day continues, Johnston is consistently called away from working the front-of-the-house for anything from phone calls to administrative tasks. Once the lunch shift ends at 2 P.M., Johnston is able to grab a quick lunch for himself, carpaccio con arugula and a Caesar salad, before focusing on other administrative tasks.

At 4 P.M., Johnston is back in front for the dinner-shift servers' staff meeting, which typically lasts between five and 15 minutes. During this meeting, Johnston questions the staff on particular items on the menu and has the staff sample two of the new additions to the wine list.

The restaurant reopens at 5 P.M. and customers are welcomed warmly by Johnston and his staff. Johnston spends the remainder of the dinner hour "buzzing around," greeting diners, opening and serving bottles of wine, adjusting lights, changing music, and evaluating the overall scene. The steady stream of customers does not slow down until closing, which is usually between 9:30 and 10 P.M. Once the pace slows down a bit, the managers have dinner with the host.

After dinner with the host, Johnston goes to the office and begins the closing procedure. He takes care of the finances and jots a few notes in the daily log about anything notable or unusual that occurred that day. After checking over the restaurant and making sure everything is ready for the next day, Johnston heads to the bar across the street where he has a Ketel One martini before heading home for the night.

*Source: Nation's Restaurant News,* "A Day in the Life: Steven Johnston," April 21, 2003, pp. 68–69.

**Discussion Question:** Is Johnston's love for everything Italian beneficial or detrimental to his restaurant?

## Management by Objectives

Properly implemented, a philosophy of management by objectives should take care of situations where there is a discrepancy between what employees want relative to clarity, commitment, and/or standards and what they feel they get.

Management by objectives (MBO) can be defined as a managerial process in which managers and employees join in pursuit of specific, mutually agreed-upon goals of limited duration, through a plan of action that is monitored in appraisal sessions following mutually determined standards of performance.[16] The definition indicates that

1. Manager and subordinate agree on company and personal objectives for the subordinate.
2. The objectives are for a specified period of time, usually a year.
3. Objectives should be specific and measurable.
4. The subordinate prepares a plan of action that is reviewed by the manager.
5. At the end of the time period there is a formal appraisal process to indicate the extent to which the objectives have been met.

The evidence is mixed as to whether or not MBO works. Conceptually, the idea appears sound. Objectives should be set; manager and employee should agree as to what the important objectives are; manager and employee should agree on what is to be measured; the plan of action designed to achieve the objectives should be monitored; and there should be a session at the end of a specified period at which the employee's efforts are evaluated. Despite mixed results regarding the overall effectiveness of the concept, there is general agreement that the mere setting of goals improves performance. MBO also assumes that people will work toward goals to which they are committed. That commitment comes from being involved in the process of setting the objectives.

## Implementing the Concept

A program of management by objectives is most appropriate when there are problems with clarity, commitment, or standards. Clarity, it will be recalled, indicates how well employees understand the company's goals and policies and feel that things are organized and running smoothly.

Commitment indicates how strongly employees feel about achieving company goals. To what extent do they accept these goals, see them as realistic, get involved in setting them, and have their performance evaluated against them?

Standards indicate the emphasis that management puts on a high quality of performance. How much pressure exists to improve performance?

**Clarity.** How will a properly implemented program of MBO improve these three dimensions of climate? When management involves employees in the objective-setting process, it becomes clear to employees what objectives are important and the role that they, the employees, play relative to management in achieving these objectives.

In many cases, management has done a poor job of communicating the objectives that are important to a company. The manager or supervisor is the key link between the company and the employee. The objective of the company is to make a profit; the employee is seeking satisfaction from the job. How are these brought together? To maximize profit, the company must determine the key result areas that must be emphasized; what employee behavior is necessary in those key areas; whether employee performance matches the behavioral objectives set; and how to communicate to employees the results of their efforts, following up with praise, coaching, or remedial actions.

At the same time, the employee has several questions: What is really expected of me? How far am I expected to go? How good is good? How am I doing? It seems that the best performance and highest degree of goal attainment exist when there is agreement between manager and employee as to the content of the employee's job.

Objectives can be set in a variety of ways. The manager could come in one morning and say, "We've had a number of complaints about the quality of service in the restaurant. From now on, I want you to pick up the pace to improve the job that you do." Will employees know what is expected of them? On the other hand, the manager could hold an employee meeting, announce that there are problems with the level of service, and solicit ideas from the employees about what is causing the complaints and how they can be resolved. The point is that when management and employees discuss in specific terms what they should focus on, employees are clear about what they should do and what they can expect from management.

**Standards.**   But what about the level of standards that would be set when employees are involved? A fair amount of research indicates that participative rather than assigned goals leads to setting higher goals and, in turn, to higher performance. In particular, some studies indicate that participative goal setting has produced higher goals among minorities and the less educated.

If we assume that most employees want to do a good job, it is fair to say that when involved in the setting of objectives, most employees will set objectives they can be proud of. Thus, involving employees may very well produce standards higher than if management alone had set them.

**Commitment.**   Generally, employees resist making commitments to goals for two reasons: They do not feel that they are capable of reaching a goal because they lack confidence, ability, or knowledge, or because they see no personal benefit or gain in terms of money, promotion, personal pride, recognition, or whatever is important to them. This relates to the concept of expectancy theory.

Allowing employees to participate gives them a feeling of control over the process that they might not ordinarily have had in their lives. Steak & Ale has found that commitment is improved when[17]

- Decisions are made as far down the company ranks as possible.
- People are told the whys and hows of change.
- People are informed about how well the company is doing.
- Employee input is sought.
- Employees' individuality is respected.
- The focus of leadership styles is on helping people perform.

Although management has to take primary responsibility for determining the key results areas, employees can be involved in helping set objectives for these key areas.

Let us return to the earlier problem with service. A manager might ask, "What would a server do that would have you say 'That is excellent service'? What would a server do that would have you say 'That is terrible service'?" Employees could easily come up with a list of specifics. They might say that excellent service includes such things as

- Calling regular customers by name
- Seating customers right away
- Smiling at customers

Terrible service might include such things as

- Forgetting who ordered what
- Not making eye contact
- Being slow to bring the check

Management can go on to ask for input on how long it should be before customers' presence is recognized, before they should be given a menu, before they receive the drinks and the meals they ordered, which customers should be smiled at (everyone!), who should get eye contact, and so on. The result will be a series of objectives—employees should make eye contact with and smile at every customer, drinks should be delivered within 4 minutes of being ordered, and servers should always remember who ordered what—that employees are committed to achieve because they have been involved in setting them. Ideally, the standards set will be high (who is going to suggest low service standards?), and employees will be clear as to exactly what they are expected to do.

**Evaluating Employee Performance.** Once set, the objectives become the performance standards against which employee performance will be evaluated. Next, management will monitor employee performance.

In deciding which method to use, various criteria should be kept in mind. First, the method should validate the selection techniques used. If an effective selection method is in place, an appraisal method should show a significant percentage of employees meeting the performance objectives of the job. If this does not happen, it indicates that the selection method is faulty and/or the appraisal method is poor.

Another purpose of an appraisal method is to provide a rationale for making personnel decisions. It is important that the method selected be legally defensible. In this regard it should be based on an analysis of job requirements. Ratings should be documented and employees should have a formal appeal procedure.

A variety of methods are commonly used. Performance can be evaluated through direct indices or personal traits against set objectives or behaviorally anchored rating scales. Direct indices are objective and can be well documented. Servers may be evaluated on the basis of number of appetizers sold, for example. Direct indices, however, cannot take into account how well employees deal with customers and fellow employees.

In the personal trait method, characteristics are identified that are considered to be an important part of the job—such as creativity, dependability, and initiative—and the employee is evaluated on the extent to which he or she possesses them. A major problem here is the subjectivity involved. The extent to which a person is creative is open to a great deal of interpretation and argument.

Behaviorally anchored rating scales (BARS) are very compatible with a program of MBO. Whereas management by objectives focuses on the end result, BARS stresses the means to reach the end. In a BARS program the behavior necessary to reach the set objective is specified and the employee evaluated on the extent to which the behavior is displayed. Take, for example, the objective of selling more appetizers. Employees may be unable to sell a customer on buying an appetizer because they lack the training or because the customer is just not that hungry. Thus, through no fault of their own, the objective is not met. BARS identifies whether or not the employees do what they should, within their power, to get the sale.

The behaviors necessary for successful suggestive selling need to be identified. Success in selling probably comes from displaying a knowledge of items on the menu, suggesting items to every customer while maintaining eye contact and smiling, and describing those items using language that paints a desirable picture. This is another area in which employee involvement can be sought. Given a few minutes and some encouragement, employees can come up with several types of behavior that would encourage or discourage the sale of extra items. These behavioral objectives or anchors become the behavioral standards against which employees will be measured.

The ratings scale is typically displayed on a single page with various scale points, ranging from excellent to unacceptable. For each scale point there are behavioral statements representing the behavior that will probably lead to that level of performance. By observing the behavior, a manager can determine whether the employee behaved in a way that would lead to the objective being met.

BARS are useful for several reasons. They focus on behavior, what employees actually do in their jobs. They stress only those things over which an employee has control. Employees have no control over whether a customer buys dessert; they do have control over whether they ask the person to buy. Specifying behavior tells employees what to do to be given a rating of excellent; employees can then adjust their behavior accordingly. If they do not perform as desired, managers can also be specific about what the employees did wrong.

Although this method is time consuming and costly to develop, BARS makes it easier for managers to implement the last part of the MBO process, providing employee feedback.

**Providing Employee Feedback.** Employees need to know how they are doing. Many managers view the appraisal session with as much trepidation as does the employee. It may be especially difficult and uncomfortable if the subordinate is older or has more experience than the manager.

Most people enjoy giving good feedback (although they may not do enough of this). However, it can be difficult to tell employees they are not doing so well. One reason is that the manager has little or no objective data on which to base an evaluation. With BARS the manager can indicate the specific objective things that the employee did or did not do.

Having employees evaluate themselves prior to the appraisal interview with the manager provides a basis for discussion of any differences in the ratings. In some cases, managers may be surprised that employees are regarding their own shortcomings. It is also a good idea to give the employee the manager's basic evaluation one to three days prior to the appraisal interview. This allows the employee to get over the initial defensiveness that comes from a negative appraisal and to approach the interview more objectively.

It can be argued that a formal annual evaluation is of questionable value. Some research is available to show that in annual interviews, praise has no effect, while criticism brings on defensive reactions that in some cases result in decreased performance in the future. For this reason it is suggested that coaching be a day-to-day activity, not once a year.

The actual interview can take one of several formats. In the tell-and-sell interview, the objective is to communicate the manager's evaluation of the employee and persuade the employee to improve. The manager acts as judge. This approach is most likely to work when the employee respects the manager and feels that the manager is, in fact, qualified to pass judgment on his or her performance.

A second approach is the tell-and-listen interview. The task is to communicate the evaluation while giving the employee an opportunity to react to it. The manager still plays the role of judge but spends time listening to the employee and attempting to summarize the employee's reactions.

In the problem-solving interview, the approach is to stimulate growth and development within the employee rather than focus on past behavior. In the role of helper, the manager uses exploratory questions to identify new ideas from the employee on how performance can be improved. This does not mean that performance is not evaluated. It does mean that the focus is not on how the employee has failed, but rather on why the employee has failed and what has to change for her or him to succeed.

While the potential for change is great, the interview is unsuccessful if the employee is unable or unwilling to bring forward ideas. Additionally, the interview may not go the way the manager thought it would. The employee may identify changes the employer is unwilling or unable to consider.

## Job Redesign

When employees rate their job low on "responsibility," they are saying that they do not feel personally responsible for the work that they do, that supervisors do not encourage them to take the initiative, and that they do not have a real sense of autonomy. When the level of responsibility felt is less than the level desired, there is a problem. The answer lies in redesigning the "problem" jobs.

**Definition.** The classical approach to designing jobs held that productivity would be increased by task specialization. Additionally, by simplifying jobs, costs would be reduced because management could avoid paying for a difficult skill that was used only sparingly in the performance of a piece of work.

More recently, with a workforce that is increasingly educated and demanding, a perception has developed that low-skill, monotonous jobs will lead to boredom and job dissatisfaction, which, it is argued, will lead to lateness, absenteeism, and reduced performance on the job. Thus the move to job redesign is to accomplish two things: task efficiency and human satisfaction.

The objectives of a program of job redesign are to design jobs to help the company get work done in the most productive way possible while helping satisfy employee needs for a good-quality work life by fashioning jobs that are interesting, challenging, and provide opportunities for employee accomplishment.

Job redesign, then, assumes that employees want jobs that are interesting, challenging, and provide opportunities for employee accomplishment. Employees who cannot or will not handle such a job are likely to become confused and frustrated at being asked to think rather than just perform. When employees feel that they are being given insufficient responsibility, when they are in a job that they feel is monotonous, segmented, and routine, the job is a good candidate for redesign.

There are two common redesign strategies: job enlargement and job enrichment. Job enlargement—horizontal job loading—involves adding more tasks to the individual job to provide a greater variety of tasks for the person doing the job. Adding one meaningless task to another meaningless task is like adding zero to zero. The answer is still zero.

Job enrichment—vertical job loading—enriches the job by taking some of the tasks performed by management and adding them to the job of the employee. Traditionally, management has planned the work, the employee performs it, and management decides whether or not it has been performed correctly. Vertical job loading seeks to build into people's jobs some of the planning and/or control functions usually performed by managers.

A program of job enrichment fits in well with a number of the motivational theories noted previously. Herzberg's work indicates that 80 percent of job satisfaction comes from achievement, recognition, and responsibility. Job enrichment can be seen as an outgrowth of this model.

Behavioralists believe that reinforcement is the key to achieving performance. They view job design as a way of making the job more intrinsically rewarding, thus leading to higher levels of performance. Others feel that cues received from the environment are diffused over areas of the brain to arouse and activate the person. The greater the variety and stimulation in a job, the higher the state of arousal and the greater the motivation.

As noted previously, expectancy theory holds that a person will behave in a certain way if he or she believes that such behavior will result in an important outcome. This theory indicates that the worker perceives that an enriched job will lead to an intrinsic reward, so the employee is committed to the job and performs better if such rewards (challenge, responsibility, etc.) are regarded as important by the employee.

**Implementation.**   The manager's task is to organize the tasks involved in performing the job and the relationships among the person doing the job and the supervisor, any subordinates, and all fellow employees, to produce jobs that will be performed in an efficient manner while contributing to employee satisfaction.

**Employee Satisfaction.**   Behavioral scientists have found that three factors are critical to satisfaction and motivation on the job. Employees must feel that what they are doing is meaningful in terms of their own set of values, they must feel personally responsible for the outcome, and they must learn how well they are performing.

If, for example, a server feels that serving food is demeaning, the person is unlikely to feel good about the job, the company, or self. It is difficult for a person to give good service when feeling this way. In a kitchen organized such that several cooks are involved in preparing a particular dish, the fact that no one has total responsibility for the outcome diminishes the rewards of the job. Finally, consider the typical relationship between kitchen and dining room. Cooks prepare the meal and hand it over to servers to give to the customer. If they get no feedback from either the customer or management, their job satisfaction goes down. Brian Watts, managing director of the catering facilities at the Bank of England, found that the quality of food improved noticeably when he redesigned the cooks' job to serve customers the food they had cooked in the kitchen.

Throughout this section we have discussed employee job satisfaction and motivation. No links have been established between job satisfaction and productivity. However, there are links between job satisfaction and such things as absenteeism, lateness, and turnover. These things cost the operation money. It can be safely assumed that anything that will improve job satisfaction will reduce costs in terms of the items mentioned previously. Additionally, it is not hard to accept that employees who feel a level of dissatisfaction with their jobs will be unable to give truly hospitable service to customers.

**Basic Job Dimensions.** Every job has five basic dimensions that affect whether or not the job produces any of the three factors noted previously. How meaningful the job appears to the person doing it depends on three of these dimensions: the variety of skills used, task identity, and task significance. The more skills that are used in performing a job, the more meaningful the job appears to the employee performing it. The job seems more important because it requires more skills. It is also less boring because of the variety of skills required. Skill variety can be improved by such things as combining tasks and/or adding customer contact to a job that did not require such contact previously. For example, instead of one person washing dishes for an eight-hour shift, perhaps he or she could wash dishes for four hours and bus dishes for four hours. Enlarging the job adds variety while allowing the dishwasher to get to the front of the house and interact with the customers.

Such a technique also relates to task identity, the extent to which the job entails doing something from beginning to end. The more that employees are involved in a job from beginning to end, the more motivated they are about what they are doing. The busser who takes dirty dishes into the kitchen does not see what happens to them after they are left with the dishwasher. By doing both jobs, the flow of dishes from use to reuse is seen in its totality. This technique may also improve relations between two employees who bicker over who should do what in the interaction of their jobs. Bussers can make the dishwasher's job easier or more difficult, depending on how they arrange the dirty dishes as they are cleared from the tables. Dishwashers, on the other hand, do not see the hectic pace in the dining room. Seeing the job "from the other side" can produce more-understanding employees.

Task significance refers to the way a job affects others in a substantial way. The more employees feel that what they are doing affects the overall goal of the restaurant in a substantial way, the more satisfaction they get from what they are doing. Before Disney employees are allowed to sell popcorn or clean Main Street, they must undergo a training program that emphasizes what they do in relation to customer satisfaction. The street cleaners are very visible to visitors and therefore, they are asked numerous questions. They are told that an important part of their job is acting as a Disney "Ambassador" in addition to their crucial role of keeping the place clean. On the other hand, what message does a manager send to back-of-the-house employees when he or she spends little or no time behind the scenes, preferring to be out front with customers?

What is said, or communicated, nonverbally is also important. Saying such things as, "I don't know how you can stand this job for eight hours a day" lets the employee know exactly what is thought about the job. If the job is so bad, what does that say to the employee about the person doing the job? If employees are told, "You start as a hostess and if you work out and when we get an open-ing, we'll move you into a server's position," they learn that much is thought of the hostess position. It is better if they are told, "We have found that you will benefit from starting out in this position. You will have a chance to work with all of our servers and see how this operation works. You set the tone for the cus-tomer's experience because you make that first impression. When you get your own station, you'll have a better understanding of the way the restaurant oper-ates." Taking those who burnish the silverware up to see the banquet room when it is set up for a party allows them to see how the silverware adds to the look of the room.

The fourth basic characteristic of a job is the amount of autonomy involved in it. The more autonomy that workers experience, the more personal responsi-bility they will feel for the outcome of the work. Employees in highly au-tonomous jobs know that they are responsible for success or failure. The management trainee who has to consult the manual for the answer to problems is taught to use the book as a crutch for judgment and initiative. The employee is not responsible for customer satisfaction; the manual is. When employees are given the responsibility and the autonomy to solve customer problems, they feel more responsible. This concept of employee empowerment pushes decision making down to the lowest possible level. Suppose, for example, that a customer complains about the length of time that he or she waits for an order to come. Many restaurants have a policy by which employees refer all complaints to a manager who seeks to appease the customer. When employees are empowered, they have, within certain boundaries, the latitude to take care of the problem. Whoever receives a complaint has ownership of it until it is solved. The server may offer to discount the meal or give a complimentary dessert to appease the customer. The feeling of control over the satisfaction of the customer will, for most employees, translate into more positive feelings about the job.

The last job dimension is feedback. The more feedback employees receive, the better they know how they are performing. For employees in tipped posi-tions feedback comes regularly in terms of the amount of tips they receive. Man-agement must pay more attention to nontipped employees, who get little or no customer feedback.

**Employee Growth Needs.**   Research results on the relationship between job satisfaction and the growth needs of employees have been mixed. Although some results show that the strength of growth needs moderates the amount of job satisfaction experienced, other studies show no effect. It appears that job sat-isfaction can be increased for all employees, but the increase is greater for those who have strong needs for growth.

**Leadership Style.**   Managers can affect employee job satisfaction and perfor-mance through the style of leadership they adopt. The appropriate leadership style depends on the scope of the job and the growth needs of the employee performing that job.[18] When an employee has high growth needs and is performing a job high in variety (a high-scope job), participative management with a great deal of autonomy for the employee would be appropriate.

When a job is varied but the employee has a low need for growth, the manager should provide direction in planning, organizing, and controlling the work of the employee.

When an employee with high growth needs is performing a task that is not fulfilling, frustration and dissatisfaction probably result. Supportive leadership will be necessary to produce a satisfied and productive employee.

When an employee with low growth needs is performing a dull and repetitive task, performance should be monitored but the manager need not supervise the employee closely. As long as the job is being performed to the level required, little or no interference from the manager is needed. This maintenance leadership style is appropriate until performance or satisfaction problems arise, in which case more direction or support can be given.

## Punishment

Many managers overrely on punishment as a means of shaping employee behavior. Punishment seeks to eliminate negative behavior by applying negative consequences to that behavior. An employee comes in late. The employee is told, "If you come in late again this month, you will be fired." The negative behavior is the lateness; the punishment is being fired; the objective is to reduce or eliminate the negative behavior—to stop the lateness.

There are several problems with an overreliance on punishment. It may eliminate the behavior. However, it may, instead, result in avoidance behavior. Our tardy employee wakes up late. Instead of coming in late and being fired, the employee may call in sick and not come in at all. Or consider the chef who is told, "Don't let me catch you with your food costs this high again." Under his breath the chef may mutter, "Don't worry, you won't catch me." The result may be actions that suppress rather than eliminate the negative behavior. There is also the problem that if employees hear from management only when things go wrong, a negative climate results.

## Positive Reinforcement

When employees rate a company climate low on "recognition," they are saying that they feel criticized and punished when they do something wrong rather than praised and rewarded when they do something right. The "solution"—positive reinforcement—assumes that people behave in a way that is most rewarding to them. Management can improve employees' performance by providing appropriate consequences to employee behavior. Research does seem to show that positive reinforcement works better than negative reinforcement in producing and maintaining behavior.

Positive reinforcement seeks to increase the occurrence of positive behavior by providing desirable consequences for that behavior. Let us return to our tardy quick bite 14.6

## Why Are Loyalty and Recognition Important?

**Learning Objective:** Describe how to implement successfully the following in a restaurant operation:

- Management by objectives
- Job redesign
- Positive reinforcement
- A climate of trust

Chick-fil-A has discovered the perfect recipe for motivating their employees. The "Team Member Loyalty and Recognition Program" was created in order to improve upon excellence in the workplace.

The Loyalty and Recognition Program allows operators to recognize and reward valued team members consistently and without trouble. As a part of the program, every operator receives a customized package of program materials quarterly. This package includes promotional posters, paycheck stuffers, recognition certificates, an implementation guide, and incentive awards (such as gift certificates or movie passes).

There are five values that drive this program:

1. Customers First: Recognize and reward team members who practice key customer service skills such as suggestively selling, value sizing, and providing fast, accurate, and polite service.
2. Teamwork: Acknowledge employees who go out of their way to show coworkers how to execute a task and those who help train new members.
3. Personal Excellence: Reward team members who strive to set an example of excellence inside and outside the workplace.
4. Stewardship: Encourage good stewardship of unit resources such as managing cash and inventory carefully, keeping the restaurant safe and clean, and properly maintaining equipment.
5. Character: Set an example to follow by rewarding team members who exhibit key character traits such as loyalty, integrity, and respect.

These five values are considered by many food service operations to be the core values that are key to the success of any restaurant.

*Source:* Winning Workforce Ideas, Employer of Choice Awards, "A Great Team Gets Better," pp. 22–25.

**Discussion Questions:** Would it be possible to modify the five values so that they could be used for employee training? How? Could these values be adapted to other restaurant chains besides Chick-fil-A?

employee. Positive reinforcement occurs when the employee is told that at the end of each week, all employees who have a perfect attendance record will be eligible for a prize drawing. The idea is to reward the desired behavior.

**Implementation.**   The starting point is an audit of existing performance in behavioral terms. We may note, for example, that servers do not suggest dessert after customers are finished with the entree.

Next, management identifies what objectives it wishes to see accomplished. Carrying the dessert example through, a goal may be set of having servers sell 10 desserts per shift.

The next step is to identify the behaviors necessary to achieve the objectives. To sell desserts it is necessary to

- Know what desserts are being offered.
- Suggest to every customer that they have a dessert.
- Describe the desserts accurately and in a way that is likely to induce purchase.

If employees do these three things, it is more likely that they will sell desserts than if they do not do these things.

The fourth step is the key to the success of positive reinforcement—reinforcing the behavior. Several types of reinforcement are possible. Continuous reinforcement involves reacting to the behavior every time it occurs. This is the type of reinforcement received when we put coins in a soda machine. Every time the correct amount of money goes into the slot, a soda appears. Continuous reinforcement is necessary to establish a new behavior.

Related to this is the idea of fixed and variable or intermittent reinforcement. Fixed reinforcement involves getting feedback on a set schedule in terms of time or number of actions. The most obvious example of fixed reinforcement is the weekly or biweekly paycheck. Because that check comes once a week, it becomes expected and, as a consequence, can lose its effect as a motivator. Intermittent reinforcement is given on an irregular basis.

In terms of motivation, variable or intermittent reinforcement is more effective in sustaining already established behavior. Consider the soda machine compared to the slot machine. If you put coins in the soda machine and nothing happens, you may give up and leave, muttering under your breath; or you may kick the machine; or if you are thirsty enough, you may put more coins in the slot. But if nothing still happens, will you put more change in? Probably not. We are used to a continuous schedule of reinforcement. When we go from continuous reinforcement to no reinforcement, the behavior stops.

Management will often work with employees to improve their behavior. After lots of work, lots of coaching, and lots of reinforcement, an employee's behavior begins to improve. But then the manager goes to work with another employee whose behavior needs to improve. Getting no more reinforcement, the first employee's new behavior may disappear.

Consider the slot machine. We put in some coins but get no response. Do we put in more? Of course! The behavior is continued far longer than we would feed the soda machine because we know that at some time there will be a worthwhile payoff. The intermittent variable response of the slot machine keeps the behavior going.

As the fifth step in the process, employees are encouraged to keep a record of their own work. This self-assessment means that employees themselves continuously reinforce their own behavior. Every time the server sells a dessert, he or she makes a note of it. The reinforcement is immediate. In this way the server sees the relationship between the behavior and the consequence. The success interval, or the distance between the behavior and the measurement, is shortened.

Finally, the supervisor looks at the performance of the employee and praises the positive aspects. For reinforcement to work, the employee has to see the relationship between the behavior and the consequence. Continuous reinforcement has to be as immediate as possible. It also has to be meaningful to the employee. The priorities of a waitress struggling as a single parent to raise two children are different from those of a college student working for "fun money."

## Development of Trust

The last of the six dimensions of organizational climate to be considered is teamwork. This is the feeling of belonging to an organization characterized by cohesion, mutual warmth, and support, trust, and pride. Such employees trust and respect each other while feeling personal loyalty and a sense of belonging to the company. When employees perceive teamwork to be low, it is management's responsibility to instill a feeling of trust and loyalty.

**Organizational Commitment.**   What factors determine whether or not an employee will be loyal to a company? There are various models of organizational commitment that determine the factors that influence how and why employees are tuned in to the needs of the company. In these models there are several common ideas. The main factors that influence a person's commitment are investments, reciprocity, lack of alternatives, and identification.

As people invest more deeply in a company in time, energy, and commitment, the less they are likely to leave as they accept future rewards—promotions, for example—for their contributions. If they leave the company, their investment will not be recovered.

The idea of reciprocity is based on the assumption that if employees feel they are getting more than they deserve—that the rewards of the job are more than expected—they will remain with the operation to repay this debt through future performance.

Lack of alternatives means that the more specific skills become to a company, the less opportunity is available to use those skills outside the operation. This is not very important, however, in the restaurant industry, where the job in one restaurant differs little from that in another.

Identification is defined as the linking of one's social identity to one's work. As identification increases, change becomes harder and commitment is strengthened.

**Implementation: Management Style.** Management's task is to integrate the employee with the company in such a way that there is evidence of mutual warmth and support. In a climate where truth and respect are present, employee feelings of belonging and loyalty will result.

Managers can implement such a climate by the style and behaviors they adopt. Many contemporary managers have idealized models in their imagination akin to the heroic manager: the conquering leader who rescues helpless, disorganized employees from all problems and leaves only when all has been accomplished by his or her own courage, intelligence, and skill. The helpless subordinates continue with their mundane tasks until another problem arises and the hero returns.

It is the feeling of control over themselves, but primarily over others, that creates this vision. When crises arise at work and tough decisions are called for, many managers feel responsible for knowing what the problem is, developing the solution, and exerting control over the situation.

When managers perceive their employees to be helpless and incapable and take full control, they elicit reciprocal behavior from their employees. Subordinates retreat to a defense of their narrow interests as managers exert complete control.

The key is for managers to act as developers, people with a strong employee-centered image. Managers learn to have impact without exerting total control, to be helpful without having all the answers, and to be powerful without needing to dominate.

The developer–manager model consists of three components that must be nurtured to achieve productive excellence: interdependence, interpersonal skills, and commitment to an overriding departmental goal. Within the operation there is a high degree of interdependence among departments and a constant stream of changes, both internal and external. This is especially true in the restaurant industry, where the satisfaction of the customer depends on the performance of many people in many departments. Managers must develop a method to handle this interdependence.

The solution is to build a team that shares the responsibility for managing departments. It is a joint responsibility group that shares in making the basic decisions and influences each member to a high level of performance. Building such a team leads to greater subordinate commitment and motivation. Joint responsibility increases individual challenge and potential learning and growth. Development occurs in technical and managerial skills. Research has indicated that groups make better decisions than individuals do when the problem is complex.

The second component in being a developer–manager is the importance of interpersonal skills. Daily interaction can be used to encourage and enhance growth in subordinates. Coaching from the developer–manager helps build competence. In this way, behavioral problems can be turned into an opportunity for growth.

The third component is getting employees committed to the overriding goal of the department. The goal unites employees because it is a vision they can share and work toward. Employees do not work for money alone; the goal generates reasons that make the work worthwhile. It is the achievement made toward the goal and the appreciation of the extra effort that become rewarding to the employee.

**Implementation: Management Behavior.**   The day-to-day behavior of managers nurtures or destroys a climate of trust and loyalty. Employees are constantly looking to determine the extent to which they should be on their guard in dealing with management. The more they perceive management as being threatening, the more time they will spend on their own emotional defenses. The more they perceive an atmosphere in which they can grow, the more emotion they can devote to the job.

Certain behaviors that management can develop encourage trust on the part of the employee:

1. Encourage employees to express doubts, feelings, and concerns. In some companies, expressing doubt about a management course of action is liable to have that person labeled a traitor to the operation. In such an atmosphere, creative ideas are stifled.
2. Tell employees the reasons behind requests. When people understand why they are being asked to perform rather than just being told what to do, they feel that management has a greater respect for them. Consequently, they respect management more and perform better.
3. When something goes wrong, be more concerned about what happened and how to prevent it than in finding and punishing the guilty party. This does not mean permitting or encouraging slackness. It does mean that the focus is on problem solving, including the participation of the affected parties, rather than on assigning blame.
4. Encourage employees to come to you for assistance while helping them to develop independent judgment.
5. Be candid about the person to whom you are talking, but never gossip about anyone. Managers are never off the record.

## LEADERS AND MANAGERS

Throughout this chapter we have referred to supervisors as "managers" while suggesting at times that they exhibit a "leadership" style. There is a difference between a manager and a leader. According to Bennis and Nanus,[19] most organizations are managed, not led. Bennis and Nanus, among others, promote the idea that what is increasingly needed are leaders, not managers. It is useful, therefore, to look at some ideas of what constitutes a leader and to relate these ideas to the task of motivating employees.

### Leadership Theories

Leadership theories have evolved over the years. Trait theories, popular from the 1920s to the 1950s, focused on the role of personal characteristics such as intelligence and dominance. Beginning in the 1950s, we saw the development of behavioral theories that suggested that the effectiveness of leaders comes from what they do rather than the personal characteristics they possess. Another development is that of situational theories—the idea that the characteristics of employees and the situation the business is in must be considered when developing an effective leadership strategy.

**Trait Theories.**   While early studies attempting to identify personal characteristics that made for successful leaders were inconsistent, later reviews have identified more consistent results. It appears that the following are important:[20]

- Vigor and persistence in the pursuit of goals
- Self-confidence
- Ability to influence others
- Ability to tolerate frustration

Taken together, they give a fuzzy picture of the personality of a leader. Although it is now felt that personality is part of being a leader, it is no longer accepted that the existence of various traits will make a person a leader, and vice versa.

**Behavioral Theories.**   Because trait theories were unable to identify what made a leader effective, the focus turned to an examination of the behaviors that seemed to work.

Early studies at the University of Michigan found that production-centered supervision, where the focus was on getting the job done, actually produced less than did employee-centered supervision, where the accent was on developing high goals and focusing highly enthusiastic attention on the employees who did the work.

A research team at Ohio State University identified two similar dimensions of supervisory behavior—consideration and structure—that were popularized by Blake and Mouton as the managerial grid. Two dimensions—consideration for production and consideration for people—were placed on a grid to form five possible supervisory styles:[21]

1. **Country club management:** Where there is a high concern for people and a low concern for production. There is a friendly atmosphere at work and little pressure to perform.
2. **Impoverished management:** Where there is a low concern for both people and production. Those in the organization put forth just enough effort to keep their jobs.
3. **Organization management:** Where there is average concern for both people and production. There is a balance between getting out the work and keeping morale at a satisfactory level.
4. **Authority-obedience:** A workplace characterized by a very efficient workforce in which employees are expected to conform to the needs of the company.
5. **Team management:** Where there is a high concern for both people and production. Employees see themselves as having a common purpose with the company and, as such, are committed to perform well.

## quick bite 14.7
### What Makes a Successful Leader?

**Learning Objective:** Summarize the major theories of leadership, indicating how they can be applied to a restaurant situation.

The Women's Foodservice Forum brought together a group of forty chief executives, presidents, and top human resource executives to decide what makes a successful leader. These forty women came up with 10 Core Competencies. A Competency was defined by the team as "a description of the criteria for successful performance" and a skill that produces "successful performance within a particular culture and business context." The following are the 10 Core Competencies essential to being a successful leader:

1. Initiative: Reflect a strong drive for personal growth and improvement.
2. Strategic Thinking: Consider a broad range of factors in decisions and judgments.
3. Building Networks: Identify and nurture a system of internal and external relationships with the intent to widen one's business circles and use these relationships to achieve successful goals.
4. Visioning/Setting Directions: Understand where the company needs to go to be successful and share that vision in a war that guides and energizes others.
5. Developing Others: Mentor and coach team members to develop their leadership skills; delegate effectively and give people challenging assignments.
6. Building High Performing Teams: Staff and develop to maximize effectiveness of the team; build teams committed to achieving organizational goals.
7. Driving for Results: Strive to succeed and overcome barriers rather than getting blocked; push self and others for results.
8. Risk Taking: Take calculated risks to support business goals; be willing to challenge the status quo and traditional ways of doing things.
9. Tough-Minded: Make hard decisions and empower team members to do the same; address problems and concerns directly.
10. Communicating and Listening: Demonstrate excellent written and oral communication skills; listen to truly understand other points of view before responding.

*Source: National Restaurant News,* Women's Foodservice Forum, "Successful to the Core," March 22, 2004 p. 42.

**Discussion Questions:** How did the group of 40 chief executives, presidents, and top human resource executives define "competency?" Having read the 10 Core Competencies, do you agree with them? If not, what should be changed?

In an attempt to synthesize earlier work, Gary P. Yukl identified the following measurable behaviors that, when used under specific conditions, will produce effective leadership:[22]

| | |
|---|---|
| Performance emphasis | Consideration |
| Inspiration | Praise–recognition |
| Structuring reward contingencies | Decision participation |
| Autonomy delegation | Role clarification |
| Goal setting | Training–coaching |
| Problem solving | Information dissemination |
| Planning | Coordinating |
| Work facilitation | Representation |
| Interaction facilitation | Conflict management |
| Criticism–discipline | |

**Situational (Contingency) Theories.** Aware that neither trait nor behavioral theories adequately explained what makes a leader, attention turned to the importance of situational variables. Basically, such theories say that there is no single style of leadership that will be effective in every situation. To be effective, leaders must adapt their behavior to changing situations.

Fiedler's contingency leadership model states that group performance is a function of both the leader and the leadership situation. The extent to which the leader is task or relationship oriented is a measure of the motivational system of the leader. The leadership situation consists of three things:[23]

1. Leader–member relations (the extent to which the group trusts and likes the leader and is willing to follow her or his instructions)
2. The extent to which the task is structured
3. Position power

The first factor is the most important. Fiedler's research has shown that task-oriented leaders are most effective where they have power by virtue of their position, good relations with the group, and a job to be done that is well structured. Relationship-oriented leaders are most effective where the situation is moderately favorable or unfavorable to the leader. These might be situations where the leader is accepted but the job objectives are vague or where the task is structured but the leader is not accepted. The major lesson to be learned from this theory is that a style of leadership that is effective under one set of circumstances may not work under a different set of conditions.

The path–goal theory identifies two variables to be taken into account when deciding on an appropriate leadership style: employee characteristics and characteristics of the work environment. Preliminary findings indicate that[24]

- A directive style of leadership is effective when the work situation is vague.

- Supportive leadership works best on employees who have jobs that are stressful, frustrating, or dissatisfying.
- Employees prefer a participative style of leadership in jobs that are not repetitive and that involve the ego of the employee.

Four points can be made regarding leadership theories:[25]

1. There is no universally accepted approach to studying leadership.
2. There are some personal characteristics that differentiate effective leaders from ineffective leaders.
3. There are two accepted dimensions of leadership:
   a. Employee—or relationship—oriented (consideration)
   b. Production—or task—oriented (structure)
4. Leadership effectiveness is some function of a leader's personal characteristics and behaviors, the feelings of the employees toward the leader, the type of job, relationships within the work group, and the organizational climate.

---

## quick bite 14.8
### Road to the Top: Sally Smith

Sally Smith made her debut in the foodservice industry after working with KPMG Peat Marwick and Miracle-Ear Inc. for 11 years. The small company environment of Buffalo Wild Wings is what initially attracted Smith to the restaurant industry. After years of working for large public corporations, she was thrilled to have to the opportunity to help an up-and-coming company through its growing pains. Although it was quite the undertaking, Smith was not intimidated by all the work that Buffalo Wild Wings needed to get on its feet. The restaurant had no functional areas; Smith had to set up the accounting, finance, marketing and human resource departments. "I saw a wonderful opportunity," Smith said.

In less than two years, Smith had worked her way up to the top post at Buffalo Wild Wings. She initiated an entire product-repositioning. The name was changed from "bw-3" to "Buffalo Wild Wings." A new logo and décor package that emphasized the front counter rather than the bar was created, and the interior was transformed into a brighter environment with more windows and softer accent colors. She also implemented a program to jump-start sales. The new program had customers place initial orders at the front counter where servers can encourage them to add more food and drinks to their order.

This repositioning resulted in more consistent customer service and a lower turnover rate among the staff. These results can be attributed to the

*(continued)*

better training provided for employees. The senior vice president of marketing, advertising, and development for Buffalo Wings says, "Sally has a passion and loyalty to employees. She is honest and full of integrity, and she loves to have fun. She also cultivates the culture of doing the right thing." Under Sally Smith's leadership, Buffalo Wild Wings Grill & Bar evolved from a local college bar into a national fast-casual establishment.

*Source: National Restaurant News,* "2003 Golden Chain: Sally Smith," September 22, 2003. pp. 72, 74.

**Discussion Question:** In what ways did the product repositioning initiated by Sally Smith result in better customer service?

## ENDNOTES

1. Dina Berta, "Employee Behavior Study Alarms Operators," *Nation's Restaurant News,* vol. 37, no. 31, August 4, 2003, p. 16.
2. Craig C. Pinder, *Work Motivation: Theories, Issues and Applications* (Glenview, IL: Scott, Foresman and Company, 1984), p. 63; David C. McClelland, *Human Motivation* (Glenview, IL: Scott, Foresman and Company, 1985), pp. 595–596.
3. Auren Uris, *101 of the Greatest Ideas in Management* (New York: John Wiley & Sons, 1986), p. 26.
4. Ibid., p. 26.
5. Arthur W. Sherman, George W. Bohlander, and Herbert J. Chudren, *Managing Human Resources,* 8th ed. (Cincinnati, OH: South-Western Publishing Co., 1988), p. 304.
6. Ibid., p. 299.
7. Ibid., p. 302.
8. Ibid., p. 304.
9. This material has been taken from Robert Christie Mill, *Managing for Productivity in the Hospitality Industry* (New York: Van Nostrand Reinhold, 1989), Chapters 6–10.
10. George H. Litwin and Robert A. Stringer, Jr., *Motivation and Organizational Climate* (Cambridge, MA: Harvard University Press, 1968).
11. Forum Corporation, *The Language of Organizational Climate,* unpublished monograph, 1979.
12. Thomas T. Peters and Robert H. Waterman, *In Search of Excellence* (New York: Harper & Row, 1982).
13. Bruce Grindy, "Hooking and Keeping Employees," *Restaurants USA,* October 1998, p. 25.
14. Dina Berta, "Study Finds Employees Not Getting a Lot of Satisfaction," *Nation's Restaurant News,* vol. 37, no. 23, June 9, 2003, pp. 8, 22.
15. Milford Prewitt, "All Work, No Play—No More, Special Report: General Managers," *Nation's Restaurant News,* vol. 37, no. 47, November 24, 2003, pp. 1, 43, 46, 48.
16. M. C. McConkie, "A Classification of the Goal-Setting and Appraisal Process in MBO," *Academy of Management Review,* vol. 4, no. 1, 1979, p. 29.
17. Mill, *Managing for Productivity in the Hospitality Industry,* pp. 143–144.
18. Ricky W. Griffen, "Relationships among Individual, Task Design and Leader Behavior," *Academy of Management Journal,* vol. 23, no. 4, 1980, p. 667.
19. Warren Bennis and Burt Nanus, *Leaders: The Strategies for Taking Charge* (New York: Harper & Row Publishers, 1985), p. 218.
20. Marc G. Singer, *Human Resource Management* (Boston: PWS-Kent Publishing Company, 1990), pp. 353–354.

21. Ibid., p. 356.
22. Gary P. Yukl, *Leadership in Organizations* (Upper Saddle River, NJ: Prentice Hall, 1981), pp. 121–125.
23. Singer, *Human Resource Management,* pp. 356–357.
24. Ibid., p. 358.
25. Ibid., p. 359.

## INTERNET RESOURCES

| | |
|---|---|
| Success Factors Performance and Talent Management | *http://www.successfactors.com* |
| Loyalty Works Incentive and Loyalty Programs | *http://www.loyaltyworks.com/* |

CHAPTER FIFTEEN

# RESTAURANT MANAGER 2010

"The three-martini lunch is the epitome of American efficiency.
Where else can you get an earful, a bellyful, and a snootful at the
same time?"
Gerald R. Ford, 38th U.S. President

## learning objectives

*By the end of this chapter you should be able to*

1. Identify the major challenges facing the industry in the restaurant industry.

2. Identify the skills and knowledge that will be required of restaurant managers to respond to these challenges.

## INDUSTRY CHALLENGES

There are a number of challenges facing managers in the restaurant industry. This section profiles a number of these issues. The final section identifies likely changes in the job of managers as they seek to answer these challenges.

### Nutrition/Obesity[1]

In March 2003 a bill was introduced in New York State that would require many restaurant chains across New York to post nutritional information on menus and signboards. By some estimates there are almost 300,000 deaths linked to obesity every year. Some critics suggest that corporate responsibility rather than personal choice is to blame. They also charge that restaurateurs have not done enough to provide customers with healthy alternatives and important nutritional information about the contents of their menus.

Nutritional labeling bills have now been introduced in several other states and the District of Columbia and at least two lawsuits have been filed against fast-food chains claiming the foods made teenagers fat. While the suits were thrown out (89 percent of Americans do not believe restaurants should be held liable for health problems due to obesity), the threat of future action is causing concern in many board rooms.

In response a number of chains have introduced more healthy menu items. Applebee's recently signed an agreement with Weight Watchers to develop low-fat, low-calorie menu items.

## Smoking Prohibition[2]

There are smoking bans in eight states at the time of writing and plans for more states to outlaw the practice. There is even disagreement between some state and local restaurant associations about whether or not smoking should be banned in restaurants. At the moment over 80 percent of chains, two-thirds of

 **quick bite 15.2**
**Restaurant 2010: Technology Forecast**

The National Restaurant Association (NRA) follows the use of technology in restaurants through the use of periodic surveys. In its most recent survey in 2002, three quarters of the survey respondents use computers to perform business operations. Half of the respondents use the Internet for communicating summary menu information, hours of operation, location and other information. From this data, the NRA predicts that half of the changes that will occur in the restaurant industry before 2010 will be the result of changes in technology.

The following processes are commonly addressed by computer applications:

- Measuring in-store product profit and loss
- Calculating in-store payroll
- Performing inventory management
- Managing accounts receivable and payable
- Monitoring attendance and time
- Processing customer orders
- Processing credit/debit card payments
- Scheduling labor
- Tracking customer patronage

- Printing in-store payroll checks
- Administering gift certificate programs
- Administering frequent diner programs
- Managing the reservation system
- Scanning bar codes

In many operations, the following processes are addressed by Internet applications:

- Comparing in-store product profit and loss
- Monitoring the weather
- Monitoring recipe trends
- Monitoring industry news
- Providing advertising and promotional information
- Performing market research
- Monitoring local news
- Providing training information
- Providing recruiting services

Technology increases productivity by enhancing both operating efficiency and customer service. The processes sure to be changed the most by technology include:

- Performing daily in-store profit and loss analysis
- Requiring both "high-tech" and "high-customer-touch" balancing
- Increasing the number of cost control and management efficiency techniques
- Merging point of sale and ordering systems
- Simplifying point of sale information collection
- Increasing point of sale information accuracy and collection speeds

To the survey respondents, the increased use of computers and Internet applications means that all restaurant technology users will soon require major system updates every three to five years. Also, at least one employee will have to devote a major portion of his or her duties to keeping the applications running efficiently and training staff in their use.

*Source:* Liddle, Alan J., "NRA Tech Poll Bolsters Think-Tank's 2010 Forecast," *Nation's Restaurant News,* vol. 36, no. 47, November 25, 2002, pp. 4, 42.

**Discussion Question:** What are some of the downsides to using computer technology so much in an operation?

independent restaurants, and one-fifth of state associations believe smoking will be banned in restaurants by 2014.

In states where smoking has been banned, bars and nightclubs have been hit the hardest. Where restaurants are in municipalities close to areas where smoking is not banned, many have lost business to where the practice is allowed. On the other hand, some restaurants are finding new nonsmoking customers who had previously boycotted facilities that allowed smoking.

Mindful of the fact that 20 percent of the U.S. population still smoke, some restaurants accommodate smokers in sidewalk and patio areas, where the New York State law allows up to 25 percent of such space to be set aside for smokers.

## Animal Rights[3]

People for the Ethical Treatment of Animals (PETA) employs attention-getting tactics to protest what they claim is the poor treatment of animals. They find that passing out literature near restaurants and organizing boycotts is more effective than lobbying Congress.

After taking on burger chains to improve practices in cattle slaughter-houses, they turned their attention to improving conditions for chickens.

McDonald's recently mandated guidelines for its suppliers who provide it with more than 2.5 billion pounds of chicken, beef, and poultry a year. For example, they mandate that egg suppliers double the living space for each caged hen. They will not buy eggs from farmers who debeak chickens. Animal behaviorists have designed slaughterhouses in ways that reduce anxiety in animals.

## Human Resources[4]

By most accounts restaurant jobs are not considered prestigious occupations. In one study, being an *owner* of a fast-food restaurant was rated lower than being a loan officer, travel agent, social worker, or teacher. The problem of finding qualified managers and employees will intensify in the future unless something can be done to change the image of the industry.

Despite the problem, industry wages are very competitive. The average total compensation for assistant managers and general managers in 2003 was $41,885 and $68,077 respectively.

## Food Safety[5]

In 1986 the state of California mandated that businesses must post warning signs if their products contain one or more of 700 chemicals deemed potentially harmful. The Sardine Factory restaurant in Monterey, in an attempt to avoid fines and lawsuits posted the following:

"Chemicals Known To The State of California To Cause Cancer,
Or Birth Defects, Or Other Reproductive Harm May be Present
In Foods Or Beverages Sold Or Served Here."

One national survey ranks restaurants fifth behind grocery stores and consumers themselves for actively ensuring food safety.

## quick bite 15.3
### Restaurant Management 2010: Restaurant Technology

**Learning Objective:** Identify the major challenges facing the industry in the restaurant industry.

The use of technology in restaurants will require both that technology providers deliver solutions that create value and that restaurant owners strictly assess what technologies work best for their particular operations, be they up-scale single locations or multi-unit chains.

Providers will only create value for restaurant owners if they become IT partners with the owners rather than mere suppliers. They will need to specialize in working with restaurant operators and providing tools that make business sense not the most in sales commissions. The providers will need to supply IT that expands the operators' access to data and extends the capabilities of their existing systems rather than replacing them.

Correspondingly, restaurant owners will need to build on existing IT investments rather than replacing them. This will mean concentrating on acquiring open software applications that will run on existing systems or on light web-based designs that augment the performance of existing equipment. Owners will also need to work with vendors who cooperate in creating small IT projects that create clever combinations of hardware and software that extend existing computer power. For example, develop systems that combine temperature and humidity sensors with reporting and alert software.

Restaurants will also need to avoid vendors that lock them into proprietary systems. Instead focus on open, integrated applications that run hardware and software systems that link the restaurants' in-store and other employees with two-way, real-time data instruments such as computers, pagers, cell phones and text-messaging services.

Restaurants and vendors will need systems that function as more than point-of-sale data collection devices. Such systems will need to focus on speed of service, food safety, loss prevention and energy usage.

Keeping up with restaurant IT trends will not be enough. Restaurants will need to insist that their IT partners assist in developing systems to improve the entire restaurant operation and enhance the dining experience of customers. Only then will the promise of restaurant IT be turned into value.

*Source:* Melvin, Jim, "Riding Wave of Future Can Be Risky; Smart Tech Choices help Operators avoid Wipeout," *Nation's Restaurant News,* vol. 38, no. 10, March 8, 2004, p. 26.

**Discussion Question:** "Restaurants and vendors will need systems that function as more than point-of-sale data collection devices. Such systems will need to focus on speed of service, food safety, loss prevention and energy usage." Do you agree? Support your answer.

## Food Technology[6]

Increasing numbers of people feel that genetically modified foods are safe to eat. Indeed, the percentage of Americans who regard such foods as safe is about equal to those who believe it to be unsafe. Over 90 percent of American are in favor of mandatory labeling of such foods, a position that the National Restaurant Association opposes.

## Serving Alcohol

The National Restaurant Association was initially opposed to legislation reducing blood alcohol content (BAC) from 0.1 to 0.08. The federal standard was lowered to 0.08 in 2002 with withholding of federal highway funds to states that did not follow along. Increasing numbers of state associations have stopped their opposition with the realization that federal highway funds are needed.

While some believe that the goal of Mothers Against Drunk Driving (MADD) is to outlaw drinking outside of the home, the organization claims they are not against responsible alcohol consumption by those legally old enough to drink. They are in favor of working with restaurants to set up designated-driver programs and server training.

## Food Sustainability[7]

There are increasing concerns about operating business in a way that present-day actions do not threaten future generations. One flash point concerns fisheries. A recent boycott of swordfish by environmental groups targeted all swordfish despite the fact that, although North American beds were overfished, Pacific beds were fine.

In the past mangroves were destroyed to build shrimp farms despite the fact that the water around them was too acidic for shrimp farms. Chilean sea bass is also on the boycott list while farm-raised salmon has come under increased attack.

Recent fears about mad cow disease in the U.S. have spurred sales of "natural" beef—raised without antibiotics and fed a vegetarian diet. Increasing numbers of customers are willing to pay higher prices for such items.

# INDUSTRY SOLUTIONS

## The Manager's Job

According to the National Restaurant Association, the basic functional areas of a restaurant manager's job consist of[8]

1. **Cost control and financial management:** Monitoring, controlling, and reporting on store profitability indicators
2. **Supervising shift operations:** Running each shift efficiently and effectively
3. **Organizing and planning each shift:** Preparing for the shift so that it will run smoothly.

4. **Unit coordination and control:** Communication among and between managers, supervisors, and other resources within the organization.

5. **Customer relations:** Improving the dining experience for customers.

6. **Motivating employee performance:** Improving the performance of employees.

7. **Employing and developing crew members:** Obtaining, selecting, training, and keeping employees.

8. **Communicating with outside sources:** Keeping in touch with corporate and community sources outside the unit.

9. **Monitoring and maintaining facility and equipment:** Keeping physical assets operational and in compliance with internal and external regulations and laws.

In the following sections we examine the job of the restaurant manager in each of the following areas:

- Administration
- Finance
- Human resources

- Facility maintenance
- Sanitation and food safety
- Service
- Marketing
- Food and beverage
- Working conditions
- Background and education
- Industry trends

**Administration.**   In the area of administration, managers will have to become computer proficient. As more operations move to comprehensive computer-based information, managers will have to be able to find, oversee, and use information from a variety of databases on a regular basis. Managers will use computers to perform a variety of tasks, from scheduling employees and forecasting customer demand to collecting sales data and keeping inventories.

A report from the National Restaurant Association identifying what the industry will look like in 2010 indicates that, in the area of technology, the top five predications are as follows:[9]

- Restaurateurs will be challenged to remain people-oriented, becoming both high-tech and high-touch.
- Technology will be tied into ordering systems.
- Point of sale (POS) systems will be tied into ordering systems.
- POS technology will be much simpler, faster, and more accurate.
- Employee selection and background verification will be computer assisted.

Managers will increasingly have to supervise a more culturally diverse workforce. Managers will have to become more sensitive to the characteristics of different cultures and customs. Many feel that managers who are bilingual will be at an advantage in communicating with, and therefore motivating, their employees.

---

## quick bite 15.5
### Restaurant 2010: Restaurant Knowledge Management

**Learning Objective:** Identify the skills and knowledge that will be required of restaurant managers to respond to these challenges.

The common definition of "knowledge management" (KM) states that it is a collection of practices that an organization uses to improve the capabilities of the organization's human resources. KM is a continuous process of creating, storing, finding, acquiring and using work experiences to enhance the value of the organization.

---

Most restaurant organizations value preparation for the future. These organizations should put a similar value on learning lessons from past performance. In order to do so, restaurants need to capture and record the collective memory currently present in the organization, because by 2014 fully half of the Baby Boomer generation will retire and with them will go their experience, insight and work culture.

The following is a list of some of the things that restaurant organizations can do to foster KM in a practical manner:

- Videotaping or otherwise recording retirement and award ceremonies and speeches
- Collecting and archiving every menu edition, employee manual and photos that document the organization's history
- Interviewing (and recording the interviews with) key personnel with ten or more years experience about company milestones, history, and growth challenges
- Mentoring new employees using these materials
- Interviewing current successful team members about service, teamwork and customer focus (using, for example, the leading question "What story do you wish everybody here knew?")
- Photographing, indexing and archiving team members, dining rooms, kitchens, uniforms and customers for use by mentors and new team members
- Surveying periodically senior executives about "The 10 Stupidest Things We've Done" and the newest employees about "The 10 Stupid Things We Do" and recording these impressions for review by each new generation of managers and mentors
- Computerizing this information into an organizational memory bank

How will this information be used? It will be used in part to reinvent employee training methods—turning them away from often stale manuals, videos and PowerPoint-assisted lectures. Instead, training will consist of live coaching, video game simulations, e-learning exercises, instant messaging between new employees and their work teams and daily new worker and team input to a portion of the organizational memory bank dedicated to the best practices.

*Sources:* "Smart Businesses File Knowledge Away for Future Reference," *Nation's Restaurant News,* vol. 38, no. 15, April 12, 2004, pp. 14, 22. "Trainers, Change with the Times, or the Times will Change You," *Nation's Restaurant News,* vol. 38, no. 9, March 1, 2004, pp. 20, 31.

**Discussion Question:** Is KM intrusive on the privacy of employees? Explain your opinion.

Managers will be more involved in teaching and training their employees. This will require them to develop better communication skills to enable them to do a better job in interacting with employees. Specific skills would include public speaking, presentation, interpersonal skills, and leadership abilities.[10] More time will be spent training employees and less time dealing with paper.

**Finance.**   The reason that managers will need more computer skills is that operations, primarily the chains, will increasingly have online computer-based financial systems. Managers who are able to perform spreadsheet analysis will be more effective in understanding and reporting on a unit's financial condition.

It is likely that, by 2010,[11]

- Technological advances will allow managers to monitor profit and loss on a daily basis.
- Real estate costs will escalate more rapidly as competition for prime sites increases.
- More resources will be spent on training employees, particularly in food safety and accident prevention.
- Costs for waste disposal will rise.
- Increased labor costs will lead operators to acquire more labor saving equipment.

**Human Resources.**   Human resources will become increasingly important to tomorrow's managers. Managers will have to move from being authoritarian to becoming coaches and develop better people skills for dealing with employees as well as customers. It is expected that finding qualified employees will be more difficult.

More attention will be paid to reducing turnover and keeping qualified employees. The manager's task will be to create a climate within the operation that will foster team spirit and motivate workers. This will involve such things as paying on the basis of performance, and providing better fringe benefits, improved work schedules, ongoing training, extensive evaluations, and better retirement benefits.

By 2010 it is likely that[12]

- Training and communications will be key factors in retention of hourly employees.
- More women and minorities will move into upper management.
- Greater cultural diversity will require management to foster an atmosphere of cooperation and accommodation within the workplace.
- Restaurants will provide more opportunities for managing a diverse workforce and solving problems.
- Employees will demand benefits that give them more free time and a better family lifestyle.

**Facility Management.** Mangers will get more involved in waste management and recycling. This will cover such things as ensuring that recyclable materials are properly sorted and helping encourage recycling by consumers. In this regard operators will have to become more familiar with government regulations regarding waste management.

Safety and security will also be a concern. Because of increasingly high liability costs, managers, with safety committees made up of employees, will be more aware of security issues both within and immediately outside their units.

There will be a greater emphasis on the implementation of preventive maintenance programs as a way of reducing maintenance and repair costs.

By 2010 it is likely that[13]

- Equipment will be on wheels for ease of movement and will have quick disconnect systems for cleaning and flexibility.
- Inventory management will become more automated.
- Casual and comfortable will continue as prominent design and décor themes.
- Equipment will be required to monitor and record critical control points (HACCP) electronically.
- More items will be premade by commissaries or manufacturers, reducing handling time at the restaurant site.

**Sanitation and Food Safety.** Increasingly, restaurant managers will have to have a sanitation certificate. Most states will require sanitation testing. In addition, managers will have to communicate the importance of this topic to employees, who will receive more training in this area. It is expected that more natural cleaning agents will be developed as a consequence of restrictions on the use of pesticides and cleaners.

**Service.** As service increasingly becomes a method of differentiating one restaurant from another, managers will have to become adept to getting feedback from customers and providing service to an increasingly diverse customer base. To allow employees to deliver the level of service needed, managers will have to empower them, giving them the training to be flexible in dealing with customers as well as the authority to handle requests and complaints. This means that managers will spend more time on customer relations and on setting the standards required to ensure that employees perform to the level needed to produce satisfied customers. They will spend more time talking to customers to get feedback on the service provided and giving that feedback to employees.

**Marketing.** Success in marketing comes from the manager's ability to understand and satisfy local tastes. To accomplish this, managers will have to understand the desires of neighborhood and local customers. They will be given greater latitude in implementing plans to accomplish this.

We can expect that[14]

- Customers will look for higher-quality takeout food.

- The percent of the dollar spent away from home will continue to rise.
- Convenience will continue to dominate customer trends.
- Customers will be more knowledgeable and value conscious.
- Changing demographics will lead to more marketing to older customers.

**Food and Beverage.** As consumers become more knowledgeable about nutrition, managers will have to develop more expertise about the nutritional content of ingredients and menu items. Quality control and product consistency will grow in importance. As a way of cutting down on costs, inventory control will become an even greater concern. In line with greater flexibility at the local level, mangers will be given more authority to promote specific food and beverage items.

It is most likely that, by 2010,[15]

- At midscale restaurants, there will be a significant upgrade in product quality and emphasis on "fresh."
- There will be greater demand for authentic items and flavor profiles.
- The customer's interest in new menu items will continue.
- Menus will become more regionalized.
- More high quality bakery products, especially whole grain products, will be available.

**Working Conditions.** Although the number of hours worked per week is not expected to decline, managers will have a better quality of life. Salaries and benefits will become more competitive, and mangers will have more formal education. The job will continue to be stressful, although training in how to deal with stress on the job may help managers deal with this issue.

**Background and Education.** To deal with a more diverse customer and employee base, managers will need better interpersonal and communication skills. A manager will be more of a generalist and less of a specialist, creating the climate necessary to accomplish the profit objectives of the unit. Managers will have to become more democratic and flexible in dealing with employees and be able to "present an image of grace under pressure to both staff and customers."[16] The typical restaurant management will become more highly educated while certification of employees will become increasingly important.[17]

**Industry Needs.** It is most likely that[18]

- Consistent and predictable earnings will be more critical as institutional investors continue to have a big impact on stock values.
- Per-seat investment will increase with higher equipment investment needed to meet food safety requirements.
- Public offerings will continue to finance the expansion of large chains.

- Newer restaurants will rely on higher cost secondary financing because large banks will only finance those with a proven track record.
- Emphasis on sale/leaseback financing will continue.

More managers will be needed in casual dining table services, nursing care, and fast food, whereas fewer positions will be available in military foodservice and fine dining.

## The Bottom Line

Managers who implement the principles and practices outlined in this book, paying special attention to the areas noted in this chapter, will lead the industry in the next decade. Good luck in your efforts!

---

### quick bite 15.6
### Road to the Top: Danielle Johnson

The changing demographic of the restaurant industry indicates that by 2010 more general managers (GMs) will be younger professionals. What will it mean for someone under thirty to be a GM for the best fine-dining restaurant in an area? This is the issue that faces 27-year-old Danielle Johnson, the GM for the seasonal fine-dining Arrows restaurant in Ogunquit, Maine. Johnson was recently named by *Nation's Restaurant News* as one of the top 50 GMs in the country.

Johnson's relationship with the various Arrows stakeholders looks like this:

Owners and other stakeholders: Johnson demonstrates a die-hard work ethic to the owners—up to 16 hours per day, 6 days a week. She's prepared to organize one or more critical product areas, such as the wine cellar and wedding bookings, and to tackle receipt of the product or inquiry to sales, and then expand sales of the product. Johnson is prepared to deal with a number of stakeholders—supply purveyors, wine distributors, special booking customers and staff members—and to coordinate dealings with all them. Johnson delivers 50 percent of her GM efforts to guests, 25 percent to staff (including service training) and 25 percent to maintaining the restaurant's front house operations, physical plant and coordination with the owners. She stresses to the owners the need to give exceptional employees creative outlets for their talents. Johnson always accepts increased responsibility from the owners and is prepared to give responsibility to her staff.

Guests: Johnson makes it a policy to treat every customer as an honored guest. When guests arrive, she greets them cordially. She is attentive to the

*(continued)*

customer at all times during the dining experience and exhibits patience with guests' requests. Johnson graciously pampers special event guests, such as the mothers of the groom and bride for wedding parties. Above all, Johnson always aims to give each dining customer the best dining experience he or she has ever had.

Staff: Johnson creates a sense of responsibility in new hires starting with the interview process. She does so by defining her expectations on day one and reminding the new hires of their duties until it becomes second nature. Johnson uses veteran staff to lead newcomers. But she always leads by example and does not cut corners. If the general manager cuts corners, so will her staff. Johnson educates her staff in mannered speech, and this includes valets and receptionists, the very first staff members customers encounter. She also exposes each staff member to the operations of every division. Johnson makes it a habit to teach all staff members what is in every dish. With respect to wine training, Johnson encourages her employees to taste the wines and dishes and lets them suggest wine-pairing ideas. She trusts her staff's creativity, and often asks them for ideas and suggestions.

*Source:* Kooker, Naomi, "Danielle Johnson," *Nation's Restaurant News,* vol. 38, no. 4, January 26, 2004, pp. 20–21.

**Discussion Question:** What are some challenges that could face a GM who is younger than his or her employees?

## ENDNOTES

1. "The New Revolution? Industry on Alert in an Age of Activism," *Nation's Restaurant News,* vol. 37, no. 38, pp. 86–92.
2. Ibid., pp. 94–100.
3. Ibid., pp. 106–114.
4. Ibid., pp. 116–120.
5. Ibid., pp. 122–126.
6. Ibid., pp. 128–132.
7. Ibid., pp. 146–149.
8. "Job Analysis Report for Unit Manager and Assistant Manager," Educational Foundation of the National Restaurant Association, November 1988.
9. National Restaurant Association, *Restaurant Industry 2010: The Road Ahead* (Washington, DC: National Restaurant Association, 1999), p. 33.
10. National Restaurant Association, *Foodservice Manager 2000, Current Issues Report* (Washington, DC: National Restaurant Association, 1992), p. 5.
11. National Restaurant Association, *Restaurant Industry 2010: The Road Ahead* (Washington, DC: National Restaurant Association, 1999), p. 32.
12. Ibid., pp. 33–34.
13. Ibid., p. 32.
14. Ibid., p. 34.
15. Ibid., p. 35.

16. National Restaurant Association, *Foodservice Manager 2000, Current Issues Report* (Washington, DC: National Restaurant Association, 1992), p. 16.

17. National Restaurant Association, *Restaurant Industry 2010: The Road Ahead* (Washington, DC: National Restaurant Association, 1999), p. 12.

18. Ibid., p. 31.

## INTERNET RESOURCES

| | |
|---|---|
| Restaurant Edge | *http://www.restaurantedge.com/* |
| Aloha | *http://www.alohapos.com/public_site/index_final.asp* |
| Micros | *http://www.micros.com/* |
| Nutrition Information | *http://www.nal.usda.gov/fnic/* |
| American Management Association | *http://www.amanet.org/* |

# INDEX

**A**

accessories, 181–82
accounts receivable, 306
activities, 106–7
advertising, 88–96, 100
    agencies, 86–88
    campaigns, types of,
        88–89
    claims, 105
    commercials, 92
    direct mail, 94–95, 99
    media, 88, 89, 90–93
    signs, 94
affirmative action, 334
Age Discrimination in
    Employment Act of 1967,
    332
American Association of Retired
    Persons, 327
American Marketing Association,
    53
American Psychological
    Association, 341, 342
Americans with Disabilities Act,
    36, 192, 328
animal rights, 426
Aramark, 30
assets, 297
    fixed, 309

**B**

baby boomers, 35, 41, 61
back of the house, 192, 193–202
balance sheet, 297–98
behaviorally anchored rating scales
    (BARS), 404
Bennigan's, 43
Bioterrorism Preparedness and
    Response Act of 2002, 272
Bob Evans Farms/Restaurants, 16,
    40
bona fide occupational
    qualification (BFOQ), 333
booths, 182–83
budgets, 56–57, 73–75, 76, 79, 80,
    81, 83–85
    capital, 316–19
Burger King, 49, 104, 115, 245
busperson, 145
bussers, 157, 165–66, 235

**C**

cafeterias, 7, 8, 9, 177
captain, 145, 165, 166
Centers for Disease Control (CDC),
    271
Central Life Interest Measure, 168
Cereality, 21
chairs, 176, 177, 182

channels, 72, 73
Child Labor laws, 332
Chili's Grill and Bar, 41
Civil Rights Act of 1964, 332, 341
coffee shops, 7, 8, 9
colors, 189–92
communication, 85
competition, 60
computers, hand-held, 170
consumers
    behavior, 44–45
    *See also* customers
contamination
    chemical, 275
    physical, 275
contract caterers, 15
cost control, 22, 24, 212
    balance sheet, 292, 306–7
    financial statements, 292, 293–94
    income statement, 292, 294,
        298–306
    profitability, 293
    ratios, 292, 294, 298–99, 301, 306,
        308, 310
    reducing waste, 233
    standardized recipes, 231
costs, 19, 120, 312
    benefit analysis, 85
    break-even analysis, 312

costs (*continued*)
    break-even charts, 310, 312, 316
    break-even point, 73, 292, 311,
        314–16
    cutting, 23–24
    depreciation, 297, 317
    fixed, 312, 315, 317
    labor, 312–13
    occupational, 297
    prime, 118–20
    rent, 297
    of sales, 295–96
    variable, 317
coupons, 97, 98–99, 100
crisis management, 285–86. *See also*
    management
crowding, 186
customers, 100, 103, 104, 105, 116,
        146, 147–48, 158, 160, 170, 171,
        179, 225
    accommodation of, 157, 167, 178
    attitudes, 76
    communication with, 80–81, 151,
        152, 157, 163
    data, 58–59
    expectations, 152, 156, 161, 172,
        173
    importance of, 157
    loyalty of, 4
    and menus, 111, 112
    perceived value, 115–16, 150–51
    profile of, 55–60
    psychological needs, 34, 41, 148,
        175
    relations, 151
    requirements, 164
    satisfaction of, 4, 71, 83, 149–50,
        151, 171
    seating, 155
    understanding of, 31
    *See also* consumers
customization, 35

**D**
deterministics, 154
development program, 358
dinnerhouses, 8, 9
dinnerware, 179
dishwashers (mechanical), 249,
        254
dishwashing, 234–36

**E**
economy study, 317
e-mail, 97

employee recognition programs,
        170–71
employees, 158, 167, 199, 225
    acceptance, 165
    behavior, 385
    clothing, 287
    commitment, 402–3
    communication, 158
    development, 379
    disabled, 328–30
    empathy, 168
    empowerment, 171–72
    evaluating performance, 403–4
    feedback to, 404–5
    goals, 165, 393–94
    growth needs, 409
    hand washing, 287
    health, 286–87
    importance of, 157
    literacy, 324
    minorities, 325–26, 334–35
    morale, 196
    objectives, 402
    older, 326–27
    part-time, 327–28
    personal hygiene of, 153, 267,
        280, 287, 288–89
    potential, 324
    pricing of checks, 126
    productivity, 193
    profile, 323
    recruiting, 336–37, 339
    reinforcement of, 392–93, 394,
        410–12, 413
    sales ability, 104, 141, 170
    satisfaction, 407–8
    service, 24, 26–27, 153, 155, 172
    standards, 166, 402
    turnover, 24
    women, 324–25, 331
energy management, 238, 259–65
energy sources, 243–44
entertainment
    cost, 184–85
    music, 185–86
Environmental Protection Agency
        (EPA), 259, 265
EPA. *See* Environmental Protection
        Agency
Equal Employment Opportunity
        Commission, 325, 333
Equal Pay Act of 1963, 330
equipment, 195–96, 262
    cleaning, 283–84
    cost, 240–41

    functionality of, 241
    kitchen, 238, 239–40
    maintenance, 253–54, 256–58
    materials, 242–43
    types of, 244–50
ergonomics, 203, 204
ethnic populations, 37–39
expenses, 303–5

**F**
Fair Labor Standards Act, 332
fast-food operations, 7, 8, 9, 21, 40,
        47, 115, 180, 192, 240
Federal Trade Commission (FTC),
        91
Fishbowl, 97
fisheries, 428
flatware, 180
flow
    principles of, 198–200
    product, 206
food allergies, 269–71
Food and Drug Administration
        (FDA), 268, 27, 279
foodborne diseases/illnesses, 271,
        272, 273–75
    preventatives, 277–80
    procedures for, 267
Food Insights, 151
foodservice chains, 12, 19, 319
    chicken, 17
    dinnerhouses, 13, 15
    family, 16
    grill-buffet, 16–17
    pizza, 16, 98
    sandwich, 13
    *See also* hotels
foodservice industry, 2, 151
    employment with, 322
    market categories, 29, 31–33
    outlets in United States, 2
foodservice operations/operators,
        7, 114, 139, 142, 143, 151, 309
    safety, 241–42, 280–81, 288–90
    sanitary standards for, 241,
        433
foodservice systems, 212, 213,
        226–31

**G**
genetically engineered foods,
        268–69, 428
gift certificates, 100
glassware, 180
gross profit, 296